Post-conflict Administrations in International Law

Post-conflict Administrations in International Law

International Territorial Administration, Transitional Authority and Foreign Occupation in Theory and Practice

By

Eric De Brabandere
Assistant Professor of International Law
Leiden University, the Netherlands

MARTINUS NIJHOFF PUBLISHERS

LEIDEN • BOSTON
2009

This book is printed on acid-free paper.

Library of Congress Cataloging-in-Publication Data

Brabandere, Eric de.
Post-conflict administrations in international law: international territorial administration, transitional authority, and foreign occupation in theory and practice / by Eric De Brabandere.
p. cm.
Includes bibliographical references and index.
ISBN 978-90-04-17023-0 (hardback : alk. paper) 1. Internationalized territories.
2. International trusteeships. I. Title.

KZ3673.B73 2009
341.4'2–dc22

2009005950

ISBN 978 90 04 17023 0

PRINTED IN THE NETHERLANDS

It should be borne in mind that there is nothing more difficult to handle, more doubtful of success, and more dangerous to carry through than initiating changes in a state's constitution. The innovator makes enemies of all those who prospered under the old order, and only lukewarm support is forthcoming from those who would prosper under the new. [...] [W]henever those who oppose the changes can do so, they attack vigorously, and the defence made by the others is only lukewarm.

[G]overnments set up overnight, like everything in nature whose growth is forced, lack strong roots and ramifications. So they are destroyed in the first bad spell. This is inevitable unless those who have suddenly become princes are of such prowess that overnight they can learn how to preserve what fortune has suddenly tossed into their laps, and unless they can lay foundations such as other princes would have already been building on.

Niccolo Machiavelli[1]

[1] Machiavelli, N., *Il Principe*, Translated by George Bull (London: Penguin Books Ltd., 2004), pp. 24 and 27.

Contents

PART II

INTERNATIONAL LAW, POST-CONFLICT ADMINISTRATIONS AND PEACE-BUILDING. DEFINING THE LEGAL FRAMEWORK

PART III

POST-CONFLICT ADMINISTRATIONS IN PRACTICE: INTERNATIONAL ADMINISTRATIONS, THE 'LIGHT FOOTPRINT' APPROACH, AND THE OCCUPATION OF IRAQ

Acknowledgements

This book has been finalised at Leiden University, but draws on research conducted at Ghent University between 2002 and 2007, and previously at the University of Geneva between 2001 and 2002. First of all, I would like to express my warmest thanks to Marc Cogen from Ghent University for his very much appreciated and valued support and advice throughout my research and our professional collaboration. Warm thanks go also to Nico Schrijver at Leiden University for his comments on earlier versions of this manuscript, to Eduard Somers and Frank Maes at Ghent University for their suggestions on further improvements to my research, and to Laurence Boisson de Chazournes at the University of Geneva for her advice and guidance during my studies in Geneva.

Special thanks go to Maître Pierre Philippe Harmel for his support and advice throughout the years I worked with him at his law firm at the same time as undertaking my research at the university.

Finally, I want to express my warmest gratitude to my family, and, most importantly, I would like to thank Katia Gevaert for her inestimable encouragement, trust and understanding throughout my research and the writing of this book, especially at the moments when I needed it most.

Abbreviations

ABA/CEELI	American Bar Association's Central European and Eurasian Law Initiative
AIHRC	Afghan Independent Human Rights Commission
CIVPOL	UN Police Officers, also referred to as UNPOL
CNRT	Conselho Nacional de Reconstrução do Timor (National Congress for Timorese Reconstruction), formerly Conselho Nacional de Resistência Timorense (National Council of Timorese Resistance)
CPA	Coalition Provisional Authority (Iraq)
CRTR	Commission for Reception, Truth and Reconciliation (CAVR in Portuguese) (East Timor)
DDR	Disarmament, Demobilisation, and Reintegration
DMU	Detainee Management Unit (East Timor)
DPKO	United Nations Department of Peacekeeping Operations
EC	European Community
ECHO	Humanitarian Office of the European Commission
ECHR	European Convention for the Protection of Human Rights and Fundamental Freedoms
ECJ	European Court of Justice
ETTA	East Timor Transitional Administration
EU	European Union
FALINTIL	Forças Armadas da Libertação Nacional de Timor-Leste (Armed Forces for the National Liberation of Timor Leste) – military wing of the FRETILIN
FRETILIN	Frente Revolucionária de Timor-Leste Independente (Revolutionary Front for an Independent East Timor)
IAC	Interim Administrative Council (Kosovo)
ICCPR	International Covenant on Civil and Political Rights
ICESCR	International Covenant on Economic, Social and Cultural Rights
ICJ	International Court of Justice
ICRC	International Committee of the Red Cross
ICTR	International Criminal Tribunal for Rwanda
ICTY	International Criminal Tribunal for the former Yugoslavia

IDLO	International Development Law Organisation
IDP	internally displaced person
IFRC	International Federation of Red Cross and Red Crescent Societies
ILAC	International Legal Assistance Consortium
ILC	International Law Commission
IOM	International Organisation for Migration
IPTF	United Nations International Police Task Force (Bosnia and Herzegovina)
ISAF	International Security Assistance Force (Afghanistan)
JIAS	Joint Interim Administrative Structure (Kosovo)
KFOR	Kosovo Force (International security presence in Kosovo, under NATO command)
KJPC	Kosovo Judicial and Prosecutorial Council
KLA	Kosovo Liberation Army (UCK in Albanian)
KPP-HAM	Indonesian Commission of Enquiry into Human Rights Violations in East Timor
KPS	Kosovo Police Service
KPC	Kosovo Protection Corps
KTC	Kosovo Transitional Council
KWECC	Kosovo War and Ethnic Crimes Court
NCC	National Consultative Council (East Timor)
OCHA	UN Office for the Coordination of Humanitarian Affairs
OHCHR	United Nations Office of the High Commissioner for Human Rights
ONUC	Opération des Nations Unies au Congo
ORHA	Office for Reconstruction and Humanitarian Assistance (Iraq)
OSCE	Organisation for the Security and Cooperation in Europe
PCIJ	Permanent Court of International Justice
PIC	Peace Implementation Council (Bosnia and Herzegovina)
SOFA	Status of Forces Agreement
SRSG	Special Representative of the Secretary-General
SSR	Security Sector Reform
TAL	Law of Administration for the State of Iraq for the Transitional Period
UDHR	Universal Declaration of Human Rights
UN	United Nations
UNAMA	United Nations Assistance Mission in Afghanistan
UNAMI	United Nations Assistance Mission for Iraq
UNDP	United Nations Development Programme
UNEF	United Nations Emergency Force (Middle East)
UNHCR	United Nations High Commissioner for the Refugees
UNICEF	United Nations Children's Fund

UNITAF	Unified Task Force (Somalia)
UNTAG	United Nations Transition Assistance Group (Namibia)
UNMIBH	United Nations Mission in Bosnia and Herzegovina
UNMIK	United Nations Interim Administration Mission in Kosovo
UNMISET	United Nations Mission of Support in East Timor – Res. 1410 (2002)
UNMIT	United Nations Integrated Mission in Timor-Leste – Res. 1704 (2006)
UNODC	UN Office on Drugs and Crime
UNOSOM I	United Nations Operations in Somalia
UNOSOM II	Enlarged United Nations Operations in Somalia
UNOTIL	United Nations Office in Timor-Leste – Res. 1599 (2005)
UNPROFOR	United Nations Protection Force (Bosnia and Herzegovina)
USAID	United States Agency for International Development
UNTAC	United Nations Transitional Authority in Cambodia
UNTAES	United Nations Transitional Administration for Eastern Slavonia, Baranja and Western Sirmium
UNTAET	United Nations Transitional Authority in East Timor
UNTAG	United Nations Transition Assistance Group (Namibia)
UNTEA	United Nations Temporary Executive Authority (West Irian)
WFP	World Food Programme
WHO	World Health Organisation

Introduction

The international administration of territory, in which comprehensive administrative powers are exercised by, on behalf of or with the agreement of the United Nations (UN) has recently re-emerged in the context of reconstructing (parts of) states after conflict. The cases of Kosovo and East Timor have frequently been described as ground-breaking and unique in peace-building and post-conflict reconstruction literature, and have triggered both interest and criticism. The subsequent post-conflict operations in Afghanistan and Iraq have prompted similar mixed reactions, in respect of both their achievements and their differing approaches. In Kosovo and East Timor, the UN was endowed with wide-ranging executive and legislative powers. In Afghanistan, it was decided to rely principally on local capacity with minimal international participation. In Iraq on the other hand, the occupying forces exercised administrative powers based on both the laws of occupation and Security Council resolutions. In Afghanistan and Iraq, the UN itself was not granted any direct administrative powers.

These four operations share similar objectives and are the latest examples of comprehensive international efforts aimed at rebuilding societies emerging from years of conflict and internal strife. In addition to the similarities in the objectives, these four cases are characterized by the creation of 'transitional' or 'interim' administrations to oversee the reconstruction process. The level of internationalisation of these transitional structures was nevertheless dependent on the approach taken. In Kosovo and East Timor, these interim structures were purely international. Afghanistan, in which it was decided to rely on a maximum participation of local actors with a minimum of international participation – referred to as the 'light footprint' approach[2] – was an explicit reaction against the internationalisation of administrative structures in Kosovo and East Timor, and thus resulted in the creation of entirely national interim and transitional structures. In Iraq, a United States-led administration – the Coalition Provisional Authority – was established, in conjunction with a domestic consultative 'Governing Council'. After one year, responsibility for the administration of Iraq was retransferred to domestic interim and transitional structures.

[2] Report of the Secretary-General, The Situation in Afghanistan and its Implications for International Peace and Security, UN Doc A/56/875-S/2002/278 (18 March 2002), para. 98.

The increasing involvement of international actors in various forms of international missions set up to supervise reconstruction or peace-building processes has resulted in an expanding debate on the subject. Nevertheless, less attention has been paid to the context in which these missions have been set up, the legal framework of these operations and the practical implications of this in the particular context. Similarly, the influence of the differing legal framework applicable to international actors on these missions has often been neglected. It therefore seems necessary, first, to both clearly establish and delineate the origins of the concept, and to analyse the context in which it has resurfaced, namely post-conflict peace-building or reconstruction. Secondly, the international legal framework needs to be methodically established, and must take into account the conditions in which these administrations need to operate. Thirdly, an enquiry into the practice of recent cases is vital to ensure a practical analysis of post-conflict administrations and to understand how these projects work 'on the ground'. The influence of the international character of the administration and the legal framework applicable to these administrations can indeed only be thoroughly analysed when the operative context is taken into account. To analyse and understand the ways in which the reconstruction processes have been addressed in Kosovo, East Timor, Afghanistan and Iraq, one needs to start with the mandates given to these missions, and the ultimate goals of these exercises, which extends well beyond the mere physical rehabilitation of the territory. These recent cases reveal an explicit aim to set up viable and functioning democratic institutions. Finally, the use of post-conflict administrations, and the presence of international actors in a post-conflict context do raise questions in terms of accountability of international actors, exit strategies, local ownership, appropriateness of internationalising domestic institutions and applicable legal framework. It is thus necessary, after having identified the concept, its legal framework, and its practice, to draw lessons as to its compatibility with the aim pursued.

The Context of Post-Conflict Administration

It is important to emphasise at this preliminary stage that international administrations are only the method to achieve a certain objective. The term 'international administration' or 'international territorial administration' refers only to the *regime* of the administration, and describes the nature of authority exercised by international actors. International administration can thus be defined as the regime of administration of a territory conferred upon one or more states, or to one or more international organisations.[3] International administration is thus

[3] Cf. 'Administration internationale', in Salmon, J. (ed.), *Dictionnaire de droit international public* (Brussel: Bruylant, 2001), p. 42.

merely the counterpart of the 'conventional' national or local administration. The concept of international administration has thus to be seen as a 'method' – like the 'light footprint' approach – within the broader framework of peace-building missions. In the case of Iraq, the United-States-led administration was equally international, but we will reserve the term 'international administration' for the cases of Kosovo and East Timor, in which the transitional administration was in fact purely international, and a subsidiary organ of an international organisation. Equally, the use of 'transitional administration' denotes the interim or non-elected character of the governmental structures created in the emergency phase, pending the holding of elections to set up democratic institutions, as opposed to a government elected or appointed after free and fair elections, according to the state's constitution. The notion of post-conflict administration thus clearly identifies both the method used and the environment in which they operate, since it stands for those administrations set up in a post-conflict environment.

Considering that Kosovo, East Timor, Afghanistan and Iraq are part of a similar process, any analysis must transcend the purely institutional approach. Full UN-led administration, the 'light footprint' approach, and the foreign occupation of Iraq are processes with a similar aim. Any analysis of this topic which is limited to the institutional dimension of either international administrations or foreign occupation misconceives the similarities in the aims and objectives of these cases. The creation of 'transitional' or 'interim' administrations is similar in the four cases; only the level of 'internationalisation' of these structures differs, resulting in the application of a different legal framework. The international administration of territory certainly is an established practice, with certain, but very limited normative implications. Any restriction of an analysis to the mere concept of international administrations thus overlooks the varying legal framework applicable to such administrations, in function of the use made of it. It is therefore in our view paramount to study the concept of international administrations with reference to the contexts in which they operate, in this case a post-conflict environment. It is equally this context which confirms the similarities between the cases of Kosovo and East Timor, and Afghanistan and Iraq. However it is true that international administrations, and this will be evidenced in the historical analysis contained in the first part, have traditionally served other purposes than peace-building or post-conflict reconstruction. Some authors thus view the concept of international territorial administration merely as an independent institution which serves a particular policy.[4] Other authors focus on the use of international administrations as a method to serve to fill a

[4] See e.g. Wilde, R., *International Territorial Administration. How Trusteeship and the Civilizing Mission Never Went Away* (Oxford: Oxford University Press, 2008). Cf. Stahn, C., *The Law and Practice of International Territorial Administration. Versailles to Iraq and Beyond* (Cambridge: Cambridge University Press, 2008).

power vacuum or have construed it as a response to a governance problem.[5] The basic premise of this book is that it is specifically by placing these operations in the situation in which they operate, that one can see how the international legal framework influences the reconstruction process, and which questions this practice raises. In addition, not placing the current missions in a peace-building perspective leads to ignore the very reasons why international administrations can be considered as manifesting the re-emergence of an old notion.

The approach used in this book does not therefore suggest, first, that the use of international administration of territory is limited to post-conflict scenario's, and secondly, that the creation of international administrations is always a response to a (post-conflict) governance problem. The use that is made of the post-conflict label in this book only aims at situating the administrations in their operational context; it does not imply that we view the creation of such an administration as a response to an administrative vacuum, that it necessarily is a *result* of the conflict or that it can only be established after the end of all hostilities. Rather, this book is founded on the pragmatic viewpoint that international administration is an already existing concept which recently resurfaced as a method of to re-build states or territories in a post-conflict environment, which is the context in which these should be analysed.

Outline of the Argument

In the first part of this book we will examine the extent to which the international administration of a territory is truly pioneering, considering the allegations about the unique character of such comprehensive mandates. Often, such an assessment is based on the fact that the reconstruction of states and territories has never been addressed in such a way. Though this may seem correct if one limits the analysis to the current context, historical examples will nevertheless show that the exercise of administrative functions by international actors has frequently taken place in the past. The first part will therefore aim to establish the historical context in which the current forms of international administration need to be placed. The historical precedents are essential to the evaluation of the current operations. Mapping the current missions from a historical standpoint will not only clearly ascertain that the concept of delegating sweeping powers to international actors cannot be seen as entirely new, but will also enable us to analyse to what extent the current missions could have been better planned and executed if their historical origins had been taken into account. The historical

[5] See e.g. Chesterman, S., Ignatieff, M. and Thakur, R. (eds.), *Making States Work: State Failure and the Crisis of Governance* (Tokyo / New York / Paris: United Nations University Press, 2005).

analysis is equally aimed at determining that the current resurgence of international administrations is the result of an evolution in addressing post-conflict and peace-building scenarios. We will indeed establish that a continuous expansion of peacekeeping mandates, which have gradually shifted from *keeping* peace to *building* peace, has resulted in the complete take-over of administrative functions by international actors encompassing the commitment to engage in large-scale and comprehensive reforms in all governmental sectors. The identification of such an evolution is important for us to see to what extent the *objectives* of international administration have shifted over the years.

The second part addresses the applicable legal framework, which is fundamental, as it has a direct influence on the exercise of administrative powers by international actors. Establishing the legal framework applicable to international administrations and peace-building missions requires an analysis of various branches of international law, ranging from the UN's legal capacity to undertake and authorise such intrusive missions and the transitory nature of these missions, to the application of human rights law and the laws of armed conflict. The different forms of the engagement of international actors resulted in different applicable legal frameworks. In the case of Iraq, we will see that the laws of occupation have played a substantial role in determining the powers of the Coalition Provisional Authority (CPA). Another example is the legal status of Kosovo, which has directly influenced the capacity of the United Nations Interim Administration Mission in Kosovo (UNMIK) to engage in reform of the economic sector for instance. The legal obligations of international actors involved in international administration will equally form an important aspect of our research, as issues of accountability of foreign actors involved in international administration have frequently been raised in order to criticise such intrusive powers. This part is thus intended not merely to categorise and identify the complex rules which apply in post-conflict reconstruction, but also to locate the legal limits inherent in the exercise of administrative functions by international actors. Therefore, the second part does not aim to be an in-depth analysis of these various international legal issues. Rather we will adopt a 'functional approach', which implies that these subjects will only be analysed in function of the subject of this book.

The pith of this book is the examination of the various ways in which reconstruction has been approached in Kosovo, East Timor, Afghanistan and Iraq, which is grouped in the third part. The discussion of the practice of post-conflict reconstruction in these four cases is not intended to be comprehensive. Our third part will necessarily be selective, as we aim to illustrate certain developments and concerns, in particular those related to application of the legal framework and the involvement of the UN. The selection of these four cases does not imply that other cases are less important. Precedents need to be seen as significant steps in the evolution described in the first part of the book. In addition, this selection of leading cases does not imply that we will not refer to other cases when necessary, in order to illustrate the evolution in UN reconstruction efforts established in part one. The analysis of the implementation of the mandates will be grouped in three chapters. The first chapter will deal with civil administration, including economic reconstruction, security aspects, emergency aid and the issue of refugees. The second chapter will deal will with the reconstruction of the judicial system, and other issues pertaining to the rule of law. In the third chapter, we will analyse institution-building and democratic governance in the four cases.

The fourth and final part of this book addresses overarching issues of post conflict administrations. In a sense, the last part groups several 'concluding' chapters. The aim is to suggest improvements to the concept by proposing a comprehensive legal framework for post-conflict administrations. It is not, however, the purpose to establish a 'model' post-conflict mission. Rather, the last part is based on a lessons-learned exercise, not only from the analysed practice, but also from the established legal framework and origins of these missions, and the interaction between these.

Methodology, Approach and Selection of Cases

The rationale behind this methodology is twofold. Firstly, it ensures a practical analysis of the effective implementation of the mandates entrusted to the different forms of post-conflict administration, based on both the international mission's approaches and achievements. Secondly, it allows us to see how the theoretical findings in respect of the legal framework established in the first part influenced in a very different way the capacities of the administrations to deal with the reconstruction processes in each case. This four-tiered approach reflects the need to analyse the concept of peace-building in post-conflict scenarios within a broader framework.

The selection of these particular four cases hinges on various reasons. From the viewpoint of the UN's involvement in post-conflict reconstruction, Kosovo and East Timor represent the first cases of full administration by a UN subsidiary organ, representing a culmination in the evolution of peacekeeping mandates, which we described in our first part.[6] As far as the later two operations

[6] See also Bothe, M. and Marauhn, T., 'The United Nations in Kosovo and East Timor—Problems of a Trusteeship Administration', 6 *International Peacekeeping* 152 (2000), p. 218 *et s*. The authors clearly distinguish the Kosovo and East Timor administrations from the previous cases, especially that of Bosnia and Herzegovina, which has often been compared to the administrations in Kosovo and East Timor, as the foreign civil presence is not the sole authority in the territory, leading to the co-existence of two parallel authorities.

in Afghanistan and Iraq are concerned, they are to be considered as alternative approaches to post-conflict reconstruction, considering that in Afghanistan the emphasis was placed on a maximum participation of local actors with a minimum of international participation – the 'light footprint' approach – as a kind of reaction against the broad authority granted to the Special Representative of the Secretary-General in Kosovo and East Timor. While the case of Afghanistan is sometimes equated with an international administration, we nevertheless favour the view that Afghanistan represents an alternative approach to addressing post-conflict reconstruction, since the interim and transitional structures were purely national.[7] Transitional Afghan authorities had been set up, but the UN was not entrusted with direct administrative powers. Iraq represents yet another approach to addressing a similar post-conflict reconstruction mandate,[8] as the administrative functions were exercised by the occupying powers, on the basis of the laws of occupation and a Security Council Resolution. However, it has to be acknowledged that the case of Iraq presents certain similarities with those of Kosovo and East Timor, considering the direct exercise of powers by the United States and United Kingdom.[9] The overall mandates and major objectives of the missions in Kosovo, East Timor, Afghanistan and Iraq do, however, reveal major similarities, as we will point out throughout this book. In addition, they have all taken place in the context of enlarged peace-building mandates in post-conflict situations.

The general approach of this book is thus descriptive and analytical rather than normative. It aims principally to describe the evolution in the use of international administration, the legal framework applicable to post-conflict administration and the practice of recent cases of post-conflict administration and reconstruction. The book is thus mainly based on an empirical analysis. The second and fourth parts will necessarily include normative elements. However, these normative elements are intended to represent the state of the law rather than to propose a new normative framework. In the same line, we will address the subject from

---

[7] Also Dahrendorf, N. *et al.*, 'A Review of Peace Operations: A Case for Change: Overall Introduction and Synthesis Report', *Conflict Security & Development Group, King's College London* (13 March 2003).

[8] On the relationship between Iraq and other cases of international territorial administration see Ratner, S.R., 'Foreign Occupation and International Territorial Administration: The Challenges of Convergence', 16 *European Journal of International Law* 697 (2005) and Wilde, R. and Delcourt, B., 'Le retour des "protectorats". L'irrésistible attrait de l'administration de territoires étrangers', in Delcourt, B., Duez, D. and Remacle, E. (eds.), *La guerre d'Irak. Prélude d'un nouvel ordre international?* (Bern: PIE Peter Lang, 2004), p. 219, and in particular Part III 'L'Irak: nouvel avatar de l'administration étrangère de territoires', p. 237.

[9] See also de Wet, E., 'The Direct Administrations of Territories by the United Nations and its Member States in the Post Cold War Era: Legal Basis and Implications for National Law', 8 *Max Planck Yearbook of United Nations Law* 291 (2004).

a functional perspective. This implies that we will only discuss those issues and themes necessary for our research, and that theoretical debates will be only be engaged upon if these are necessary for the subject matter.

Part I

Mapping the Concept: The Administration of Territory and the Reconstruction of States from a Historical Perspective

Despite assertions in legal literature with regard to the exceptional character of the mandates of the missions in Kosovo and East Timor,[10] and as previously mentioned in the general introduction, the international administration of territory has a long history, going back to 1815 with the establishment of the 'Independent Republic of Cracow' at the Congress of Vienna.[11] In fact, when the Statute of the Free Territory of Trieste was adopted after the Second World War, scholars also engaged in an analysis of the uniqueness of that administration from a historical perspective to see to what extent the Statute could be compared to previous cases in order to establish the legal framework in which the international presence in Trieste had to operate.[12]

The first major precedents were formed either as a response to the World Wars or as a consequence of the decolonisation process. From her creation, the League of Nations was entrusted by the Versailles Peace Treaty[13] with the administration of two territories, the Saar Basin and the Free City of Danzig. The UN was also entrusted with the administration of two territories after the end of the Second World War. However, unlike the mandates under the League of Nations after the First World War, the first two administration projects under UN auspices were never implemented. It is nevertheless interesting to mention them briefly as they represent an important step in the UN-led administration of territories,

[10] See for example: Matheson, M. J., 'United Nations governance of postconflict societies', 95 *American Journal of International Law* 76 (2001); Chopra, J., 'The UN's Kingdom of East Timor', 42 *Survival* 27 (2000) and Kondoch, B., 'The United Nations Administration of East Timor', 6 *Journal of Conflict and Security Law* 245 (2001).

[11] See for these historical precedents: Ydit, M., *Internationalised Territories: from the "Free city of Cracow" to the "Free city of Berlin". A study in the Historical Development of a modern Notion in International Law and International relations (1815–1960)* (Leyden: A. W. Sythoff, 1961), pp. 22–39.

[12] As stated by J. Leprette, "On est tenté, pour déterminer la filiation juridique de ce nouvel élément de la communauté des Nations qu'on appelle le Territoire libre de Trieste, de remonter dans le passé et de se référer aux expériences antérieures. C'est une démarche naturelle de l'esprit: elle tend à faire surgir d'une judicieuse confrontation les caractères qui permettent d'apparenter le nouveau statut à des régimes plus anciens. Lorsque ces instituions en cause on été élaborées d'une façon empirique, sans constituer l'application d'un système juridique préétabli, cette méthode d'investigation s'impose a fortiori." (Leprette, J., *Le Statut International de Trieste* (Paris: Pedone, 1949), p. 147).

[13] Versailles Peace Treaty (28 June 1919), 225 CTS 188 (1919) [hereafter 'Versailles Peace Treaty'].

and clearly demonstrate the UN's capacity to administer territories, which had long been criticised and challenged.

Our first task is to point out that the concept of international administration as such is relatively old and has been used in various ways by the UN to resolve, for example, territorial disputes or to assist a population in exercising its right to self-determination in the decolonisation process. We should indeed keep in mind that the purpose of the current missions is fundamentally different, although some historical cases clearly resemble more recent operations. The importance of establishing that the concept of administering territory on behalf of the local population is itself not pioneering resides in the fact that important lessons about the basic principles of international administrations and peace-building missions could have been deducted from these cases and will need to be taken into account when discussing the applicable legal framework.

The second aim of this part is to establish the evolution of mandates entrusted to UN missions. Having started out as peacekeeping missions in which no administrative power was exercised by international organisations, missions have become involved in long-term post-conflict reconstruction processes. The administration of post-conflict societies is the latest policy shift to be observed in the UN-led or -assisted missions. The recent post-conflict reconstruction missions are the next step in the evolution of peacekeeping mandates, which started with the UN experience in Cambodia. Cases before Cambodia nevertheless predicted such evolution, aimed at attaining long-term goals in terms of creating stable and democratic societies, and therefore tackling the root-causes of conflicts. Clearly, operations in the 1990's underestimated the importance of political, economical, social and civil reconstruction in building a sustainable peace.[14] As the former Secretary-General put it "[w]hile United Nations efforts have been tailored so that they are palpable to the population to meet the immediacy of their security needs and to address the grave injustices of war, the root causes of conflict have often been left unaddressed. Yet, it is in addressing the causes of conflict, through legitimate and just ways, that the international community can help prevent a return to conflict in the future".[15] The concept of peace-*building* has been described by the Security Council as "aimed at preventing the outbreak, the recurrence or continuation of armed conflict and therefore encompass[ing] a wide range of political, developmental, humanitarian and human rights programmes and mechanisms".[16] The International Commission on Intervention and State

[14] See Paris, R., 'Post-Conflict Peacebuilding', in Weiss, T. G. and Daws, S., *The Oxford Handbook on the United Nations* (Oxford: Oxford University Press, 2007), p. 417.

[15] Report of the Secretary-General, 'The rule of law and transitional justice in conflict and post-conflict societies', UN Doc. S/2004/616 (23 August 2004), para. 4.

[16] SC Presidential Statement, UN Doc. S/PRST/2001/5 (20 February 2001), para. 5.

Sovereignty goes even further and presages an evolution into a *responsibility* to rebuild.[17] In reality, post-conflict peace-building has a dual role. It is first of all a reactive instrument, by re-establishing and consolidating peace after conflict, but at the same time it has a preventive function, namely to address the underlying root-causes of the conflict. In a recent debate in the Security Council on the need for a comprehensive approach in peace-building, the US representative stated that "peacekeeping without peace building is a recipe for potential waste".[18] This evolution will be clearly revealed throughout our analysis.

The historical cases can therefore all be placed in one of two categories. Either they conceptually illustrate the international administration paradigm from a historical perspective, or they show that the recent practice is an evolution in expanding peacekeeping mandates. In the latter, the various types of international involvement can be distinguished on the basis of the authority exercised by international actors. While the starting point is the monitoring of elections by international actors such as the UN, the exercise of full and direct authority can be seen as the culmination of this evolution, witnessed by the administrations of Kosovo and East Timor, the other cases "exhibiting varying magnitudes of control".[19] For methodological purposes, the precedents discussed will be grouped systematically, as we endeavour to establish the historical context of past administrative operations and the expansion of peacekeeping mandates, and chronologically, as the evolution can best be viewed from the starting point of peace-building missions. The first chapter contains an overview and discussion of the cases aimed at fixing the concept of international administration in international law. The cases we will discuss here were very much related to various forms of territorial disputes or to the preservation of an 'internationalised' status for territories. The concept of comprehensive international involvement aimed at re-establishing peace and security emerges only in the cases discussed in the second chapter. The subsequent cases, showing the evolution in complex peace operations, will therefore be grouped in the second chapter. In our third chapter we will turn to the cases of Kosovo, East Timor, Afghanistan and Iraq. The inclusion of these cases in a separate chapter within this first part is intended

---

[17] "Too often in the past the responsibility to rebuild has been insufficiently recognized, the exit of the interveners has been poorly managed, the commitment to help with reconstruction has been inadequate, and countries have found themselves at the end of the day still wrestling with the underlying problems that produced the original intervention action." (International Commission on Intervention and State Sovereignty, 'The Responsibility to Protect' (December 2001), para. 5.2).

[18] Statement by the US representative to the Security Council, SC Meeting Record, 'Peace-building: towards a comprehensive approach', UN Doc. S/PV.4272 (5 February 2005), p. 11.

[19] Caplan, R., 'International Authority and State Building: The Case of Bosnia and Herzegovina', 10 *Global Governance* 54 (2004).

not just to emphasise the necessity of situating them within the evolution we will describe, based on the *objectives* of the administrative powers conferred upon the different missions. It also outlines the context in which they were set up and the delimitation of the powers conferred on international and national actors.

Chapter 1

Early Forms of International Administration

This historical overview is not intended to be exhaustive. Instead, it focuses on cases which, in our view, are necessary and useful to our research question, in the sense that they provide practical support on issues we will discuss throughout this book. We have identified several cases in which either the League of Nations or the UN has exercised far-reaching administrative powers. The end of the First World War resulted in the assumption of administrative functions by the League of Nations in the Saar Basin, the 'Free City of Danzig' and Upper Silesia. After the Second World War, the UN developed plans to administer the cities of Jerusalem and Trieste, although they were finally abandoned. As a *casus specialis*, the Second World War resulted in the administration of Germany by the Allied Powers, which went far beyond the provisions of the laws of occupation. The first comprehensive administrative mission led by the UN outside the traditional peacekeeping sphere was the administration of West Irian.

A. *The Saar Basin and the Free City of Danzig*

The League of Nations was in charge of the administration of the Saar Basin between 1922 and 1935. After the end of the First World War, and after long negotiations between the Allied Powers, France obtained the right to exploit the mines in the German Saar Basin for 15 years, as compensation for the damage caused to the coalmines in Northern France during the War. Although the majority of its population was German or at least spoke German, the Saar Basin had always been disputed territory between France and Germany. The appointment of an *independent* and *neutral* 'Governing Commission' of the League of Nations to administer it for 15 years has to be regarded as a practical solution impeding French aspirations to annex the territory, which they had demanded during the negotiation of the Versailles Peace Treaty.[20]

---

[20] During the Paris Peace Conference in 1919, the French delegations wanted to create a buffer zone between Germany and France, with the Rhine as a natural border. The creation of an

As the territory itself was not transferred to France, it was decided, on an American proposal, to establish an interim administration, the 'Governing Commission', for the 15-year period. The American, and to a lesser extent the British, delegation viewed the League of Nations as an adequate instrument for holding back Germany, and were convinced that the annexation of the Saar Basin by France would leave Germany with a sense of frustration, which could lead to another war. The administration of the Saar Territory was thus strictly limited in time, contrary to that of the Free City of Danzig, which was intended to become a permanent 'internationalised' territory. The appointed Saarland Governing Commission had broad governmental powers. The Versailles Treaty endowed the Commission with "all the powers of government hitherto belonging to the German Empire, Prussia, or Bavaria, including the appointment and dismissal of officials, and the creation of such administrative and representative bodies as it may deem necessary".[21] Although a local *Landesrat*, which consisted of elected representatives, had been created, the Governing Commission did not rely on this local Assembly. Neither was the Commission bound by the advice of the *Landesrat*.[22] Formally, the Saar Basin remained a part of the German territory as article 49 of the Versailles Treaty stated that "Germany renounces in favour of the League of Nations, in the capacity of trustee, the government of the territory defined above". The Saar Basin was thus not under the sovereignty of the League of Nations, which was merely the administrative authority for the territory.[23] This division between sovereignty and exercise of state competences by an international organisation is very similar in the case of Kosovo.

The administration of the Saar Basin by the Governing Commission lasted the envisaged 15 years, pending the organisation of a plebiscite, as provided for by the Versailles Peace Treaty.[24] The plebiscite was to function as an evaluation of the transitional period in which the population would decide between union with France, reunion with Germany, or the status quo, in other words continu-

independent and neutral Rhine State had also been envisaged, which, together with the neutral States of Belgium and Luxembourg, would have formed an adequate safeguard against any possible future German invasion. The French indeed argued that the Rhine had always been the borderline between Gaul and Germany, and that its annexation could also be regarded as adequate reparation for the damage caused by Germany. See in general on the negotiations on the Saar Basin: MacMillan, M., *Paris 1919: Six months that changed the world* (New York: Random House Trade, 2002), pp. 169 *et s.*

21 Para. 19, Chapter II, Annex to the articles 45–50, Peace Treaty of Versailles (28 June 1919).

22 Walters, F. P., *A History of the League of Nations* (London / New York / Toronto: Oxford University Press, 1952), p. 586.

23 See Strupp, K. (ed.), *Wörterbuch des Völkerrechts* (Berlin: de Gruyter, 1960–1962), pp. 128–133. Contra: Ydit, *supra* note 11, pp. 44–46.

24 Versailles Peace Treaty, para. 34, Annex to Article 50.

ation of the regime of international administration.[25] The plebiscite resulted in an overwhelming majority of 90.8 % in favour of reunion with Germany.[26]

The administration of the Saar Basin was far more significant than that of Danzig, although both had been agreed upon in the same period. History shows that Danzig had always been disputed territory between Prussia, later Germany, and Poland, as Danzig was preponderantly German in character but Poland needed to maintain a passage to the sea. In 1466 and again in 1807, the city had already been constituted as a Free City or Free State with, *inter alia,* the right to enter into international agreements. Following a long period of systematic annexation and cession by both Poland and Prussia, the Versailles Treaty reconstituted Danzig as a 'Free City'.[27]

The Versailles Treaty placed Danzig "under the protection of the League of Nations".[28] The powers granted to the League of Nations were to be exercised together with Poland, which was responsible for the conduct of Danzig's external affairs. Danzig was also included in the Polish customs regime. A 'High Commissioner' and a 'Commission' were appointed, both of which had only very specific powers, most of them being relative to the implementation of the statute as embodied in the Versailles Treaty. The High Commissioner had two main areas of responsibility. His first main task was the elaboration of the Constitution of the Free City of Danzig. The second was to deal in the first instance with all differences arising between Poland and the Free City of Danzig with regard to the Versailles Treaty or any arrangements or agreements made in accordance with the Versailles Treaty.[29] Notwithstanding its success in the elaboration of the Constitution, the League of Nations gradually lost its interests in Danzig, and this led to the annexation of the territory by Germany before the Second World War. For almost ten years however, the League of Nations had duly fulfilled its mandate.

In the case of Danzig, the mediation role of the League of Nations was still preponderant to the administering role, as the limited administrative tasks of the High Commissioner were merely transitional pending the adoption of a

---

25 Para. 34 of the annex to article 50, Versailles Peace Treaty: "At the termination of a period of fifteen years from the coming into force of the present Treaty, the population of the territory of the Saar Basin will be called upon to indicate their desires in the following manner: A vote will take place by communes or districts, on the three following alternatives: (a) maintenance of the regime established by the present Treaty and by this Annex; (b) union with France; (c) union with Germany."

26 Walters, *supra* note 22, pp. 586–598.

27 See for an overview: Verzijl, J. H. W., *International Law in Historical Perspective, Part II – International Persons* (Leyden: A. W. Sijthoff, 1969), pp. 501–502 and Ydit, *supra* note 11, pp. 186 *et s.*

28 Article 102 Versailles Peace Treaty.

29 Article 103 Versailles Peace Treaty.

constitution. After the adoption of the Constitution by the League of Nations Council, the High Commissioner's tasks were limited to being the arbitrator in disputes arising between Danzig, Poland and Germany. The High Commissioner was finally expelled by the Germans after their reoccupation of the territory.[30] The Danzig administration was not as impressive as that in the Saar Basin. The major differences between the two cases are probably the consequence of their differing purposes. The settlement of the final status of the territories placed under international administration had a direct influence on the scope of administrative powers. Danzig was indeed intended to become a completely independent territory, and the temporary administration provided by the League of Nations was envisaged to facilitate its transition towards independence, while guaranteeing its international status. The competences of the Danzig Commission and the High Commissioner were limited in scope, as the future territorial status of the territory was pre-defined. The Saar Basin on the other hand had no pre-defined final status and was never expected to achieve independence. It was therefore almost logical that the Governing Commission would have all the governing powers until the final status of the territory was decided according to the results of the plebiscite.

B. *The Upper Silesia Mixed Commission*

Apart from the two abovementioned territorial arrangements after the First World War, the Versailles Treaty provided for the appointment of several Commissions to organise plebiscites to resolve certain territorial disputes between Germany, Denmark and Poland. International Commissions were appointed for Schleswig at the Danish border and for Eastern Prussia and Upper Silesia at the Polish border.[31] The Versailles Peace Treaty gave the Commissions all the powers exercised by the German or the Prussian Government in order to organise the plebiscite, except those of legislation or taxation.[32]

Although the first two plebiscites did not pose any problems, as the votes were clearly in favour of incorporation into one particular State, the Upper Silesian situation was far more complex. The plebiscite had resulted in a small majority of votes in favour of incorporation into Germany.[33] In view of these results, and after an armed uprising by the Polish inhabitants of Upper Silesia, the League of Nations decided not to incorporate the territory into Germany. It nominated

[30] Ydit, *supra* note 11, pp. 195 *et s.*
[31] Article 88 Versailles Peace Treaty.
[32] Article 3 Annex to article 88, Versailles Peace Treaty.
[33] See Walters, *supra* note 22, pp. 152 *et s.*

a 'Special Rapporteurs' Committee', which recommended the division of the territory between Poland and Germany. The territory was thus divided along the lines of the outcome of the plebiscite. In order to ensure the stability of the economy in Upper Silesia, the Council of the League of Nations recommended the conclusion of a Convention between Poland and Germany regarding the free movement of people and the free importation and exportation of coal from Upper Silesia to either country.[34] To facilitate and assure the implementation of the Convention a 'Mixed Commission' was appointed, composed of two German nationals, two Polish nationals and a neutral president appointed by the League of Nations.[35] The Convention also created an International Arbitral Tribunal consisting of one Polish and one German national, and a League-appointed president.[36] The League of Nations retained the right to veto any law of Germany or Poland regarding Upper Silesia and was the final arbitrator for disputes concerning the implementation of the Agreement. The Commission ended its mandate in 1937, and the mission was generally considered a success.[37] The League of Nations' involvement in this case is an early form of limited administrative powers granted to international actors to oversee the implementation of a convention. The context, however, remains that of a territorial dispute. The situation nonetheless shows some similarities with several later cases such as those of Eastern Slavonia or Bosnia.

C. *The Proposed UN Administration of the Cities of Jerusalem and Trieste*

General Assembly Resolution 181 (II) containing the territorial partition plan between Israel and Palestine, envisaged a solution for the problem of Jerusalem by establishing the city as a demilitarised *corpus separatum* under a specific international regime and statute.[38] The UN itself was mandated to administer the city, under the supervision of the Trusteeship Council. However, control by the Trusteeship Council did not imply that Jerusalem could have been considered a trust territory in accordance with Chapter XII of the UN Charter.[39] The

34 Convention concerning Upper Silesia signed at Geneva, 15 May 1922, 9 LNTS 466. The full text is also available in Strupp, K., *Documents pour servir à l'histoire du droit des gens* (Berlin: Sack, 1923) [Hereafter 'Convention concerning Upper Silesia'].

35 Artt. 562–605, Part V, Convention concerning Upper Silesia.

36 *Ibid.*

37 See: Kaeckenbeeck, G. S., 'Upper Silesia under the League of Nations', 243 *Annals of the American Academy of Political and Social Science* 129 (1946).

38 GA Res. 181 (II), UN Doc. A/RES/181 (II) (A+B) (29 November 1947), Part III.

39 See Seyersted, F., 'United Nations Forces: Some Legal Problems', 37 British Yearbook of International Law 351 (1961), 452.

resolution adopted by the General Assembly provided *inter alia* for the elaboration of a statute and the nomination of a Governor by the Trusteeship Council. The statute was to be revised after ten years. In accordance with Resolution 181 (II), the Trusteeship Council formally adopted a draft statute for the City of Jerusalem, placing the city "under the administration of the United Nations".[40] Among other specific executive powers relating to the ensuring of peace, order and good government, the Governor had the power to conduct the City's external relations, including the protection abroad of the interests of the City and its citizens.[41] The Statute equally envisaged the creation of a purely local 'Legislative Council' to exercise legislative power in accordance with the Statute.[42] The draft statute was however never implemented because, after the hostilities in 1948, it failed to obtain the necessary majority in the plenary meeting of the General Assembly.

The Statute for the Free Territory of Trieste was adopted at the signature of the peace treaty with Italy at the end of the Second World War.[43] Trieste was established as a 'Free Territory' and placed under the direct responsibility of the Security Council, which was to ensure the territory's integrity and independence.[44] The Security Council subsequently approved the Statute.[45] A Governor had to be appointed by the Security Council who, as the representative of the Security Council, "shall be responsible for supervising the observance of the present Statute including the protection of the basic human rights of the inhabitants and for ensuring that public order and security are maintained by the Government of the Free Territory in accordance with the present Statute, the Constitution and laws of the Free Territory".[46] Legislative powers were to be exercised by a local popular assembly, while executive powers were entrusted to a 'Council of Government'.[47] Again, the proposal was never implemented. Notwithstanding agreement on the Statute of Trieste which was formally part of the peace treaty with Italy, the Security Council never managed to appoint a Governor because of a lack of agreement between its members. Consequently, the territory was administered by the United States, the United Kingdom and Yugoslavia until

---

[40] Trusteeship Council, Statute for the City of Jerusalem, UN Doc. T/592 (4 April 1950), Article 1. The Trusteeship Council was to exercise the administrative powers of the UN through the appointment of the Governor.

[41] *Ibid.*, Article 37.

[42] *Ibid.*, Article 21.

[43] Treaty of Peace with Italy, signed at Paris (10 February 1947), 49 UNTS 126.

[44] Article 2, Annex VI Permanent statute of the Free Territory of Trieste, annexed to the Treaty of Peace with Italy.

[45] SC Res. 16, UN Doc. S/RES/16 (1947).

[46] *Ibid.*, article 17.

[47] *Ibid.*, articles 12 and 13.

the signature in 1954 of the London Agreement, in which Trieste was divided between Yugoslavia and Italy.[48] Despite the fact that these administration projects were never carried out, they at least constitute evidence of the legal capacity of the UN to administer territories, although discussions in that regard had raised many doubts about the legality and conformity with the UN Charter of these comprehensive administrative missions.

D. *Post-war Germany*

After the capitulation of Germany on 8 May 1945, the allied forces entirely occupied the German territory. As we will see later, the 1907 Hague Regulations[49] contain specific articles limiting the occupier's powers when involved in a belligerent occupation of foreign territory. Apart from the demilitarisation of Germany, the holding of war crimes trials leading to the creation of the Nuremberg Tribunal, and reparation for the damage caused by the Second World War, the aim of the post-war occupation of Germany was to re-establish a democratic environment through the restoration of strong political institutions.[50] The Berlin (Potsdam) Conference held in 1945 determined that the administration in Germany should be directed towards the decentralisation of the political structure and the development of local responsibility, based on democratic principles.[51] In addition to the establishment of a central German Government, the creation of administrative departments under the direction of the Control Council was also

---

[48] Memorandum of Understanding (with annexes and exchange of notes) regarding the Free Territory of Trieste (5 October 1954), 235 UNTS 99.

[49] Convention (IV) respecting the Laws and Customs of War on Land and its annex: Regulations concerning the Laws and Customs of War on Land, The Hague (18 October 1907), 187 CTS 227 (1907) [hereafter referred to a 'Hague Regulations'].

[50] At the Conference of Yalta, the Allied had nevertheless been very clear about their intentions towards Germany: "We are determined to disarm and disband all German armed forces; break up for all time the German General Staff [...]; remove or destroy all German military equipment; eliminate or control all German industry that could be used for military production; bring all war criminals to just and swift punishment and exact reparation in kind for the destruction wrought by the Germans; wipe out the Nazi Party, Nazi laws, organizations and institutions, remove all Nazi and militarist influences from public office and from the cultural and economic life of the German people; and take in harmony such other measures in Germany as may be necessary to the future peace and safety of the world." (Communiqué issued at the end of the Crimea (Yalta) Conference (4–11 February 1945), www.ena.lu/mce.cfm).

[51] Protocol of the Proceedings of the Berlin (Potsdam) Conference (1 August 1945), section II, A, 9, www.yale.edu/lawweb/avalon/20th.htm.

envisaged.[52] Therefore it was assumed even then that the situation represented more an international administration than an international occupation.[53]

German territory was divided into four zones, each under the responsibility of an Allied State, while a Control Council was established to supervise the administration of the different zones. The Control Council issued a directive in which it described the different normative instruments it could issue in order to exercise its functions.[54] On that basis, the Control Council issued a total of 46 laws relating to *inter alia* the abrogation of discriminatory laws, the reorganisation of the judiciary and tax collection.[55] On the political and institutional levels, each Zone progressed at a different speed. The American Zone quickly transferred power to the local *Landräte* through the organisation of elections. Elections were equally rapidly held in the Soviet Zone. In the British Zone members of the local institutions had simply been appointed by the British Commander-in-Chief, while the legislative powers of the *Länder* were recognised only in December 1946, as in the French Zone. The political reconstruction of Germany was nevertheless rapidly abandoned with the start of the Cold War and the withdrawal of the Soviet Union from the Control Council. The Federal Republic of Germany eventually regained its full independence in 1955 following the signature of an Agreement between France, the United Kingdom and the United States.[56]

Interestingly, the question of the applicable law posed problems as early as in the case of the post-war occupation of Germany. While certain laws were abrogated immediately, it was agreed that the laws adopted after 30 January 1933 were to be applied provided that they did not create injustice or discrimination. It was not however clearly established that the laws prior to 30 January 1933 were equally applicable. Eventually, it was determined that, in the American Zone, all laws applicable upon the establishment of the occupation remained applicable until replaced by subsequent laws.

---

[52] *Ibid.*

[53] See Virally: "Plutôt que d'occupation [...] il vaudrait mieux parler d'administration internationale" (Virally, M., *L'administration internationale de l'Allemagne du 8 mai 1945 au 24 avril 1947* (Paris: Pedone, 1948), p. 3).

[54] Directive Nr. 10 of 22 September 1945. For an overview, see: Virally, *supra* note 53, pp. 63–64.

[55] See Annex A, II – Lois, in Virally, *supra* note 53.

[56] Convention on the Rights and Obligations of Foreign Forces and Their Members in the Federal Republic of Germany, with annexes (26 May 1952), as amended by the Paris Protocol (23 October 1954), 332 UNTS 3.

E. *The United Nations Temporary Executive Authority in West Irian*

West Irian was a non-self-governing territory placed under the administration of the Netherlands. An Agreement between Indonesia and the Netherlands providing for the transfer of the administration of the territory from the Netherlands to Indonesia resulted in the establishment of the international administration of West Irian.[57] The UN was entrusted with the overall administration of the territory for a period of one year in order to facilitate the transfer of all powers to Indonesia. After this first year, the agreement provided for an 'act of self-determination', *i.e.* the organisation of a referendum in which the population of the territory would have to decide on its future. In order to carry out this administrative mandate, the Secretary-General, in accordance with the Agreement between Indonesia and the Netherlands, established the United Nations Temporary Executive Authority (UNTEA), which formally acted under the authority of the UN General Assembly.[58] The head of UNTEA, the UN Administrator, was granted "full authority under the direction of the Secretary-General to administer the territory for the period of the UNTEA administration".[59] The Agreement explicitly empowered UNTEA to promulgate new laws and regulations and to amend existing laws and regulations within the spirit and framework of the agreement, while existing laws and regulations remained applicable.[60]

Even if the experience in West Irian lasted only seven months, the UN established an important historical precedent in the international administration of a territory. Indeed, even if this precedent is rooted in the decolonisation process, the experience in West Irian is of substantial value, both for its recognition of the capacity of the UN to administer a territory outside the scope of the trusteeship system, and for the range of the powers granted to the administering authority. In addition, a very interesting feature of the UNTEA administration was the inclusion of a provision requiring the Administrator to "replace as rapidly as possible top Netherlands officials [...] with non-Netherlands, non-Indonesian officials during the first phase of the UNTEA administration which will be completed on 1 May 1963."[61] The Administrator was authorised to employ Dutch officials only on a temporary basis. The Agreement also required that as many West Irianese as possible should be brought into administrative and technical positions.[62] The reliance on local capacity to staff local institutions is

---

[57] Agreement (with annex) concerning West New Guinea (West Irian) (15 August 1962), 437 UNTS 274 [Hereafter 'Agreement concerning West Irian'].

[58] GA Res. 1752, UN Doc. A/RES/1752 (XVII) (21 September 1962).

[59] Article V, Agreement concerning West Irian.

[60] *Ibid.*, Article XI.

[61] *Ibid.*, Article IX.

[62] *Ibid.*

a recurrent feature of current reconstruction missions. Although in this case the main aim was not to establish an independent territory, with national institutions, the inclusion of such a provision presaged similar engagements in more complex operations.

Chapter 2

Evolving Peace Operations

The cases discussed in this chapter can be differentiated from the previous ones in the sense that they were set up in different contexts and with different objectives. In addition, while the older cases were necessary to establish the historical origins of the concept of international administration, the subsequent cases will illustrate the evolution in the granting of administrative powers to international actors in the context of comprehensive peace-building missions. The use of international administrations as a method to solve territorial questions is less apparent in these cases. In those cases where the administrations were nevertheless set up to oversee a territorial transition process, the mission's administrative mandate went far beyond the mere territorial transition, and included various peace-building elements. The operation in the Congo was the first operation mixing peacekeeping elements and other relatively limited state-building activities. The subsequent case of Namibia presents the first instance of (very) limited administrative powers in conjunction with election supervision. The actual start of the expansion of administrative mandates lies in the Cambodian experience. Subsequent cases are Somalia, the *sui generis* administration of Bosnia and Herzegovina and the first case in which the UN was granted more comprehensive administrative powers: the administration of Eastern Slovenia, Baranja and Western Sirmium.

A. *ONUC: Assisting the Congolese Government*

The Democratic Republic of the Congo became independent of Belgium on 30 June 1960. The days following independence were characterised by disorder and an attempted secession by Katanga province. This led to intervention by Belgian troops, without the consent of the newly independent state, in order to restore law and order and to protect the Belgian nationals who were still living in the Congo. After an explicit demand from the Congolese Government to the

Security Council, the latter adopted Resolution 143,[63] calling upon Belgium to withdraw its troops from the territory of the Congo.[64] Resolution 143 equally authorised the UN Secretary-General to take the necessary steps to "provide the Government with such military assistance as may be necessary until [...] the national security forces may be able [...] to meet fully their tasks".[65] Within 48 hours, the first contingents of UN troops began to arrive in Leopoldville, at the same time as UN civilian experts were deployed to help ensure the maintenance of essential public services.

The mandate of the UN Mission ('*Operation des Nations Unies au Congo*' – ONUC) was later modified and enlarged by the Security Council to include the preservation of the territorial integrity and political independence of the state, assistance to the Congolese Government in the maintenance of law and order, the prevention of a civil war, and the removal of all foreign military and paramilitary personnel and mercenaries.[66] These subsequent resolutions were adopted following a deterioration in the security situation, and the assassination of the Congolese Prime Minister Patrice Lumumba in Katanga Province. The Security Council authorised ONUC to use force if necessary to implement its mandate, especially in the secessionist Katanga province where foreign mercenaries were engaged in armed activities. ONUC was a large-scale military and civilian operation employing, at its peak, almost 20,000 UN Forces.[67] The tasks given to ONUC in that particular context were revolutionary and hitherto unprecedented in the history of the Organisation. However, ONUC was a painful operation for the UN, which suffered 250 fatalities and the loss of its Secretary-General Dag Hammarskjöld. Ultimately, after the reintegration of Katanga into the national territory of the Congo in February 1963, ONUC started to bow out and had withdrawn completely by 30 June 1964.

The effect of the mission, although positive concerning the reintegration of Katanga and the re-establishment of law and order, is however doubtful in the longer term. The subsequent control of President Mobutu Sese Seko, and the revival of hostilities in the 1990s led to the establishment of yet another UN Mission. The Congo has certainly not been able to maintain the stability it partially achieved at the withdrawal of ONUC in 1964, underlining the need to engage in more comprehensive operations than just the restoration of law and order, despite the presence of UN civilian advisors to counsel the Congo-

---

63 SC Res. 143, UN Doc. S/RES/143 (1960).

64 This was reiterated in later resolutions: SC Res. 145, UN Doc. S/RES/145 (1960) and SC Res. 146, UN Doc S/RES/146 (1960).

65 SC Res. 143, UN Doc. S/RES/143 (1960), para. 2.

66 See for example: SC Res. 161, UN Doc. S/RES/161 (1961) and SC Res. 169, UN Doc. S/RES/169 (1961).

67 See www.un.org/depts/DPKO/Missions/onucF.html.

lese Government on security matters. Nevertheless, the Congo's breakdown is unquestionably also an effect of the decolonisation process, but the question should also be asked whether ONUC's achievements were sufficient to build local capacity in order to create functioning government institutions.

B. *The United Nations Council for South West Africa*

After the General Assembly revoked South Africa's mandate over South West Africa,[68] the territory was placed under the direct administration and responsibility of the UN. The 'United Nations Council for South West Africa', established in 1967 by General Assembly Resolution 2248 (S–V), was designed to administer the territory until independence, with the maximum possible participation of the Territory's population.[69] The action undertaken by the General Assembly was subsequently 'recognised' in Security Council Resolutions 264 and 269.[70] However, as a consequence of the refusal of South Africa to withdraw its administration and its presence from Namibia, the UN administration could not access Namibian territory in order to exercise its administrative powers over it. Confronted with the impossibility of exercising legislative or executive powers *de facto*, the United Nations Council for Namibia nevertheless exercised its powers *de jure*. The Council *inter alia* issued a 'Decree for the Protection of the Natural Resources of Namibia', established the 'Institute for Namibia' to provide training for Namibians, and issued travel and identity documents for Namibians residing outside the territory.[71]

Finally, after a long period of negotiations and after the adoption of a settlement proposal,[72] the Security Council in 1978 adopted Resolution 431 requesting the appointment of a Special Representative for Namibia and the submission by the Secretary-General of a report on the implementation of the settlement

---

[68] South West Africa had been a colony of Germany since 1884 and was placed under mandate of South Africa in December 1920. The mandate was then revoked by General Assembly Resolution A/RES/2145 (XXI) on 27 October 1966. See International Court of Justice, *Legal Consequences for States of the Continued Presence of South Africa in Namibia (South West Africa) notwithstanding Security Council Resolution 276 (1970)*, Advisory Opinion, 21 June 1971, 1971 *ICJ Reports* 16.

[69] GA Res. 2248, UN Doc. A/RES/2248 (S–V) (19 May 1967). The 'United Nations Council for South West Africa was renamed 'United Nations Council for Namibia' in 1968 in accordance with the wish of its population.

[70] Cf. SC Res. 264, UN Doc. S/RES/264 (1969), para. 1, reaffirmed by SC Res. 269, UN Doc. S/RES/269 (1969).

[71] See Engers, J. F., 'The United Nations Travel and Identity Documents for Namibians', 66 *American Journal of International Law* 570 (1971), pp. 570–578.

[72] UN Doc. SC/12636 (10 April 1978).

proposal. The settlement proposal charged the Special Representative for Namibia with several civilian tasks, including the organisation of free and fair elections in order to achieve independence. The report submitted by the Secretary-General resulted in the creation in 1978 of the 'United Nations Transition Assistance Group' (UNTAG)[73] to assist the Special Representative of the Secretary-General to carry out the mandate conferred on him by Security Council Resolution 431. Following the South African opposition to the settlement proposal and the persistence of its illegal presence in Namibia, the Special Representative could assume his duties only in 1989.[74] Elections were finally held, and the elected Constituent Assembly drafted a constitution for the independent state.

Although the setting up of the administration in Namibia was a direct outcome of the decolonisation process, the case is still of major significance. The administration of Namibia was established by the General Assembly without reference to an inter-party agreement, and, as was the case in West Irian, it was established without the explicit consent of the parties involved, although an agreement was finally reached with South Africa to allow the deployment of UNTAG.[75] One nevertheless has to acknowledge that the entire operation in fact relied on a combination of administrative powers conferred on both the 'Council for Namibia' through a General Assembly Resolution, and UNTAG through a Security Council Resolution.

C. *Cambodia: Focusing on Elections*

The 'Agreement on a Comprehensive Political Settlement of the Cambodia Conflict' of 16 February 1991,[76] and more specifically Annex 1 to the Agreement, required the appointment of "a United Nations Transitional Authority in Cambodia (hereinafter referred to as 'UNTAC') with civilian and military components under the direct responsibility of the Secretary-General of the United Nations".[77] For this purpose the Secretary-General was asked to designate a Special

---

[73] SC Res. 435, UN Doc. S/RES/435 (1978).

[74] SC Res. 632, UN Doc. S/RES/632 (1989).

[75] Although this does not, in our view, preclude the fact that, initially, the administrative powers were based on a resolution rather than an agreement. Resolution 435 (1978) in its preamble merely refers to the 'relevant communications' from the South African Government to the Secretary-General. Zaum nevertheless considers that the administration was set up with the consent of the population (Zaum, D., *The Sovereignty Paradox: The Norms and Politics on International Statebuilding* (Oxford: Oxford University Press, 2007), p. 55).

[76] Agreement on the Comprehensive Political Settlement of the Cambodia Conflict, UN Doc. A/46/608-S/23177 (23 October 1991); 31 ILM 174 (1992).

[77] *Ibid.*, Article 6.

Representative to act on his behalf. Following the report of the Secretary-General, the Security Council adopted Resolution 745 effectively authorising the establishment of UNTAC.[78] The mandate given to UNTAC included many aspects relating to human rights, the organisation and conduct of free and fair elections, military arrangements, limited civil administration, the maintenance of law and order, the repatriation and resettlement of Cambodian refugees and internally displaced persons and the rehabilitation of essential Cambodian infrastructure. Clearly, this operation already covered many of the necessary building blocks for the reconstruction of territories in a peace-building context.

The administrative functions envisaged in the Paris Agreements required the exercise of control over existing administrative structures having impact on the outcome of the elections. UNTAC had been accorded the right to issue binding directives as necessary.[79] Concerning the electoral process, UNTAC had been authorised to establish, "in consultation with the SNC, a system of laws, procedures and administrative measures necessary for the holding of a free and fair election in Cambodia".[80] UNTAC even had the power to suspend or abrogate provisions of existing laws, which could defeat the objects and purposes of this Agreement.[81] Elections, in which 19 political parties participated, were held in May 1993, and were described as free and fair.[82]

Even if UNTAC was faced with several difficulties in exercising its powers and in achieving its mandate, the 22,000-member mission terminated in 1993 as the goals of the Paris Agreements had been fulfilled.[83] The relative success of this mission can be seen as a major achievement for the UN, as UNTAC was the first peacekeeping operation with such a large mandate relating to civil administration and the organisation of free and fair elections. The powers entrusted to UNTAC can only be compared to precedents like the Saar Basin and West Irian. The context in which the mission was set up nevertheless clearly differentiates it from those earlier cases. The long-term achievements of the mission have not however been as positive as its immediate successes. Although the foundations were laid for democratic institutions, the disarmament of militias was not achieved under UNTAC, and this resulted in the resurgence of violence after

[78] SC Res. 745, UN Doc. S/RES/745 (1992).

[79] Agreement on a Comprehensive Political Settlement of the Cambodia Conflict, Section B.

[80] *Ibid.*, Section D, Article 3, a.

[81] *Ibid.*, Section D, Article 3, b.

[82] Peou, S., 'The UN's modest impact on Cambodia's democracy', in Newman, E. and Rich, R., *The UN Role in Promoting Democracy: Between Ideals and Reality* (Tokyo / New York / Paris: United Nations University Press, 2004), p. 264.

[83] SC Res. 880, UN Doc. S/RES/880 (1993).

UNTAC's withdrawal.[84] In addition, no progress was made in the (transitional) justice sector. The lesson to be learned from this experience is the need to have adequate exit strategies. In Cambodia efforts were still too much centred on the organisation of elections only, while areas such as the justice sector were not or were only slightly touched upon.[85]

D. *Restoring Peace and Stability in Somalia*

Somalia is without doubt one of the clearest examples of failing governmental institutions. Since the military overthrow of the dictator General Mohamed Siad Barre in 1991, Somalia had been without an effective central government. From that time onwards, it was racked by substantial internal violence between the different political factions and the complete collapse of the state's structure.[86] The Security Council decided to intervene firstly by establishing a purely humanitarian mission, the United Nations Operation in Somalia (UNOSOM I).[87] In December 1992, the Security Council authorised the deployment of a multinational force, the Unified Task Force (UNITAF), organised and led by the United States. UNITAF was given permission to use all necessary means to establish a secure environment for humanitarian relief operations in Somalia.[88] The second and expanded United Nations Operation in Somalia (UNOSOM II)[89] was approved by the Security Council as the successor to UNITAF and UNOSOM I. UNOSOM II is a crucial mission, because it was not established by the Security Council following an agreement between the parties.

Unlike UNOSOM I, the expanded UNOSOM II mission was not limited to humanitarian assistance and the observation of the cease-fire agreement. Its mandate was much more complex and included elements of restoration of the state's institutions. More specifically, the mission was mandated to "assist the people of Somalia to promote and advance political reconciliation, through broad participation by all sectors of Somali society, and the re-establishment of

[84] See on the elections organised by UNTAC: Peou, S, 'The UN's modest impact on Cambodia's democracy', in Newman and Rich, *supra* note 82, p. 269.

[85] See for an assessment, Boua, C., 'Cambodia, ten years after UNTAC', in Azimi, N., Fuller, M. and Nakayama, H. (eds.), *Post Conflict Reconstruction* (New York / Geneva: United Nations Publications, 2003), p. 121.

[86] See Yannis, A., 'State Collapse and Prospects for Political Reconstruction and Democratic Governance in Somalia', 5 *African Yearbook of International Law* 23 (1997), pp. 23–47.

[87] SC Res. 751, UN Doc. S/RES/751 (1992).

[88] SC Res. 794, UN Doc. S/RES/794 (1992).

[89] SC Res. 814, UN Doc. S/RES/814 (1993).

national and regional institutions and civil administration in the entire territory".[90] In February 1994, the mission's mandate was reshaped, and the mission was *inter alia* asked to assist in the reorganization of the Somali police and judicial system and to assist in the political process in Somalia, in particular the installation of a democratically elected government.[91] In the absence of an effective government and administration, and pending the creation of the Transitional National Council, which was envisaged by the Addis Ababa Agreement of 27 March 1993,[92] UNOSOM II assumed some administrative and legislative powers in Somalia in respect of *inter alia* the applicable penal laws.[93] Before and after the revision of its mandate, the mission took several measures relating to *inter alia* the judiciary, the elaboration of a new constitution, and the training and reinstitution of a police force.[94]

UNOSOM II is a significant mission in the development of peace-building towards international post-conflict administration. From the purely legal point of view, we should highlight the fact that the Security Council based Resolution 814 in part on Chapter VII. However, UNOSOM II is not a mission with a solely coercive mandate; Chapter VII was essential in this case because the military presence had to be authorised to use force if necessary in order to implement the resolution. The administrative objectives assigned to UNOSOM II were however not completely achieved. The difficulties UNOSOM II faced were considerable, since it needed to act as a government without the necessary mandate, and thus resources, to perform this task. UNOSOM II was eventually withdrawn in early March 1995. Probably one of the most important lessons to be learned from the experience in Somalia, in respect of peace-building missions, is that the success of such missions is not possible unless they have a clear mandate and full control over the territory.

[90] *Ibid.*, Art. 4, c).

[91] SC Res. 897, UN Doc. S/RES/897 (1994).

[92] Addis Ababa Agreement concluded at the first session of the Conference on National Reconciliation in Somalia (27 March 1993), in *The United Nations and Somalia 1992–1996*, United Nations Blue Books Series, Vol. VIII (New York: United Nations, Dept. of Public Information, 1996), pp. 241–242.

[93] See on the question whether such powers were in conformity with UNOSOM's mandate, Sarooshi, D., 'The United Nations and the Development of Collective Security. The Delegation by the UN Security Council of Its Chapter VII Powers' (Oxford: Clarendon Press, 1999), p. 63.

[94] See for an overview of the administrative tasks performed by UNOSOM: Further report of the Secretary-General on the United Nations Operation in Somalia submitted in pursuance of paragraph 14 of Resolution 897 (1994), UN Doc. S/1194/614 (24 May 1994). See also Han, S. K., 'Building a Peace that Lasts: The United Nations and Post-Civil War Peace-Building', 26 *NYU Journal of International Law and Politics* 837 (1993–1994).

E. *Co-administration in Bosnia and Herzegovina*

Negotiations after the end of the hostilities in Bosnia, with the presence of the United Nations Protection Force (UNPROFOR) to monitor the ceasefire, led to the signature of the 'General Agreement for Peace in Bosnia and Herzegovina' ('Dayton Agreement') in December 1995.[95] The Dayton Agreement, besides the general provisions of a peace treaty, contained a list of annexes defining the role of the international community in rebuilding the state. The annexes included provisions relating to the involvement of international organisations, the military presence, the supervision of elections, the preservation of national monuments by UNESCO and the future constitution of Bosnia. The Dayton Agreement was subsequently endorsed by the Security Council under a Chapter VII Resolution.[96]

Annex 10 to the Dayton Agreement provided for the appointment of a High Representative to facilitate its implementation.[97] The High Representative was given the right to act as final authority in the interpretation of the Agreement. It should be stressed that the High Representative was not a UN body, as the UN was seen as discredited by its performance as peacekeeper in the Balkans.[98] The major tasks of the High Representative were to monitor the implementation of the peace settlement and to co-ordinate the activities of the organisations and agencies in Bosnia and Herzegovina. In addition to the High Representative, the Agreement established a Peace Implementation Council (PIC), mandated to oversee his work. The High Representative's powers were expanded following the Bonn Summit of the Peace Implementation Council in 1997 (the so-called 'Bonn Powers'), which for example enabled the High Representative to remove from office public officials who violated legal commitments and the Dayton Peace Agreement. In addition, he was given a mandate to impose and change laws if Bosnia and Herzegovina's legislative bodies failed to do so.[99]

Next to the Office of the High Representative, and in accordance with the Dayton Agreement, a UN Mission in Bosnia and Herzegovina (UNMIBH) was established in combination with a UN International Police Task Force (IPTF).[100] The main objectives of the IPTF were to monitor, observe and inspect law

---

[95] General Agreement for Peace in Bosnia and Herzegovina, UN Doc. S/1995/999 (14 December 1995) [hereafter 'Dayton Agreement'].

[96] SC Res. 1031, UN Doc. S/RES/1031 (1995).

[97] Art. 1, Annex 10, Dayton Agreement.

[98] Cousens, E. M. and Cater, C. K., *Towards Peace in Bosnia: Implementing the Dayton Accords* (Boulder: Lynne Riener Publishers, 2001), p. 46.

[99] Cf. PIC Bonn Conclusions (10 December 1997), www.ohr.int/pic/default.asp?content_id=5182.

[100] SC Res. 1035, UN Doc. S/RES/1035 (1995).

enforcement activities and facilities, and to advise and train law enforcement personnel.[101] UNMIBH was an umbrella mission, and had authority over the UN IPTF Commissioner. The Mission was equally given a limited civilian mandate, mainly aimed at the co-ordination of UN activity in the field of humanitarian relief, refugees, human rights, elections, rehabilitation of infrastructure and economic reconstruction.[102] The mission was finally withdrawn on 31 December 2002, and the main activities were transferred to a European Union (EU) mission.[103]

In the evolution of comprehensive peace-building, the Bosnian case is clearly a *sui generis* form of limited international administration, comprising the exercise of administrative powers by a 'High Commissioner' and a UN mission. In addition, the Dayton Agreement essentially relied on co-administration by national and international actors, based on co-operation more than extensive administering authority for the international presence. As such the case is closer to the Cambodian precedent than to the 'full' UN-led administrations in Kosovo and East Timor.[104] Nevertheless the lessons from Bosnia are important. Plans to withdraw early after the holding of elections and the limited powers of the international actors underline the necessity of establishing both a clear mandate from the start and an effective exit strategy.

F. *The Transitional Administration for Eastern Slovenia*

An Agreement concluded between the Croatian Government and the Serb Authority[105] requested the Security Council to establish an international administration to govern the region during a transitional period of 12 months, and to authorise an international force to maintain peace and security during that period and otherwise to assist in the implementation of the Agreement. The Basic Agreement on the Region of Eastern Slavonia, Baranja and Western Sirmium provided for the peaceful integration of that region into Croatia. The Security

---

[101] Annex 11, Dayton Agreement.

[102] Report of the Secretary General pursuant to Security Council Resolution 1026 (1995), UN Doc. S/1995/1031 (13 December 1995).

[103] See on the achievements of UNMIBH: Report of the Secretary General on the United Nations Mission in Bosnia and Herzegovina, UN Doc. S/2002/1314 (2 December 2002).

[104] See also on the relation between the experience in Bosnia and Kosovo and East Timor: Bothe and Marauhn, *supra* note 6, p. 224 and Chesterman, S., *You the People – The United Nations, Transitional Administration, and State-Building* (Oxford: Oxford University Press, 2004), p. 79.

[105] Basic Agreement on the Region of Eastern Slavonia, Baranja and Western Sirmium, UN Doc. S/1995/951 (12 November 1995).

Council, by adopting Resolution 1023 (1995), 'welcomed' the agreement and 'recognised' the request made by the parties to establish a Transitional Administration.[106] The 'United Nations Transitional Administration for Eastern Slavonia, Baranja and Western Sirmium' (UNTAES) was set up on 15 January 1996 by Security Council Resolution 1037, with both military and civilian components, under the global authority and supervision of a Transitional Administrator. The civilian component was to establish a temporary police force, monitor the prison system, undertake tasks relating to civil administration and to the functioning of public services, facilitate the return of refugees and organise elections, assist in their conduct, and certify the results.[107] The additional tasks of UNTAES included economic reconstruction and facilitating the demining of the territory.[108] In order to accomplish the mandate, the Transitional Administrator was granted, alongside important executive powers, some limited legislative powers. As the Secretary-General's December 1995 Report states: "if there are any areas in which Croatian law has been modified or supplemented by legislation enacted by the local Serb authorities during the period since 1991 or by other law, it would be necessary to establish a programme and modalities for the earliest possible restoration of the law of the Republic of Croatia. The transitional administrator might also need to have legislative power to enact regulations for carrying out the functions attributed to him by the agreement; the validity of such regulations would expire at the end of the transitional period, unless the Croatian authorities decided otherwise".[109]

Despite the fact that the experience in Eastern Slavonia has been somehow neglected in the literature, it illustrates important aspects of the international administration paradigm. The Easter Slavonia administration is noteworthy because Resolution 1037 was adopted by the Security Council acting under Chapter VII of the UN Charter. As we will see in the next part, international administrations can be based on several provisions of the UN Charter, according to whether or not the parties involved in the conflict consented to the establishment of the mission. The explicit mention of Chapter VII of the UN Charter is significant, as the mission was also based on an agreement between the parties. However, as in Somalia, in this case, Chapter VII was seen as indispensable, not because there was no agreement between the parties, but because the Security Council had to authorise the use of force in order to guarantee the implementation of the Agreement and to make sure that UNTAES would

---

[106] SC Res. 1023 UN Doc. S/RES/1023 (1995).

[107] *Ibid.*, Article 11 (a)–(f).

[108] *Ibid.*, Article 12.

[109] Report of the Secretary-General pursuant to Security Council Resolution 1025 (1995), UN Doc. S/1995/1031 (13 December 1995), para. 17.

achieve its mandate.[110] The experience in Eastern Slavonia equally was generally described as successful, because it managed to reintegrate the territory into Croatia in a peaceful and smooth manner; this was, it should be remembered, its first and foremost task.

---

[110] According to the Secretary-General, "[i]n more hostile circumstances, operations under Chapter VII of the Charter of the United Nations can help to solve commitment and cooperation problems by directly implementing agreements, or raising the costs of violating peace agreements. In these cases the use of force to resist attempts by the parties to prevent the operations from fulfilling their mandates should be – and typically is – authorized and resourced in support of or as a substitute for a comprehensive peace treaty, as in the United Nations Transitional Administration for Eastern Slavonia, Baranja and Western Sirmium (UNTAES) in Croatia or the United Nations Interim Administration Mission in Kosovo (UNMIK), respectively" (Report of the Secretary-General, 'No exit without strategy: Security Council decision-making and the closure or transition of United Nations peacekeeping operations', UN Doc. S/2001/394 (20 April 2001), para. 17).

Chapter 3

UN International Administrations, the 'Light Footprint' Approach and the Occupation of Iraq

This chapter continues to assess the evolution described in the previous chapters and is aimed at situating the cases of Kosovo, East Timor, Afghanistan and Iraq within it. Full administrative powers were assumed by the UN in the cases of Kosovo and East Timor. Alternative approaches are the 'light footprint' in Afghanistan, and the post-conflict occupation of Iraq by the coalition forces. In the latter two cases, the UN was only granted a limited role in the post-conflict phase.

A. *The United Nations Interim Administration in Kosovo*

Following NATO's armed intervention in Kosovo in March 1999, the Security Council adopted Resolution 1244 establishing the 'United Nations Interim Administration Mission in Kosovo' (UNMIK).[111] Resolution 1244 was adopted after the acceptance by the Federal Republic of Yugoslavia of the plan presented by Martti Ahtisaari and Victor Chernomyrdin,[112] which contained the general principles of an agreement on the Kosovo crisis.[113] In the post-conflict peace-building context, the international administration of Kosovo is, at present, the

[111] SC Res. 1244, UN Doc. S/RES/1244 (1999).

[112] "Agreement on the principles (peace plan) to move towards a resolution of the Kosovo crisis presented to the leadership of the Federal Republic of Yugoslavia by the President of Finland, Martti Ahtisaari, representing the European Union, and Viktor Chernomyrdin, Special Representative of the President of the Russian Federation", UN Doc. S/1999/649 (3 June 1999).

[113] NATO's intervention in Kosovo followed the refusal of Yugoslavia to sign the 'Rambouillet Accords' (Interim Agreement for Peace and Self-Government in Kosovo, UN Doc. S/1999/648 (7 June 1999). During the NATO air strikes, the G8 foreign ministers had a meeting in Petersberg, resulting in a "Statement by the Chairman on the conclusion of the meeting of the G-8 Foreign Ministers held at the Petersberg Centre on 6 May", UN Doc. 1999S/1999/516

most comprehensive mission ever deployed by the UN. The powers granted to UNMIK and the Special Representative of the Secretary-General encompass a wide range of executive and legislative powers, the scope of which is unprecedented in that context. A complementary and important aspect making UNMIK a historic case lies in the fact that the Security Council Resolution is adopted under Chapter VII, almost 'imposing' the mission onto the Federal Republic of Yugoslavia,[114] even if the latter had previously accepted the Ahtisaari-Chernomyrdin proposal.

The Security Council agreed to the deployment of an international civil and an international security presence under UN auspices. The Secretary-General was requested to appoint a Special Representative who was to lead the civil presence and co-ordinate closely with the security presence.[115] The security presence was to operate independently of the civil presence, under the general authority of NATO. More specifically, Resolution 1244 called upon UNMIK to promote the establishment of substantial autonomy and self-government in Kosovo, perform basic civilian administrative functions, facilitate a political process to determine Kosovo's future status, co-ordinate the humanitarian and disaster relief of all international agencies, support the reconstruction of key infrastructure, maintain civil law and order, promote human rights, and assure the safe and unimpeded return of all refugees and displaced persons to their homes in Kosovo.[116] To implement its mandate, UNMIK initially brought together four 'pillars' under its leadership, as envisaged by the Secretary-General in his report following the adoption of Resolution 1244. Each of the four pillars was entrusted to international organisations working together as a sort of 'federation' under the general authority and co-ordination of the Special Representative of the Secretary-General, the head of UNMIK. Initially, the responsibilities were divided as follows: 'humanitarian assistance' led by the Office of the United Nations High Commissioner for Refugees (UNHCR), 'civil administration' under the direct leadership of the UN, 'democratisation and institution building' led by the Organisation for Security and Co-operation in Europe (OSCE), and

(6 May 1999), providing for a set of principles for a political solution for the Kosovo crisis. These principles are annexed to Resolution 1244.

[114] The Federal Republic of Yugoslavia was a federal state consisting of the republics of Serbia and Montenegro, and was formed following the collapse of the former Socialist Federal Republic of Yugoslavia. In 2003, the Federal Republic of Yugoslavia was reinstated as the State Union of Serbia and Montenegro, which was in turn dissolved following the independence of Montenegro in 2006. We will nevertheless refer to the Federal Republic of Yugoslavia when discussing issues occurred under the Federal Republic of Yugoslavia, while we will refer to 'Serbia' when we discuss aspects of the state's current involvement.

[115] SC Res. 1244, UN Doc. S/RES/1244 (1999), paras. 5 and 6.

[116] *Ibid.*, para. 11 (a)–(k).

'reconstruction and economic development' led by the EU. At the end of the emergency stage, Pillar I was phased out, and replaced in May 2001 by a new Pillar I 'police and justice', formerly part of the civil administration pillar.

The competences of UNMIK and of the Special Representative included the power to regulate within the areas of responsibility laid down by Resolution 1244. In doing so, the Special Representative was even granted the right to change, repeal or suspend existing laws to the extent necessary for the carrying out of his functions. The Special Representative also had the right, where existing laws were incompatible with his mandate conferred by Resolution 1244, or with the aims and purposes of the interim civil administration, to alter the existing laws.[117] The Special Representative confirmed these extensive powers by vesting UNMIK with all legislative and executive authority with respect to Kosovo, including the administration of the judiciary, in order to achieve its mandate.[118]

As long as no political solution was found for the future status of the territory, no definitive and global transfer of authority to the Kosovar Institutions could take place. It should however be remembered that an international administration is by definition a temporary arrangement. Political negotiations under UN auspices led in March 2007 to a proposal by the Secretary-General's Special Envoy for a sort of 'conditional' independence. The Special Envoy equally requested the presence of an EU mission to oversee the implementation of the agreement.[119] Russian opposition however prevented the formal adoption of the status settlement proposal by the Security Council. Soon afterwards, an agreement was reached by the members of the 'Contact Group' – the United States, the United Kingdom, France, Germany, Italy, and the Russian Federation – to have a troika composed of the European Union, the Russian Federation and the United States to lead further negotiations on the future status of Kosovo.[120] The Contact Group reported to the Secretary-General on the progress of negotiations with Belgrade on 10 December 2007 but was not able to propose a consensual solution. Eventually, on 17 February 2008, Kosovo unilaterally declared independence with the adoption of a declaration in the Kosovo General Assembly. By May 2008, some 43 States had recognised Kosovo as an independent state. The envisaged EU mission, EULEX, had in the meantime been moderately deployed in the country, but was subjected to much legal controversy. Indeed,

[117] Report of the Secretary-General of the United Nations Interim Administration Mission in Kosovo, UN Doc. S/1999/779 (12 July 1999), paras. 39–40.

[118] UNMIK Regulation 1999/1 on the authority of the interim administration in Kosovo, UN Doc. UNMIK/REG/1999/1 (25 July 1999).

[119] Comprehensive Proposal for the Kosovo Status Settlement, UN Doc. S/2007/168/Add. 1 (26 March 2007).

[120] UNMIK News Coverage, 'Ban Ki-moon endorses new initiative on determining Kosovo's future status' (1 August 2007).

as Resolution 1244 is the basis for the international presence in Kosovo, any change in the mission's mandate, including its replacement by a smaller EU mission, will need approval of the Security Council. Any consent by the host state will be the subject of controversy, considering the limited amount of official recognition of Kosovo's independence by other states. In addition, when establishing UNMIK, the Security Council did not work with the more common one-year renewable terms, but instead agreed that the mission would last until it was revoked by the Security Council.

B. *The United Nations Transitional Authority in East Timor*

The 'United Nations Transitional Authority in East Timor' (UNTAET) was established in 1999 with the adoption of Security Council Resolution 1272.[121] The creation of UNTAET followed the conduct of a 'popular consultation' among the East Timorese on 30 August 1999, through which they expressed their clear wish to begin a process of transition towards independence.[122] According to Security Council Resolution 1272, UNTAET was "endowed with overall responsibility for the administration of East Timor and will be empowered to exercise all legislative and executive authority, including the administration of justice".[123] UNTAET's responsibility for the administration of East Timor during its transition to independence encompassed an all-inclusive mandate in order to provide security and maintain law and order, to establish an effective administration, to assist in the development of civil and social services, to ensure the co-ordination and delivery of humanitarian assistance, rehabilitation and development assistance, and to support capacity-building for self-government.[124] UNTAET's mandate was largely identical to that of UNMIK. A major difference however was the military component, which in this case was formally part of UNTAET and therefore under the direct authority of the Special Representative. UNTAET was initially composed of three pillars under the responsibility of the Special Representative: the Military Pillar, the Humanitarian Assistance and Emergency Rehabilitation Pillar and the Governance and Public Administration Pillar. Gradually, authority was transferred to local institutions, and, finally, democratically elected institutions. On 20 May 2002, East Timor became an independent country, marking the end of a three-year transitional administration

---

121 SC Res. 1272, UN Doc. S/RES/1272 (1999).

122 See also on the organisation of the referendum: Agreement between the Republic of Indonesia and the Portuguese Republic on the question of East Timor, Annex I to the Report of the Secretary General, UN Doc. A/53/951–S/1999/513 (5 May 1999).

123 SC Res. 1272, UN Doc. S/RES/1272 (1999), Article 1.

124 *Ibid.*, Article 2.

by the UN. The new nation changed its name to Timor-Leste and became the 191st UN Member State on 27 September 2002.

The precarious situation of the independent state upon UNTAET's withdrawal nevertheless necessitated continuing international supervision. UNTAET was replaced by the 'United Nations Mission of Support in East Timor '(UNMISET),[125] established under Security Council Resolution 1410 (2002), which was *inter alia* mandated to provide assistance to core administrative structures critical to the viability and political stability of East Timor, to provide interim law enforcement and public security, and to contribute to the maintenance of the external and internal security of East Timor.[126] On 20 May 2005, UNMISET concluded its mandate in Timor-Leste and was succeeded by a 'follow-on special political mission', the United Nations Office in Timor-Leste (UNOTIL).[127] After a year, the mission was replaced by the United Nations Integrated Mission in Timor-Leste (UNMIT), which was established under Security Council Resolution 1704 (2006)[128] with a more comprehensive mandate including support to the Government and relevant institutions with a view to consolidating stability, enhancing a culture of democratic governance, and facilitating political dialogue among Timorese stakeholders, the restoration and maintenance of public security in Timor, capacity-building in the field of police and defence, and the promotion of a 'compact' between Timor-Leste and the international community.[129] The 'compact', called 'Working Together to Build the Foundations for Peace and Stability and Improve Livelihoods of Timorese Citizens', was adopted at the March 2008 Timor-Leste and Development Partners' Meeting. The document contains a number of national priorities on security, safety and social issues.[130]

C. *Afghanistan: the 'Light Footprint' Approach*

One month after the 11 September 2001 attacks on the World Trade Center and the Pentagon, a United States-led coalition embarked on a military intervention in Afghanistan aimed at eradicating the terrorist network Al-Qaeda, harboured by the Taliban regime in Afghanistan. A month later, the Taliban were effectively

---

[125] SC Res. 1410, UN Doc. S/RES/1410 (2002).

[126] The Secretary-General requested a slight revision of UNMISET's tasks in his April 2004 report. See: Report of the Secretary-General on the United Nations Mission of Support in East Timor, UN Doc. S/2004 /333 (29 April 2004).

[127] SC Res. 1599, UN Doc. S/RES/1599 (2005).

[128] SC Res. 1704, UN Doc. S/RES/1704 (2006).

[129] *Ibid.*, para. 4, f.

[130] The document is available at www.unmit.org.

removed from power. The question immediately arose what the role of the UN would be in the reconstruction of Afghanistan. From the start, it was clear that Afghanistan would not be a 'full' UN-led international administration like UNMIK or UNTAET. Although this kind of operation could have been a solution,[131] the focus was on the greatest possible participation of local actors and less international involvement. The main reason for this minimalist approach is probably that, after the fall of the Taliban regime, local power was logically assumed by various local leaders and commanders. Illegal economy and drug trafficking also flourished after the fall of the Taliban. If the political process was to succeed, all local leaders had to accept the proposed political course of action, although, as we will see, relying on a national interim authority does not necessarily imply the disappearance of parallel structures. In addition, Afghanistan was a sovereign state, the territorial status of which was never questioned. East Timor on the other hand was not yet a sovereign state, whereas Kosovo's final status had yet to be determined. A limited UN assistance mission was therefore seen as far more acceptable to the local population and leaders than a full-scale UN administration. As the Secretary-General put it, the UN's tasks was aimed to "bolster Afghan capacity [...], relying on as limited an international presence and on as many Afghan staff as possible, [...], thereby leaving a light expatriate 'footprint'".[132] This 'light footprint' approach was particularly favoured by UN Special Envoy Lakhdar Brahimi who led the Bonn talks. Brahimi stated that the UN's role "should be to provide the government with support and assistance, not to seek to govern in its place or impose upon it our own goals and aspiration". He further stated that "the peace and reconstruction process stands a far better chance of success when it is nationally owned rather than led by external actor".[133] As we will see, this assumption was flawed. The consequence of this approach was that the Bonn Agreement did not give the UN a mandate to exercise administrative authority over the territory, nor a direct responsibility for the administration of the territory.

The peace conference held in Bonn on 5 December 2001 under UN auspices resulted in an agreement which provided *inter alia* for a Special Independent Commission for the Convening of an Emergency *Loya Jirga*, a traditional Afghan National Assembly.[134] The Emergency *Loya Jirga* was envisaged as convening in

---

[131] See Chesterman, S., 'Tiptoeing through Afghanistan: The Future of UN State-Building', *International Peace Academy – Report from the Transitional Administrations Project* (September 2002), p. 3.

[132] Report of the Secretary-General, UN Doc. A/57/487–S/2002/278, *supra* note 2, para. 98 d.

[133] Aita, J., 'United Nations' Brahimi says Afghanistan will need help for years', United States Mission to the European Union (9 September 2002).

[134] Agreement on Provisional Arrangement of Afghanistan pending the Re-establishment of Permanent Government Institutions, UN Doc. S/2001/1154 (5 December 2001) [hereafter 'Bonn Agreement'].

June 2002 for the nomination of a Transitional Authority to govern the state until democratic elections were held.[135] Pending the nomination of the Transitional Authority, an Interim Authority was established as "the repository of Afghan sovereignty".[136] The Interim Authority was entrusted "with the day-to-day conduct of the affairs of the state", and had "the right to issue decrees for the peace, order and good government of Afghanistan".[137] The Bonn Agreement also included provisions on the drafting of a new constitution, the convening of a Constitutional *Loya Jirga* by the end of 2003, and democratic elections, to be held in 2004.[138]

The participants in the UN Talks on Afghanistan requested the UN Security Council to authorise the deployment of an 'Assistance Force' to support the maintenance of security for Kabul and its surrounding areas. Although the Bonn Agreement confirmed that the primary responsibility for providing security and law and order throughout the country resided with the Afghans themselves, the assistance of the international community was requested to help the new Afghan authorities in the reconstruction of a national police and defence force. The Bonn Agreement therefore consented to the concomitant deployment of an international security force, the International Security Assistance Force (ISAF),[139] which was subsequently endorsed by the Security Council.[140] At first, ISAF had a presence only in Kabul and its surrounding areas. Later, the mission gradually deployed outside Kabul.

Following the signature of the Bonn Agreement, the Security Council unanimously endorsed the Agreement[141] and established the 'United Nations Assistance Mission in Afghanistan' (UNAMA),[142] in conformity with the outcome of the Bonn Conference and according to the Secretary General's report on the proposed structure for the UN presence in Afghanistan.[143] UNAMA's core mandate consists of the provision of assistance to the Interim Authority, the fulfilment of the tasks entrusted to the UN by the Bonn Agreement, and the co-ordination of all UN humanitarian and reconstruction activities in Afghanistan.[144] The mission was established with two main pillars: a 'political affairs pillar' and a 'relief, recovery and reconstruction pillar', both under the

---

135 Art. I, 4, Bonn Agreement.
136 *Ibid.*, Art. I, 3.
137 *Ibid.*, Art. III, C, 3.
138 *Ibid.*, Art. I, 4 and 6.
139 *Ibid.*, Annex 1.
140 SC Res. 1386, UN Doc. S/RES/1386 (2001).
141 SC Res. 1383, UN Doc. S/RES/1383 (2001).
142 SC Res. 1401, UN Doc. S/RES/1401 (2002).
143 Report of the Secretary-General, UN Doc. A/57/487–S/2002/278, *supra* note 2.
144 *Ibid.*, para. 97 and Art. III, C, 9, Bonn Agreement.

responsibility of a Special Representative of the Secretary-General.[145] The tasks of the first pillar were dedicated to the implementation of the political transition laid out in the Bonn Agreement, but also included the investigation of human rights violations and the combating of illicit drug trafficking. Pillar II is mainly responsible for the co-ordination of UN assistance programmes and capacity development in the public sector. Although UNAMA established a framework for the co-ordination of humanitarian aid, there was no true structure to the international community's involvement and donor assistance with regard to the other matters. However, we will see that many areas addressed under the international administrations in Kosovo and East Timor were equally present in the case of Afghanistan. The reconstruction efforts were based on a 'lead-nation approach', leaving the responsibility for certain areas to a specific country: the United States was the lead donor nation for reconstructing the Afghan National Army, Germany for the police, the United Kingdom for counter-narcotics, Italy for justice, and Japan for the disarmament, demobilisation and reintegration of ex-combatants (DDR).

With the holding of parliamentary and provincial elections, the Bonn process formally ended in September 2005. Despite the relative 'successes' of the political transition, as we will see, obstacles to a sustainable peace remain, since several critical aspects included in the Bonn Agreement have not been met: voter registration, civil service reform, judicial reform and the holding of district council elections. In order to provide a continuing framework for the reconstruction of Afghanistan and the role of the international community, a conference was held in London in January 2006 to launch the 'Afghanistan Compact'.[146] The document is not as such legally binding, as it has been neither signed nor endorsed by any government. The Afghanistan Compact identified three priority areas in which progress still had a long way to go: 1/ security, governance, 2/ rule of law and human rights, and 3/ economic and social development.[147] The Compact contains in its first annex a set of benchmarks and timelines for each priority area. The majority of the benchmarks request results by the end of 2010. As a follow-up to the London Conference, the Government of Afghanistan engaged in the elaboration of a final 'Afghanistan National Development Strategy'.[148] Each sector and sub-sector of the Afghan administration, ministries and independent agencies elaborated a strategy for the achievement of the goals and standards of

---

145 Report of the Secretary-General, UN Doc. A/57/487–S/2002/278, *supra* note 2, para. 99. Each pillar is headed by a Deputy Special Representative of the Secretary-General.

146 Endorsed by the Security Council as a Framework Document: SC Res. 1659, UN Doc. S/RES/1659 (15 February 2006) [hereafter 'Afghanistan Compact'].

147 Preamble, Afghanistan Compact.

148 The Interim Afghanistan National Development Strategy had been presented at the London Conference.

the Afghanistan Compact.[149] The Afghanistan Compact equally created a 'Joint Coordination and Monitoring Board', with a mixed composition, and co-chaired by a senior Afghan Government official appointed by the President and by the Special Representative of the Secretary-General.[150] UNAMA's mandate was subsequently extended and redefined in function of the new agreement and contains six key elements: providing political and strategic advice for the peace process, providing good offices, assisting Afghanistan's government towards implementation of the Afghanistan Compact, promoting human rights, providing technical assistance, and continuing to co-ordinate all UN humanitarian relief, recovery, reconstruction and development activities.[151] The structure however, remains essentially the same.[152]

D. *The Foreign Occupation of Iraq*

After the fall of Saddam Hussein's regime following military intervention – 'Operation Iraqi Freedom' – led by the United States and the United Kingdom, the question immediately arose how the problem of the reconstruction and administration of the territory would be tackled. From the start we need to highlight that the legality and legitimacy of the military intervention will not be discussed, as this would be outside the scope of this book, although we should note that it remains highly controversial. The reconstruction process in Iraq is a specific case in which a completely different approach was followed, although the major objectives are essentially the same as those in the other cases. The UN's role in Iraq is very limited. The administration of the territory was the primary responsibility of the occupying powers, the United States and the United Kingdom. The occupying power nevertheless had limited powers to administer the territory, as a consequence of the 1907 Hague Regulations and the Fourth Geneva Convention,[153] but, as we will see, the Security Council both confirmed the coalition's mandate and expanded its administrative powers.

After, and even before, the beginning of Operation Iraqi Freedom, different plans were discussed for the post-conflict scenario. It was clear from the start that there would not be a provisional government led by Iraqis similar to the Afghan model, nor a UN-led administration. Eventually, the coalition opted

---

149 See www.ands.gov.af/strategies/strategies.asp.

150 Annex III, Afghanistan Compact.

151 SC Res. 1662, UN Doc. S/RES/1662 (2006).

152 Report of the Secretary-General, The situation in Afghanistan and its implications for international peace and security, UN Doc. A/60/712–S/2006/145 (7 March 2006), paras. 53 *et s.*

153 Convention (IV) relative to the Protection of Civilian Persons in Time of War. Geneva (12 August 1949), 75 UNTS 287 [hereafter 'Fourth Geneva Convention'].

for a United States-led administration with minimal UN participation. The first administrative structure introduced by the United States was the 'Office for Reconstruction and Humanitarian Assistance' (OHRA), which was set up to handle the administration of the country in the emergency phase, and especially to deal with the humanitarian crisis. The US and the UK, as occupying powers, created the 'Coalition Provisional Authority' (CPA), led by Ambassador L. Paul Bremer III, which was entrusted with the governing powers. As the primary governing institution, the CPA had all executive, legislative and judicial competences necessary for the execution of its mandate.[154] OHRA was superseded by the CPA on 11 May 2004.[155]

Security Council Resolution 1483 (2003)[156] contains the basic provisions for the administration of the territory and clarifies the different responsibilities in Iraq. Resolution 1483 confirmed that the CPA had the primary responsibility in the administration of Iraq, and the Security Council called on the CPA to fulfil its obligations under the Hague Regulations and the Geneva Conventions. At the same time the Security Council considerably expanded the CPA's mandate by calling on the occupying powers to promote the welfare of the Iraqi people through the effective administration of the territory. Some authors nevertheless claim that Resolution 1483 did not change the rights and duties of the administering authority because the relevant paragraphs of that resolution were not precise enough to supplant the rules relating to foreign occupation.[157] Other authors claim that a Security Council resolution can never derogate from the laws of armed conflict, and that Resolution 1483 could thus in any event not be interpreted as extended the power of the occupying forces.[158] Nevertheless, the wording of Resolution 1483 leaves no doubt that the CPA's powers were extended or at least modified. Indeed, one cannot ignore that "promote the welfare of the Iraqi people through the effective administration of the territory, including in particular working towards the restoration of conditions of security

[154] "The CPA is vested with all executive, legislative and judicial authority necessary to achieve its objectives, to be exercised under relevant U.N. Security Council resolutions, including Resolution 1483 (2003), and the laws and usages of war". CPA Regulation Number 1, 'The Coalition Provisional Authority', CPA/REG/16 May 2003/01 (16 May 2003).

[155] For an overview of the CPA's status, see Halchin, L. E., 'The Coalition Provisional Authority (CPA): origin, characteristics, and institutional authorities', *Congressional Research Service*, CRS report for Congress, Doc. Nr. RL32370 (2005).

[156] SC Res. 1483, UN Doc. S/RES/1483 (2003).

[157] See e.g. Kolb, R., 'Occupation in Iraq since 2003 and the powers of the UN Security Council', 90 *International Review of the Red Cross* 29 (2008), p. 48.

[158] See e.g. Condorelli, L., 'Le statut des Forces des Nations Unies et le droit international humanitaire', in Emanuelli, C. (ed.), *Les casques bleus: policiers ou combattants / Blue Helmets: Policemen or Combatants?* (Montréal: Wilson & Lafleur, 1997), pp. 105–106. Cf. David, E., *Principes de droit des conflits armés* (Bruxelles: Bruylant, 2002), pp. 85 *et s.*

and stability and the creation of conditions in which the Iraqi people can freely determine their own political future" goes well beyond the general powers of an occupying force.[159]

Resolution 1483 required the UN to co-ordinate humanitarian and reconstruction assistance, promote the safe, orderly and voluntary return of refugees and displaced persons, work with the CPA and the Iraqis to restore and establish national and local institutions for representative governance, facilitate the reconstruction of key infrastructure, promote economic reconstruction, encourage international efforts to contribute to basic civilian administrative functions, promote the protection of human rights, and encourage international efforts to rebuild the capacity of the Iraqi civilian police force and legal and judicial reform. A more detailed description of the UN's functions was provided by the Secretary-General in his report pursuant to Resolution 1483.[160] The report recommended the creation of a 'United Nations Assistance Mission for Iraq' (UNAMI), in order to help the Special Representative accomplish the tasks entrusted to him by Security Council Resolution 1483. The report and the creation of UNAMI were subsequently endorsed by Security Council Resolution 1500.[161] The Secretary-General explicitly confirmed that the maintenance of security and stability in Iraq was not the responsibility of the UN but of the CPA. Although the Secretary-General had proposed the inclusion of additional areas, such as police reform, judicial and legal reform, economic reconstruction and good governance within UNAMI's mandate,[162] this was not accepted by the CPA and the Iraqi Governing Council.[163] The UN was thus entrusted with a merely co-ordinating mandate with a special focus on humanitarian aid. Furthermore, civil administrative powers were not listed among UNAMI's tasks. The UN was thus left with a task consisting mainly of 'promoting', 'facilitating',

[159] See also Wolfrum, R., 'Iraq – from Belligerent Occupation to Iraqi Exercise of Sovereignty: Foreign Power versus International Community Interference', 9 *Max Planck Yearbook of United Nations Law* 1 (2005), p. 16. See however the discussion by R. Kolb on the question whether the Resolution was precise enough to include an explicit derogation from the laws of armed conflict: Kolb, *supra* note 157. See also for an overview of the relation between the powers of the occupying forces under the laws of occupation and the Security Council: Fox, G. H., 'The Occupation of Iraq', 36 *Georgetown Journal of International Law* 195 (2004–2005), pp. 524–262.

[160] Report of the Secretary-General pursuant to paragraph 24 of Security Council Resolution 1483 (2003), UN Doc. S/2003/715 (17 July 2003).

[161] SC Res. 1500, UN Doc. S/RES/1500 (2003).

[162] Report of the Secretary-General, UN Doc. S/2003/715 (17 July 2003), *supra* note 160, para. 99.

[163] Report of the Secretary-General pursuant to paragraph 24 of Security Council Resolution 1483 (2003) and paragraph 12 of Resolution 1511 (2003), UN Doc. S/2003/1149 (5 December 2003), para. 6.

'working intensively', and 'encouraging'. The Secretary-General appointed Sergio Vieira de Mello as his special representative for Iraq and head of UNAMA. Vieira de Mello, and 21 other UN staff and visitors were killed in August 2003 by a truck bomb in Baghdad, a tragic incident which resulted in a decrease in UN involvement in Iraq.

The complex structure and interaction between the different institutions involved, necessitated practical arrangements. This issue had not been addressed by the Security Council. Iraq was the first time the UN was called to work together with an occupying power in the administration of territory in a post-conflict environment. When Sergio Vieira de Mello presented the Secretary-General's report on the role of UNAMI, he clearly indicated that UNAMI "cannot be, and do not wish to be, a substitute for the Coalition Provisional Authority in this field, the United Nations stands ready to lend modest assistance, in terms of its expertise, in the area of developing an effective national law and order capacity. We have much training experience in that area, not least in the field of human rights".[164] He added, "[i]t is not a clear mandate, but at the same time the situation in Iraq is exceptional, and therefore it requires an exceptional approach".[165] Logically, this co-operation, especially considering UNAMI's unclear mandate, would raise practical difficulties. As the Secretary-General put it:

> this is a unique situation. It is the first time we are working on the ground with an occupying Power, side-by-side, trying to help the population in the territory. Therefore, there are certain things that we will have to work out on the ground. We have to define and work out our relationship with the coalition Authority or the occupying Power, and also our relationship with occupied Iraq. [...]. Some of the activities are very clear. The humanitarian mandate is very clear. We have a direct responsibility for it and we are going to carry it out as we are doing. In other areas, we have to work in partnership with the coalition and, of course, with Iraqi civil society and leaders. And, of course, these relationships will have to be worked out on the ground [...].[166]

The CPA, which had administered Iraq since the fall of the Ba'athist regime, was dissolved following the adoption of Resolution 1546. An appointed Iraqi Interim Government assumed authority for governing the country. Following the dissolution of the CPA, UNAMI's mandate was reshaped in accordance with Security Council Resolution 1546. From that time onwards, the reconstruction was very similar to Afghanistan, and although never explicitly stated, it was similar to the 'light footprint' approach.[167] As with the follow-up to the Bonn

[164] Presentation of the report of the Secretary General by Mr Sergio Vieira de Mello: UNSC Meeting Record, UN Doc. S/PV.4791 (22 July 2003), p. 5.

[165] *Ibid.*, p. 8.

[166] UN Press Release, UN Doc. SG/SM/8720 (27 May 2003).

[167] Also Stahn, *supra* note 4, p. 368.

process in Afghanistan, the international community launched an 'International Compact in Iraq' in May 2007.[168] The Iraq Compact was drafted in March 2007 by the Government of Iraq in co-operation with the UN and the World Bank. The Compact is again, as in the case of Afghanistan, not a binding legal instrument, as it merely established a framework for the international community's involvement in Iraq. The Compact is the follow-up to the completion of the political process envisaged under Security Council Resolution 1546. The Compact includes a number of commitments on the part of the Iraqi Government, covering many areas with respect to human rights, transitional justice, finance, economic reform and political issues, which had not been efficiently addressed in the recent international involvement.

[168] Government of Iraq, 'The International Compact with Iraq. A Shared Vision A Mutual Commitment' (May 2007) [Hereafter 'Iraq Compact'].

Part II

International Law, Post-conflict Administrations and Peace-building. Defining the Legal Framework

The way in which the already complex international legal framework of international administrations and peace-building missions interfere in national legal systems generates an even more complex co-application of different legal norms. The legal rules with regard to the establishment of these missions will directly influence the conduct of the operation, through the administration or mission's capacity to address certain aspects of the reconstruction process. However, often the constituting instruments do not define the pertinent rules applicable to the conduct of peace-building missions and international administrations. The Security Council, for instance, when adopting a resolution authorising the setting up of an international administration, does not specifically define the framework in which the missions will need to operate. In addition, the legal status of the territories concerned will influence the conduct of the reconstruction process. The legal status of Kosovo, for instance, has directly influenced the legal limits of the United Nations Interim Administration Mission in Kosovo (UNMIK).

Establishing the legal framework applicable to such comprehensive peace-building missions and international administrations therefore requires a broad legal analysis, ranging from the UN's legal capacity to undertake and authorise such intrusive missions to the simultaneous application of the laws of armed conflict and human rights law. We will endeavour not only to identify the legal basis of the creation of peace-building and international administration missions, but also to determine the legal status of the territories under administration. The legal limits inherent in such comprehensive missions will be determined through an analysis of the legal rules applicable in post-conflict reconstruction and their interrelation. The legal obligations of international actors involved in international administration will equally form an important aspect of our research. Issues of the accountability of international actors involved in international administrations have frequently been raised in order to object to such intrusive powers. As already mentioned, the purpose of this part is not to give an exhaustive overview of the international legal issues we will discuss, but merely to analyse the legal framework of post-conflict administrations and peace-building from a functional perspective.

The first chapter of this part will address the issue of the competence of the UN to administer territory and authorise the creation of comprehensive peace-building operations. The second chapter will focus on the legal status of the territories under international administration. The third chapter will address what could be called additional obligations of peace-building missions, with a focus on the temporary nature of the authority exercised and the long-term objective of comprehensive peace-building. The next two chapters are dedicated to the legal framework within which these missions have to operate, in terms of human rights law and the laws of occupation.

Chapter 4

The Competence of the United Nations to Engage in Comprehensive Peace-building and International Territorial Administration

The legal basis upon which the UN can authorise the setting up of peace-building missions and international administrations will be analysed in the first section. The powers of the Security Council under the UN Charter will first be analysed, in which regard we will establish not only the legal foundation of these missions in the UN Charter, but also the connection between Security Council action and state failure, domestic jurisdiction, and self-determination. The powers of the General Assembly will then be briefly considered. Although the General Assembly did not play any role in recent operations, former missions have indeed been set up under the General Assembly's auspices.

A. *The Capacity of the United Nations to Administer Territory outside the Trusteeship System*

Even if there has been some reluctance in the past to accept the UN's capacity to take over the administration of a territory, one can easily assert that this controversy is actually at an end.[169] The capacity of the UN to set up a mission responsible for the administration of a territory on behalf of the Organisation is indeed no longer questioned as such, although some remain reluctant to accept the expanding scope of the UN's powers, especially those of the Security Council.[170] The debate is nevertheless worth mentioning as it relates to the discussion

---

[169] See also de Wet *supra* note 9, pp. 306 *et s.*

[170] See for an overview of this issue Sarooshi, D., *The United Nations and the Development of Collective Security. The Delegation by the UN Security Council of its Chapter VII Powers* (Oxford: Clarendon Press, 1999).

on the possible use of the Trusteeship System in the context of peace-building operations.

One of the most fervent opponents of the capacity of the UN to administer territory outside the Trusteeship System was Hans Kelsen. In discussing the powers granted to the UN in the administration of the Free Territory of Trieste, Kelsen argued that the UN did *not* possess the capacity to set up an international administration, as the UN Charter already provided for a system of territorial administration, the Trusteeship System. The Trusteeship System established under article 81 of the UN Charter was, according to Kelsen, "the only case where the United Nations is authorized by the Charter to exercise the rights of sovereignty over a territory".[171] Interestingly, at that time, Article 24 of the UN Charter, in which UN Members confer on the Security Council the primary responsibility for the maintenance of international peace and security, was seen as the legal basis for the administration of the Free Territory of Trieste. It was argued that the situation presented a threat to international peace and security, and that, considering that the Security Council was given the responsibility to deal with the situation on the basis of Article 24 UN Charter, that provision was sufficient to authorise the exercise of administrative powers by the UN.[172] This can in fact be seen as an application of the doctrine of 'implied powers'[173] which, as we will see, is currently one of the legal bases of Security Council action with regard to the administration of territory. The *a contrario* reasoning proposed by Kelsen can nevertheless no longer be upheld, bearing in mind the evolution in the interpretation of several UN Charter provisions. Indeed, as will be pointed out in the next chapter, several provisions of the UN Charter can be seen as a legal basis for the establishment of an international administration. The Trusteeship System cannot be considered as the only regulatory framework for all administrative powers exercised by the UN. The Trusteeship System was meant only to control the decolonisation process, and it cannot therefore be concluded that the system was intended as the *only* means of exercising administrative powers. In addition, the explicit provision in the Trusteeship System authorising the *UN* to be administrator can be seen as a confirmation of the Organisation's capacity to assume governmental functions.[174]

---

[171] Kelsen, H., *The Law of the United Nations* (London: Stevens & Sons Limited, 1951), pp. 833–834.

[172] For a discussion, see Halderman, J. W., 'United Nations Territorial Administration and the Development of the Charter', *Duke Law Journal* 95 (1964).

[173] See the statements of the representatives in the Security Council, reprinted in Halderman, *supra* note 172.

[174] Lauterpacht, E., 'The contemporary practice of the United Kingdom in the field of International law – Survey and comment', 5 *International and Comparative Law Quarterly* 405 (1956), p. 28.

But before examining the different provisions of the Charter which can be seen as legal bases for such comprehensive peace-building missions, it may be interesting to investigate the relationship between the current peace-building missions, international administrations and the inoperative Trusteeship System and Council. It has indeed been argued that, if the UN wanted to expand these types of missions, it would be preferable to adopt a framework for future operations instead of having to rely on an *ad hoc* deployment of international staff.[175] The Trusteeship Council, which had the task of supervising the administration of territories placed under the Trusteeship System, suspended all activities a month after the independence of Palau on 1 October 1994, the last remaining UN trust territory. The Trusteeship Council still formally exists, as the relevant articles of the UN Charter have not been amended or abolished, although it remains out of action. Some scholars have therefore argued that the trusteeship system could be used for the administration of territories other than those summed up in the Charter.[176]

The International Trusteeship System was established in the UN Charter for the administration of trust territories placed thereunder by an individual agreement in accordance with the relevant provisions of the Charter.[177] The International Trusteeship System applied to only three limited categories of territories: (1) territories formerly held under the mandate of the League of Nations (2) territories detached from enemy states as a result of the Second World War, and (3) territories voluntarily placed under the system of International Trusteeship by states responsible for their administration.[178] It should also be added that, contrary to the Mandates System of the League of Nations, which accepted only one or more states as the administering authority, the trusteeship system explicitly provided that the administering authority could be one or more States or the UN itself.[179] The possibility of re-using that system for the purpose of post-conflict

[175] Cf. the recommendations contained in the 'Brahimi Report' (Report of the Panel on United Nations Peace Operations, UN Doc. A/55/305 – S/2000/809 (21 August 2000) [Hereafter 'Brahimi Report'].

[176] See in particular for the possibility to apply the International Trusteeship System on the Kosovo case: Franckx, E., Pauwels, A. and Smis, S., 'An international trusteeship for Kosovo: attempt to find a solution to the conflict', 52 *Studia Diplomatica* 155 (2001), pp. 155–166 and Kelly, M.J., *Restoring and Maintaining Order in Complex Peace Operations. The Search for a Legal Framework*, (London / The Hague / Boston: Kluwer Law International, 1999), pp. 101–103. See for a general and comprehensive study on the 'revitalisation' of the Trusteeship System: Parker, T., 'The Ultimate Intervention: Revitalising the Un Trusteeship Council for the 21st Century', *Centre for European and Asian Studies, Norwegian School of Management, Report 3/2003* (April 2003).

[177] See Chapters XII (International Trusteeship System) and XII (The Trusteeship Council) of the UN Charter.

[178] Article 77, para. 1 UN Charter.

[179] Article 80 UN Charter.

reconstruction may seem very attractive at first, but the legal impediments to the application of the Trusteeship System as established in the UN Charter are insurmountable. Many conditions set out in the UN Charter indeed hinder any possible reapplication of this system.

The first legal obstacle is Article 78 of the UN Charter, which provides that the system of international trusteeship shall not apply to territories which have become members of the UN as, according to Article 78, the relationship between Members of the UN "shall be based on respect of the principle of sovereign equality". While some territories we will discuss – East Timor and Kosovo – were not members of the UN,[180] Article 78 in fact excludes any application of the system to UN member States. The second obstacle lies in the requirement that the territory be placed *voluntarily* under UN trusteeship. An individual agreement has to be signed by the future trust territory and by the states concerned with its administration or by the UN.[181] This obstacle would, for instance, hamper every administration of a territory when the administering authority, if one were effective, did not consent to it. In states lacking any effective and representative government, as in the case of Somalia at the establishment of the UNOSOM II operation, no consent can be given. Imposing international administration on a territory by a Security Council resolution under Chapter VII of the UN Charter would thus be impossible.

These obstacles are prohibitive for any application of the system as established in the UN Charter. The only possible way out is an amendment of the Charter, but history has already shown that this is *de facto* not feasible. Moreover, when considering an amendment of the Charter, one has to take into account the psychological close link between the concept of trusteeship and the decolonisation process aspect of any revitalisation of the UN Trusteeship System. While the context in which the Trusteeship System was envisaged cannot be compared to the peace-building missions themselves, the purpose of the trusteeship system reveals similarities with post-conflict administrations and reconstruction.[182] The trusteeship system's main purpose was the progressive transfer of former colonies towards independence or self-government. Article 76 of the UN Charter contains the basic objectives of the System: the furtherance of international peace and security, the promotion of the political, economic, social and educational advancement of the inhabitants of the trust territories, and their progressive development towards self-government or independence. In addition, encour-

[180] See on the controversy of the membership of the Federal Republic of Yugoslavia, of which Kosovo was a Province upon establishment of UNMIK: International Court of Justice, 'Application of the Convention on the Prevention and Punishment of the Crime of Genocide' (Bosnia and Herzegovina *v.* Serbia and Montenegro), Judgement, 26 February 2007, www.icj-cij.org.

[181] See article 77, para. 2 UN Charter.

[182] See in particular Wilde, *supra* note 4.

aging respect for human rights and for fundamental freedoms for all without distinction as to race, sex, language or religion, and guaranteeing equal treatment in social, economic, commercial and justice matters for all UN Members and their nationals were main aims of the trusteeship system. Despite these parallels, the reapplication of the trusteeship system will be seen by many states as a new form of colonisation, which will get in the way of every attempt or effort to amend the Charter in order to change the conditions of application of the trusteeship system.

B. *The Legality of the Establishment of Post-conflict Administrations and Missions*

While the capacity of the UN to administer territory outside the Trusteeship System can no longer be questioned, this does not mean that only one well-defined legal basis for it can be envisaged. Several UN Charter provisions can function as a legal basis. The particular article or provision of the UN Charter on which the exercise of such extensive powers can be based has already been broadly discussed in legal literature. Nevertheless, it is necessary to briefly recall these, and to consider the implication of the legal basis on questions such as self-determination, domestic jurisdiction and the capacity of the Security Council to deal with certain cases. Certainly, the various legal bases differ substantially according to whether it is the General Assembly or the Security Council which established the mission and whether or not the host state consents to the deployment of an international administration. One should in addition keep in mind that the Charter provisions we will discuss need to be read in conjunction with Articles 29 and 98 of the UN Charter. Article 29 authorises the Security Council to establish subsidiary organs as it deems necessary for the performance of its functions. Article 98 contains the principle that the Secretary-General can perform such other functions as are entrusted to him by the Security Council.

1. *UN Security Council*

(a) *Peacekeeping, Chapter VII and Implied powers*

The 'first generation' peacekeeping operations were mainly based on the mediation role of the UN. The power of the Security Council to set up peacekeeping operations has frequently been referred to as the inexistent 'Chapter VI bis' or 'Chapter VI ½' powers.[183] Peacekeeping operations were generally established by the Security Council acting under Chapter VI of the UN Charter, 'Pacific

[183] Since no article of the Charter adequately describes the peacekeeping activities and in view of the fact that a formal application of Chapter VII was impossible following the continuing

Settlement of Disputes', which empowers the Security Council to make recommendations on the settlement of international disputes, and on the consent of the host state. Indeed, the recommendatory powers envisaged in Chapter VI of the UN Charter do not authorise the Security Council to *impose* measures on its members. Article 36 of the UN Charter authorises the Security Council to *recommend* appropriate procedures or methods of adjustment. All action taken by the Security Council when acting under Chapter VI must therefore also be consented to by the state in question. 'Classical' peacekeeping operations were therefore created only with the explicit consent of the host state, generally after the signature of an agreement. It should also be remembered that, in any case, Article 2, para. 7 of the UN Charter provides that the UN is not authorised to intervene in matters which are essentially within the domestic jurisdiction of a state. Although the scope of the notion of 'domestic jurisdiction' has evolved throughout the years, it nevertheless prohibits the Security Council from taking measures which interfere in the domestic jurisdiction of states, except with the explicit consent of the state, or when the Security Council acts under Chapter VII.[184]

The legal basis for several cases discussed in the first part is similar to that for 'traditional' peacekeeping operations. The authorisation of the operation in Cambodia (UNTAC) seems to have been based on the same provisions as traditional peacekeeping operations. The relevant Security Council Resolutions explicitly referred to the consent of the host state as evidenced by the signature of the Paris Agreement.[185] The mandate of the Cambodia mission nevertheless went far beyond the traditional notion of peacekeeping as defined by former Secretary-General Boutros-Ghali.[186] In the case of Afghanistan, the legal basis is rather unclear. The deployment of the military component, the International Security and Assistance Force (ISAF), was explicitly based on Chapter VII.[187] The creation of the UN assistance mission, on the other hand, seems to have been based on the 'consent' of the host state, as provided for in Annex II of

use of the veto right by the permanent members, these operations were considered as lying between the powers granted to the Security Council under Chapters VI and VII.

184 Article 2, para. 7 UN Charter.

185 SC Res. 745, UN Doc S/RES/745 (1992), preamble.

186 "[T]he deployment of a United Nations presence in the field, hitherto with the consent of all the parties concerned, normally involving United Nations military and/or police personnel and frequently civilians as well." (Report of the Secretary-General pursuant to the statement adopted by the Summit Meeting of the Security Council on 31 January 1992, 'An Agenda for Peace: Preventive diplomacy, peacemaking and peace-keeping', UN Doc. A/47/277-S/24111 (17 June 1992), para. 20).

187 See SC Res. 1386, UN Doc S/RES/1386 (2001), preamble.

the Bonn Agreement.[188] The UN mission in Afghanistan therefore appears to be based on Chapter VI of the UN Charter.

The latest international peace-building missions have mainly been established under Chapter VII of the UN Charter. This was the case for the operations in Eastern Slovenia, Baranja and Western Sirmium, Kosovo, East Timor and Iraq.[189] We should add that Chapter VII can be invoked only in case of threats to the peace, breaches of the peace, and acts of aggression. Chapter VII therefore differs from Chapter VI not only with regard to the measures that can be taken or authorised, which can involve the use of force, but also with regard to competence *ratione materiae*. When authorising a mission under Chapter VII of the UN Charter, the Security Council does not mention the precise article on which its action can be based.[190] Several articles can therefore be considered to authorise peace-building missions and international administrations, according to whether or not the consent of the host state has been obtained. Article 39 of the UN Charter states that "[t]he Security Council shall determine the existence of any threat to the peace, breach of the peace, or act of aggression and shall make recommendations [...]". This article gives the Security Council

---

188 See SC Res. 1383, UN Doc. S/RES/1383 (2001), para. 3: "Reaffirms its full support to the Special Representative of the Secretary-General and endorses the missions entrusted to him in annex 2 of the abovementioned Agreement". See also SC Res. 1401, UN Doc S/RES/1401 (2002) and SC Res. 1471, UN Doc. S/RES/1471 (2003). One could however question the validity of the consent of the host state, as the participants in the Bonn Agreement were not official governmental actors, although they were considered as representatives of the Afghan people. In addition, one could ask the question why the Security Council, in its resolutions on the deployment of the military force, indicates that Afghanistan represents a threat to international peace and security while, when the Security Council established and extended UNAMI, no reference to a threat to international peace and security was made.

189 Nevertheless, Resolution 1500 establishing the UN mission in Iraq, does not explicitly refer to Chapter VII. The subsequent Resolution 1546, which delineates the mandate of the mission and the respective powers of the CPA, was on the other hand explicitly adopted under Chapter VII.

190 See on the creation of UNMIK and the authorisation of KFOR: European Court of Human Rights, Agim Behrami and Bekir Behrami against France and Ruzhdi Saramati against France, Germany and Norway, Decision on the admissibility, 2 May 2007, Application n[os] 71412/01 and 78166/06, para. 130: "While the Resolution referred to Chapter VII of the Charter, it did not identify the precise Articles of that Chapter under which the UNSC was acting and the Court notes that there are a number of possible bases in Chapter VII for this delegation by the UNSC: the non-exhaustive Article 42 (read in conjunction with the widely formulated Article 48), the non-exhaustive nature of Article 41 under which territorial administrations could be authorised as a necessary instrument for sustainable peace; or implied powers under the Charter for the UNSC to so act in both respects based on an effective interpretation of the Charter. In any event, the Court considers that Chapter VII provided a framework for the above-described delegation of the UNSC's security powers to KFOR and of its civil administration powers to UNMIK."

first the power to deal with a certain situation – a threat to the peace, a breach of the peace or an act of aggression – and secondly the power to make recommendations to the parties concerned. Operations authorised under Article 39 of the UN Charter are therefore based not only on the Security Council's recommendatory power, but also on the consent of the state concerned. Next to recommendations, Article 39 of the Charter also gives the Security Council the power to decide, after determining a threat to the peace, a breach of the peace or an act of aggression, to take 'measures' in accordance with articles 41 and 42 of the Charter.

Article 41 of the UN Charter gives the Security Council the power to impose measures not involving the use of armed force. When the consent of the host state cannot be obtained for any reason whatsoever, and if a situation presents a threat to the peace, breach of the peace, or in the event of an act of aggression, this article can thus also be considered an adequate legal basis to authorise such a mission. The administration of a territory as a part of 'measures not involving the use of armed force' has however not always been accepted. Indeed, Article 41 merely provides that such measures may include complete or partial interruption of economic relations and of rail, sea, air, postal, telegraphic, radio, and other means of communication, and the severance of diplomatic relations. However, the opinion that the Security Council's powers under Article 41 are limited can no longer be defended. The list of measures contained in Article 41 clearly is non-exhaustive. First, this interpretation given to Article 41 of the UN Charter is consistent with the Charter's *travaux préparatoires*. When the Chapter VII powers of the Security Council were discussed, a proposition to include the administration of territory as part of the measures not involving the use of force was rejected as it could be seen as limiting the Security Council's powers under that article.[191] In addition, such an interpretation was expressly confirmed by the International Criminal Tribunal for the Former Yugoslavia[192] and by the International Criminal Tribunal for Rwanda,[193] which both had to rule on the legality of their own foundation in the UN Charter. The Appeals Chamber of the International Criminal Tribunal for the Former Yugoslavia indeed found that "[i]t is evident that the measures set out in Article 41 are merely illustrative

[191] Cf. Report of the rapporteur on Commission III/3, Session of 23 May 1945, in Documents of the United Nations Conference on International Organisation, San Francisco, 1945, Vol. 12, Doc. Nr. 539 III/3/24, pp. 354–355.

[192] International Criminal Tribunal for the Former Yugoslavia, 'Prosecutor v. Dusko Tadic a/k/a "Dule", Decision on the Defence Motion for Interlocutory Appeal on Jurisdiction', Case n° IT-94-1, 2 October 1995.

[193] International Criminal Tribunal for Rwanda, 'Prosecutor v. Kenyabashi', Case. n° ICTR-96-15-T, 18 June 1997.

examples which obviously do not exclude other measures. All the Article requires is that they do not involve 'the use of force'. It is a negative definition".[194]

If the Security Council considers that the measures provided for in Article 41 would be inadequate or have proved to be inadequate, the Security Council can authorise military action under Article 42 of the UN Charter. Such military action may include such demonstrations, blockades, and other operations by air, sea or land forces, as may be necessary to maintain or restore international peace and security. This article is thus the appropriate legal basis for the military components of peace-building operations and international administrations, as evidenced in the case of Afghanistan mentioned above, in which the military and civil missions were established under distinct resolutions. In the case of Kosovo, although a clear distinction was made between UNMIK, the civil presence, and KFOR, the military presence, which operated under different command, both UNMIK and KFOR were established by the same Chapter VII Resolution. In East Timor, on the other hand, the military component was integrated into the UNTAET structures, which consisted of both military and civil components. In the case of Iraq, the military operation can also be considered as a measure under Article 42 of the UN Charter. Reference to Chapter VII in these cases is essential to allow the military presence to resort to the use of force.

In the case of Kosovo, the Federal Republic of Yugoslavia explicitly consented to the deployment of both the civil and military presences.[195] The consent of the host state was nevertheless not absolutely necessary as UNMIK was established under a Chapter VII resolution. However, in that particular case, we see two reasons for this dual authorisation. First, this can be explained by the ambiguities concerning the Federal Republic of Yugoslavia's Membership of the UN, as both the Security Council[196] and the General Assembly[197] had clearly indicated that it could not automatically be seen as the successor of the Socialist Federal Republic of Yugoslavia. The Federal Republic was nevertheless considered the *de facto* successor of the Socialist Federal Republic by the Secretariat.[198] The Federal Republic was nevertheless formally accepted as a *new* UN Member on 1 November 2000. Secondly, one could also consider that in a *practical* sense,

---

194 International Criminal Tribunal for the Former Yugoslavia, 'Prosecutor v. Dusko Tadic a/k/a "Dule", Decision on the Defence Motion for Interlocutory Appeal on Jurisdiction', Case n° IT-94-1, 2 October 1995, para. 35.

195 See SC Res. 1244, UN Doc. S/RES/1244 (1999), preamble.

196 See *e.g.* SC Res. 757, UN Doc. S/RES/757 (1992) and SC Res. 777, UN Doc. S/RES/777 (1992).

197 See *e.g.* GA Res. 47/1, UN Doc. A/RES/47/1 (22 September 1992).

198 See International Court of Justice, 'Application of the Convention on the Prevention and Punishment of the Crime of Genocide' (Bosnia and Herzegovina v. Serbia and Montenegro), Judgement, 26 February 2007, www.icj-cij.org.

an operation such as UNMIK cannot adequately operate without the consent of the sovereign state. The latter also seems to have been the reason Indonesia's consent was sought in the case of UNTAET, despite the very doubtful character of Indonesian sovereignty over East Timor.

The question has been raised whether there is a need to identify a specific article in the UN Charter as authorising the establishment of international administrations and other peace-building missions. We have already seen that in the case of Trieste the representatives of the Security Council did not consider it necessary to base the Security Council's power to authorise such an operation on one specific UN Charter provision. In its advisory opinion in the *Reparation for injuries suffered in the service of the United Nations* case, the International Court of Justice noted that "the Organization must be deemed to have those powers which, though not expressly provided in the Charter, are conferred upon it by necessary implication as being essential to the performance of its duties".[199] This principle thus implies that even if the power to administer territories was not expressly included in the UN Charter, the UN would nevertheless be able to exercise administrative authority if it were essential to the performance of its duties. As no provision of the Charter explicitly authorises the UN to create an international *administration*, it has been argued that instead of searching for a specific basis for these missions, the doctrine of the implicit powers can be sufficient to authorise the establishment of these types of operations.[200] Therefore, it can indeed be argued that if the Security Council can actually deal with a certain case, such as the settlement of an internal conflict as a threat to international peace and security, one cannot exclude its capacity to set up an administrative mission to maintain international peace and security.[201]

(b) *State Failure as a Threat to International Peace and Security*

Reliance on Chapter VII implies that the situation presents a threat to international peace and security. The establishment of international administrations

---

[199] International Court of Justice, 'Reparation for injuries suffered in the service of the United Nations', Advisory Opinion, 11 April 1949, 1949 *ICJ Reports* 174, p. 182.

[200] See Brownlie, I, *Principles of Public International Law* (Oxford: Oxford University Press, 2003), p. 167; Ruffert, M., 'The administration of Kosovo and East-Timor by the International Community', 3 *International and Comparative Law Quarterly* 613 (2001), pp. 620–621 and Schrijver, N., 'Commentary on the Lecture 'The Complex Role of the Legal Adviser when international Organisations Administer Territory' by R. Wilde', 95 *Proceedings of the American Society for International law* 259 (2001).

[201] Also Ruffert, *supra* note 200, p. 621. See on the *customary* powers of the Security Council to adopt these measures, and an evaluation of General Assembly support to these missions, de Wet *supra* note 9. For a critique, see Conforti, B., *The law and practice of the United Nations* (The Hague / London / Boston: Kluwer Law International, 2005), pp. 205–206.

and peace-building operations cannot therefore be envisaged in every case of malfunctioning states.[202] This brings us to the question whether the Security Council's competence may include measures with regard to purely internal situations, and to the relationship between post-conflict administrations and the notion of 'failing' or 'failed' states. Often the concept of international administration has been directly linked to the idea of 'state failure'.[203] The concept of the failed state is relatively new in international relations and gained importance at the beginning of the 1990s with Helman and Ratner's article 'Saving Failed States'.[204] Since then, this paradigm has been widely used in various ways to define the phenomenon of states which are unable to maintain themselves as members of the international community. As states constitute the basic actors of the international legal system, state failure is considered to cause a real threat to the very existence and continuation of this system.[205] Although there is no clear definition of 'failed states', the general description relates to the internal dissolution and collapse of a state and the impossibility for that state to deliver essential public services to its population. It is however not the purpose of this section to analyse the concept of state failure extensively. We will instead analyse to what extent 'state failure', as a threat to international peace and security, can trigger Security Council action.

State failure is often considered to have its roots partly in the decolonisation process and the principle of the self-determination of peoples.[206] The latter, although a fundamental principle of international law, has led to the creation of a massive number of states within a short term.[207] The self-determination of

---

[202] Matheson *supra* note 10, p. 83.

[203] See for example Bain, W., 'Trusteeship: A Response to Failed States?', *Paper Presented at the Conference on Failed States and Global Governance, Perdue University* (10–14 April 2001).

[204] Helman, G. B. and Ratner, S. R., 'Saving Failed States', 89 *Foreign Policy* 3 (1993).

[205] See in general on the phenomenon of State Failure: Rotberg, R. I. (ed.), *When States Fail: Causes and Consequences* (Princeton / Oxford: Princeton University Press, 2003); Rotberg, R. I. (ed.), *State Failure and State Weakness in a Time of Terror* (Harvard: World Peace Foundation, 2003) and Chesterman, *et al.*, *supra* note 5.

[206] Another factor is the Cold War and the substantial support of potentially failed states by the Soviet Union and the United States. Of course, foreign aid, especially from the United States and Russia during the Cold War, was essential for the viability of these newly independent states, but in the meantime financial, political and military support did not provide sufficient assistance for the creation of functioning and long-lasting institutions. The Cold War helped to maintain weak governments in failed states. But this did not provide sufficient support for the creation of functioning political institutions, and it merely prolonged the fragile viability of these states. See Helman and Ratner, *supra* note 204.

[207] The membership of the UN, which has almost quadrupled since the signature of the UN Charter in San Francisco, illustrates this rather well. In 1919, the world community consisted of 55 recognised nations. This number increased to 69 in 1950. After the independence of

peoples, considered as a primary goal of the international community since the adoption of the UN Charter, has been widely applied since the creation of the UN in 1945. The main idea behind the doctrine of self-determination was that peoples could best govern themselves without the interference of any foreign powers, and that they had an inalienable right to do so.[208] Decolonisation did not necessarily coincide with institution-building processes, as witnessed in the case of The Congo. Regardless of the capacity of local actors to have the necessary institutions to govern themselves, the emphasis lay on the immediate independence of states.[209] However, the explosive growth of nation-states has also increased the danger of failing state institutions, emphasising the need for a functioning internal political structure to increase the stability of states.

The concept of failed states has been widely criticised for several reasons.[210] It is true that the notion implies a certain hierarchy in the international community between 'failed', 'weak', 'collapsed' and 'strong' states. Without it being necessary to consider the intrinsic value of a state, it is undoubtedly correct to argue that not all states are characterised by the same stability. On the internal level, 'failed states' are generally considered to represent a grave danger to the wellbeing of the local population, especially with regard to respect for human rights. However, in the context of the competence of the Security Council to take action in respect of a threat to international peace and security, the label of state failure cannot be limited to mere internal aspects. The simple fact that a state is malfunctioning internally is insufficient for one to hold that it cannot maintain itself as a member of the international community. It is indeed only when a state presents a threat to international peace and security that the international community can impose measures though the Security Council.

Montenegro in 2007, the number of UN Member States reached 192. For an overview see Rotberg, R. I., 'Failed States, Collapsed States, Weak States, Causes and Indicators', in Rotberg, R. I. (ed.), *State Failure and State Weakness in a Time of Terror* (Harvard: World Peace Foundation, 2003), pp. 1–25.

208 Helman and Ratner, *supra* note 204.

209 In fact, General Assembly Resolution 1514 (XV) containing the Declaration on the Granting of Independence to Colonial Countries and Peoples demonstrates this viewpoint by stating that: "the subjection of peoples to alien subjugation, domination and exploitation constitutes a denial of fundamental human rights, is contrary to the Charter of the United Nations and is an impediment to the promotion of world peace and co-operation. [...] Inadequacy of political, economic, social or educational preparedness should never serve as a pretext for delaying independence" (GA Res. 1514 (XV)), 'Declaration on the Granting of Independence to Colonial Countries and Peoples', UN Doc. A/4684 (14 December 1960).

210 See *e.g.* Englebert, P. and Tull, D. M., 'Postconflict Reconstruction in Africa. Flawed Ideas about Failed States', 32 *International Security* 106 (2008) and Wilde, R., 'The Skewed Responsibility Narrative of the 'Failed States' Concept', 9 *ILSA Journal of International & Comparative Law* 425 (2003).

The notion of 'failed' of 'failing' state is thus not as such useful in considering whether a situation can prompt Security Council action.

The expansion in the interpretation of a threat to international peace and security nevertheless shows that the Security Council can deal with a situation that may, at first sight, seem purely internal. It is generally acknowledged that the Security Council has a large discretionary power to assert whether a situation presents a threat to international peace and security, although some have stressed that the Security Council needs to act with good faith.[211] The notion of 'threat to the international peace and security' is in fact difficult to recognise as it does not necessarily include the use of armed force within a territory.[212] In the case of Cambodia, the Security Council still noted that the UN's involvement was aimed at restoring and maintaining peace in *Cambodia*, while no reference to *international* peace and security was made.[213] Nevertheless, the evolution in the interpretation of the notion of 'threat to the international peace and security' has led to the consideration of purely internal situations as presenting a threat to peace and security.[214] It has been noted that the notion of 'peace' in the sense of Chapter VII is far more than the absence of war between two or more States.[215] In the case of Iraq in 1991 for instance, the Security Council was "gravely concerned by the repression of the Iraqi civilian population in many parts of Iraq, including most recently in Kurdish populated areas, which led to a massive flow of refugees towards and across international frontiers and to cross-border incursions, which threaten international peace and security in the region".[216]

The significant expansion of the Security Council's competence to deal with a certain situation is noteworthy, as post-conflict reconstruction is aimed at the consolidation of *internal* structures to maintain *international* peace and security.[217] This contrasts with the former position of the Security Council in the case of Cambodia.[218] The situation in Kosovo which was equally of an internal character, was described by the Security Council as a threat to international peace and security. In that case, one can easily understand that internal situations

---

211 Kirgis, F. L., 'Security Council Governance of Postconflict Societies: A Plea for Good Faith and Informed Decision Making', 3 *American Journal of International Law* 579 (2001), p. 581 and Matheson, *supra* note 10, p. 3.

212 Conforti, *supra* note 201, p. 172.

213 SC Res. 745, UN Doc. S/RES/745 (1992), preamble.

214 See Frowein, J. A., 'Article 39', in Simma, B., *The Charter of the united Nations* (Oxford: Oxford University Press, 1994), pp. 610–611.

215 Ruffert, *supra* note 200, p. 617.

216 Preamble, SC Res. 688, UN Doc. S/RES/688 (1991).

217 Cf. Dupuy, P. M., *Droit international Public* (Paris: Dalloz, 2000), paras 558–566.

218 Although it should be noted that the abovementioned Security Council resolution in Iraq in 1991 was passed prior to the establishment of the UNTAC-operation in Cambodia. It nevertheless forecast the evolution we described.

can result in serious regional instability, which can be interpreted as a threat to international peace and security. Nevertheless, some authors have pointed out that, considering the intrusive character of the measures taken, the Security Council should be required effectively to determine the threat to international peace and security.[219]

(c) *Security Council Action and Domestic Jurisdiction*

The question whether the Security Council can, even when acting under Chapter VII of the UN Charter, interfere with state sovereignty, and for instance make changes in a state's legal system, is distinct from the previous one. While the previous section dealt with the power of the Security Council to consider a situation as part of its Chapter VI or Chapter VII powers, this section will look at the possible conflict between the measures taken by the Security Council and the principle of domestic jurisdiction. This question lies at the heart of (the limits to) its expanding role. The conformity of Security Council action with the concept of 'domestic jurisdiction' has been often raised, especially in relation to Kosovo, considering that the Security Council extracted the province from the Federal Republic of Yugoslavia's sovereignty by placing it under an international administration mandated to exercise all state competences. Another clear example is the Security Council's endorsement of the Constitution of Bosnia and Herzegovina annexed to the Dayton Agreement.[220]

The starting point is Article 2, para. 7 of the UN Charter which provides that nothing contained in the Charter shall authorise the UN to intervene in matters which are essentially within the domestic jurisdiction of any state. Article 2, para. 7 of the Charter further expressly states that the principle of 'domestic jurisdiction' shall not prejudice the application of enforcement measures under Chapter VII. Accordingly, this provision includes that if Security Council is authorised to take action under Chapter VII of the UN Charter, it will not be subject to any limitation by reason of the principle of 'domestic jurisdiction'. In cases where the peace-building missions were established under Chapter VI, Article 2, para. 7 UN Charter would not pose a problem, as we saw that the consent of the host state is a necessary condition. From a formal legal point of view, the principle of domestic jurisdiction cannot therefore block the creation of an international administration or a peace-building operation.

However is the Security Council's scope of action unlimited when it acts under Chapter VII? In his dissenting opinion in the *South West Africa* case in 1971,

---

[219] See Kirgis, *supra* note 211, pp. 580–581.

[220] See Annex 4, Dayton Agreement; SC Res. 1031, UN Doc. S/RES/1031 (1995) and for a comment: de Wet, *supra* note 9, pp. 332 *et s.*

Judge Sir Gerald Fitzmaurice defended the theory that the Security Council does not have the capacity to make changes to the territorial rights of a State:

> *Even when acting under Chapter VI1 of the Charter itself*, the Security Council has no power to abrogate or alter territorial rights, whether of sovereignty or administration. Even a war-time occupation of a country or territory cannot operate to do that. It must await the peace settlement. This is a principle of international law that is as well-established as any there can be, – and the Security Council is as much subject to it (for the United Nations is itself a subject of international law) as any of its individual member States are. The Security Council might, after making the necessary determinations under Article 39 of the Charter, order the occupation of a country or piece of territory in order to restore peace and security, but it could not thereby, or as part of that operation, abrogate or alter territorial rights; – and the right to administer a mandated territory is a territorial right without which the territory could not be governed or the mandate be operated. It was to keep the peace, not to change the world order, that the Security Council was set up.[221]

As evidenced by the mandates entrusted to international actors in the cases of Kosovo, East Timor, Afghanistan and Iraq, it seems that Judge Fitzmaurice's opinion can no longer be upheld. We have already mentioned that Article 2 para. 7 of the UN Charter precludes any UN intervention in matters which are essentially within the domestic jurisdiction of any state, while making an explicit exception for Chapter VII action. In adhering to the UN Charter, the UN Member States accept the authority of the Security Council, and in particular the powers contained in Chapter VII. It should also be remembered that Article 25 of the UN Charter contains the acceptance by all members of the obligation to carry out the decisions of the Security Council in accordance with the Charter.

In addition, next to reliance on the exception of Article 2 para. 7 of the UN Charter to authorize an operation with intrusive territorial powers, it should be remembered that what formerly lay within the domestic jurisdiction of states can have ceased to be a part of that category.[222] Indeed, the group of matters that are within the domestic jurisdiction of states has evolved over the years, and certainly since the drafting of the UN Charter. There is a tendency towards a growing restriction of the 'domestic jurisdiction' category, and especially in such areas as human rights, which at present can be considered as no longer falling

221 International Court of Justice, 'Legal Consequences for States of the Continued Presence of South Africa in Namibia (South West Africa) notwithstanding Security Council Resolution 276 (1970)', Advisory Opinion, 21 June 1971, 1971 *ICJ Reports* 16. 'Dissenting opinion' of Judge Sir Gerald Fitzmaurice, 1971 *ICJ Reports* 220, para. 115.

222 Kirgis, *supra* note 211, p. 579.

within the domestic jurisdiction of states.[223] The same can be said with regard to the protection of minorities.

In contrast to what Sir Gerald Fitzmaurice argued in his dissenting opinion in the *South West Africa* advisory opinion of 1971, it can thus be argued that the Security Council is capable of affecting or altering the rights of a state by adopting changes in the legal systems of states or by granting a certain autonomy to a population within such states. This presumption can be based either on the exception provided for in Article 2 para. 7 UN Charter or on the fact that these matters no longer fall within the domestic jurisdiction of a state. One can argue that a change in, for example, the internal political structure of a state no longer falls within its domestic jurisdiction if it is justified to guarantee a certain autonomy for a population in accordance with the right of self-determination.[224] However, the question remains whether such action does not infringe the right of self-determination.

(d) *The Security Council and Self-determination*

The link between international administrations and self-determination becomes apparent in different ways, essentially in the habitual distinction between the *external* and *internal* aspects of the right to self-determination. As seen in the first part, the self-determination of peoples, in its traditional external form, has led to the creation of various forms of international operations to oversee the independence of former colonies. The case of East Timor can easily be seen as a form of 'classical' self-determination,[225] following the conduct of a UN-led and internationally supervised popular consultation in which the East Timorese voted overwhelmingly for independence.[226] The role of *internal* self-determination, *i.e.* the right of the people freely to determine their own political structure, becomes apparent when contrasted with the exercise of administrative powers by international actors and 'territorial' or political solutions adopted by the Security Council.

The right of self-determination is often considered a *jus cogens* norm, or at least a fundamental principle of international law.[227] The International Court

---

[223] Dupuy, *supra* note 217, para. 72; Kirgis, *supra* note 211, p. 579 and Conforti, *supra* note 201, p. 172.

[224] Matheson, *supra* note 10, pp. 83–85.

[225] Salamun, M., *Democratic Governance in International Territorial Administration* (Baden-Baden: Nomos Verlagsgesellschaft, 2005), p. 47.

[226] Abline, G., 'De l'Indépendance du Timor-Oriental', 107 *Revue Générale de Droit International Public* 349 (2003).

[227] See *e.g.* Dupuy, *supra* note 217, p. 126; Cassesse, A., *Self-Determination of Peoples. A Legal Appraisal* (Cambridge: Cambridge University Press, 1995), pp. 135–136 and Orakhelashvilli, A., *Peremptory Norms in International Law* (Oxford: Oxford University Press, 2006), 51.

of Justice has equally stressed the *erga omnes* character of the external right of self-determination.[228] The exact current content of the right to self-determination has however not yet clearly been established. In other words, while the right of self-determination could easily and undeniably be granted to peoples in the context of decolonisation, the question remains what this right actually amounts to today. After the decolonisation process, the question was raised whether the right to self-determination would include a right to independence or secession, as had been the case in the decolonisation process. An analysis of relevant case law and the opinions of the Badinter Commission in the Former Yugoslavia, excludes a right to secession as part of the right of self-determination outside the context of decolonisation.[229]

While the right to external self-determination was important in determining independence for former colonies, some have argued that self-determination has shifted to the right of peoples freely to determine the internal structure of their state. Very early on, Cassesse defined the internal aspect of self-determination as "the right to choose [the] form of government and to determine the social, economic, and cultural policies of the state".[230] This follows Article 1 common to International Covenants, which states: "[a]ll peoples have the right of self-determination. By virtue of that right they freely determine their political status and freely pursue their economic, social and cultural development".[231] The current content of the internal aspect of self-determination is nevertheless still not agreed and its existence as a legal concept is challenged.[232] Nevertheless, on the basis of both international human rights covenants, there seems to be strong support for the internal aspect of the right of self-determination as the follow-up of the right of self-determination in a post-colonial era, aimed at avoiding the further fragmentation of states.[233] The right to independence would therefore be reserved

---

228 International Court of Justice, 'Case concerning East Timor' (Portugal v. Australia), Judgment, 30 June 1995, 1995 *ICJ Reports* 90.

229 Klabbers, J., 'The Right to be Taken Seriously: Self-Determination in International Law', 28 *Human Rights Quarterly* (2006), pp. 198–199. Also Shaw, M. N., *International Law* (Cambridge: Cambridge University Press, 2003), p. 444.

230 Cassesse, A., 'The Self-Determination of Peoples', in Henkin, L. (ed.) *The International Bill of Right. The Covenant on Civil and Political Rights* (New York: Columbia University Press, 1981), p. 97.

231 Article 1, common to the ICCPR and the ICESCR.

232 See Crawford, J., *The creation of states in International Law*, 2nd edition (Oxford: Clarendon Press, 2006), p. 121 *et s.* See also d'Aspremont, J., *L'état non démocratique en droit international* (Paris: Pedone, 2008), p. 278.

233 See on this: Pellet, A., 'The opinions of the Badinter Arbitration Committee. A Second Breath for the Self-Determination of Peoples', 3 *European Journal of International Law* 178 (1992) discussing the role of the Badinter opinions. Also Cogen, M., *The Comprehensive Guide to International Law* (Brugge: Die Keure, 2008), p. 91.

to former colonies, while other peoples would have a right to their own cultural identity and other collective rights within the framework of an existing state.[234] The question is thus whether the right of *internal* self-determination plays a role in defining the internal structures of a state, when international administrations exercise administrative powers or when the Security Council endorses political choices made in relation to the internal political structures of a state.

It has indeed sometimes been questioned whether the Security Council can 'impose' a form of UN administration upon the population of any state without the clear acquiescence of that population, given the peremptory character of the right of self-determination.[235] Of course, if one views the concept of international administration as a method of imposing a government on a population without its explicit consent, this could indeed be seen as a violation of the right of internal self-determination. However, we question that the establishment of an international administration over a state or entity amounts *per se* to a violation of the right of self-determination.[236] The *establishment* of an international administration must in our view be considered as a means of achieving self-determination, internal as well as external, and does not therefore automatically amount to a violation of the principle of self-determination of peoples.[237] Provided that the right of internal self-determination is admitted as a legal principle, in the case of Kosovo, the creation of the international administration is a way to implement the right of the Kosovar people to internal self-determination.[238] Equally, the setting up of the administration in East Timor is a method of implementing the external right of self-determination of the East Timorese. The temporary character of an international administration, as well as relevant Security Council resolutions, provides sufficient support for our argument. The question indeed is linked to the aim of peace-building missions through the setting up of an international administration which is not the creation of a definitive substitute

---

234 Cf. Dupuy, *supra* note 217, p. 130. For a critique on internal self-determination, see also Klabbers, *supra* note 229.

235 Gill, T. D., 'Legal and Some Political Limitations on the Power of the UN Security Council to Exercise its Enforcement Powers under Chapter VII of the Charter', 26 *Netherlands Yearbook of International Law* 75 (1995).

236 On this issue, see the discussion in Salamun, *supra* note 225. See also Zimmermann, A. and Stahn, C., Yugoslav Territory, United Nations Trusteeship or Sovereign State? Reflections on the Current and Future Legal Status of Kosovo, 70 *Nordic Journal of International Law* 454 (2001).

237 Also Bothe and Marauhn, *supra* note 6, pp. 238–239.

238 Tomuschat, C., 'Yugoslavia's Damaged Sovereignty over the Province of Kosovo', in Kreijen, G. (ed.), *State, Sovereignty, and International Governance* (Oxford: Oxford University Press, 2004), p. 345. Also Stahn, C., 'Constitution without a State? Kosovo under the United Nations Constitutional Framework for Self-Government', 14 *Leiden Journal of International Law* 541 (2001).

government in a territory or state. We will argue *infra* that such missions are by definition temporary in character, as they are designed to delegate governmental functions to the local population. The various international administrations which were created were explicitly aimed at the development or rehabilitation of national democratic institutions, following the holding of free and fair elections. We might even add that, in the light of the evolution described in our first part, international administrations are actually useful for dealing with claims of internal and external self-determination as they are aimed at the creation of functioning democratic institutions.[239]

The same can be said for the most recent cases of post-conflict reconstruction with non-international transitional administrations, such as Afghanistan and Iraq. Although they are not UN-led administrations supplanting the local government, their goal is essentially the same: transition towards a functioning democratic state. The case of Afghanistan of course cannot as such be seen as contravening the right of self-determination, as no foreign administration has been set up. Instead, the Bonn Agreement immediately envisaged national interim authorities to oversee its implementation. Nevertheless, one could ask whether the endorsement by the Security Council of certain transitional authorities could contravene the right of self-determination. The case of Iraq is somewhat different. The reconstruction process under the CPA was accepted and authorised by the UN Security Council, but again is aimed at restoring an effective civil administration in the territory. In the case of foreign military occupation, the right of self-determination is also expressed through the provisions relating to the obligation on the occupier to maintain the *status quo*. The rehabilitation of the institutions or the establishment of an elected government following the holding of free and fair elections can therefore be considered to be in conformity with the right of self-determination.[240]

The imposition of a *particular* form of government is a distinct question, which is related to the *exercise* of administrative functions by the international administration rather than to the conformity of the concept of foreign or international administration with the right of self-determination. The question has been raised on several occasions, such as the adoption by the Security Council of a resolution calling for the creation of a federal, multi-ethnical state in Iraq, therefore enforcing regime change. Another example is the issue of the privatisation of public companies and the signature of Free Trade Agreements by

[239] Also Bothe and Marauhn, *supra* note 6, p. 239 and Stahn, C., 'The United Nations Transitional Administrations in Kosovo and East Timor: a First Analysis', 5 *Max Planck Yearbook of United Nations Law* 182 (2001).

[240] See Wheatley, S., 'The Security Council, Democratic Legitimacy and Regime Change in Iraq', 17 *European Journal of International Law* 531 (2006).

UNMIK.[241] Some have argued that the adoption of a particular form of government, as in the case of Iraq and to a lesser extent in Kosovo and East Timor, encroaches upon the right of self-determination.[242] While this can be true to some extent, as the people did not indeed freely determine the political system and its representatives in an interim phase, the issue cannot be addressed from a purely hierarchy of norms viewpoint, considering the contested existence of the *internal* right to self-determination, and thus by necessary implication the *jus cogens* character of such a norm.[243] Therefore, the 'conflict' between these two norms is better solved from the point of view of balancing the interests of the international community in maintaining international peace and security and the 'right' of internal self-determination.[244] To a certain extent, we could even consider that the endorsement of a federal entity in Iraq would actually not only contribute to the stability of the country, but also ensure the fair and balanced representation of all ethnical parties in Iraq. The same observation can be made with regard to the reservation of certain seats in the provisional institutions for Kosovo Serbs.

2. *UN General Assembly*

The latest operations in which the UN was invested with far-reaching administrative competences were all authorised by the Security Council. Nevertheless, the question whether the General Assembly is competent to authorise the establishment of a peace-building missions is still relevant to a certain extent, given that several precedents were established by the General Assembly. This was the case with the administration of West Irian, the 'Council for Namibia' and the proposed administration of Jerusalem. One has to keep in mind that the circumstances of the specific case will directly influence the establishment of administrative missions by either the General Assembly or the Security Council.

---

241 Free Trade Agreement between The United Nations Interim Administration Mission in Kosovo (UNMIK) on behalf of the Provisional Institutions of Self-Government in Kosovo and The Council of Ministers of the Republic of Albania, UN Doc. UNMIK/FTA/2003/1 (4 July 2003) and Interim Free Trade Agreement between The United Nations Interim Administration Mission in Kosovo (UNMIK) on behalf of the Provisional Institutions of Self-Government in Kosovo and the Government of FYROM, UN Doc. UNMIK/FTA/2005/1 (31 August 2005).

242 See Gill, *supra* note 235. See in general on the potential between the notion of self-determination and foreign administration, d'Aspremont, J., 'La création internationale d'Etats démocratiques', 109 *Revue générale de droit international public* 889 (2005).

243 See however, on the consequences of a violation of *jus cogens* norms by the Security Council: de Wet, E., *The Chapter VII powers of the United Nations Security Council* (Oxford: Hart Publishers, 2004), pp. 187 *et s.*

244 Cf. Wheatley, *supra* note 240.

The UN Charter specifies that, besides the general functions entrusted to it, the General Assembly "may consider the general principles of co-operation in the maintenance of international peace and security, including the principles governing disarmament and the regulation of armaments, and may make recommendations with regard to such principles to the Members or to the Security Council or to both".[245] Article 11 para. 2 of the UN Charter further states that "the General Assembly may discuss any questions relating to the maintenance of international peace and security brought before it by any Member of the United Nations, or by the Security Council, [...] and, except as provided in Article 12, may make recommendations with regard to any such questions to the state or states concerned or to the Security Council or to both". Accordingly, with regard to its capacity to deal with a situation, the General Assembly is competent to discuss all matters relating to the maintenance of international peace and security, and to make recommendations in that regard, except when the Security Council is exercising the functions assigned to it by the UN Charter in respect of that dispute or situation.[246] The recommendatory power of the General Assembly, with regard to the maintenance of international peace and security, can be compared to the analogous powers of the Security Council under Chapter VI of the UN Charter. The instruments which can be employed by the General Assembly are extensive, and there does not seem to be a limitation in that regard, as long as it is a non-binding instrument and merely recommendatory.[247]

Nevertheless, even if the General Assembly is competent to deal with a certain matter, the question remains what kind of action can be taken, and whether or not the establishment of an international administration falls within such authorised action. The whole debate can be brought back to the meaning of the second sentence of Article 11, para. 2 of the Charter, which states that "any such question on which action is necessary shall be referred to the Security Council by the General Assembly either before or after discussion". The precise meaning of the word 'action' in that Article has been problematic for many years, especially in the period in which the General Assembly aspired to exercise comprehensive powers due to the Security Council's inability to act. However, at this stage, it is clear that the term 'action' refers to action with respect to threats to the peace, breaches of the peace, and acts of aggression, *i.e.* Chapter VII action.[248] It means that the General Assembly is not competent to resort to measures involving the use of force, even if it desires to respond to a situation which constitutes a threat

[245] Article 11, para. 1 UN Charter.

[246] Article 12, para. 1 UN Charter.

[247] Conforti, *supra* note 201, p. 211.

[248] Hailbronner, K. and Klein, E., 'Article 11', in Simma, *supra* note 214, p. 242 and Conforti, *supra* note 201, pp. 214–215.

to the peace, a breach of the peace, and acts of aggression. This was expressly confirmed by the International Court of Justice in the *Certain expenses* case in which the Court held that

> "the word 'action' must mean such action as is solely within the province of the Security Council, namely that indicated by the title of Chapter VII of the Charter: 'action with respect to threats to the peace, breaches of the peace, and acts of aggression'".[249] The Court equally considered that if "the word 'action' in Article II, paragraph 2, were interpreted to mean that the General Assembly could make recommendations only of a general character affecting peace and security in the abstract, and not in relation to specific cases, the paragraph would not have provided that the General Assembly may make recommendations on questions brought before it by States or by the security Council. Accordingly, the last sentence of Article II, paragraph 2, has no application where the necessary action is not enforcement action."

In light of these considerations, one can conclude that the General Assembly would be authorised under the UN Charter to establish such operations with the consent of the government.[250] The competence of the General Assembly to carry out military operations however remains excluded.[251]

---

249 International Court of Justice, *Certain Expenses of the United Nations (Article 17, paragraph 2, of the Charter)*, Advisory Opinion, 20 July 1962, 1962 *ICJ Reports* 165.

250 Also Stahn, *supra* note 239, p. 140. See for a discussion on the lack of competence of the General Assembly: Conforti, *supra* note 201, pp. 216–217.

251 Bothe, M., 'Peace-Keeping', in Simma, *supra* note 214, p. 592.

Chapter 5

The Legal Status of Territories and States under International Administration

While the legal status under international law of the states and territories under international administration is less relevant in the cases of Afghanistan and Iraq, this is paramount in respect of Kosovo and East Timor. In the past, various names have been given to the cases discussed in the first part: 'internationalised territory', 'protectorate', 'trust territory', '*de facto* state' and so forth. One should however clearly distinguish the status of the territory, its denomination and the name of the administrating regime. We will analyse to what extent the states and territories in which the UN has exercised far-reaching administrative powers are endowed with a particular international legal status, and subsequently, whether the legal status has implications for the exercise of state competences and the international legal personality of the entity.

A. *'Trust Territories', 'Protectorates' and 'International(ised) Territories'*

As mentioned in our introduction, the term 'international administration' or 'international territorial administration' refers only to the *regime* of the administration, which is particular type of operation within the broader framework of peace-building missions. Equally, the use of 'transitional administration' only denotes the interim or non-elected character of the administration. These indications are therefore useful to describe the nature of authority exercised by international actors and to delineate the context in which these operations have been set up, but they nevertheless do not indicate whether a specific legal regime is attached to these descriptions.

Generally, the Montevideo Convention is seen as the legal instrument containing the characteristics of statehood: "[t]he State as a person of international law should possess the following qualifications: a) a permanent population, b) a defined territory, c) government and d) capacity to enter into relations with the other States".[252] With regard to Kosovo, and East Timor, it can be argued that, in the absence of an effective domestic government, they cannot be qualified as states.[253] On the other hand, in the cases of Afghanistan and Iraq it is clear that their statehood has not been suspended or altered following the setting up of the missions, which have, in addition and to a certain extent, not supplanted the national authorities.

Several scholars have argued that territories under international administration, such as Kosovo, could be described as *de facto* trust territories.[254] As already extensively explained *supra*, the trusteeship system is a specific institution contained in the UN Charter, which requires the implementation of several conditions, such as the conclusion of a formal trusteeship agreement. As these requirements are not met in the cases we discussed, none of these territories can therefore, *in a legal sense,* be regarded as trust territories under the UN system. They remain Security Council operations under Chapter VI or Chapter VII. However, we also acknowledged that the finality and purposes of the Trusteeship System bears much resemblance to many of the latest administrative missions, such as those in Kosovo and in East Timor.[255] Similar objectives are present in the cases of Afghanistan and Iraq, although in these cases the UN was not formally entrusted with administrative authority. Even if the similarities between the two categories are many, the legal notion of trusteeship has, in our view, to be reserved for the purposes set out in the UN Charter. An often cited precedent to back the assertion that the recent missions are *de facto* trusts is the Saar Basin. In that case, however, it was explicitly stipulated that "Germany renounces in favour of the League of Nations, in the capacity of trustee, the government of the territory defined above".[256] In addition, considering the specific characteristics of that case, in which the territory was placed under international administration to ensure the temporary international status of the territory, it is doubtful whether the concept of *trust* in that case can be applied *mutatis mutandis* to the recent forms of international administration. The administration in the Saar Basin indeed had an entirely different purpose than the current missions.

---

[252] Montevideo Convention on the Rights and Duties of States, 26 December 1933, 165 LNTS 19. See also Brownlie, *supra* note 200, p. 74 and Dupuy, *supra* note 217, pp. 30–33.

[253] Ruffert, *supra* note 200, p. 627.

[254] See in particular on the Kosovo case: Franckx, E., Pauwels, A. and Smis, S., 'An international trusteeship for Kosovo: attempt to find a solution to the conflict', 52 *Studia Diplomatica* 155 (2001), pp. 155–166 and Kelly, *supra* note 176.

[255] See also Ruffert, *supra* note 200, p. 629 and Maziau, N. and Pech, L., 'L'administration internationale de la Bosnie-Herzégovine: un modèle pour le Kosovo?', 4 *Civitas Europa* 51 (2000), pp. 51–97.

[256] Saar Article 49 of the Versailles Peace Treaty.

In addition, in spite of the mentioned similarities in the overall objectives of recent post-conflict missions and the Trusteeship System, the recent mandates given to international administrations and other post-conflict peace-building missions cannot be seen as a continuance of that system. First of all, the Trusteeship System was reserved for certain specific categories of states and territories, which were administered until either self-government or independence. Secondly, despite the references to international peace and security in both post-conflict operations and the Trusteeship System, the use made of 'international peace and security' in the Trusteeship System is different than in the current context of post-conflict administrations. Although the establishment of a trusteeship was seen as generally 'strengthening universal peace',[257] the inclusion of "to further of international peace and security" as one of the objectives of the trusteeship system in Article 76 of the UN Charter was principally intended to point out that a trust territory would need to "play its part in the maintenance of international peace and security", as provided for by article 84 UN Charter.[258] Conversely, the creation of post-conflict administrations is a measure aimed at maintaining or re-establishing international peace and security, which falls under the ambit of the Security Council's Chapter VII powers. The application of the Trusteeship System might thus not be the ideal framework for the current administrations.

The concept of *trust* as such has nevertheless been seen as useful, if considered outside the formal scope of the Trusteeship System embodied in the UN Charter.[259] Such a 'modern' form of trusteeship has been defined as "a relationship in which a natural person or a legal person is responsible for the general well-being of a group of people who are incapable – perhaps, through no fault of their own – of directing their own affairs".[260] However, although we do favour the view that certain inherent aspects of the concept of *trust* can in fact be part of the *subsidiary* applicable legal framework, the notion of trust as such is not appropriate to be used in the current cases. The concept of trust indeed implies a certain hierarchy in the international community of states, as it is based on the assumption that certain people are not able to govern themselves. The recent peace-building missions and international administrations are, on the contrary, based on the assumption that the people are capable of governing themselves. The

---

[257] Rauschning, D., 'Article 76' in Simma, *supra* note 214, p. 940.

[258] *Ibid.* See also Toussaint, C. E., *The Trusteeship System of the United Nations* (Westport: Greenwood Press, 1976), pp. 54–55 and Rauschning, D., 'Article 84', in Simma, *supra* note 214, p. 961.

[259] Cf. Grant, T. D., 'Extending Decolonisation: How the United Nations Might Have Addressed Kosovo', 28 *Georgia Journal of International and Comparative Law* 8 (1999).

[260] Bain, W., 'The Idea of Trusteeship in International Society', 368 *The round Table* 67 (2003), p. 68. See also for the concept of a 'modern protectorate': Grant, *supra* note 259, p. 50.

aim of these missions is not to direct peoples while creating a form of dependence, inherent in the notion of trust, but to assist peoples in achieving self-government as a method of maintaining international peace and security.[261]

The notion of 'protectorate' has also often been used as a qualification for these territories.[262] A protectorate can be defined as "a legal status largely of historical interest whereby a dependant state retains control over its internal affairs, while leaving its external protection in the hands of another state".[263] A protectorate is thus a relationship between states by which one state takes on the protection of another and the protected state cedes to the protector the competence over its external relations.[264] This qualification can therefore not be upheld for the recent cases of post-conflict administration. A protectorate is a particular legal construction with very specific features which apply only to certain precise bilateral structures between states. Beside the close link with the colonisation period, the historical use of the concept links the notion of protectorate to a form of dependence.[265] There are also legal impediments. One of the basic characteristics of a protectorate, as derived from the abovementioned definition, is that it is essentially a relationship between two *states*. While one might consider that the concept could *mutatis mutandis* be applied in the case where an international organisation was the 'protector', the inherent characteristics of a protectorate cannot be associated with the concept and objectives of peace-building. Although some scholars have pointed out that the case of Bosnia and Herzegovina may be similar to a modern protectorate,[266] we consider that the aim of a protectorate is not comparable with the objectives of the recent cases. The UN does not aim at protecting a dependent state or entity, but explicitly works towards independence, self-determination or self-government.

Although we have doubts about its usefulness, the most appropriate term to be used for territories under international administration is probably 'internationalised territory',[267] or such similar notions as 'internationalisation', 'internation-

---

261 Cf. Gordon, R. E., 'Some Legal Problems with Trusteeship', 28 *Cornell International Law Journal* 301 (1995), pp. 345–346.

262 The Independent International Commission on Kosovo, *The Kosovo Report: Conflict, international response, lessons learned* (Oxford: Oxford University Press, 2001), pp. 259 *et s.*

263 Bledsoe, R. and Boczek, B., *The International Law Dictionary* (Santa Barbara: ABC-Clio, 1987), p. 43.

264 See 'Protectorat', in Salmon, *supra* note 3, p. 42; Basdevant, J., *Dictionnaire de la terminologie du Droit International* (Paris: Sirey, 1960), p. 485 and Cogen, *supra* note 233, p. 96.

265 Cf. Whiteman, M. M. (ed.), *Digest of International Law* (Washington: Department of State Publications, 1963), para. 27.

266 Ruffert, *supra* note 200, p. 628.

267 See on the concept of 'internationalised territories': Delbez, L., 'Le concept d'internationalisation', *Revue générale de droit international public* 5 (1967); Crawford, J., *The creation of states in International Law* (Oxford: Clarendon Press, 1979); Dunoff, J. L., Ratner, S. R. and Wippman, D.,

alised cities' or 'international territories'. There is not however a very precise or exact definition of an 'internationalised territory', which is probably due to the diverse conditions and specificities of each case of international administration. Ydit described internationalised territories as "populated areas established for an unlimited duration as special State entities in which supreme sovereignty is vested in (or de facto exercised by) a group of States or in the organised international community. The local element in these territories is restricted in its sovereign powers by the provisions of an International Statute (Charter, Constitution, etc.) imposed upon it by the Powers holding the supreme sovereignty over the territory."[268] While we cannot agree with the transfer of sovereignty to international actors or with the unlimited character of the internationalisation, this description can indeed be applied to some of the precedents we discussed in our first part, such as Danzig and the projected administration of Trieste. Such a definition is not however applicable to more recent international administrations. Another and more general description is proposed by Rousseau, who used the similar notion of '*territoire international*', and described it as a territory subtracted from any exclusive state competence which had a regime of direct international administration exercised by an international authority.[269] According to Brownlie, the label 'internationalised territory' can be applied to cases where "a special status was created by multilateral treaty and protected by an international organisation",[270] as in the cases of Dazing and Trieste. It can also be applied to cases with an "exclusive administration of a territory by an international organisation or an organ hereof", such as the proposed regime for Jerusalem. Shaw uses the term 'international territories' as meaning "when a particular territory is placed under a form of international regime".[271] Shaw adds that the conditions under which this has been done have varied widely, from autonomous areas within states to relatively independent entities. Other taxonomies have been proposed in the literature, such as 'permanent internationalisation' as opposed to 'temporary internationalisation',[272] but these denominations do not add any substantial element to the qualification of internationalised territories. Though no clear and

International Law: norms, actor, process – A problem-Oriented Approach (New York / Gaithersburg / Aspen: Law & Business, 2002); Stahn, C., 'International Territorial Administration in the former Yugoslavia: Origins, Developments and Challenges ahead', 61 *Zeitschrift für ausländisches öffentliches Rechts und Völkerrechts.* 107 (2001), p. 119; Ruffert, *supra* note 200, p. 629 and Zimmermann and Stahn, *supra* note 236, pp. 428-429.

268 Ydit, *supra* note 11, p. 323.

269 Rousseau, C., *Droit International Public, Tome II – Les sujets de droit* (Paris: Sirey, 1974), p. 413.

270 Brownlie, *supra* note 200, p. 60.

271 Shaw, *supra* note 229, p. 162.

272 Dunoff, Ratner and Wippman, *supra* note 267, pp. 244–245.

all-inclusive definition of the concept of 'internationalised territory' exists, it is often seen as the most appropriate term to use to categorise these entities considering the neutrality of the notion towards the issue of legal personality.[273]

While such a description can be envisaged in the cases where the UN has fully taken over the administration of a territory or state, we nevertheless question whether it is useful. Indeed, in the current cases, internationalisation as such is not the aim of the exercise, but the means to achieve another objective. In addition, there are no legal consequences attached to the notion. Categorisation by means of a notion with no legal implications is therefore in our view unnecessary. There is no need explicitly to ascertain a legal qualification, distinct from the qualification of the states or territories under existing categories. East Timor, for instance, was, prior to the establishment of UNTAET, a non-self-governing territory occupied by Indonesia.[274] The establishment of UNTAET did not alter its legal status, as it was explicitly aimed at providing a transition to independence through the exercise of governmental powers. Kosovo, which was formally a Province of the Republic of Serbia within the Federal Republic of Yugoslavia, equally maintained its status under UNMIK's administration. The only consequence of the establishment of the international administration in Kosovo was the suspension of the Federal Republic of Yugoslavia's competences, but this did not alter Kosovo's territorial status. Nevertheless, the concept of 'internationalised territory' can be useful to describe situations such as Danzig or Trieste, as the guarantee of a specific international status was the main purpose of the exercise. It is not however helpful in recent operations in which the administration was internationalised.

B. *Sovereignty and the Suspension or Limitation of Exclusive State Competences*

The relationship between sovereignty and the exercise of administrative functions by international actors has frequently been misconceived in recent cases. Sovereignty is as such closely related to international legal personality, and can be described as the right to exercise, to the exclusion of any other state, the functions of a state.[275] Sovereignty is thus an intrinsic aspect of a state, distinct

---

[273] Cf. Ruffert, *supra* note 200 and Stahn, *supra* note 267.

[274] See International Court of Justice, 'Case concerning East Timor' (Portugal v. Australia), Judgment, 30 June 1995, 1995 *ICJ Reports* 90, para. 37.

[275] Cf. 'Island of Palmas Case' (Netherlands v. U.S.), Arbitral Award, 4 April 1928, 22 *American Journal of International Law* 967 (1928), p. 875.

from the competences of the state which are both territorial and personal and distinct from its administration.[276]

Certain situations can nevertheless moderate a state's exclusive competence, one of them being the transfer of administrative powers. In recent decades several institutions were formed which directly limited a state's exclusive competences, such as foreign military occupation, protectorates and the trusteeship and mandate systems. These structures implied the right of another entity, a State or an international organisation, to exercise certain competences. However, none of them implied a sovereign right to the territory in question.[277] In the similar cases of UN-led international administrations, the temporary suspension of the exclusive state competences in favour of the UN does not therefore imply the transfer of sovereignty over the territory to the UN. The international character of these territories does not question the title to and ownership of the territory, nor does it question sovereignty, despite the fact that the exercise of the administrative authority does not coincide with the ownership of or sovereignty over the territory.[278] As a consequence, the transfer of administration or state competences to an international organisation or the presence of foreign actors in the administration does not imply the *transfer* of the state's sovereignty to the international organisation.[279] The state itself, when the entire state or a part of its territory is under international administration, does not disappear, nor does it transfer elsewhere its inherent right to those competences.

It has also been argued that the sovereignty of states or territories under international administration would be suspended in favour of the administrator or that the international organisation would exercise sovereignty in place of the state.[280] However, this seems to result from an erroneous interpretation of the concept of sovereignty. On the contrary, the transmission by a state of its administering power and competences to another entity can be seen as the *exercise* of the rights of a sovereign state. This can be either by consenting to the deployment of an international administration, or by granting the power to the UN Security Council to establish such mission by signing the UN Charter. It cannot therefore be assumed that sovereignty over the territory under international administration is temporarily vested in or exercised by the UN. As Rousseau stated with regard

---

276 Brownlie, *supra* note 200, p. 107 and Crawford, *supra* note 232, p. 33.

277 Dupuy, *supra* note 217, p. 65. See also Knoll, B., *The Legal Status of Territories Subject to Administration by International Organisation* (Cambridge: Cambridge University Press, 2008), p. 41 *et s.*

278 Zimmermann and Stahn, *supra* note 236, p. 429.

279 See however, Chopra, *supra* note 10, arguing that sovereignty has passed to the UN.

280 See for instance. Yannis, A., 'The Concept of Suspended Sovereignty in International Law and its Implications in International Politics', 13 *European Journal of International Law* 1037 (2002), pp. 1037–1052.

to former cases in which an international organisation exercised administrative functions, "il n'apparaît pas, comme certains auteurs l'ont pensé [...] que les régimes d'internationalisation constituent une catégorie juridique impliquant l'exercice effectif de la souveraineté [...] par la communauté internationale organisée."[281] In addition, from the point of view of the UN as an international organisation, it is obvious that when an international organisation is entitled to function as the administering authority over a state or part of a state, this title is not the equivalent of territorial sovereignty. The territorial delimitation of these competences does not imply that the international organisation has sovereignty over that territory.[282]

The case of Kosovo is of course a unique situation, but even in this case it cannot be claimed that UNMIK has sovereignty over this province, which remains an integral part of Serbia.[283] This is implicitly confirmed by the Security Council as it authorises "an agreed number of Yugoslav and Serb military and police personnel [...] to return to Kosovo to perform the functions in accordance with annex 2".[284] In addition to the abovementioned principles and reasoning, and although UNMIK *de facto* exercises all competences normally attributed to the sovereign, Resolution 1244 of the Security Council strengthens the idea that UNMIK merely temporarily exercised the competences of the sovereign.[285] Indeed, the UN can function as the administering authority of a territory only when the State concerned has no or only partial exclusive competence. We argue that for the duration of the international administration of the territory the state's sovereignty persists, but its exclusive competences are partially or totally suspended and exercised by the foreign actors.

As far as East Timor is concerned, it remained a non-self-governing territory throughout UNTAET's administration towards independence. It may be deduced from the General Assembly's Friendly Relations Declaration[286] that a non-self-governing territory enjoys separate legal status in international law with a

---

[281] Rousseau, *supra* note 269, p. 413.

[282] Nguyen Quoc Dinh, Dallier, P. and Pellet, A., *Droit International Public* (Paris: L.G.D.J., 1999), n° 393.

[283] See also in that sense: Zimmermann and Stahn, *supra* note 236, p. 429. Contra: Ringelheim, J., 'The legal status of Kosovo', in European University Institute (ed.), *Kosovo 1999–2000, The Intractable Peace* (Florence: European University Institute, 2001), pp. 7 *et s.* and Brand, M.G., 'Institution-Building and Human Rights Protection in Kosovo in the Light of UNMIK Legislation', 70 *Nordic Journal of International Law* 460 (2001), p. 463.

[284] SC Res. 1244, UN Doc. S/RES/1244 (1999), para. 4.

[285] See for a discussion: Zimmermann and Stahn, *supra* note 236, p. 429.

[286] G.A. Res. 2625(XXV), 'Declaration on Principles of International Law Concerning Friendly Relations and Co-operation Among States in Accordance with the Charter of the United Nations', UN Doc. A/5217 (24 October 1970).

certain legal personality.[287] However, the issue of East Timor's sovereignty, before achieving independence, remains uncertain. According to the principles applicable to non-self-governing territories,[288] one could assume that Portugal retained formal sovereignty over East Timor. Even after Indonesia's military intervention the Security Council continued to regard Portugal as the Administering Power under Chapter XI of the UN Charter,[289] although it subsequently asked UN Member States to respect East Timor's territorial integrity.[290] In addition, some have questioned the very notion of the sovereignty of the administering powers in non-self-governing territories.[291]

With regard to Iraq, the concept of sovereignty has frequently been used and misused by the CPA and the Security Council. In one of its resolutions, the Security Council "reaffirm(ed) the independence, sovereignty, unity, and territorial integrity of Iraq", although it stated that at the end of occupation "Iraq will reassert its full sovereignty".[292] Sovereignty as such was never transferred to the CPA, as the CPA was merely the administering authority in Iraq.[293] Although a comparison with the occupation of Germany by the four major Allied Powers after the Second World War is not totally accurate, it is clear that in that case the exercise of state functions by the Allied powers did not equally amount to a transfer of the sovereignty to the allied powers. As Brownlie puts it, "the important features of 'sovereignty' in such cases are the continued existence of a legal personality and the attribution of territory to that legal person and not to the holders for the time being".[294] In the case of Iraq, a reference to the transfer of *authority* instead of *sovereignty* would therefore have been more appropriate.[295]

C. *International Legal Personality*

When an *entire state*'s territory is placed under a certain form of international administration, the question relating to its international legal personality is relatively clear. As we saw in earlier chapters, the state and its sovereignty persist throughout the administration. Only the administration, as part of a state's

---

[287] Crawford, *supra* note 232, p. 618.
[288] *Ibid.*, 614.
[289] See *e.g.* SC Res. 384, UN Doc. S/RES/384 (1975).
[290] SC Res. 389, UN Doc. S/RES/389 (1976).
[291] Crawford, *supra* note 232, p. 613.
[292] SC Res. 1546, UN Doc. S/RES/1546 (2004), preamble and para. 2.
[293] Also Roberts, A., 'The End of Occupation: Iraq 2004', 54 *International and Comparative Law Quarterly* 27 (2005), p. 35.
[294] Brownlie, *supra* note 200, p. 107.
[295] Roberts, *supra* note 293, p. 41.

exclusive competences, is transferred to the administering authority, whereas the state retains sovereign over its territory. A state is granted international legal personality by the basic fact of the grouping of the constitutive elements of state. The transfer by a state of its administration, even with the conduct of its external relations and treaty-making power, does not imply the creation of a new legal person. In this case, it is obvious that the state concerned still possesses international legal personality; the legal personality of the state subsists.[296]

When considering the establishment of an international administration over a *part of a state's territory*, such as in Kosovo or Eastern Slavonia, Baranja and Western Sirmium, the question whether these territories enjoy *distinct* international legal personality is less evident. Apart from states, which are granted international legal personality by the mere fact that they are states, functional reflections can also be the basis for the recognition of international legal personality in other entities. This doctrine was initially developed for the benefit of international organisations by the International Court of Justice in its 'Reparation for Injuries' advisory opinion, but it has been argued that these principles could be applied to other entities.[297]

We should thus focus on whether the administration of the territory entails a specific international legal status. International administration as such is not the decisive factor to be evaluated, since such mandates may also be exercised without creating a new legal person. The scope and purposes of the international administration are the relevant criteria which need to be examined, for only the specific status of the territory in question is likely to establish a distinct legal person. When a special status is created for an entity by a multilateral treaty or by a UN resolution, and if that special status is accompanied by sufficient independence and international legal capacity, a distinct legal person can be formed.[298] An example of this is the establishment of Danzig as a 'Free City', endowed with treat-making capacity, an independent nationality law, a constitution and a defined territory and population.[299] The special status of Danzig was the guarantee by the League of Nations that the international status and constitution of Danzig would not be altered. Though Poland remained competent for the conduct of its foreign relations, this did not get in the way of Danzig being a distinct legal person. This position was confirmed by the Permanent Court of International Justice, which noted that "the fact that the legal status of Danzig is sui generis does not authorise it to depart form the ordinary rules governing

[296] Also Brownlie, *supra* note 200, p. 107.

[297] See Ruffert, *supra* note 200, p. 630 and Zimmermann and Stahn, *supra* note 236, p. 448.

[298] Brownlie, *supra* note 200, p. 60.

[299] Cf. Schwarzenberger, G., *International Law, Volume I: International Law as Applied by International Courts and Tribunals*, 3rd Edition (London: Steven & Sons Limited, 1957), pp. 109–112.

relations between States [...]. With regard to Poland, the Danzig Constitution, despite its peculiarities, is and remains the Constitution, of a foreign State."[300] A few years earlier, the Permanent Court of International Justice had already implicitly recognised the international legal personality of Danzig in its 'Advisory Opinion on the Free City of Danzig and the International Labour Organisation'.[301] However, such specific international status is often missing in recent cases, since as we argued in the previous chapter, internationalisation is not the aim of the current post-conflict administrations.

Kosovo's belonging to the Federal Republic of Yugoslavia was explicitly confirmed despite the territory being placed wholly under UN administration. Formally, therefore, Kosovo was still a Province of Serbia. However, the competences of Serbia over that part of its territory were exercised by UNMIK, while Serbia's *de jure* sovereignty was not questioned. We argued above that Serbia's competences over Kosovo were merely suspended for as long as UNMIK administers it. In this case, it seems clear that no new and distinct legal person is established.[302] However, a few scholars have argued that Kosovo does have a distinct international legal personality. Zimmermann and Stahn for instance view this grant of limited international legal personality as a consequence of Kosovo's internationalisation. This international legal personality, limited to matters which are directly linked to UNMIK's mandate, would, according to the authors, *inter alia* be demonstrated by UNMIK's capacity to conclude international treaties.[303] However, capacity to conclude international treaties does not automatically define a distinct international person, although we agree that it is often an elementary indication of international legal personality since it gives international *effectivité* to the territorial entity. The situation in Kosovo should however be compared to that of federal states. In federal states, the component states have no distinct legal personality while the authority to enter into treaties or agreements with

---

[300] Permanent Court of International Justice, 'Treatment of Polish National and other Persons of Polish Origin or Speech on the Danzig Territory', Advisory Opinion, 4 February 1932, 1932 *PCIJ Reports*, pp. 23–24.

[301] Permanent Court of International Justice, 'Free City of Danzig and International Labour Organization', Advisory Opinion, 30 August 1930, 1930 *PCIJ Reports* 4. The case concerned the possibility for the Free City of Danzig to become a member of the ILO. The Permanent Court of International Justice recognised that Danzig as such could become a member, but due to its special status regarding the conduct of its foreign relations by Poland, Danzig could not duly participate in the work of the ILO. Indeed, the Polish Government would have to accept every action taken by Danzig as a member of the ILO.

[302] Cf. Islami, I., 'The Insufficiency of International Legal Personality of Kosova as Attained Through the European Court of Human Rights: A Call for Statehood', 80 *Chicago-Kent Law Review* 83 (2005).

[303] Zimmermann and Stahn, *supra* note 236, pp. 449–451.

other states essentially depends on the constitution of the federal state.[304] This does not however imply that component states are not authorised to enter into agreements or have liaison offices in neighbouring countries. Similarly, one can say that UNMIK may enter into practical international agreements with, for instance, neighbouring countries provided that is consistent with its mandate under Security Council Resolution 1244, which, in this case, is the relevant legal instrument. The practice also supports this conclusion. UNMIK has signed a limited number of agreements with its neighbouring countries[305] and has concluded technical agreements.[306] These limited competences are nevertheless not the equivalent of an international legal personality.[307]

As far as East Timor is concerned, it remained a non-self-governing territory under UNTAET administration. According to the already mentioned General Assembly's Friendly Relations Declaration, a non-self-governing territory enjoys separate legal status in international law with a certain legal personality.[308] East Timor may seem similar to Kosovo, but is in fact different in respect of its international legal personality. When UNTAET was established, it was clear that East Timor would become an independent state at the termination of the

[304] For an overview on the evolution of this question, see: Wouters, J. and De Smet, L., 'The legal position of federal states and their federated entities in international relations – the case of Belgium', in Vandamme, T. A. J. A. and Reestman, J.-H. (eds.), *Ambiguity in the Rule of Law. The Interface between National and International Legal Systems* (Groningen: Europa Law Publishing, 2001), p. 121.

[305] Interim Free Trade Agreement between The United Nations Interim Administration Mission in Kosovo (UNMIK) on behalf of the Provisional Institutions of Self-Government in Kosovo and the Government of FYROM, UN Doc. UNMIK/FTA/2005/1 (31 August 2005) and Free Trade Agreement between The United Nations Interim Administration Mission in Kosovo (UNMIK) on behalf of the Provisional Institutions of Self-Government in Kosovo and The Council of Ministers of the Republic of Albanian, UN Doc. UNMIK/FTA/2003/1 (4 July 2003).

[306] See e.g. Agreement between the United Nations Interim Administration Mission in Kosovo and the Council of Europe on technical arrangements related to the European Convention for the Prevention of Torture and Inhuman or Degrading Treatment or Punishment (23 August 2004). The preamble emphasises that the agreement "does not make UNMIK a Party to the Convention and that it is without prejudice to the future status of Kosovo to be determined in accordance with Security Council resolution 1244 (1999)".

[307] Also Ruffert, *supra* note 200, p. 630.

[308] G.A. Res. 2625(XXV), 'Declaration on Principles of International Law Concerning Friendly Relations and Co-operation Among States in Accordance with the Charter of the United Nations', UN Doc. A/5217 (24 October 1970): "The territory of a colony or other Non-Self-Governing Territory has, under the Charter, a status separate and distinct from the territory of the State administering it; and such separate and distinct status under the Charter shall exist until the people of the colony or Non-Self-Governing Territory have exercised their right of self-determination in accordance with the Charter, and particularly its purposes and principles".

transitional period. In addition, a major difference from UNMIK was that UNTAET's mandate under Resolution 1272 explicitly authorised it "to take all necessary measures to fulfil its mandate".[309] Equally, in his report prior to the establishment of UNTAET, the Secretary-General provided for the power to conclude international agreements with States and international organisations as necessary for the carrying out of the functions entrusted to UNTAET.[310] This can again be evidence of a limited international legal personality, but we question whether this is the result of the 'internationalisation' of the territory or just a confirmation of the limited international legal personality of East Timor as a non-self-governing territory. Nevertheless, practice shows that UNTAET has been very careful in concluding international agreements. While UNTAET did engage in negotiations for the follow-up treaty on the Timor Gap, it did not as such sign the treaty, which was left to the Timorese Government upon independence. The exercise of administrative functions by the UN does not therefore seem to amount *by itself* to a distinct limited international legal personality.

309 SC Res. 1272, UN Doc. S/RES/1272 (1999), para. 4.

310 Report of the Secretary General on the situation in East Timor, UN Doc. S/1999/1024 (4 October 1999), para. 35.

Chapter 6

The Temporary Nature of Authority

Although this chapter is particularly directed towards the cases of Kosovo and East Timor, many principles need to be considered as also applicable in the case of Iraq. The CPA was not just an occupying force, but was also acting under a Security Council mandate. One of the most essential characteristics of recent peace-building missions, and post-conflict international administrations is their temporary nature. Often, contemporary peace-building missions are initially authorised by the Security Council for a limited and renewable period.[311] UNMIK is an exception, as it was established for "an initial period of 12 months, to continue thereafter unless the Security Council decides otherwise".[312] However, this does not mean that the mission in Kosovo was envisaged as a quasi-permanent form of international administration. The uncertain final status at the time of the establishment of UNMIK necessitated a much longer international presence, but it was clearly pointed out that the missions would transfer authority only from Kosovo's provisional institutions to permanent institutions established under a political settlement of Kosovo's final status.[313]

The temporary nature of current missions is mainly a direct consequence of the fact that these operations were established by the Security Council under Chapter VII of the UN Charter. Chapter VII allows the Security Council to take measures aimed at maintaining or restoring international peace and security. Once international peace and security are re-established or once a threat to international peace and security no longer exists, the mission must by definition come to an end.[314] This is indeed in accordance with the central aim of modern peace-building missions and international administrations. The powers granted are exercised with a specific purpose, reconstructing states emerging from years

---

[311] See *e.g.* SC Res. 1272, UN Doc. S/RES/1272 (1999), para. 17: "Decides to establish UNTAET for an initial period until 31 January 2001".

[312] SC Res. 1244, UN Doc. S/RES/1244 (1999), para. 19.

[313] *Ibid.*, para. 11, f).

[314] Bothe and Marauhn, *supra* note 6, p. 236.

of conflict or internal strife, and creating stable democratic institutions as a method of maintaining international peace and security. This is in fact, as we argued in the first part of this book, one of the basic distinctions between early forms of full or partial international administration and current missions. The creation of sustainable democratic institutions is the main long-term objective of the current missions, and necessarily implies a lengthy, although not indefinite, presence of international actors.

A consequence of the temporary nature of international administration is that the foreign administration must refrain from taking measures which would prejudice or alter the (final) status of the territory. Such limitations can also directly result from the mandate itself, contained in an agreement or resolution. This principle is very much related to the continuation of territorial sovereignty. International actors do not operate as sovereigns over these territories, since they exercise only administrative authority without acquiring title over the territory. This principle is of crucial importance in the case of Kosovo, where no agreement had been reached on its final status prior to the establishment of the international administration. Though the Security Council agreed that Kosovo should enjoy substantial autonomy, it also reaffirmed the territorial sovereignty of Serbia over the province. The interim administration in Kosovo was thus required to refrain from taking measures which would prejudice or predetermine Kosovo's future status. The opposite would be a violation not only of Security Council Resolution 1244, but also of the territorial integrity of Serbia.

Some authors argue that the temporary nature of the authority of international actors incorporates a fiduciary type of authority.[315] This idea of fiduciary authority originates from the private law institution of trust, which implies that a person, called the 'trustee', holds property for and on behalf of another person.[316] Trust also implies that these rights are exercised by the trustee for the benefit of the other. The main difference from *international* trusteeship is that in the latter case, the trustee is not a private person but a state or an international organisation, and that the object of the trust is not property but administering authority over a state or territory.[317] In a previous chapter we nevertheless pointed out that the concept of 'trust' could not as such be applied to current

[315] See Stahn, *supra* note 267 and Knoll, B., 'Legitimacy and UN-Administration of Territory', 8 *German Law Journal* 39 (2007), p. 45.

[316] See for example De Pover, M.-F., *Trust – Fiducie* (Brussel: Larcier, 2001), pp. 47–49.

[317] Kelsen, *supra* note 171, p. 566. Judge McNair, in a separate opinion in the South West Africa-case, identified several general principles which can be derived from the notion of trust in private law, and which could be applied in international law:

"(a) that the control of the trustee, *tuteur* or *curateur* over the property is limited in one way or another; he is not in the position of the normal complete owner, who can do what he likes with his own, because he is precluded from administering the property for his own personal benefit;

comprehensive peace-building missions. However, we did acknowledge that some overarching principles could probably be applied in those missions. The principle that international actors administer the territory on behalf and for the benefit of the population, and not for themselves, is very relevant, but it is not a consequence of the application of the concept of trust or the fiduciary character of the authority. The existence of such an obligation is derived from the relevant Security Council Resolutions and the context in which these missions were set up. The provision of basic civil services, humanitarian relief and reconstruction, as well as the long-term objectives, is obviously intended for the population and for the international community which has entrusted the Security Council with the maintenance of international peace and security. The objectives of such missions thus necessarily implies governance on behalf of and for the benefit of the population.

The basic principles derived from the fiduciary character of the authority can nevertheless be seen as applicable only in a subsidiary manner. This rule can for instance be applied to the administration by UNMIK of the properties belonging to Serbia. UNMIK did not acquire title to these properties, and one can therefore consider that the administration of Serbian property needed to take into account the rights and interests of Serbia.[318] In practice however, international administrations have not been very enthusiastic about the fiduciary character of their authority. In the case of Kosovo, for example, intrusive measures have been taken with regard to the privatisation of public companies. In Iraq, far-reaching measures have been adopted to achieve the liberalisation of the economy. In both cases, the administrations were apparently not convinced that their powers were limited by the fiduciary nature of their authority. The administering authority is indeed primarily bound by the main objectives of the missions, and the mandates under Security Council Resolutions are to take precedence over the fiduciary principle. In the event of ambiguity in the mandate, the fiduciary character can however be seen as a useful method of interpretation of the mandate.

(b) that the trustee, *tuteur* or *curateur* is under some kind of legal obligation, based on confidence and conscience, to carry out the trust or mission confided to him for the benefit of some other person or for some public purpose;

(c) that any attempt by one of these persons to absorb the property entrusted to him into his own patrimony would be illegal and would be prevented by the law." (International Court of Justice, 'International Status of South West Africa', Advisory Opinion, 11 July 1950, 1950 *ICJ Reports*, p. 128. Separate opinion by Sir Arnold McNair, 1950 *ICJ Reports* 146, p. 149).

In that particular case however, this referred to the mandates system of the League of Nations and the UN Trusteeship System. It is doubtful whether these principles apply to every form of international administration.

318 Cf. Lagrange, E., 'La mission intérimaire des Nations Unies au Kosovo, nouvel essai d'administration directe d'un territoire', 45 *Annuaire Français de Droit International* 335 (1999), p. 350.

Chapter 7

Human Rights Obligations of International Actors

At present there is no international organisation which is a party to international human rights treaties, which is the consequence of the fact that human rights instruments are generally open only to States, with the exclusion of international organisations. In addition, human rights obligations are traditionally addressed to states. The International Covenant on Civil and Political Rights (ICCPR)[319] for example, provides that the Convention is open for signature by any UN Member State or member of any of its specialised agencies, by any State Party to the Statute of the International Court of Justice, and by any other State which has been invited by the General Assembly of the UN to become a Party to the Covenant.[320] A similar limitation is contained in the European Convention for the Protection of Human Rights and Fundamental Freedoms (ECHR)[321] which is open for signature only by states members of the Council of Europe.[322] Does this however preclude the application of basic human rights standards to the activities of international organisations, and in particular when these organisations administer states or territories? We will first analyse whether foreign and international actors, and in particular the UN, engaged in the administration of territory are bound by international human rights standards. We will then examine to what extent international actors can accordingly be held accountable for violations of these rights in the exercise of their functions.

---

319 International Covenant on Civil and Political Rights (19 December 1966), 999 UNTS 17 [hereafter 'ICCPR'].

320 See article 48, para. 1, ICCPR.

321 European Convention for the Protection of Human Rights and Fundamental Freedoms and its protocols (4 November 1950) 213 UNTS 222 [hereafter 'ECHR'].

322 See article 59, ECHR.

A. *Human Rights Obligations in Peace-building Missions*

While it might seem appropriate to require that international actors not violate human rights, given that they are mandated to implement and introduce human rights into the territories under administration, the legal foundation for this assertion is not self-evident. Although none of the resolutions establishing international administrations explicitly confirm the application of internationally recognised human rights standards to the administering authority, we will analyse to what extent the UN can be considered to be legally bound by human rights norms, either as a matter of customary international law, or by its constitutional treaty, the UN Charter.[323] We will later turn to the question of the application of human rights to military components. Such a distinction is indeed necessary, as the civil components of peace-building missions and international administrations are subsidiary organs of the UN, while the military components cannot automatically be considered as such.

1. *The UN Charter*

Although certain 'programmatic' provisions contained in the UN Charter can certainly create an obligation to respect human rights *as a matter of policy*, it is far from clear that the Charter contains any *legal* obligation in this respect.[324] The preamble to the UN Charter emphasises the determination of the UN "to reaffirm faith in fundamental human rights". Article 1 further declares one of the purposes of the UN to be "achieve international co-operation in solving international problems of an economic, social, cultural, or humanitarian character, and in promoting and encouraging respect for human rights and for fundamental freedoms for all without distinction as to race, sex, language, or religion". This commitment is reaffirmed again in Article 55: "the United Nations shall promote [...] universal respect for, and observance of, human rights and fundamental freedoms for all without distinction as to race, sex, language, or religion". These explicit commitments by the UN have directed several scholars to conclude that the organisation is, at least as a matter of policy, under an obligation to respect human rights law.[325] Although it is true that States are the

---

[323] For an overview of other additional approaches see Cameron, L., 'Human Rights Accountability of International Civil Administrations to the People Subject to Administration', 1 *Human Rights & International Legal Discourse* 267 (2007).

[324] Kolb, R., Porretto, G. and Vité, S., *L'application du droit international humanitaire et des droits de l'homme aux organisations internationales: Forces de paix et administrations civiles transitoires* (Bruxelles: Bruylant, 2005), p. 259.

[325] See for instance, Cerone, J., 'Minding the gap: outlining KFOR accountability in post-conflict Kosovo', 12 *European Journal of International Law* 469 (2001), p. 473.

primary and more or less exclusive actors in ensuring respect for human rights, it has been argued that the UN cannot consider itself outside the scope of these provisions.[326] Bearing these provisions in mind it would thus seem obvious to require from the UN respect for human rights, in particular when performing legislative and administrative functions. The question however is whether this obligation is also a *legal* obligation. The provision contained in Article 1 is at most a non-compulsory commitment of the UN to establish international consciousness of basic human rights standards. The same objection can be made for the provision contained in Article 55, which merely includes an obligation for the UN to *promote* respect for human rights standards, which consequently, based on a textual interpretation, can also not be seen as compulsory. In a narrow legal sense, the UN Charter cannot function as a legal basis for the application to the UN of human rights standards.

On the other hand, we understand the argument that it is hardly imaginable that the UN, while having the responsibility to promote and encourage respect for human rights, would consider itself not to be bound by these standards when it comes down to its own activities.[327] Nevertheless, such a consideration will not be very helpful to understand the human rights obligations of an international administration that has to operate in a post-conflict environment. Equally, the policy argument ignores the legal rules applicable under international administration, which cannot be limited to human rights obligations. The respective obligations of international administrations are more complex than would seem at first hand, and are not limited to the international organisation's constitutional obligations. It thus seems necessary to establish a clear legal basis for the application of human rights standards to international organisations.

2. *Human Rights as Customary International Law*

An international organisation has international legal personality distinct from that of its member states. As stated by the International Court of Justice in the 'Reparations for Injuries' case, "the Organization is an international person. That is not the same thing as saying that it is a State, which it certainly is not, or that its legal personality and rights and duties are the same as those of a State. [...] What it does mean is that it is a subject of international law and capable of

326 See for example, Stavrinides, Z., 'Human Rights Obligations under the United Nations Charter', 3 *International Journal of Human Rights* 38 (1999).

327 Cf. Irmscher, T. H., 'The Legal Framework for the Activities of the United Nations Interim Administration Mission in Kosovo: The Charter, Human Rights, and the Law of Occupation', 44 *German Yearbook of International Law* 353 (2001), p. 369 and Kolb, Porretto, and Vité, *supra* note 324, p. 259.

possessing international rights and duties".[328] An international organisation's legal personality is not identical to that of a State, as it is limited by the organisation's competences.[329] The distinct legal personality of an international organisation, recognised in the *Reparations* case, has become a general principle of international law, and applies therefore also to other international organisations which are presumed to possess international legal personality.[330] In addition, it is a well-established principle that international legal personality confers not only rights, but also, as a counterpart, the duty to respect international law,[331] a principle which has equally been confirmed by the International Court of Justice: "International Organisations are subjects of international law and, as such, are bound by any obligations incumbent upon them under general rules of international law, under their constitution or under agreements to which they are parties."[332] It thus flows from the organisation's status as a subject of international law as opined by the ICJ, that international organisations can be considered bound by customary international law or general international law.

At this stage, many internationally recognised human rights standards, such as on prolonged arbitrary detention, the prohibition of retroactive penal laws and the core due process guarantees, have without doubt attained customary status in international law.[333] With regard to the Universal Declaration of Human Rights (UDHR),[334] which is formally not a legally binding instrument, several authors have claimed that the overwhelming majority who voted in favour of it and the continuous affirmation over the years transformed it – or at least

---

[328] International Court of justice, 'Reparation for injuries suffered in the service of the United Nations', *supra* note 199.

[329] *Ibid.*

[330] Bettati, M., 'Création et personnalité juridique des organisations internationales', in Dupuy, R.-J. (ed.), *Manuel sur les organisations internationales – A Handbook on International Organizations* (Dordrecht / Boston / London: Martinus Nijhoff Publishers, 1998), pp. 51–52.

[331] Dupuy, *supra* note 217, p. 175.

[332] International Court of justice, 'Reparation for injuries suffered in the service of the United Nations', *supra* note 199, para. 90.

[333] Cf. Meron, T., *Human Rights and Humanitarian Norms as Customary Law* (Oxford: Clarendon Press, 1989), pp. 94–96; Cerone, J., 'Reasonable Measures in Unreasonable Circumstances: a Legal Responsibility Framework for Human Rights Violations in Post-conflict Territories under UN Administration', in Blokker, N. M. and Schermers, H. (eds.), *Proliferation of International Organizations – Legal Issues* (The Hague / London / Boston: Kluwer Law International, 2001); The American Law Institute, Restatement of the Law, Third, Foreign Relations Law of the United States, para. 702 (St. Paul: American Law Institute Publishers, 1987), and, for a commentary on the Restatement, Henkin, L., Restatement of the Foreign Relations Law of the United States (Revised): Tentative Draft No. 3, 76 (No. 3) American Journal of International Law 653 (1982).

[334] GA Res. A/217 (III), 'Universal Declaration of Human Rights', UN Doc. A/RES/3/217 A (10 December 1948).

part of it – into customary international law.[335] In addition, several 'hardcore' provisions of human rights law, among which are the prohibition of torture and inhumane or degrading treatment, the prohibition of racial discrimination and the prohibition of slavery, are generally considered *jus cogens*,[336] identified as such by the absence of permissible derogations from these rights.[337] As far as these peremptory norms of international law are concerned, it is generally admitted they bind international organisations,[338] insofar as the rule can be applied to the organisation.

One major problem arises when one applies human rights as customary norms to international organisations. Obviously, the defined customary rules of international human rights law are principally addressed to States, and have therefore become customary law because of *state* practice and the corresponding *opinio juris* of *states*. One way to tackle the issue is to consider the customary norms of human rights as customary law of the international organisation itself, and more specifically, in this case, the UN. This is however difficult to ascertain, especially with regard to UN-led international administrations, as the recent relevant practice is limited to the latest cases of Kosovo and East Timor. These cases could perhaps be considered relevant practice for an *emerging* customary obligation. Previous experience[339] in the administration of territory is insufficient to establish a customary legal obligation relative to the application of human

335 See in particular Hannum, H., 'The Status of the Universal Declaration of Human Rights in National and International law' 25 *Georgia Journal of International & Comparative Law* 287 (1995–1996), p. 322 and Tomuschat, C., *Human Rights: Between Idealism and Realism Actors* (Oxford: Oxford University Press, 2003), p. 4. See also Clapham, A., *Human Rights Obligations of Non-State Actors* (Oxford: Oxford University Press, 2006), p. 86 and Franck, T., 'The Emerging Right to Democratic Governance', 86 *American Journal of International Law* 46 (1992), p. 61.

336 See Kondoch, B., 'Human Rights Law and Un Peace Operations in Post-Conflict Situations', in Blokker, N. M. and Schermers, H. (eds.), Proliferation of International Organizations – Legal Issues (The Hague / London / Boston: Kluwer Law International, 2001) and Dupuy, *supra* note 217, p. 175. See also International Court of Justice, 'Certain Expenses of the United Nations (Article 17, paragraph 2, of the Charter)', Advisory Opinion, 20 July 1962, 1962 *ICJ Reports* 151, para. 32.

337 See for example article 15, para. 12, ECHR.

338 Schermers, H., 'The Legal Bases of International Organization Action', in Dupuy, *supra* note 330, p. 402.

339 Previous practice can be found with regard to the proposed administrations of Trieste and Jerusalem, although these cases were never implemented. With regard to West Irian, human rights observance was mainly limited to the respect by the United Nations Temporary Executive Authority (UNTEA) of the rights the citizens enjoyed before the take-over of the administration. UNTEA was however also requested to ensure *inter alia* the rights to freedom of expression and association. The UN administration in West Irian lasted only eight months.

rights to transitional administrations.[340] The following approach seems more convincing. Several scholars have argued that once a norm has become customary international law it applies to all subjects of international law, irrespective of their nature.[341] The rights and obligations of an international organisation would thus be the consequence of the organisation's 'subjectivity'. Hence, international organisations, while not directly participating in the formation of custom, could be considered bound by customary law, including human rights law.

However, customary rules can of course only bind an international organisation to the extent that these rules can be applied to the organisation. In order to establish the exact contents of the international organisation's obligation, one has to go back to the specific international legal personality of international organisations, drawn from the aforementioned 'Reparations' case. While an international organisation's rights under international law need to be interpreted in function of its competences, the same is true with regard to its duties or obligations under international law. The possession of international legal personality does not imply that the organisation enjoys the same rights and duties as a State. Bearing in mind the abovementioned principles relating to an international organisation's obligation to respect international law, we argue that an international organisation's human rights obligations need to be examined in function of the activity performed. This approach equally has the advantage of being universal, in the sense that this obligation does not arise out of a 'constitutional' analysis of an international organisation's constitutional treaty. Human rights are mainly intended to regulate the exercise of public authority. In the case of international administrations, an international organisation assumes direct responsibility for the administration of a territory, thus replacing the government of a State or territory in the exercise of public authority. When international administrations are entrusted with legislative and executive powers, they exercise competences which are usually a State's exclusive prerogative. The same can be said when international organisations perform more limited administrative functions. Considering the nature of the performed activity, it therefore seems obvious, taking into account the competences exercised by the international

---

340 See also Kolb, Porretto, and Vité, *supra* note 324, p. 264.

341 Schermers, H., 'The Legal Bases of International Organization Action', in Dupuy, *supra* note 330, p. 402. See also Tomuschat, C., 'International Law: Ensuring the Survival of Mankind on the Eve of a New Century: General Course on Public International Law, 281 *Recueil des Cours de l'Académie de Droit International* (2001), pp. 134–135. See also Buzzini, on the formation of what the author calls "droit objectif", which the author considers to be applicable "à tous les sujets d'un ordre juridique, indépendamment de leur assentiment individuel à être soumis à ces règles." (Buzzini, G., 'La théorie des sources face au droit international général', 106 *Revue Générale de Droit International Public* 582 (2002), p. 582).

organisation, to consider it bound by *customary* human rights standards as it performs administrative functions *in place of* a State.[342]

In practice, the international administrations in Kosovo and East Timor have both adopted regulations stating that human rights laws apply throughout the territory. However, in its 2006 report submitted to the Human Rights Committee on the Human Rights in Kosovo, UNMIK explained that, while international human rights treaties were a part of the applicable law, "this does not imply that these treaties and conventions are in any way binding on UNMIK. It must be remembered throughout that the situation of Kosovo under interim administration by UNMIK is sui generis. Accordingly, it has been the consistent position of UNMIK that treaties and agreements, to which the State Union of Serbia and Montenegro is a party, are not automatically binding on UNMIK. In each case, a specific determination as to the applicability of the principles and provisions must be made."[343] While it is not clear on what basis this assertion was made, it seems that reliance on the *sui generis* character of the mission is certainly insufficient considering the abovementioned doctrine. Nevertheless, the statement does not seem to exclude any application of human rights to the administration as a matter of customary law, as it only relates to international *treaty* law.

3. *Human Rights and Foreign Military Components*

The status of foreign military components participating in international operations is, in terms of the applicable legal framework, different from that of the civil personnel. The legal status of the military presence in Kosovo for instance is not identical to that of UNMIK, since KFOR is a subsidiary organ of NATO, exercising powers delegated to it by the UN Security Council. The same reasoning we held in respect of the civil components of international administration can of course be applied to military forces if they can be regarded as UN subsidiary organs, and if they exercise functions to which human rights can be applied. This would for instance be the case if military personnel would run detention facilities or exercise policing activity. However, an often-overlooked issue is the possible concomitant application of the laws of armed conflict in certain cases, namely when there is an armed conflict or a situation of occupation. In that case, the legal framework applicable in armed conflict or under occupation

---

342 See also Irmscher, *supra* note 327, p. 370 and Bongiorno, C., 'A culture of impunity: applying international human rights law to the United Nations in East Timor', 33 *Columbia Human Rights Law Review* 643 (2001–2002), pp. 643–644.

343 Human Rights Committee, Report Submitted by the United Nations Interim Administration Mission in Kosovo to the Human Rights Committee on the Human Rights Situation in Kosovo since June 1999, UN Doc. CCPR/C/UNK/1 (13 March 2006), paras. 123–124.

needs to be regarded as a *lex specialis*. A detailed analysis of this question would nevertheless fall outside the scope of this book. At this stage it is sufficient to mention the growing consensus in favour of the application of human rights law to situations of occupation.[344] This was confirmed by the International Court of Justice in its advisory opinions in the 'Legality of the Threat or Use of Nuclear Weapons' case[345] and the case concerning the 'Legal Consequences of the Construction of a Wall in the occupied Palestinian Territory'.[346] The Human Rights Committee similarly confirmed the complementary and inclusive character of both legal frameworks.[347]

The human rights obligations of military contingents can be tackled from the perspective of obligations of the individual states to observe human rights law,[348] as they are composed of national forces which have international obligations, including respect for the laws of armed conflict.[349] In principle, the scope of application of the main human rights instruments is limited to persons who are subject to the jurisdiction of a State party to these instruments. Several decisions or recommendations have nevertheless extended their application to the agents of a State, party to one of these human rights treaties, for acts committed on the territory of another State. With regard to the ICCPR, the Human Rights Committee has repeatedly argued that the jurisdiction of states can be extended beyond the territorial boundaries of the State party to the ICCPR. In 'Delia Salidas Lopez v. Uruguay', where a Uruguayan national living in Argentina was captured and tortured, the Committee held that the violation by Uruguay of certain rights enshrined in the Covenant could not be waived by reason of the fact that the violations were committed outside its territory. The Committee further stated that it "would be unconscionable to so interpret the responsibility under article 2 of the Covenant as to permit a State party to perpetrate violations of the Covenant on the territory of another State, which violations it could not

---

344 Ratner, *supra* note 8 and Wilde, R., 'The Applicability of International Human Rights Law to the Coalition Provisional Authority (CPA) and Foreign Military Presence in Iraq', 11 ILSA *Journal of International and Comparative Law* 489 (2005), pp. 489–490.

345 International Court of Justice, 'Legality of the Threat or Use of Nuclear Weapons', Advisory Opinion, 8 July 1996, 1996 *ICJ Reports* 226.

346 International Court of Justice, 'Legal Consequences of the Construction of a Wall in the occupied Palestinian Territory', Advisory Opinion, 9 July 2004, www.icj-cij.org.

347 Human Rights Committee, General Comment 31: Nature of the General Legal Obligation on States Parties to the Covenant, UN Doc. CCPR/C/21/Rev.1/Add. 13 (2004), para. 11.

348 See: Cerone, *supra* note 325, p. 475.

349 Sassoli, M., 'Droit international pénal et droit pénal interne: le cas des territoires se trouvant sous administration internationale', in Henzelin, M. and Roth, R. (eds.), *Le droit pénal à l'épreuve de l'internationalisation* (Paris / Brussels / Geneva: LGDJ / Bruylant / Georg, 2002), p. 43.

perpetrate on its own territory".[350] Although this case concerned the violation of rights of a state's *own* citizens residing on foreign territory, the principle posed by the Committee is considered broad enough to include all violations of the ICCPR on foreign territory by a State party.[351]

As far as the ECHR is concerned, the European Court of Human Rights extensively examined the extraterritorial application of the convention in the landmark case of 'Loizidou v. Turkey'.[352] The case concerned alleged violations of the ECHR, such as unlawful detention and denial of access to property, by the Turkish presence in Northern Cyprus. Turkey invoked declarations it had made restricting the application of the Convention to acts or omissions of public authorities in Turkey performed within the boundaries of the national territory of the Republic of Turkey.[353] The Court explicitly linked the obligation to ensure the application of the ECHR to the effective control over the territory, and recalled that "although article 1 sets limits on the reach of the Convention, the concept of "jurisdiction" under this provision is not restricted to the national territory of the High Contracting Parties. [...] [T]he responsibility of a Contracting Party may also arise when as a consequence of military action – whether lawful or unlawful – it exercises effective control of an area outside its national territory. The obligation to secure, in such an area, the rights and freedoms set out in the Convention derives from the fact of such control whether it be exercised directly, through its armed forces, or through a subordinate local administration."[354] The developed 'effective control' criterion was confirmed by the same Court in the 'Bankovich' case, in which the Court found that the ECHR reflected the "ordinary and essentially territorial notion of jurisdiction, other bases of jurisdiction being exceptional and requiring special justifications in the particular circumstances of each case".[355] The Court subsequently examined whether the applicants were capable of coming within the jurisdiction of the respondent State, and concluded that the victims of the bombing of the RTS in the Federal Republic of Yugoslavia by NATO Air Forces were not within the jurisdiction of a Contracting State.[356]

---

350 Human Rights Committee, 'Delia Salidas de Lopez v. Uruguay', Communication No. 52/1979, UN Doc. CCPR/C/OP/1 (29 July 1981), para. 12.3.

351 Cerone, *supra* note 325, p. 476.

352 European Court of Human Rights, 'Loizidou v. Turkey', 23 February 1995, 1995 ECHR Series A No. 310.

353 See Moloney, R., 'Incompatible reservations to Human Rights Treaties: severability and the problem of State consent', 5 *Melbourne Journal of International Law* 155 (2004).

354 European Court of Human Rights, 'Loizidou v. Turkey', 23 February 1995, 1995 ECHR Series A No. 310, para. 62.

355 European Court of Human Rights, 'Bankovich and others. v. Belgium and 16 other contracting States', 12 December 2001, ECHR 2001–XII, para. 61.

356 *Ibid.*, paras. 74–75.

A similar approach was followed by the Inter-American Commission of Human Rights in 'Coard et al. v. the United States'. The Commission held that "each American State is obliged to uphold the protected rights of any person subject to its jurisdiction. [...] [This] may, under given circumstances, refer to conduct with extraterritorial locus where the person concerned is present in the territory of one state, but subjected to the control of another state – usually through the acts of the latter's agent abroad."[357] The threshold applied by the Inter-American Commission is lower than that by the European Human Rights Court as it requires effective control over an individual, irrespective of his nationality or geographical location.[358]

The International Court of Justice equally confirmed the extraterritorial application of human rights standards in its 2004 Advisory Opinion on the 'Legal Consequences of the Construction of a Wall in the occupied Palestinian Territory'. The International Court contended that the ICCPR, the ICESCR and the Convention on the Rights of the Child applied to Israel's conduct in the occupied Palestinian Territory. The Court found "that the International Covenant on Civil and Political Rights is applicable in respect of acts done by a State in the exercise of its jurisdiction outside its own territory."[359] With respect to the ICESCR, however, the Court asserted that, while it does not contain a provision on its scope of application and although the rights guaranteed therein are essentially territorial, "it is not to be excluded that it applies both to territories over which a State party has sovereignty and to those over which that State exercises territorial jurisdiction".[360] Interestingly, the Court linked the application of the ICESCR to the exercise of *territorial* jurisdiction, and thus not *individual* jurisdiction.

The abovementioned principles, applied to recent cases in which a military component was concomitantly established, would have encompassed an obligation for the military components to observe the human rights contained in the instruments discussed, provided that the sending States were bound by them.[361] Although the application of the *effective control* test, as contained in the 'Loizidou' case, does not create an overall obligation on all contingents to ensure respect for human rights law, the jurisdiction of military forces over individuals, and

---

357 American Commission of Human Rights, 'Coard et al. v. the United States', Case 10.951, Report No. 109/99 (29 September 1999).

358 Cf. Cerone, J., 'The Application of Regional Human Rights Law Beyond Regional Frontiers: The Inter-American Commission on Human Rights and US Activities in Iraq', *ASIL Insights* (2005).

359 International Court of Justice, 'Legal Consequences of the Construction of a Wall in the occupied Palestinian Territory', Advisory Opinion, 9 July 2004, www.icj-cij.org, para. 111.

360 *Ibid.*, para. 112.

361 For a similar conclusion, with regard to KFOR in Kosovo, see Cerone, *supra* note 325, pp. 479–480.

especially detainees in the emergency phases, was unquestionable.[362] In Iraq, the application of human rights norms to the military presence equally seems beyond doubt, insofar as the conditions with regard to control exercised over individuals are met.[363] The principles relating to the extraterritorial application of human rights conventions can equally be applied to the Coalition Provisional Authority in Iraq, which can be seen as under the Authority of the Governments of both the United States and the United Kingdom.[364] However, in general, the diversity of the military contingents often leads to difficult application of these instruments. While some are bound by the ECHR, others are bound by the American Human Rights Convention. In addition, not all States have signed or ratified the ICCPR.[365]

4. *Observations on the Attribution of Conduct*

The attribution of conduct is a separate and more difficult question, which is nevertheless often mistaken with the human rights obligations of international actors. The conduct of subsidiary organs of the UN – such as the civilian components – is without doubt attributable to the UN. This principle is included in the Draft Articles on the Responsibility of International Organisations currently discussed by the International Law Commission (ILC). According to Draft Article 4, "the conduct of an organ or agent of an international organization in the performance of functions of that organ or agent shall be considered as an act of that organization under international law whatever position the organ or agent holds in respect of the organization".[366] The ILC draft articles equally provide that the UN can be held responsible for the *ultra vires* conduct of one

---

362 See for overview of the issue of detainees: Kelly, M. J., 'INTERFET Detainee Management Unit in East Timor', *Paper presented at the Swiss Seminar on the Law of Armed Conflict, Chavannes-de-Bogis* (27 October 2000). The author nevertheless considers that the Geneva Conventions did not formally apply, as Indonesia had consented to the deployment of INTERFET. The author does point out that the Conventions provided a useful framework after the collapse of Indonesian authority in East Timor.

363 See Wilde, *supra* note 344.

364 Although the US did not as such consider the CPA to be a Federal Agency in US constitutional terms. See Roberts, *supra* note 293, p. 35.

365 In East Timor, for example, the States which contributed to the military component were Australia, Bangladesh, Bolivia, Brazil, Chile, Denmark, Egypt, Fiji, Ireland, Japan, Jordan, Kenya, Malaysia, Nepal, New Zealand, Norway, Pakistan, Philippines, Portugal, Republic of Korea, Russian Federation, Singapore, Slovakia, Sweden, Thailand, Turkey, United Kingdom, United States and Uruguay.

366 GA, 'Report of the International Law Commission', Official Documents of the General Assembly, Fifty-sixth Session, Supplement No. 10, UN Doc. A/59/10 (2004), p. 103.

of its agents or organs when acting in its official capacity.[367] On the other hand, 'off-duty' conduct of UN staff cannot entail the responsibility of the UN.[368] Although these draft articles cannot be considered as representing a codification of customary international law, there does not seem to be an obstacle in accepting a *mutatis mutandis* application of the relevant rules of attribution of conduct in case of state responsibility.

With regard to military contingents placed at the disposal of the UN, the model contribution agreement relating to military contingents provides that the UN is liable to third parties. This is, however, more a question of attribution of responsibility than attribution of conduct, and has legal effects only between the parties to the agreement.[369] The acts of military contingents can therefore still engage the responsibility of the sending State if the conduct is attributable to that State. According to Draft Article 5, the criterion to see whether the conduct of organs or agents of a State placed at the disposal of an international organisation is attributable to that organisation, is the exercise of 'effective control'.[370] The 'effective control' criterion should be analysed in the light of the factual circumstances. If the UN is considered to be in effective control of the military operation, then the conduct of that military component is directly attributable to the UN.

This seems to have been the approach followed by the European Court of Human Rights in the 'Behrami' and 'Saramati' cases.[371] The first case concerned the death of a Kosovar citizen by reason of the presence of an unexploded cluster bomb unit, and the inadequate demining of the territory by both UNMIK and KFOR. The second case related to the alleged unlawful arrest of a citizen by the UNMIK Police following an order issue by the KFOR Commander. In both cases, the applicants submitted that the actions involved the responsibility of the sending states. The Court found that the responsibility for demining fell solely into the hands of UNMIK, while detention fell within KFOR's mandate. The Court concluded that both UNMIK and KFOR action was in principle attributable to the UN. UNMIK was rightly considered a subsidiary organ. Although one can criticize the factual appraisal by the Court of the entity having 'effective

---

367 Draft article 6, *ibid.*, p. 116. See also International Court of Justice, 'Difference relating to immunity form Legal Process of a Special Rapporteur of the Commission on Human Rights', Advisory opinion, 29 April 1999, ICJ Reports 66 (1999), para. 66.

368 GA, 'Report of the International Law Commission', Official Documents of the General Assembly, fifty-sixth session, Supplement No. 10, UN Doc. A/59/10 (2004), p. 119.

369 *Ibid.*

370 *Ibid.*, p. 109.

371 European Court of Human Rights, 'Agim Behrami and Bekir Behrami against France' and 'Ruzhdi Saramati against France, Germany and Norway', Decision on the admissibility, 2 May 2007, Application n°s 71412/01 and 78166/06.

control' in the case of the military contingents, KFOR's actions were equally considered by the Court to be attributable to the UN because KFOR exercised lawfully delegated Chapter VII powers of the Security Council, which held ultimate control over the operation.[372] The court concluded "that the applicant's complaints must be declared incompatible ratione personae with the provisions of the Convention."[373] While the Court's underlying legal reasoning in respect of the attribution of conduction might indeed seem feeble, the Court equally indicated that relevant Security Council Resolutions are the primary source for analysing the human rights obligations of the international administration. The Court opined that the European Convention cannot "impos[e] conditions on the implementation of a UNSC Resolution which were not provided for in the text of the Resolution itself."[374] This reasoning, if extended beyond the European Court of Human Rights, would however in any event not be applicable in the case of Iraq unless the conduct in question could be considered an exercise of lawfully delegated Chapter VII powers by the Security Council.

The question remains how the organisation should deal with alleged breaches of human rights obligations of its subsidiary organs in practice. The immunity system will often bar individuals from directly addressing claims to national judicial bodies. Alternative mechanisms need to be put in place concomitantly to address alleged human rights violations, but the possibility of creating such mechanisms in post-conflict societies if however not an easy task.

B. *Immunities*

The UN and its international staff are generally considered to have jurisdictional immunity. This is drawn from the UN Charter itself, which explicitly stipulates that "the Organization shall enjoy in the territory of each of its Members such privileges and immunities as are necessary for the fulfilment of its purposes. [...] [O]fficials of the Organization shall similarly enjoy such privileges and immunities as are necessary for the independent exercise of their functions in connexion with the Organization".[375] In addition, the Convention on Privileges and Immunities of the United Nations[376] provides a complete immunities system, including provisions with respect to immunity for 'UN officials' and *functional*

---

372 *Ibid.*, para. 140.

373 *Ibid.*, para. 152.

374 *Ibid.*

375 Art. 105 UN Charter.

376 Convention on the Privileges and Immunities of the United Nations (13 February 1946), 1 UNTS 15.

immunity for 'Experts on mission'.[377] In both cases, the Secretary-General has the power to waive their immunity.[378] It should be emphasised that we are dealing with jurisdictional immunity, which is of course distinct from the question of compensation by the UN in case of harm caused by the act in question, which should be considered according to the relevant rules of attribution discussed above. The UN's immunity *as an international organisation* bars any claim against the organisation before national courts.[379]

Participants in peacekeeping forces can be considered experts on mission, falling under Section 22 of the UN Convention.[380] The immunities system therefore applies to all UN staff provided that the individual is not acting outside the scope of his or her mandate. In the same line, the UN mission in Kosovo issued a regulation providing that "UNMIK personnel, including locally recruited personnel, shall be immune from legal process in respect of words spoken and all acts performed by them in their official capacity".[381] However, the formal application of the Convention on Privileges and Immunities of the United Nations is not always self-evident. In the case of East Timor, for instance, the convention did not formally apply in the territory, as Indonesian sovereignty over East Timor had been recognised only by Australia. Indonesia had ratified the Privileges and Immunities Convention, but the state's title over the territory was thus extremely dubious. With regard to Kosovo, the former Socialist Federal Republic of Yugoslavia had acceded to the Convention on 30 June 1950, but the question whether the Federal Republic of Yugoslavia could have been considered the successor to the former Socialist Federal Republic of Yugoslavia remains unclear, in addition to the absence of clear rules of customary international law on state succession in respect of treaties.[382] In Afghanistan

---

377 *Ibid.*, Articles V and VI.

378 *Ibid.*

379 This has expressly been confirmed by the International Court of Justice: "any such claims against the United Nations shall not be dealt with by national courts" (International Court of Justice, 'Difference relating to immunity form Legal Process of a Special Rapporteur of the Commission on Human Rights', Advisory opinion, 29 April 1999, ICJ Reports 66 (1999)).

380 Schermers, H. G. and Blokker, N. M., *International Institutional Law* (Boston / Leiden: Martinus Nijhoff Publishers, 2003), p. 255. See also on the definition of 'Experts on mission' under sections 22 of the UN Convention: International Court of Justice, 'Applicability of Article VI, Section 22, of the Convention on the Privileges and Immunities of the United Nations', Advisory Opinion, 15 December 1989, 177 *ICJ Reports* 1989, para. 45.

381 UNMIK Regulation 2000/47 on the status, privileges and immunities of KFOR and UNMIK and their personnel in Kosovo, UN Doc. UNMIK/REG/2000/47 (18 August 2000), section 3.3.

382 See International Court of Justice, 'Application of the Convention on the Prevention and Punishment of the Crime of Genocide' (Bosnia and Herzegovina v. Serbia and Montenegro), Judgement, 26 February 2007, www.icj-cij.org.

and Iraq the question did not pose any significant problems, as both countries had ratified the convention, respectively in 1947 and 1949.

Privileges and immunities are often also negotiated and incorporated into a Status of Forces Agreement or a Status of Mission Agreement, with the UN or with individual troop contributing states. Prior to the establishment of UNTAET, Australia had for example signed a Status of Forces Agreement with Indonesia to regulate the deployment of Australian troops for the INTERFET mission, which provided for several privileges and immunities for the military and civilian staff, including those provided for by the UN Convention.[383] The New Zealand forces were obviously not bound by the Status of Forces Agreement concluded between Australia and Indonesia. However, New Zealand did not sign an agreement with Indonesia. Instead, the official New Zealand position was that the New Zealand Defence Forces were immune from local jurisdiction as a matter of customary international law.[384] In addition, it seems that upon deployment of the international presence, no Status of Forces or Status of Mission Agreement concerning the status of UNTAET was signed. Obviously, such an agreement could not have been signed between the UN and Indonesia, since UN organs had repeatedly challenged Indonesian title over East Timor. UNTAET immunity could thus only be based on customary law.

The 'Model status of forces agreement for peace-keeping operations' provides that in the case of a criminal offence, the host country can exercise jurisdiction after a waiver of immunity.[385] As members of a military contingent are concerned, the model agreement provides for absolute immunity and an exclusive jurisdiction of the troop-contributing country.[386] Such a regime was, for example, put in place by different orders and regulations issued by the Coalition Provisional Authority in Iraq. CPA Order No. 17 explicitly provided that the Coalition Forces and the Security Council authorised Multinational Force were subject to the exclusive jurisdiction of their sending States.[387] In effect, this amounts to

---

383 See for an overview: Kelly, M. J., McCormack, T. L. J., Muggleton, P. and Oswald, B. M. 'Legal aspects of Australia's involvement in the international force for East Timor', 841 *International review of the Red Cross* 101 (2001).

384 *Ibid.* See also on the claim that the rules relating to the immunities of UN personnel have evolved into customary international law: Dupuy, *supra* note 217, p. 188. See also with regard to UNTAET: Bongiorno, *supra* note 342, p. 661.

385 Article 47, Model status of forces agreement for peace-keeping operations, UN Doc. A/45/594 (9 October 1990).

386 *Ibid.*, Article 48. For an example of case in which the sending State exercised jurisdiction for a criminal offences, see e.g. CBC News, 'US Soldier Gets Life for Kosovo Rape and Murder' (1 August 2000), http://www.cbc.ca.

387 CPA Order No. 17, 'Status of the CPA, MNFI, Certain Missions and Personnel in Iraq w/Annex**Revised**', CPA/ORD/27 June 200/19 (27 June 2003). See however on the status of the collation forces after the CPA dissolution, Patel, M., 'The Legal Status of Coalition

complete immunity from Iraqi jurisdiction for Coalition Forces for any wrongful acts, including human rights abuses.[388] A similar provision was contained in the Immunities regulation issued by UNMIK "KFOR, its property, funds and assets shall be immune from any legal process. [...] KFOR personnel [...] shall be [...] [i]mmune from jurisdiction before courts in Kosovo in respect of any administrative, civil or criminal act committed by them in the territory of Kosovo. Such personnel shall be subject to the exclusive jurisdiction of their respective sending States."[389]

The problem often raised in this respect is whether the immunities system is appropriate when the UN is performing administrative functions in a state or a territory. Immunity is often waived in case of (serious) criminal offences.[390] In other cases, immunity has also been waived or declared inapplicable.[391] In addition, immunity is, from a legal point of view, not applicable for acts committed outside the performance of their mission.[392] Under UNTAET, for instance, in a case of rape involving a Jordanian CIVPOL officer, the individual's immunity was declared inapplicable, as the alleged act was considered to have been committed outside official functions.[393]

Apart from the waiver or inapplicability of immunities, one should remember that immunities in fact serve a purpose. The main rationale behind the immuni-

Forces in Iraq after the June 30 Handover', *ASIL Insights* (2004). CPA Order 17 nevertheless provided for a continued application until the departure of the final element from the MNF (see section 20).

388 See Economic and Social Council, Commission on Human Rights, 'Report of the United Nations High Commissioner for Human Rights and Follow-Up to the World Conference on Human Rights. The present situation of human rights in Iraq', UN Doc.E/CN.4/2005/4 (9 June 2004), para. 117.

389 UNMIK Regulation 2000/47 on the status, privileges and immunities of KFOR and UNMIK and their personnel in Kosovo, UN Doc UNMIK/REG/2000/47 (18 August 2000), section 2.

390 Rawski, F., 'To Waive or Not to Waive: Immunity and Accountability in U.N. Peacekeeping Operations', 18 *Connecticut. Journal of International Law* 103 (2002–2003), p. 118. In the case of a traffic accident involving an UNTAET staff member, resulting in the death of an East Timorese citizen, the Special Representative insisted that the Secretary-General waive the staff member's immunity (UNTAET Daily Press Briefing, 'SRSG Briefs National Council' (13 December 2000). See also Morrow, J. and White, R., 'The United Nations in Transitional East Timor: International Standards and the Reality of Governance', 22 *Australian Yearbook of International Law* 1 (2002), p. 24).

391 *Ibid.*

392 Section 22, b), Convention on the Privileges and Immunities of the United Nations (13 February 1946), 1 UNTS 15.

393 Economic and Social Council, Commission on Human Rights, 'Administration of Justice, Rule of Law and Democracy, Working paper on the accountability of international personnel taking part in peace support operations submitted', UN Doc. E/CN.4/Sub.2/2005/42 (7 July 2005), para. 31.

ties system is to protect international staff from taunting claims by the host State and to guarantee the independence of the UN and its agents. The International Court of Justice confirmed this in its *Reparations for injuries* advisory opinion, by stating that "[i]n order that the agent may perform his duties satisfactorily, he must feel that this protection is assured to him by the Organization, and that he may count on it. To ensure the independence of the agent, and, consequently, the independent action of the Organization itself, it is essential that in performing his duties he need not have to rely on any other protection than that of the Organization".[394] The independence of a UN mission as an institution and its international staff is crucial, and indeed needs to be preserved. More specifically in the area of human rights, the European Court of Human Rights, in 'Waite and Kennedy v. Germany',[395] pointed out that "the attribution of privileges and immunities to international organisations is an essential means of ensuring the proper functioning of such organisations free from unilateral interference by individual governments. [...] [T]he rule of immunity from jurisdiction, [...], has a legitimate objective".[396] The question, according to the European Court of Human Rights, is whether reasonable alternative means are available effectively to protect the individual's human rights.[397] Although this jurisprudence relates to the European Convention on Human Rights, and therefore has a limited scope of application, the Court's findings could in our view be applied to international administrations. The problem is therefore not the immunities system, but the availability of alternative means and mechanisms to protect human rights under international territorial administration.

C. *Accountability Mechanisms in Practice: Ombudspersons and Judicial Review*

A recently re-emerged method of enabling individuals to bring claims against UN staff or the organisation itself is the institution of the 'ombudsperson'.[398] Such an institution has been introduced by the international administrations in Kosovo and East Timor. In the cases where no international administration

[394] International Court of justice, 'Reparation for injuries suffered in the service of the United Nations', *supra* note 199, p. 183.

[395] European Court of Human Rights, 'Waite and Kennedy v. Germany', 18 February 1999, 1999 ECHR 13.

[396] *Ibid.*, para. 63.

[397] *Ibid.*, para. 68.

[398] For an overview of UN experience with the institution, see: Megret, F. and Hoffmann, F., 'Fostering Human Rights Accountability: An Ombudsperson for the United Nations', 11 *Global Governance* 43 (2005).

is exercising administrative authority, the necessity to create such a particular mechanism might be less apparent, but could nevertheless serve a useful purpose. In the case of Iraq, some form of independent institution could have been set up to receive claims directed towards the CPA. However, the CPA simply provided that claims directed to the CPA and other international personnel should be submitted to and dealt with by the sending states.[399]

An ombudsperson's office was established in Kosovo to investigate complaints concerning human rights violations and actions constituting an abuse of authority by UNMIK or any other official institution.[400] Although co-operation with UNMIK has apparently not always been successful, the UNMIK Ombudsperson was generally seen as an effective mechanism to address human rights violations in general.[401] However, when the Ombudsperson institution was remodelled in 2006, its jurisdiction in respect of UNMIK action was brought to an end.[402] As a replacement, UNMIK in March 2006 established a 'Human Rights Advisory Panel', composed of international jurists nominated by the President of the European Court of Human Rights, to hear complaints against UNMIK personnel.[403] The current head of the panel is former UNMIK Ombudsperson, Marek Nowicki. The panel held its first meeting only at the end of 2007,[404] more than a year and a half after its inception. The actual effect of the panel on the improvement of the UN administration's accountability for alleged human rights violations will of course be evident only after several cases. Until July 2008, the Panel had adopted decisions on only the *admissibility* of complaints, and the cases that have been declared admissible almost exclusively relate to alleged violations of the right to a fair trail before the 'Housing and Property Claims Commission' set up by UNMIK to investigate property claims. No decision on the merits had yet been taken.

UNTAET created a comparable ombudsperson, which became operational only some 17 months after the arrival of the administration.[405] The UNTAET Ombudsperson did not, however, function under an official mandate founded in an UNTAET Regulation. Its functioning, effectiveness and achievements are

---

399 CPA Order No. 17, 'Status of the CPA, MNFI, Certain Missions and Personnel in Iraq w/Annex**Revised**', CPA/ORD/27 June 200/19 (27 June 2003), section 17.

400 UNMIK Regulation 2000/38 on the establishment of the Ombudsperson Institution in Kosovo, UN Doc. UNMIK/REG/2000/38 (30 June 2000).

401 See for example, Ombudsperson Institution in Kosovo, Fourth Annual Report 2003–2004 (12 July 2004).

402 UNMIK Regulation 2006/6 on the Ombudsperson Institution in Kosovo, UN Doc. UNMIK/REG/2006/6 (16 February 2006).

403 UNMIK Regulation 2006/12 on the establishment of the Human Rights Advisory Panel, UN Doc. UNMIK/REG/2006/12 (23 March 2006), section 3.4.

404 See www.unmikonline.org/human_rights/index.htm.

405 Cf. UNTAET Daily Briefing, 'Twenty Cases Examined by Ombudsperson' (1 June 2001).

difficult to assess. From the UNTAET Daily Briefings one can however deduce that complaints against UNTAET, the Transitional Administration, the Cabinet, and agencies, programmes and institutions which collaborate with the Government could be accepted by the Ombudsperson.[406] The Ombudsperson in East Timor was generally described as ineffective, and it is clear that he did not have the same effect, or mandate, as in Kosovo.[407] The Constitution of Timor-Leste incorporated this institution in the state's official structures, as an independent organ to investigate complaints against public bodies.[408]

Another possible method of trying to ensure accountability for human rights violations can be judicial review of official acts issued by the administration before national courts and tribunals. UN privileges and immunities nevertheless should continue to apply in this scenario, in addition to those immunities resulting from Status of Forces Agreements. The exercise of public authority by an international organisation and the acts issued by these international administrations are characterised by what can be called 'functional duality'.[409] On the one hand, an international administration is a subsidiary organ of an international organisation and, on the other hand, it functions as the government of a territorial entity. The acts of the international administration are thus both international acts of the international organisations and internal acts of the state. As such, functional duality is not an innovative concept where the administration of territory is concerned. Virally, discussing the administration of Germany after the Second World War, noted that "en réalité, les autorités alliées de contrôle en Allemagne possèdent une double nature: ce sont des autorités territoriales [...] et ce sont des autorités nationales [...]. Elles utilisent alternativement et parfois cumulativement, les prérogatives attachées à chacune des ces qualités. Suivant le titre auquel elles agissent, elles sont autorités nationales ou étrangère, soit à l'égard du droit allemand, soit à l'égard du droit interne des Etats allies".[410] Although this passage offers a national perspective only, as the Allied were not at that time an international organisation with a distinct legal personality, the author already stressed the fact that decisions taken by the international administration needed to be seen as part of the German legal system.[411] The same principle of 'functional duality' can be applied in relation to acts issued under international administrations. The regulations adopted by UNMIK and UNTAET for example

406 *Ibid.*

407 Chesterman, *supra* note 104, p. 150.

408 Section 27, Constitution of Timor-Leste.

409 See on the concept of 'functional duality' in post-conflict situations, the contributions by R. Wilde and G. Verdirame in White, N. D. and Klaasen, D. (eds.), *The UN, Human Rights and Post-Conflict Situations* (Manchester: Manchester University Press, 2005).

410 Virally, *supra* note 53, para. 46.

411 *Ibid.*

are international acts of a subsidiary organ of an international legal person, yet the act in question produces effects in the territory in question, thus forming an integral part of the Kosovar and East Timorese legal systems. These acts conserve their validity even after the resumption of governmental functions by the territorial entity itself. The theory of the 'functional duality' of international administrations and the acts issued by them has recently been developed and applied by the Constitutional Court of Bosnia and Herzegovina with regard to the review by the Court of the Law on State Border Service enacted by the High Representative of the International Community.[412] The Court observed:

> Such a situation amounts to a sort of functional duality: an authority of one legal system intervenes in another legal system, thus making its functions dual. [...] [T]he High Representative [...] has been vested with special powers by the international community and his mandate is of an international character. In the present case, the High Representative – whose powers under Annex 10 to the General Framework Agreement, the relevant resolutions of the Security Council and the Bonn Declaration as well as his exercise of those powers are not subject to review by the Constitutional Court – intervened in the legal order of Bosnia and Herzegovina substituting himself for the national authorities. In this respect, he therefore acted as an authority of Bosnia and Herzegovina and the law which he enacted is in the nature of a national law and must be regarded as a law of Bosnia and Herzegovina.[413]

This kind of competence presupposes, on the one hand, the existence of a functioning judicial system and, on the other, a court or tribunal having the competence to review the international administration's acts. Often the first condition cannot be met, as the judicial system is usually collapsed or non-existent at the establishment of the majority of post-conflict peace-building missions. The difficulty of the exercise can in addition be illustrated by two cases dealt with by Timorese courts under UNTAET's mandate. In both cases, the court apparently lacked the necessary competence to review the legislation. In addition, the two cases both clearly include misinterpretations of existing legislation. The Special Representative's immunity was moreover disregarded in one of the cases, as a claim had been brought against him personally for issuing an executive order. On the other hand, these cases indicate that judicial review of official acts could be an interesting alternative to provide an effective remedy for alleged violations of human rights standards, provided that the necessary conditions are met.

[412] Constitutional Court of Bosnia and Herzegovina, Decision U9/00 (3 Nov. 2000).
[413] *Ibid.*, para. 5.

The 'Victor Alves' case[414] concerned the application of UNTAET Regulation 2000/14[415] adopted by the Special Representative to clarify and adjust the basic judicial system as laid out in Regulation 2000/11.[416] In addition to clarifying the role and powers of the investigating judges and the procedure relating to pre-trial detention, the regulation extended the detention time-limits. The Regulation was adopted with immediate effect the day before the Dili District Court was to hear the case of a former FALINTIL member, Victor Alves, whose detention had exceeded the limits set by the Indonesian Code of Criminal Procedure, which was applicable in accordance with Regulation 1999/1. The Judge refused to apply the newly passed Regulation 2000/14, as he found that the extension of the detention limits was both a violation of fundamental human rights and an impermissible interference by the executive power in order to influence the case. The Judge therefore found that Victor Alves had been unlawfully detained. Clearly, this case highlights the difficulty of such an exercise. A clear separation of powers would have prevented such a decision in which a judge simply refused to apply the law. In addition, it seems that the judgment itself contained various misinterpretations of the applicable legal instruments.[417]

In another case, a Japanese national, Takeshi Kashiwagi, had made a claim against the Special Representative of the Secretary-General, the Minister of Justice of East Timor, the Prosecutor General and a judge, based on alleged unlawful detention.[418] Kashiwagi, a freelance journalist, had been arrested following allegations of defamation and making threats to the life of the president, which was a criminal offence under the applicable Indonesian Criminal Code. The Special Representative intervened by issuing an executive order decriminalising defamation, upon which Kashiwagi was released. Kashiwagi nevertheless decided to take his case to the Dili District Court, alleging a violation of the relevant provisions of the Indonesian Criminal Code, which admits criminal defamation cases only after a *complaint* by the victim. The Dili District Court,

414 For a comprehensive overview and report of this unpublished case see Linton, S., 'Rising From The Ashes: The Creation Of A Viable Criminal Justice System In East Timor', 25 *Melbourne University Law Review* 140 (2001).

415 UNTAET Regulation 2000/14 amending Regulation No. 2000/11, UN Doc. UNTAET/REG/2000/14 (10 May 2000).

416 UNTAET, Regulation 2000/11 on the organization of courts in East Timor (UNTAET/REG/2000/11) (6 March 2000).

417 See Linton, *supra* note 414, pp. 140–143.

418 For an extensive overview and discussion of the case, see Amnesty International, 'East Timor, Justice past, present and future', *Report Nr. ASA 57/001/2001* (27 July 2001); Article 19, 'Freedom of Expression and the Media in Timor Leste' (December 2005); Bongiorno, *supra* note 342, pp. 666 *et s.*; Linton, *supra* note 414, pp. 140–143 and Fairlie, M. A., 'Affirming Brahimi: East Timor makes the Case for a Model Criminal Code', 18 *American University International Law Review* 1059 (2003), pp. 1087 *et s.* See also Zaum, *supra* note 75, p. 201.

by applying similar reasoning to that in the previous case, concluded that the executive order was illegal as is sought to override an UNTAET Regulation and therefore constituted an impermissible interference in the judiciary. The Court equally found that the procedure contained in the Indonesian Criminal Code had not been followed correctly, and therefore found all defendants liable for following incorrect procedures. Surprisingly, the Special Representative of the Secretary-General was equally found *personally* liable for issuing an executive order which conflicted with the Indonesian Criminal Code. The Court failed to act that the transitional administrator had absolute immunity, and ironically, condemned the transitional administrator for violating Kashiwagi's human rights, while the executive order issued by the transitional administrator was aimed at protecting these same rights. The case was appealed, and the Court of Appeal overturned the lower court's decision by stating that such a case should have been brought against the UN instead of against individuals. Kashiwagi's compensation claim was dismissed, although he was finally awarded compensation outside the court process.[419]

These two cases demonstrate the complexity of the review of official acts by nascent judicial systems, characterised by a lack of trained and qualified judicial personnel. The functional duality established by the Supreme Court of Bosnia and Herzegovina can be effective in assuring the compatibility of regulations with international human rights standards. However, once more, the situation 'on the ground' does not always allow for this kind of review. Under the thorny circumstances in which these operations need to manoeuvre, an adequate local court can often not be utilised to guarantee the implementation of human rights.

In some cases, a specific review mechanism was set up within the international presence. For example, under at least two UNTAET Regulations, persons were authorised to apply in writing to the Deputy Transitional Administration for a review of decisions taken by an UNTAET subsidiary unit.[420] The Deputy Transitional Administration is of course neither neutral, neither a judicial institution. In many cases, one would thus need to rely on more effective means of ensuring an official and impartial review mechanism. We are however facing a new phenomenon in international law, as the situations in which these international administrations have been used differ substantially from previous cases. A post-conflict environment does not always offer the capacity to create effective accountability mechanisms in the state or territory.

[419] Economic and Social Council, Commission on Human Rights, 'Administration of Justice, Rule of Law and Democracy, Working paper on the accountability of international personnel taking part in peace support operations submitted', UN Doc. E/CN.4/Sub.2/2005/42 (7 July 2005), para. 50.

[420] UNTAET Regulation 2000/17 on the prohibition of logging operations and the export of wood from East Timor, UN Doc. UNTAET/REG/2000/17 (8 June 2000), Section 6.1. and UNTAET Regulation 200/19 on protected places, UN Doc. UNTAET/REG/2000/19 (30 June 2000), Section 8.4.

Chapter 8

The Laws of Occupation

The laws relating to the occupation of territory after an armed conflict are fundamental for the obligations of international actors involved in post-conflict operations, although their application is often overlooked. The legal authority of peace-building missions and international administrations differs substantially from one case to another. As noted earlier, such missions are often created after an international agreement and/or a Security Council Resolution. The exercise of administrative powers can thus be a result of an explicit authorisation contained in the particular instrument. However, in some cases additional powers and authority result from the laws of armed conflict. Iraq is the most obvious case, but it is often overlooked that in East Timor, for example, the laws of armed conflict were applied before and even for a certain time after the deployment of UNTAET. It is not the purpose of this part to give an extensive overview of the legal rules applicable in occupied territory. We will instead focus first on the content of the laws of occupation, and in particular on those certain rules which may have an influence when the laws of occupation are applicable in peace-building missions. Afterwards, we will address the application of that regime to the UN and other international organisations when engaged in peacekeeping operations, peace-building missions and international administrations.

A. *Belligerent Occupation of Foreign Territory*

The rules applicable to occupying powers are for the most part incorporated in the Fourth Hague Convention of 1907 and the Regulations annexed to it,[421] the

---

[421] Convention (IV) respecting the Laws and Customs of War on Land and its annex: Regulations concerning the Laws and Customs of War on Land, The Hague (18 October 1907), 187 CTS 227 (1907) [Hereafter referred to as 'the Hague Regulations']. The rules concerning occupation are contained in articles 42–56 of the Hague Regulations of 1907.

Fourth Geneva Convention Relative to the Protection of Civilians in Time of War[422] and the First Protocol Additional to the Geneva Conventions.[423] These rules are above all important for the relationship between the occupying powers and the governing authorities, and for when the occupier acts as an administering authority. It should also be added that the laws of occupation, as determined by the Hague Regulations and by the Fourth Geneva Convention, are in essence declaratory of customary international law.

The occupying power assumes responsibility for the administration of the occupied territory, when this occupation is effective.[424] Article 42 of the Hague Regulations defines occupation of territory "when it is actually placed under the authority of the hostile army. The occupation extends only to the territory where such authority has been established and can be exercised". This definition is mainly based on the traditional idea of a declared war, and the subsequent occupation of the 'hostile state'. The Hague definition implies the effective and *de facto* submission of the territory and its population to the occupying power.[425] This effectiveness can be proven by the simultaneous fulfilment of two conditions: (1) the former government is unable to exercise its authority in that particular area, and (2) the occupying power is capable of substituting its own legal authority over that part of the occupied territory.[426] The definition proposed by the Hague Regulations, although consistent with the international legal order of that time, is nevertheless very limited, as military occupation of a foreign territory does not always follow a declared war.[427] A change took place with the adoption of the Geneva Conventions after the Second World War. Article 2 common to the four Geneva Conventions states:

> In addition to the provisions which shall be implemented in peace-time, the present Convention shall apply to all cases of declared war or of any other armed conflict which may arise between two or more of the High Contracting Parties, even if the state of war is not recognized by one of them.

---

422 Convention (IV) relative to the Protection of Civilian Persons in Time of War. Geneva, 12 August 1949, 75 UNTS 287 [Hereafter 'Fourth Geneva Convention'], in particular Articles 27–34 and 47–78.

423 Protocol Additional to the Geneva Conventions of 12 August 1949, and relating to the Protection of Victims of International Armed Conflicts (Protocol I), 8 June 1977, 1125 UNTS 3.

424 Art. 43 Hague Regulations. See also UK Ministry of Defence, *The Manual of the Law of Armed Conflict* (Oxford: Oxford University Press, 2004), n° 11.19, p. 282.

425 Vité, S., 'L'applicabilité du droit international de l'occupation militaire aux activités des organisations internationales', 86 *International Review of the Red Cross* 9 (2004), p. 11.

426 UK Ministry of Defence, *supra* note 424, n° 11.3, p. 275.

427 During the Second World War, there had been several examples of military occupation, which did not begin with war. Several territories had indeed been invaded without any or with a minimum of military resistance, for example Denmark and Czechoslovakia. See Roberts, A., 'What is a military occupation?', 55 *British Yearbook of International Law* 291 (1984), p. 252.

> The Convention shall also apply to all cases of partial or total occupation of the territory of a High Contracting Party, even if the said occupation meets with no armed resistance.

This broader definition expands the application of the convention to other types of military occupation, such as the occupation of foreign territory not preceded by a war, as explicitly referred to in paragraph 2 of Common Article 2. However, it is generally accepted that the Conventions apply to all kinds of occupation, even those during armed conflict, based on the first paragraph of article 2.[428]

Belligerent occupation, or *occupatio bellica*, is the most classical form of foreign occupation and implies occupation by a belligerent state of the territory of another belligerent state after the end of armed conflict. The Fourth Geneva Convention differentiates between occupation following armed conflict and occupation generated with no armed resistance. In the first case, according to Article 6 para. 3 of the Fourth Geneva Convention, the occupation ceases one year after the general close of military operations (the 'one-year rule'). The Convention underlines that if the occupation extends beyond that time, the occupying Power shall nevertheless be bound by a limited number of provisions of the Convention[429] for the duration of the occupation, and to the extent that the occupying power exercises the functions of government in such territory. In the case of an occupation engendered with no armed resistance, and although the Fourth Geneva Convention does not mention this explicitly, the laws of occupation apply as long as the occupation remains effective.[430] This flows from customary international law, from which article 6, para. 3 derogates in the case of occupation following armed conflict.[431] In the case of Iraq, although Security Council Resolution 1546 suggested a formal end of occupation,[432] the present coalition forces remain bound by the rules of humanitarian law, in particular those prescribed by the Fourth Geneva Convention.[433] Article 3 of the 1977 Additional Protocol I returns to an extent to the concept of effective occupation,

---

428 Pictet, J. (ed.), *Les conventions de Genève du 12 août 1949: commentaire. IV La Convention de Genève Relative à la Protection des Personnes Civiles en Temps de Guerre* (Geneva: International Committee of the Red Cross, 1956), p. 27 and Roberts, *supra* note 427, p. 253.

429 Articles 1 to 12, 27, 29 to 34, 47, 49, 51, 52, 53, 59, 61 to 77, 143 of the Fourth Geneva Convention.

430 As stated by Roberts, "it is the reality, not the label, that counts" (Roberts, *supra* note 293, p. 47).

431 See Pictet, *supra* note 428, p; 70 and Vité, *supra* note 425, pp. 12–13.

432 SC Res 1546, UN Doc. S/RES/1546 (2004), para. 2.

433 Also Roberts, *supra* note 293, p. 48. See for an overview of the different legal basis for the application of the laws of occupation to the Coalition Forces after the announced 'end of occupation': Sassoli, M., 'Legislation and Maintenance of Public Order and Civil Life by Occupying Powers', 16 *European Journal of International Law* 688 (2005), pp. 684–686.

without any exceptions. For States party[434] to the 1977 Additional Protocol I the time limit in the Fourth Geneva Convention is abolished.

The substance of the law of occupation is characterised by two basic principles: first, the obligations to respect the territorial status and the national laws of the occupied territory (maintenance of the *status quo*) and, second, the obligation to respect the personal rights of the population,[435] which are detailed in several articles.[436] We will focus on the first type of provisions, which concern the territorial status of the occupied territory.

1. *The Territorial Status of Occupied Territories*

Both the Hague Regulations and the Fourth Geneva Convention adopt the principle that occupation of territory does not result in the transfer of sovereignty. The sovereignty of the occupied state is merely 'suspended',[437] although, as noted above, issues of sovereignty and competence are often misconceived. The principle of suspended sovereignty is a corollary of the prohibition on acquisition of territory by the use of force, which is also laid down in Article 2, para. 4 of the UN Charter. The Hague Regulations stipulate that the occupier has to be regarded as "administrator and usufructuary of public buildings, real estate, forests, and agricultural estates belonging to the hostile State, and situated in the occupied country. It must safeguard the capital of these properties, and administer them in accordance with the rules of usufruct".[438] This rule, although more restrictive, in fact serves the same objective as the abovementioned concept of the fiduciary nature of the exercised authority, discussed with regard to the nature of authority in international administration. In the case of a foreign occupation, the fiduciary nature of authority is thus to be applied as a consequence of this express provision.

---

434 It has not yet been convincingly argued that the provisions of the First Additional Protocol are customary international law, which implies that States not party to this Protocol are still bound by article 6, para. 3 of the Fourth Geneva Convention, which contains the one-year rule. Cf. Roberts, *supra* note 427, pp. 271–273.

435 Cf. Kolb, R., *Ius in bello, le droit international des conflits armés* (Bruxelles: Bruylant, 2003), pp. 191 *et s.*

436 Such as the prohibition of forcible transfers, deportations (art. 49, para. 1) or transfer of parts of the civilian population of the occupier into the occupied territory (art. 49, para. 6), the prohibition on compelling the population to serve in the armed or auxiliary forces of the occupier (art. 51) and the prohibition on destruction by the occupying power of real or personal property belonging individually or collectively to private persons (Art. 53).

437 Also Kolb, *supra* note 435, p. 191 and UK Ministry of Defence, *supra* note 424, no 11.25, p. 283.

438 Art. 55 Hague Regulations.

2. *The Obligation to Respect the National Laws of the Occupied Territory*

With regard to the existing legal system of the occupied territory, the Hague Regulations establish the principle of continuity of the legal system of the occupied territory, *unless absolutely prevented.* In addition, the Hague Regulations empower the occupier to "take all the measures in his power to restore, and ensure, as far as possible, public order and safety".[439] As rightly pointed out by some authors,[440] the original French text refers to "l'ordre et la vie public". The French text seems thus to have a broader meaning than the translated notion of 'public order and safety'.

Article 64 of the Fourth Geneva Convention specifies an analogous obligation concerning penal laws, although the second paragraph of that article allows the occupier to legislate when it is "essential to enable the Occupying Power to fulfil its obligations under the present Convention, to maintain the orderly government of the territory, and to ensure the security of the Occupying Power, of the members and property of the occupying forces or administration". It has however been argued that the limitation to the penal laws cannot be interpreted *a contrario*, in the sense that other laws do not remain in force, since the Geneva Conventions contain a general principle which has to be applied to the entire existing legal framework of the occupied territory.[441] In addition, the provisions of the Geneva Conventions with regard to penal laws are to be considered as *lex specialis* with regard to the general provision of Article 43 of the Hague Regulations.[442] The second paragraph of Article 64 of the Fourth Geneva Convention can be considered as a specification of the notion of 'unless absolutely prevented' contained in the Hague Regulations.[443]

The legal system in states under occupation, comprising local institutions established by law, thus remains in force. The legislative powers of the occupier are limited, but the exception is extensive. This limited legislative authority is an essential barrier to wide-scale legislative reforms in territories under occupation, and needs again to be seen as an application of the usufructuary nature of the occupier's authority. However, as the practical analysis in the third part will show, certain exceptions are tolerated, especially with regard to human rights norms.

---

[439] Art. 43 Hague Regulations.

[440] Sassoli, *supra* note 433, pp. 662–663.

[441] Pictet, *supra* note 428, p. 360.

[442] Sassoli, *supra* note 433, p. 664.

[443] Pictet, *supra* note 428, p. 360. Sassoli, *supra* note 433, pp. 670–671.

B. *The Laws of Occupation and Post-Conflict Reconstruction*

It is sometimes argued that the law of occupation does not cover cases of peace-enforcement action or the administration of territory by the UN or another international organisation.[444] The application of the laws of occupation to foreign forces, having a coercive peace-enforcement mandate, is indeed delicate and controversial. As mentioned above, the Hague Regulations mainly address the issue of military occupation consequent upon a declared war, but not the issue of an *approved* military presence. However, we will point out that here there does not seem to be any convincing obstruction to the application of the laws of occupation in the case of a military occupation by military forces having a coercive peace-enforcement mandate based on article 42 of the UN Charter. The question in respect of peace-keeping forces and international administrations is less evident, and will be addressed first.

1. *Peacekeeping Operations*

In the case of classical peacekeeping operations, the legal authority for the presence of these forces is generally the signature by the receiving state of a Status of Forces Agreement (SOFA). It is commonly acknowledged that the presence of a peacekeeping force does not constitute occupation in the sense of the Hague Regulations and the Geneva Conventions.[445] However, it is not the legal instrument, namely the Status of Forces Agreement, which blocks the application of the law of occupation. The main difference consists of the central objective of a peacekeeping operation, which is neither the military occupation of a territory, nor the exercise of control or authority over certain territories. The main rationale is the interposition of a *neutral* military force in a territory, which has no ambition to occupy the territory. In other words, peacekeeping forces will not, generally, be in a situation of effective occupation of foreign territory. In addition, peacekeeping forces generally have no enforcement mandate, and are not authorised to resort to armed force. They are only accorded the right to use force in cases of self-defence. In general, there will not be an armed conflict in which the foreign forces could be seen as one of the parties.

Nevertheless, the issue is not that clear-cut, as just shown. The evaluation of whether or not there is occupation is factual and derives from the effectiveness norm. In some circumstances, peacekeeping forces could thus find themselves in a situation of 'occupation'. In that case, the occupation can be either a belligerent occupation or an occupation by consent. This can be the case, for instance,

---

[444] See for example, UK Ministry of Defence, *supra* note 424, no 11.1.2., p. 275.

[445] See Bowett, D. W., *United Nations Forces. A Legal Study of United Nations Practice* (London: Stevens & Sons, 1964), p. 490.

when the central authority in the host state has collapsed or when the agreement has been terminated, leading the UN Forces to assume certain functions such as the maintenance of security and public order.[446]

2. *Peace-building Operations and Enforcement Action*

There is a growing acceptance of the obligation on UN Forces to respect international humanitarian law when they are in a situation of armed conflict. The Secretary-General confirmed in his 1999 Bulletin that "the fundamental principles and rules of international humanitarian law set out in the present bulletin are applicable to United Nations forces when in situations of armed conflict they are actively engaged therein as combatants, to the extent and for the duration of their engagement. They are accordingly applicable in enforcement actions, or in peacekeeping operations when the use of force is permitted in self-defence".[447] The 1999 Bulletin, however, does not contain an explicit proclamation that UN Forces are bound by the Geneva Conventions or Hague Regulations, just as no provision in the Bulletin deals with the potential applicability of the law of occupation.

As with the already discussed application of human rights, the main hurdle is that the UN itself is not a party to the applicable conventions. The degree of application of the rules contained in the Hague Regulations and the Geneva Conventions is still not agreed upon. Some scholars argue that the entire legal framework of the laws of armed conflict is applicable, while others contend that the UN is bound only by those rules which are declaratory of customary international law.[448] In view of our conclusion in respect of the human rights obligations of the UN, one can *mutatis mutandis* claim that the latter alternative is preferable. It should also be added that in any case forces operating in foreign territory are composed of national contingents, which are required to respect the laws of armed conflict.[449] The only question then is whether or not there is an armed conflict or a situation of effective occupation which can trigger the formal application of the relevant international rules.

In our view there is again no well-founded obstacle to the application of the law of occupation in the case of a military occupation by UN Forces having a coercive peace-enforcement mandate. Benvenisti, in defining the occupation of territory, also clearly indicates that occupation can be exercised by "one or

---

[446] Roberts, *supra* note 427, p. 291.

[447] UNSG Bulletin, Observance by United Nations Forces of International Humanitarian Law, ST/SGB/1999/13 (6 August 1999).

[448] Roberts, *supra* note 427.

[449] Sassoli, *supra* note 349, p. 143.

more states or an international organisation, such as the United Nations".[450] It is therefore important to analyse the situation 'on the ground' to assess the effectiveness of the occupation of the territory concerned. When the UN finds itself in a situation of effective control over a territory or part of a territory without explicit consent by the host State, the UN Forces should be considered as an occupying force.[451] Several scholars have nevertheless argued that UN Forces could not be considered as occupiers because the main difference from the traditional belligerent occupation is that international forces are in a relationship of co-operation with the local population instead of a conflict of interest,[452] or that international humanitarian law is inadequate to deal with peace operations.[453] But, as already mentioned, international forces can be in a situation of effective occupation of territory, which is the basis of the application of the law of occupation. The adequacy of the existing legal apparatus is indeed highly relevant, but, as will be made clear later, the laws of armed conflict, including the laws of occupation can be a helpful tool in post-conflict scenarios.

As far as State practice is concerned, attention should be drawn to the status of UNITAF in the case of Somalia. Although the UN did not recognise the *de jure* application of the Fourth Geneva Convention, the Australian Government accepted that the laws of occupation applied fully to UNITAF, which did not meet with armed resistance from the territorial sovereign.[454] The UN for its part only considered that "in an environment of State collapse, the Fourth Geneva Convention could supply adequate guidelines for regulating relations between peacekeeping troops and the local population".[455] As INTERFET in East Timor is concerned, the Australian Government found that the laws of armed conflict were not applicable as there was no international or non-international armed conflict on East Timorese territory at the time of the intervention. The Australian Government thus applied the principles of the laws of armed conflict by way of 'guidelines'. The Australian Government equally considered that INTERFET was not in a situation of belligerent occupation of territory because Indonesia had

[450] Benvenisti, E., *The International Law of Occupation* (Columbia / Princeton: University Presses of California, 2004), p. 4.

[451] Also *Ibid.* and Sassoli, *supra* note 433.

[452] Shraga, D., 'The UN as an actor bound by international humanitarian law', *in Les Nations Unies et le droit international humanitaire, Actes du Colloque international à l'occasion du 50ième anniversaire de l'ONU* (Paris: Pedone, 1996), p. 326.

[453] Megret, F. and Hoffmann, F., 'The UN as a Human Rights Violator? Some Reflections on the United Nations Changing Human Rights Responsibilities', 25 *Human Rights Quarterly* 330 (2003).

[454] Kelly, McCormack, Muggleton and Oswald, *supra* note 383.

[455] United Nations Department of Peacekeeping Operations, The Comprehensive report on Lessons Learned from the United Nations Operation in Somalia (UNOSOM), New York (April 1992–March 1995).

consented to its deployment.[456] The New Zealand position was, on the contrary, that the laws of armed conflict did apply to INTERFET, disregarding the fact that Indonesia had consented to its deployment, especially considering that no other State, except Australia, had recognised Indonesian title to East Timor.[457]

The question remains whether the laws of occupation continue to apply in the case of a subsequent agreement with the host state, considering that, in that case, there is no longer opposition between the armed forces of the host state and those of the international force. In that regard, it should be remembered that article 47 of the Fourth Geneva Convention provides that "protected persons who are in occupied territory shall not be deprived, in any case or in any manner whatsoever, of the benefits of the present Convention by any change introduced, as the result of the occupation of a territory, into the institutions or government of the said territory, nor by any agreement concluded between the authorities of the occupied territories and the Occupying Power, nor by any annexation by the latter of the whole or part of the occupied territory". It can be argued that this provision concerns not only agreements concluded before the occupation, but also agreements concluded during hostilities.[458] Although more specific regulations can be envisaged in the agreement concluded between the international forces and the host state, the laws of occupation can be regarded as a minimum or secondary source of applicable rules. We could therefore conclude that, even when a subsequent agreement with the host state regulates the occupation, by analogy the rules of the laws of occupation remain applicable, albeit in a subsidiary manner and in conformity with the concluded agreement.[459] The laws of occupation likewise remain in force even when an occupying power's mandate is confirmed or modified by a consequent Security Council resolution, or when the presence of a military force is 'formalised' by a Security Council resolution, as was the case for KFOR in Kosovo. *Jus ad bellum* issues cannot affect the application of the laws of armed conflict, because those laws apply notwithstanding the legality or legitimacy of a conflict or an occupation, However, in line with what we argued on the previous paragraph, the application of the laws of occupation should then be interpreted according to the mandate given to such Forces.[460]

---

456 Kelly, McCormack, Muggleton and Oswald, *supra* note 383.

457 *Ibid.*

458 Roberts, *supra* note 427, p. 279.

459 This situation should not be confused with that of an agreement concerning the stationing of foreign military forces in another State, which is fundamentally different from occupation (Roberts, *supra* note 427, pp. 297–298).

460 Also: Irmscher, *supra* note 327, p. 376.

3. *Post-conflict Administration*

The objectives and mandate of an occupying power under the laws of occupation are more limited than other forms of international administration. This results from the different purposes of the two legal bodies. As mentioned above, the laws of occupation mainly focus on relations with the administering authority and on the humanitarian aspect of the occupation. International administrations have not always been set up in accordance with similar instruments. The consent of the host state, for instance, is not a characteristic of all international administrations and can therefore not be upheld as a basis for the (non-)application of the laws of occupation. In East Timor for instance, the consent of the host State has been rightly criticised, as Indonesia was not the lawful sovereign, nor had it been recognised as such.[461] In addition, the preceding military intervention and consequent military occupation vary from one case to another. It is for these reasons very difficult to establish a single criterion for the application of the laws of occupation to all international administrations. The principles discussed in the previous two sections will thus need to be applied to international administrations, in particular to the military components of such missions.

When the establishment of a post-conflict administration is preceded by military intervention, as in Kosovo for instance, we consider that the military forces are bound by the laws of occupation. The same is true in respect of the military component of UNTAET, which can be considered to have been bound by the laws of occupation. As argued in the previous section, this remains true even when a subsequent Security Council resolution endorses or extends the mandate of the military forces.[462] The laws of occupation remain the original legal regime applicable to military occupiers, and have to be interpreted in function of relevant Security Council Resolutions. On the other hand, when the host State has explicitly consented to the establishment of the administration, the situation is not really one of belligerent occupation. However, similar to what we argued in the previous section in respect of peace-building operations, the laws of occupation can equally be applied to these cases, even though *de jure* application can be contested.[463]

The case is of course different in Iraq. The application of the laws of occupation to the United States forces and administration is undeniable. However, in that case, the powers of the occupier also need to be supplemented by relevant

---

461 See also Ratner, *supra* note 8.

462 See: Cerone, *supra* note 325, pp. 483–485.

463 Cf. Levrat, B., 'Le droit International Humanitaire au Timor Oriental: entre Théorie et Pratique', 841 *International Review of the Red Cross* 77 (2001); Sassoli, *supra* note 349, p. 143 and Kelly, McCormack, Muggleton and Oswald, *supra* note 383, p. 115.

Security Council resolutions. As an example, all Coalition Provisional Authority Orders and Regulations are based both on the CPA's authority under the relevant Security Council Resolutions and on the 'laws and usages of war'.[464]

[464] See for example, the first consideration of CPA Regulation Number 1, "The Coalition Provisional Authority", CPA/REG/16 May 2003/01 (16 May 2003).

Part III

Post-conflict Administrations in Practice: International Administrations, the 'Light Footprint' Approach, and the Occupation of Iraq

The different core components that will be analysed are grouped into three chapters. This division is based on the somewhat different objectives of the components. The first cluster is principally related to essential governmental tasks, which are more or less short-term objectives and which are related to the executive power. The reconstruction of the judicial system, comprising the re-establishment of the rule of law, can be seen as a more long-term objective, and is by definition related to the judicial power. The next chapter discusses institution-building and democracy, which is a major, if not the most prominent objective of these missions, and can to a certain extent be linked to the legislative power and institutions. The short-term objectives nevertheless do not necessarily imply a short-term engagement. Capacity-building by definition requires a long-term course of action, as will be evidenced throughout this analysis. We nevertheless acknowledge that every attempt to categorise necessarily involves exceptions, and could, of course, be handled differently. In addition, our arrangement does not necessarily reflect the division of powers within the missions, although, arguably, the 'pillar structure' under UNMIK seems to be on the whole similar to our approach.

Clearly, these components have not enjoyed the same level of importance or priority in every case under examination, nor have all of these components had the same weight in relation to each other. Economic reconstruction for instance has not enjoyed a high priority in every post-conflict mission. Each section is again subdivided into several subsections, in which the implementation of the mandates in Kosovo, East Timor, Afghanistan and Iraq will be addressed.

As we briefly noted in our introduction, it is not the purpose of this book to engage in an all-inclusive analysis of the various peace-building missions undertaken in recent years, nor to undertake the establishment of a 'model', if one should exist, to address post-conflict reconstruction. This book will thus not propose an exhaustive description of all measures taken under the mandates assigned to the different missions. Instead, the focus will be on the general approach and on the major difficulties encountered, enabling us to differentiate between the approaches in Kosovo, East Timor, Afghanistan and Iraq.

Chapter 9

Civil Administration

Probably one of the most immediate tasks of post-conflict reconstruction missions is the restoration and re-establishment of basic civil administration, which consists of delivering public services to the population through an effective interim administration. In sum, it boils down to performing one of the core functions of a national government. Civil administration however cannot easily be 'detached' from other components, as it influences as much as it is influenced by other sectors such as those of judicial reconstruction and institution building.

This chapter is divided into four different sections. The first deals with civil administration *sensu stricto*, by which we mean the provision of public services. Special attention will be paid to the reform of and capacity-building in the civil service, since the transfer of authority to national institutions is part of the final objective of such missions. The second section relates to economic reconstruction, which must be seen as part of civil administration, although in the case of Kosovo a separate pillar was set up to oversee that economic reconstruction. This was however a pragmatic solution to the fact that UNMIK operated as a 'federation' of international organisations, each having a distinct field of operation. Our third section is dedicated to the re-establishment of law and order, and the reform of the security sector. The monopoly of a state in the maintenance of law and order within its territory is a vital element in the administration of the territory. As a result, special attention will be given to the establishment of local police and defence forces, and the relationship with the foreign military presence. This interaction between national and international security presences, especially in the immediate emergency period is inevitable, and a necessity. The last section discusses the provision of emergency relief and the problem of refugees and internally displaced persons.

A. *Basic Civil Administration*

Basic civil administration is an essential condition for effective governance. As will become clear throughout our analysis, emergency measures have mostly been taken by international officials upon arrival, and have in general caused no real controversy. Indeed, restoring postal services, water and energy supply, and garbage collection and reopening schools and hospitals are logical immediate steps to be taken. A recurrent and most interesting practice is the creation of claims commissions to deal with territorial disputes. These commissions are vital for the creation of sustainable peace, as their decisions influence judicial, economic and security aspects. Post-conflict societies often emerge from years of discrimination imposed by regimes of former occupiers, especially with regard to property rights, which are in addition seen in various international treaties as fundamental human rights. This has almost always led to much friction among the population. Therefore special attention will be paid to this issue.[465]

Civil administration is of course closely related to the setting up of institutions, as they will be in charge of delivering these services, and to the creation of interim institutions in the emergency phase. We will not enter into the details of the interim or transitional administrative structures set up, as they either were described in the first part, which gives an overview of the four cases we will focus on, or will be discussed in the chapter on institution-building. However, a short description of interim structures is necessary to facilitate the analysis of capacity-building in the civil service. We will equally focus on the emergency phase during which the need for the rapid restoration of essential services is paramount. Besides the main problems encountered by the interim authorities, our analysis will be centred on both immediate measures taken to restore essential public services and the building of local capacity in the civil service through the transition from international to local institutions.

1. *Kosovo: Replacing Parallel Structures*

UNMIK's second pillar, 'Civil Administration', under the direct leadership of the UN, was entrusted with the civil administration of the Province, and was the

---

[465] The issue of housing and property restitution has been the object of several interesting works entirely dedicated to it. See for example, Buyse, A., *Post-Conflict Housing Restitution. The European Human Rights Perspective, with a Case Study on Bosnia and Herzegovina* (Antwerpen: Intersentia, 2008) and Van Houtte, H., Delmartino, B. and Iasson, Y., *Post-War Restoration of Property Rights under International Law: Volume 1: Institutional features and Substantive Law* (Cambridge: Cambridge University Press, 2008) and Das, H. and Van Houtte, H., *Post-War Restoration of Property Rights under International Law: Volume 2: Procedural Aspects* (Cambridge: Cambridge University Press, 2008).

UN's primary responsibility. Security Council Resolution 1244 asked UNMIK to "[perform] basic civilian administrative functions where and as long as required".[466] The reinstatement of essential public services was quickly dealt with. The restoration of power, water and heating was rapidly, but partially, achieved in the first months after UNMIK's arrival, although serious breakdowns often occurred.[467] Many schools were immediately reopened throughout the country, while the physical reconstruction of damaged buildings had already started in October 1999.[468] All hospitals were equally reopened soon after UNMIK's deployment, and were managed by international staff to fill the vacuum caused by the emergency.[469] A separate authority for post and telecommunications was established as early as October 1999.[470]

As UNMIK was the first mission of its kind in recent years, staff had to be recruited on a case by case basis, the same problem UNTAET would be faced with a few months later.[471] The slow deployment of UNMIK outside the capital had led to the resurgence of parallel structures, mainly operated through the Kosovo Liberation Army (KLA/UCK). These parallel administrations collected tax revenues and operated health and educational services.[472] UNMIK responded to these shadow structures by introducing a municipal administrative framework, the 'Joint Interim Administrative Structure' (JIAS), aimed at implementing official policies in the provinces and integrating members of these parallels structures.[473] The municipal authorities were integrated in the JIAS, which explicitly required the dissolution of parallel entities by January 2000.[474] The problems of parallel administrative structures nevertheless continued throughout UNMIK's administration. While Kosovo Albanians' parallel structures such as schools have been

---

466 SC Res. 1244, UN Doc. S/RES/1244 (1999), para. 11, b).

467 See on the relation between the energy sector and economy Caplan, R., *International Governance of War-Torn Territories: Rule and Reconstruction* (Oxford: Oxford University Press, 2005), pp. 139–140.

468 Report of the Secretary-General on the United Nations Interim Administration Mission in Kosovo, UN Doc. S/1999/987 (16 September 1999), paras. 21–2.

469 Report of the Secretary-General on the United Nations Interim Administration Mission in Kosovo, UN Doc. S/1999/1250 (23 December 1999), para. 37.

470 UNMIK Regulation 1999/12 on the provision on postal and telecommunications services in Kosovo, UN Doc. UNMIK/REG/1999/12 (14 October 1999).

471 In May 2000, almost a year after UNMIK's establishment, the civil administration pillar had a staff of 292 internationals out of the 435 envisaged. See Report of the Secretary-General on the United Nations Interim Administration Mission in Kosovo, UN Doc. S/2000/538 (6 June 2000), para. 28.

472 OSCE Mission in Kosovo, Department of Human Rights and Rule of Law, 'Parallel Structures in Kosovo' (October 2003).

473 Report of the Secretary-General, UN Doc. S/1999/1250, *supra* note 469, para. 35.

474 Report of the Secretary-General on the United Nations Interim Administration Mission in Kosovo, UN Doc. S/2000/177 (3 March 2000), para. 12.

satisfactorily integrated in the official administration, Serb parallel structures, mainly property registration and schools, persisted in the Serb municipalities because of ethnical bias within the official structures and Serbian interference in UNMIK's administration.[475]

When UNMIK arrived, Kosovo completely lacked any local civil administration, as a consequence of the departure of all Yugoslav administrators and civil servants. The ethnical bias towards Kosovo Serbs, who were a majority in the former civil service, would in any case have necessitated a complete reform of the administration. UNMIK quickly involved the local population, especially Kosovo Albanians, in the area of civil administration. Following the signature of an agreement on 15 December 1999, the first Kosovar multi-ethnic governmental structure was created, the already mentioned Joint Interim Administrative Structure (JIAS), aimed at giving the Kosovars a direct input into UNMIK decision-making.[476] The structure comprised three main bodies – the Kosovo Transitional Council, the Interim Administrative Council and administrative departments. The administrative departments were co-headed by local and international officials. The first *operational* departments were those relating to civil administration: Health and Social Welfare, Education and Science, Local Administration and the Central Fiscal Authority.[477] Kosovo Serbs were very reluctant to join the interim institutions, and withdrew shortly after the creation of the first interim structures.[478] By May 2000, the Joint Interim Administrative Structure's departments already employed 58.300 local staff, although at the senior level local capacity building was slower.[479] In order to bolster local capacity while preserving and ensuring the multi-ethnical character of Kosovo, UNMIK drafted a regulation laying the basis for recruitment into the civil service.[480] Besides establishing the conditions for recruitment procedures, the regulation contains in an annex a short 'Civil Service Code of Conduct' to be respected by all civil servants. An 'Institute for

---

475 OSCE Mission in Kosovo, Department of Human Rights and Rule of Law, 'Parallel Structures in Kosovo' (October 2003).

476 UNMIK Regulation 2000/1 on the approval Kosovo Joint Interim Administrative Structure, UN Doc UNMIK/REG/2000/1 (14 January 2000).

477 Civil administration was later handled by the Institutions of Provisional Self-Government, instituted under the 'Constitutional Framework for Provisional Self-Government'. See UNMIK Regulation 2001/19 on the executive branch of the provisional institutions of self-government in Kosovo, UN Doc. UNMIK/REG/2001/19 (13 September 2001).

478 Report of the Secretary-General, UN Doc. S/1999/1250, *supra* note 469, para. 3.

479 Report of the Secretary-General on the United Nations Interim Administration Mission in Kosovo, UN Doc. S/2002/1126 (9 October 2002), para. 9.

480 UNMIK Regulation 2001/36 on the Kosovo Civil Service, UN Doc. UNMIK/REG/2001/36 (22 December 2001).

Civil Administration', led by the OSCE, was equally set up to conduct training sessions for civil servants.[481]

As briefly mentioned, a recurrent component of post-conflict reconstruction is the setting up of claims commissions in order to establish property rights and provide compensation for those who lost them under former discriminatory laws. Following NATO's armed intervention, Serbian officials withdrew completely from Kosovo, taking with them the entire collection of cadastral documents.[482] UNMIK therefore decided to create an internationalised 'Housing and Property Claims Commission'[483] in conjunction with a registration office, the 'Housing and Property Directorate'.[484] The great importance of this commission in the reconstruction process can easily be illustrated by the number of submitted claims: by the end of June 2003 – the deadline for the submission of claims – the Commission had received 28,587 claims in addition to the 3,000 properties placed under the Commission's administration. The handling of the claims was less of a success, at least in the early days. By September 2002, only 644 of the 19,862 claims had been resolved and only 322 decisions implemented – less than 2 per cent.[485] The underestimate of the importance of the number of claims received by the Claims Commission required the permanent availability of external funding to enable all the claims to be adjudicated upon.[486] On 6 June 2006 the Housing and Property Claims Commission had finally adjudicated on all received claims at first instance, and was replaced by the new 'Kosovo Property Claims Commission', composed of Kosovars only.[487]

UNMIK's capacity to engage in the rapid, although partial, restoration of essential services needs to be highlighted, especially considering the generally alarming condition of public companies in Kosovo. The basic rehabilitation of

---

[481] Report of the Secretary-General on the United Nations Interim Administration Mission on Kosovo, UN Doc. S/2002/62 (15 January 2002), para. 34.

[482] Report of the Secretary-General on the United Nations Interim Administration Mission in Kosovo, UN Doc. S/2001/926 (2 October 2001), para. 17.

[483] See in general on this: Das, H. and Van Houtte, H., *Post-War Restoration of Property Rights under International Law: Volume 2: Procedural Aspects* (Cambridge: Cambridge University Press, 2008), pp. 16 *et s.*

[484] UNMIK Regulation 1999/23 on the establishment of the housing and property directorate and the housing and property claims commission, UN Doc. UNMIK/REG/1999/23 (15 Nov. 1999). For an overview through a human rights lens see OSCE Mission in Kosovo, Department of Human Rights and Rule of Law, 'Property Rights in Kosovo' (30 June 2003).

[485] Report of the Secretary-General on the United Nations Interim Administration Mission in Kosovo, UN Doc. S/2002/1126 (9 October 2002), para. 41.

[486] Report of the Secretary-General on the United Nations Interim Administration Mission on Kosovo, UN Doc. S/2006/906 (20 November 2006), para. 78.

[487] Report of the Secretary-General on the United Nations Interim Administration Mission on Kosovo, UN Doc. S/2007/395 (29 June 2007), Annex I, para. 65.

the civil service sector was immediate, and progressed well during the mission's presence.[488] UNMIK also swiftly integrated local actors in the civil administration departments, by increasing local ownership over essential civil services to pave the way for a transfer to the local administration. Local capacity-building has been slow but promising, although in the field of minority employment efforts need to be sustained. It should however be noted that recreating a functioning civil administration from scratch necessitates long-term commitments. Emergency measures to ensure rapid rehabilitation are paramount, but reforms require a continuing engagement. The 2006 decentralisation exercise in Kosovo was for instance difficult to achieve.[489] In addition, the IMF recommended headcount reduction resulted in a hiring freeze from 2006 in order to keep expenditure under control.[490] This shows that sustainability requires long-term strategic planning and continuing international assistance and support.

2. *East Timor: The Importance of a Long-term Engagement*

Beyond emergency measures, the restoration of governance and administration through the reconstruction of essential infrastructure, the provision of basic social services, the recruitment of civil servants and the reinstatement of a law enforcement system were considered immediate priorities for UNTAET.[491] The emergency measures taken by UNTAET were mainly aimed at the rehabilitation of essential public services. These immediate responses were however only partial with regard to severe logistical problems and did not ameliorate the catastrophic infrastructural condition of the territory. Water and electricity were rapidly although very partially restored.[492] UNTAET equally managed to restore the majority of the schools by April 2000.[493] Other emergency measures were aimed at a swift restoration of port and airport activity, as well as health services.[494] The reconstruction of the physical infrastructure however posed major problems, considering the overall destruction of public facilities in the territory. Road infrastructure, and in general the rehabilitation of the other existing infrastructures,

[488] Cf. the Secretary General's reports on UNMIK.

[489] Report of the Secretary-General on the United Nations Interim Administration Mission on Kosovo, UN Doc. S/2006/906 (20 November 2006), para. 13

[490] Report of the Secretary-General on the United Nations Interim Administration Mission on Kosovo, UN Doc. S/2007/134 (9 March 2007), para. 62.

[491] Report of the Secretary-General on the United Nations Transitional Administration in East Timor, UN Doc. S/2000/53 (26 January 2000), paras. 40–62.

[492] *Ibid.*, para. 48.

[493] Report of the Secretary-General on the United Nations Transitional Administration in East Timor, UN Doc. S/2000/738 (26 July 2000), para. 36.

[494] Report of the Secretary-General, UN Doc. S/2000/53, *supra* note 491, paras. 57–61.

such as the port and airport, necessitated longer-term cost-intensive investments.[495] The restoration of the telecommunications network covering the entire territory could not, for instance, be achieved before UNTAET's withdrawal.

The problems witnessed in Kosovo relating to the planning of the mission resurfaced in East Timor. Not only was UNTAET not able rapidly to deploy to its maximum capacity, its own staff needed to be trained in governmental functions, as staff recruited early in the mission were apparently considered poorly qualified for certain specific tasks.[496] A few months after UNTAET's arrival, some 391 officials still needed to be recruited, especially in the fields of public services.[497] Full deployment of the mission took more than a year.[498]

Soon after the arrival of Special Representative Sergio Vieira de Mello in East Timor, contacts with local personalities were established in order to involve the Timorese in the reconstruction process. The Transitional Administrator rapidly established a 'National Consultative Council' (NCC),[499] consisting of a majority of local officials, to oversee the decision-making process during the transitional period. UNTAET immediately created district administrations, staffed by UNTAET officials, in conjunction with district advisory councils composed of Timorese nationals.[500] In July 2000, UNTAET's first Pillar ('Governance and Public Administration') was replaced by the 'East Timor Transitional Administration' (ETTA), headed by the Special Representative of the Secretary-General. The East Timor Transitional Administration comprised nine portfolios, four of which were directed by UNTAET officials, the remaining five being entrusted to the East Timorese. The East Timorese portfolios included 'Internal Administration', 'Social Affairs' and 'Infrastructure'.[501] In October 2000 a 'National Council' was established as an early form of national legislative assembly to replace the former National Consultative Council.

The transfer of administrative functions to an East Timorese administration necessitated a reliable civil service infrastructure, which appeared to be one of the

[495] Report of the Secretary-General, UN Doc. S/2000/738, *supra* note 493, paras. 29–30.

[496] Smith, M. G. and Dee, M., *Peacekeeping in East Timor. The Path to Independence* (Boulder: Lynne Rienner Publishers, 2003), p. 64. Major General M. G. Smith was Deputy Force Commander for UNTAET. See also Dahrendorf, N. *et al.*, 'A Review of Peace Operations: A Case for Change: East Timor' (Conflict Security & Development Group, King's College London, 10 March 2003), para. 176.

[497] Report of the Secretary-General, UN Doc. S/2000/53, *supra* note 491, para. 67.

[498] Dahrendorf *et al., supra* note 496, para. 176.

[499] UNTAET Regulation 1999/2 on the establishment of a National Consultative Council, UN Doc. UNTAET/REG/1999/2 (2 December 1999).

[500] Report of the Secretary-General, UN Doc. S/2000/53, *supra* note 491, para. 41.

[501] Report of the Secretary-General, UN Doc. S/2000/738, *supra* note 493, para. 3. See also Smith and Dee, *supra* note 496, p. 65.

major difficulties.[502] Local capacity was far from sufficient, and had been identified as one of the top priorities by the 'Joint Assessment Mission', conducted under the auspices of the World Bank.[503] In trying to rely on local capacity from the start while boosting an exclusively Timorese civil service, UNTAET soon decided to set up an independent Civil Service Commission.[504] The Commission was in charge of the development and recruitment of a new, and much leaner,[505] civil service. The Civil Service Commission has however been criticized for several reasons: its mixed composition, the application of formal criteria not adapted to the local traditions, and its inadequate legal and institutional framework.[506] In addition, the complexity of fund channelling and strict UN procedures resulted in problems in the payment of salaries in the civil administration.[507] Soon it became apparent that the training of civil servants necessitated a distinct programme, especially in respect of managerial and technical positions. The 'Civil Service Academy of the East Timor Public Administration' was inaugurated in May 2000, to conduct seminars and workshops in management and governance.[508] By July 2002, the administration employed some 5,275 civil servants.[509] In the last months of UNTAET's presence, but without its involvement, the drafting of a 'Civil Service Act' started under the guidance of the United Nations Development Programme (UNDP). After many amendments to the draft,[510] the Act was finally adopted by the National Parliament in April 2004.[511]

502 *Ibid.*, p. 63.

503 World Bank, 'Report of the joint assessment mission to East Timor' (8 December 1999), para. 16.

504 UNTAET Regulation 2000/3 on the establishment of a Public Service Commission, UN Doc. UNTAET/REG/2000/3 (20 January 2000).

505 The former Indonesian Administration was oversized given the small territory of East Timor, 3.4% of the population compared to an Asian average of 2.6% (World Bank, 'Report of the joint assessment mission to East Timor' (8 December 1999), para. 16). It was obvious from the start that UNTAET could not re-employ the same number of civil servants recruited under Indonesian occupation, as this would have been unsustainable both for UNTAET and the future Timorese Government. Cf. Report of the Secretary-General, UN Doc. S/2000/53, *supra* note 491, para. 42.

506 Zaum, *supra* note 75, p. 209.

507 Report of the Secretary-General, UN Doc. S/2000/738, *supra* note 493, para. 35.

508 *Ibid.*, para. 19.

509 *Ibid.*

510 For an overview see Zaum, *supra* note 75, p. 211.

511 Democratic Republic of East Timor, National Parliament, Law No. 8/2004 Approving the Statute of the Civil Service (16 June 2004), an unofficial English translation is available at www.easttimorlawjournal.com.

With regard to property rights, UNTAET faced severe problems, as no registration mechanism existed at its arrival.[512] The idea of a Property Claims Commission had already been envisaged before January 2000.[513] Within UNTAET, a 'Land and Property Unit' was established to allocate property rights on a temporary basis. The Land and Property Unit suggested the creation of a Claims Commission, the 'Land and Property Commission' both to maintain the land registry and to resolve land disputes. The idea was rejected by the National Council, as it viewed it as contrary to traditional land ownership.[514] The reluctance to address the issue was even more problematic as traditional dispute settlement was not able efficiently to absorb the settlement of claims.[515]

While the integration of national capacity in and the creation of administrative structures have perhaps been a success for UNTAET, building an efficient public service was one of the most difficult aspects of UNTAET's mandate.[516] The overall assessment of UNTAET's performance in the public administration sector has been described as mixed,[517] although the difficulty of UNTAET's task, considering the above-described setbacks, needs to be emphasised. The Joint Assessment Mission indeed found that "[t]he window of opportunity for reform must be balanced against the need for speedy action to restore services, which does not allow for a lengthy analysis, consultation and planning exercise".[518] Upon independence, the East Timor civil service was however clearly not capable of ensuring an independent and effective administration. UNTAET did not manage to introduce a legal framework for the civil service, while the Civil Service Act passed by the National Parliament in 2004 is considered an insufficient basis for an independent civil service.[519] The development of an effective and neutral civil service nevertheless requires time in a new state. Time is however not the only factor. The Secretary-General acknowledged that progress had been severely hampered by the politicization and centralization of decision-making in the

[512] On this issue see Wright, W., 'Some Land Tenure Issues in Post-Conflict East Timor', 1 *East Timor Law Journal* (2006).

[513] Report of the Secretary-General, UN Doc. S/2000/53, *supra* note 491, para. 63.

[514] Pritchard, S., 'United Nations Involvement in Post-Conflict Reconstruction Efforts: New and Continuing Challenges in the Case of East Timor', 24 *University of New South Wales Law Journal* 188 (2001).

[515] Harrington, A., 'Ethnicity, Violence, & Land and Property Disputes in Timor-Leste', 2 *East Timor Law Journal* (2007).

[516] Report of the Secretary-General on the United Nations Transitional Administration in East Timor, UN Doc. S/2002/432 (17 April 2002).

[517] Dahrendorf *et al., supra* note 496, para. 210.

[518] World Bank, 'Report of the joint assessment mission to East Timor' (8 December 1999), para. 17.

[519] Zaum, *supra* note 75, p. 213.

Timorese institutions.[520] UNTAET's early withdrawal left Timor Leste with the burden of continuing civil service reform, while no international organisation was left to enforce a regulatory framework.

3. *Afghanistan: The Challenges of Reform*

The consequence of UNAMA's very limited mandate was an inadequate international civil presence in Afghanistan, in particular when compared to Kosovo and East Timor. Civil administration was deliberately not included in the UN's mandate, and was the primary responsibility of the Afghan institutions. Little was achieved in the interim period. As stated in the Bonn Agreement, an 'Emergency Loya Jirga' had to be convened within the first six months, the organisation of which was a priority for the international community after the signature of the Bonn Agreement. The implementation of the other provisions of the Bonn Agreement was more or less postponed until after the holding of the Emergency Loya Jirga.[521] The Interim Administration nevertheless initiated several emergency measures, in cooperation with various UN agencies. Among other measures, a back-to-school campaign was launched in the early days of the Interim Administration, a decree setting out the framework for a free press and radio was passed, and a new Ministry of Women's Affairs was set up.[522] A few months later, various health programmes had been initiated by UN organisations and agencies, and several water and sanitation installations had been (re) constructed.[523]

The administrative system, established under the 1964 Constitution, was as such still respected by civil servants across the country,[524] and was estimated to consist of some 240,000 employees at all levels, including teachers, health workers and employees of state-owned enterprises.[525] It was generally acknowledged

---

[520] Report of the Secretary-General on Timor-Leste pursuant to Security Council resolution 1690 (2006), UN Doc. S/2006/628 (8 August 2006), para. 33.

[521] Dobbins, J. *et al.*, *America's Role in Nation-Building: from Germany to Iraq* (Santa Monica: Rand, 2003), p. 142.

[522] Report of the Secretary-General, UN Doc. A/57/487-S/2002/278, *supra* note 2, paras. 12–9.

[523] Report of the Secretary-General, The situation in Afghanistan and its implications for international peace and security, UN Doc. A/56/1000-S/2002/737 (11 July 2002), para. 53 and Report of the Secretary-General, Emergency International Assistance for Peace, Normalcy and Reconstruction of War-Stricken Afghanistan, UN Doc. A/57/410 (17 September 2002), para. 36.

[524] *Ibid.*, para. 33.

[525] The number of civil servants was estimated by a Working Group established soon after the Interim Administration's installation in order to assess the financial support to be provided. Cf. Report of the Secretary-General, UN Doc. A/57/487-S/2002/278, *supra* note 2, para. 26.

that the civil service needed urgent reform and transformation, and was as such explicitly included in the Bonn Agreement, which asked for the creation of a Civil Service Commission "to provide the Interim Authority and the future Transitional Authority with shortlists of candidates for key posts in the administrative departments, as well as those of governors and Uluswals, in order to ensure their competence and integrity".[526] Besides the recurrent financial problems with regard to the payment of salaries of the civil servants,[527] the application of the criteria laid down in the Bonn Agreement proved to be even more challenging. Appointments of civil servants in the emergency phase, *before* the establishment of the Civil Service Commission, were widely criticized as they did not take into account the criteria of the Bonn Agreement.[528] The envisaged Civil Service Commission was eventually set up by Presidential Decree in May 2002, and was reformed in June 2003 as the 'Independent Administrative Reform and Civil Service Commission'.[529] The new commission was given the power to remove corrupt senior Government officials, as well as those who did not meet minimum educational and other qualifications.[530] Progress was nevertheless perceptible only when the Transitional Administration decided to replace incompetent and corrupt officials in Kabul and the Provinces by the end of 2003.[531]

The civil service remains a worrying issue. The January 2006 Afghanistan Compact, in line with the Bonn criteria on civil service recruitment, asked for the establishment of a "clear and transparent national appointments mechanism will be established within 6 months, applied within 12 months and fully implemented within 24 months for all senior level appointments to the central government and the judiciary, as well as for provincial governors, chiefs of police,

526 Section III, C), 5), Bonn Agreement. See also Report of the Secretary-General, UN Doc. A/57/487–S/2002/278, *supra* note 2, para. 26.

527 The Afghan Interim Authority had no funds of its own, and the civil servants had not been paid for five to six months (Report of the Secretary-General, UN Doc. A/57/487–S/2002/278, *supra* note 2, para. 12). See also on the financial aspects of the civil service: McKechnie, A., 'Humanitarian Assistance, Reconstruction & Development in Afghanistan: A Practitioner's View', in Azimi, Fuller and Nakayama, *supra* note 85, p. 222.

528 Report of the Secretary-General, UN Doc. A/57/487–S/2002/278, *supra* note 2, paras. 3 and 33.

529 Islamic Transitional Government of Afghanistan, Presidential Decree, 'Regulation of the functions and activities of the Independent Administrative Reform and Civil Service Commission' Decree Regulation n. 26 (16 June 03).

530 *Ibid.* See also Report of the Secretary-General, The situation in Afghanistan and its implications for international peace and security, UN Doc. A/57/850–S/2003/754 (23 July 2003), para. 5.

531 Report of the Secretary-General, The situation in Afghanistan and its implications for international peace and security – Emergency international assistance for peace, normalcy and reconstruction of war-stricken Afghanistan, UN Doc. A/58/616 (3 December 2003), para. 4.

district administrators and provincial heads of security". The Compact equally asked that, by the end of 2010, "merit-based appointments, vetting procedures and performance-based reviews will be undertaken for civil service positions at all levels of government, including central government, the judiciary and police, and requisite support will be provided to build the capacity of the civil service to function effectively."[532] The reinstatement of these fundamental aspects relating to the civil service can only be an indication of the failure of the former authorities effectively to implement the conditions set out in the Bonn Agreement. A few days before the deadline set in the Compact, the President signed a decree on a new appointment mechanism for all senior level appointments, the first benchmark defined in the Afghanistan Compact.[533] The question however, is whether this will influence the nomination procedures in the civil service. Just a few months before the adoption of the Decree, political influence on appointments was again revealed when fourteen candidate police officers who had failed in the selection process were nevertheless appointed to key positions in the National Police Force. In addition, some of those officers were well-known human rights offenders and/or had links to criminal and illegal armed groups. Although the government expressed its concern over the appointments, the Ministry of the Interior nevertheless decided to confirm them, albeit for a probationary period of four months.[534]

The January 2006 Afghanistan Compact equally asked the Government to initiate a process for the registration of land and titles before the end of 2007.[535] The issue has remained unaddressed since the Bonn Agreement, and was complicated by the complexity of the Afghan legal system, the massive return of refugees and internally displaced persons, occupation of properties and landlessness.[536] In sharp contrast to the setting up of claims commissions under UNMIK for instance, no such mechanism was put in place. Although a special court, the 'Special Property Disputes Resolution Court', had been set up in November 2003 to address property issues,[537] its effectiveness in property

---

532 Annex I, Afghanistan Compact.

533 Transcript of the Press Conference by Tom Koenigs the Special Representative of the Secretary-General for Afghanistan (18 September 2006).

534 Report of the Secretary-General, The situation in Afghanistan and its implications for peace and security, UN Doc. A/61/326–S/2006/727 (11 September 2006), para. 32.

535 Annex I, Afghanistan Compact.

536 See in general Economic and Social Council, Commission on Human Rights, Report by the Special Rapporteur, Miloon Kothari, 'Adequate housing as a component of the right to an adequate standard of living', Addendum, Mission to Afghanistan (31 August–13 September 2003), UN Doc. E/CN.4/2005/64/Add.4 (8 February 2005).

537 The new court was created to replace the former and malfunctioning Property Court. See Presidential Decree No. 89 of 30 November 2003.

claims resolution has been extremely low.[538] Individuals were very reluctant to submit claims to the Court because of a lack of confidence in the judiciary and the impossibility of effectively implementing the Special Court's decisions as a consequence of wide-scale corruption.[539]

Despite the early adoption of emergency measures, the rehabilitation of the civil service still has a long way to go. In 2006, the Secretary-General acknowledged that the "nascent democratic institutions created by the Bonn process are not able to meet the basic needs of the population as a whole".[540] This short overview reemphasised the need to engage in a comprehensive reconstruction exercise covering all areas. It is fair to say that no progress can be made in civil administration if the judiciary is not effective, or if corrupt civil servants continue to be employed in the public sector. Capacity building within the civil administration should have been a priority in Afghanistan, as a precursor to the creation of democratic institutions.[541] The recently adopted Afghanistan Compact does contain new challenges and timelines for the Afghan Authorities, but the question remains whether the Government will be able to ensure the correct application of its decisions throughout the country.

4. *'De-ba'athification' of Iraqi Society*

Before the military intervention, Iraq had a civil administration which worked well on both the national and local levels.[542] All areas of civil administration were covered by the existing structures. According to Resolution 1483, the CPA was nevertheless asked by the Security Council to "promote the welfare of the Iraqi people through the effective administration of the territory". The UN's early reduction in numbers and the relocation of international staff following the suicide attack against UNAMI's headquarters in Iraq logically minimised the UN's involvement in the immediate post-conflict situation. The main challenge was to revitalise the existing structures, undermined by years of dictatorial interference. The 'de-ba'athification' undertaken by the CPA, which was aimed

---

538 For an extensive overview of the procedures see the assessment conducted by The Norwegian Refugee Council and UNHCR: 'A Guide to Property Law in Afghanistan' (2005).

539 Economic and Social Council, Commission on Human Rights, Report by the Special Rapporteur, Miloon Kothari, 'Adequate housing as a component of the right to an adequate standard of living', Addendum, Mission to Afghanistan (31 August–13 September 2003), UN Doc. E/CN.4/2005/64/Add.4 (8 February 2005), paras. 33–4.

540 Report of the Secretary-General, UN Doc. A/60/712–S/2006/145, *supra* note 152, para. 48.

541 Saikal, A., 'Afghanistan's weak state and strong society', in Chesterman, *et al., supra* note 5, p. 205.

542 Chesterman, S., 'Post-war relations between occupying powers and the United Nations', in Thakur, R. and Sidhu, W. P. S., *The Iraq Crisis and World Order: Structural, Institutional and Normative Challenges* (Tokyo / New York / Paris: United Nations University Press, 2006), p. 490.

at removing all Ba'ath Party members from the civil service,[543] had resulted in a partial breakdown of the administration.[544] As in the pervious cases, emergency measures were rapidly taken. Hospitals were re-equipped and restocked. Water and electricity installations had not suffered significantly from the military operation and were therefore equally swiftly restored to pre-war levels.[545]

In line with the UN's experience in Kosovo, a Claims Commission was set up under CPA rule to resolve property disputes.[546] The 'Iraq Property Claims Commission' was instituted to deal with property which had been seized by the former Ba'athist government officials. The statute of the commission contains very detailed provisions on the restitution of such property.[547] Although the Claims Commission process has been described as a failure,[548] by the end of May 2007 the Commission had nevertheless received 132,038 claims, 34,649 of which had already been decided at first instance.[549]

The 'de-ba'athification' undertaken by the CPA resulted in the removal from their positions of many senior officials, as well as teachers and doctors. They were also barred from future employment in the public sector. CPA advisors were put in charge of the ministries until the formation of the Interim Government, including the appointment of ministers, in September 2003.[550] However, the official institutions needed to be staffed by competent Iraqi civil servants. The most urgent need was thus to restore government services by appointing new civil servants to support the reconstruction process. Obviously, the coalition was not adequately prepared to undertake such comprehensive tasks. The CPA engaged

---

[543] CPA Order Number 1, 'De-Ba'athification of Iraqi Society', CPA/ORD/16 May 2003/01 (16 May 2003). For a critique, see Diamond, L., 'What Went Wrong in Iraq', in Fukuyama, F. (ed.), *Nation-Building beyond Afghanistan and Iraq* (Baltimore: John Hopkins University Press, 2006), p. 173.

[544] Report of the Secretary-General, UN Doc. S/2003/715 (17 July 2003), *supra* note 160, para. 68.

[545] *Ibid.*, paras. 63–65.

[546] Amended statute: CPA Regulation Number 12, 'Iraq Property Claims Commission', CPA/REG/23 June 2004/12 (23 June 2004).

[547] On the legality of the setting up of the commission, in light of the laws of occupation, see Sassoli, *supra* note 433.

[548] See e.g. Stigall, D. E., 'Courts, Confidence and Claims Commissions: the Case for remitting to Iraqi civil Courts the Tasks and Jurisdiction of the Iraqi Property Claims Commission', *The Army Lawyer* 30 (2005). The limited scope of the Commission *ratione temporis* has been criticised, since it accepted only claims for property confiscated under the Ba'athist regime between 17 July 1968, and 9 April 2003, *de facto* allowing only a limited number of claims from Jews, as the majority of them had departed before 1968 (see Perleman, A., 'Iraq Allows Jews To File Property Claims', *Forward – The Jewish Daily* (17 June 2005)).

[549] IMO, 'Iraq Property Claims Programme', iom-iraq.net/ipcp.html.

[550] Dobbins, J. *et al.*, *The UN's Role in Nation-Building: from the Congo to Iraq* (Santa Monica: Rand, 2005), p. 201.

in several reforms of the ministries. The Ministry of Atomic Energy, for instance, was dissolved and replaced by a Ministry of Science and Technology,[551] but it did not provide training for civil servants.[552] The take-over of the administration by the Iraqi institutions after the end of the occupation and the CPA's dissolution left the national ministries and the UN with the task of continuing to build local capacity for which no foundation had been laid by the CPA.

The UN in contrast has been actively involved in training programmes for civil servants. Despite its early staff reduction, the UN Country Team (consisting of all UN agencies and organisations active in Iraq, under the coordination of UNAMI) conducted over 300 training seminars and workshops between December 2004 and June 2005.[553] The capacity-building seminars were conducted in various fields, such as management and accountability in the civil service. However, in addition to its limited mandate, the worsening security situation severely limited the UN's capacity to engage actively in local capacity-building.

An overall assessment of the civil administration permits one to conclude that, although progress has been made in the restoration of public services and capacity-building within the civil service, mainly through the UN's activities, the lack of a general approach in the reconstruction of the civil administration has considerably limited significant achievements in that regard. The CPA's and UNAMI's limited mandates have proved inadequate. Although training programmes are still being conducted, there has been no significant progress. The May 2007 International Compact recognised that "the resolution of security and political challenges, good governance and the provision of basic services are pre-requisites for progress in all other areas".[554] The Compact equally includes a commitment by the Iraqi Government to formulate a comprehensive civil service reform programme, "including: [...] [a]dopting a merit-based hiring and promotion practices and clearly delineate the functions of agencies supervising the public service and capacity building".[555] The explicit mention of the Iraqi Government's commitments to the creation of a viable and competent civil service is unquestionably an indicator of the insufficiency of the current services offered by the public sector.

---

551 CPA Order Number 24, Ministry of Science and Technology, CPA/ORD/13 August 2003/24 (24 August 2003).

552 Besides the reform of civil servant salary scales in several ministries. See CPA Press Release, 'An Historic Review of CPA Accomplishments' (28 June 2004).

553 Report of the Secretary-General pursuant to paragraph 30 of Security Council Resolution 1546 (2004), UN Doc. S/2005/141 (7 Mar. 2005), para. 39 and Report of the Secretary-General pursuant to paragraph 30 of Resolution 1546 (2004), UN Doc. S/2005/373 (7 June 2005), para. 50.

554 Preamble, Iraq Compact.

555 *Ibid.*, Section 4.2.3.

B. *Economic Reconstruction*

The inclusion of economic aspects in comprehensive peace building missions is a very recent phenomenon in international law.[556] This addition can be seen as underlining a tendency to recognise the economic dimension of international peace and security.[557] The emergence of a 'comprehensive concept of security', including economic aspects, although apparent from the recently discussed cases, has however been criticised for its alleged lack of plausible causality between security and economic and social conditions.[558] We nevertheless favour the view that comprehensive peace-building missions require an all-inclusive approach, including economic aspects, for the reason that economic rehabilitation is closely interrelated with other aspects of peace-building, such as security.

It has been stressed that, in contrast to the other components of complex missions, there is no adequately defined legal framework under which economic reconstruction has to operate.[559] In the second part, we argued that international administrations are nonetheless to a certain extent bound by human rights standards and, depending on the case, also by the laws of occupation. These frameworks do not, however, provide a satisfactory structure for economic issues, although the laws of occupation have of course influenced the CPA's power to deal with certain (economic) issues. In the absence of a clear legal framework and mandate, the temporary character of post-conflict administration can be taken into account when wholesale modifications to the economic system are envisaged. The relevant Security Council resolutions likewise provide information on the limits of the administrations' or missions' competences in that field, although references with regard to economic reconstruction remain rather vague.

Re-creating a viable economy in states emerging from years of conflict necessitates the adoption of both short-term emergency measures and measures aimed at long-term objectives. The short-term measures are often intended to provide

---

556 Under the UNTAES administration for instance, economic issues were limited to employment only. See Smoljan, J., 'Socio-economic aspects of peacebuilding: UNTAES and the organisation, of employment in Eastern Slavonia', 10 *International Peacekeeping* 27 (2003).

557 See Boisson de Chazournes, L., 'Taking the International Rule of Law Seriously: Economic Instruments and Collective Security', *International Peace Academy Policy Paper* (October 2005). See on the legal basis for including economic aspects in reconstruction mandates: Perez, A. F., 'Legal Frameworks for Economic Transition in Iraq – Occupation under the Law of War vs. Global Governance under the Law of Peace', 18 *The Transnational Lawyer* 53 (2004–2005). For a critique on the interference of the Security Council in economic affairs, see Conte, A., *Security in the 21st Century: The United Nations, Afghanistan and Iraq* (Aldershot: Ashgate, 2005), p. 90.

558 Koskenniemi, M., 'The Police in the Temple Order, Justice and the UN: A Dialectical View', 6 *European Journal of International Law* 20 (1995).

559 Boisson de Chazournes, *supra* note 557, p. 9.

the basis for a swift re-launching of the economy by introducing a tax and customs system, establishing financial institutions and trust funds, providing small enterprises with adequate means to re-start their businesses and attracting foreign investments. The long-term agenda, often the transition to a market economy, is as important as the short-term measures. Organising efficient public spending while securing sufficient sources of income is essential in paving the way for domestic institutions to take over the economic component, after the withdrawal or reduction of international presence and funding. We will again focus on the emergency measures and the general approach taken in different cases, and highlight some of the specific dilemmas encountered, such as the issue of privatisation in Kosovo.

1. *Kosovo's Transition towards a Free-market Economy*

As a consequence of years of conflict and under-investment in industry and the damage caused by NATO's military intervention, the economic situation in Kosovo was very precarious at UNMIK's establishment. In addition, the departure of the Serbs from the administration had left the territory with no functioning financial system.[560] Economic reconstruction in Kosovo was very intrusive. The EU was charged with the economic component of the mission in Kosovo (Pillar IV 'economic reconstruction'), tasked with "[s]upporting the reconstruction of key infrastructure and other economic reconstruction".[561] The main aim was the establishment of a market-based economy, in line with the EU's expectations.[562] The EU's approach in Kosovo was based on the conclusions of the European Council in Copenhagen, which set out the economic conditions for membership of the EU, and those of the April 1997 Council of Ministers defining the conditions for contractual relations with the EU.[563] The EU's focus was placed on both the restoration of elementary public services and the privatisation of public companies.[564]

In the emergency phase, UNMIK issued a regulation permitting the unrestricted use of foreign currencies in transactions.[565] The Deutschmark was

[560] Report of the Secretary-General, UN Doc. S/1999/779, *supra* note 117, para. 16.

[561] SC Res. 1244, UN Doc. S/RES/1244 (1999), para. 11, g).

[562] Report of the Secretary-General of the United Nations Interim Administration Mission in Kosovo, UN Doc. S/1999/779 (12 July 1999), para. 103.

[563] European Commission, Kosovo (under UNSCR 1244) 2005 Progress Report, Doc. Nr. SEC (2005) 1423 (9 November 2005), p. 27.

[564] *Ibid.*

[565] UNMIK Regulation 1999/4 on the currency permitted to be used in Kosovo, UN Doc. UNMIK/REG/1999/4 (2 September 1999).

established as the official currency of the Kosovo institutions and agencies.[566] The Special Representative based this much contested decision[567] on the fact that the Deutschmark was already used in commercial transactions and that the Yugoslav Dinar would not be attractive to foreign investors.[568] Following the re-establishment of a customs administration and revenue collection,[569] UNMIK, in addition to the donor grants, added customs and tax revenues to its incomes in the emergency phase. The rehabilitation of the financial sector was seen as a priority in order to enhance economic reconstruction. UNMIK quickly established a 'Central Fiscal Authority' to oversee the management of the Kosovo Budget,[570] and a 'Supervisory Board for Payment Operations' and 'Banking and Payment Authority' to reorganise the banking and payment systems.[571] UNMIK equally adopted regulations on the creation of private enterprises and corporations, the international sale of goods and foreign investments, supplementary to the existing applicable legal framework.[572] By March 2001, the emergency economic reconstruction programme was considered to have come to an end, and the focus shifted towards long-term sustainability.[573]

The creation of an economically viable entity of course requires long-term engagements. In addition, the transformation from a weak socialist economy, with an artificially high level of employment in state-owned enterprises, to a free-market economy necessitates many transformations. The majority of state-owned enterprises and socially-owned enterprises were as such not viable in a

---

[566] UNMIK Administrative Direction 1999/2 implementing UNMIK Regulation 1999/4 of 2 September 1999 on the currency permitted to be used in Kosovo, UN Doc. UNMIK/DIR/1999/2 (4 October 1999).

[567] The decision was surprising considering the affirmation of the FRY's sovereignty over the Province. Many saw the introduction of a foreign currency as paving the way for Kosovo's independence.

[568] Kouchner, B., *Les Guerriers de la paix* (Paris: Editions Grasset & Fasquelle, 2004 – édition Le Livre de Poche), p. 310.

[569] UNMIK Regulation 1999/3 on the establishment of the customs and other related services in Kosovo, UN Doc. UNMIK/REG/1999/3 (31 August 1999).

[570] UNMIK Regulation 1999/16 on the establishment of the central fiscal authority of Kosovo and other related matters, UN Doc. UNMIK/REG/1999/16 (6 November 1999).

[571] UNMIK Regulation 1999/11 on exercising control over payments facilities and services, UN Doc. UNMIK/REG/1999/11 (13 October 1999) and UNMIK Regulation N° 1999/20 on the banking and payments authority of Kosovo, Doc. UNMIK/REG/1999/20 (15 November 1999).

[572] See for an overview of legislation in the commercial sector: United States Agency for International Development (USAID), 'Commercial Legal and Institutional Reform Assessment. Diagnostic Assessment Report for Kosovo' (September 2004).

[573] Report of the Secretary-General on the United Nations Interim Administration Mission in Kosovo, UN Doc. S/2001/218 (13 March 2001), para. 52.

market economy.[574] Privatisation was seen as one of the most urgent measures for transition towards a market economy.[575] There were nevertheless doubts about the conformity of the privatisation of public companies with UNMIK's mandate under Security Council Resolution 1244. This was the result of the maintenance of the Federal Republic of Yugoslavia's sovereignty over the Province, which several UNMIK lawyers interpreted as limiting the administration's capacity to engage in wide-scale economic reforms.[576] UNMIK nevertheless embarked on massive privatisations of these former state- and socially-owned enterprises.[577] It established a 'Kosovo Trust Agency'[578] to privatise 90 per cent of the total assets of these enterprises, and 50 per cent of socially-owned enterprises by the end of 2006.[579] The 'Kosovo Trust Agency' was charged with the administration and restructuring of these enterprises "as trustee for their owners". The Agency was also given a mandate to decide on their privatisation.[580] In line with the doubts raised by UNMIK lawyers, the establishment of the 'Kosovo Trust Agency' created strong opposition from the UN Legal Advisor and the Yugoslav institutions, which claimed that UNMIK ignored ownership over the assets of the enterprises, and lacked the legal capacity to engage in their privatisation.[581] The privatisation process was therefore delayed until 2004, when the Kosovo Trust Agency's mandate was redefined. The issue of the conformity of the privatisation with UNMIK's mandate stresses the importance of exit strategies, and a clear-cut mandate, as these will have a direct influence

---

[574] SRSG Michael Steiner explained that "We need to face reality and call a spade a spade. Most of Kosovo's socially owned enterprises are dinosaurs. Even if we had the capital needed to rebuild them – and we don't have it – we could not make viable enterprises out of them. It is time to acknowledge that the old economic approach has failed." (UNMIK Press Release, 'SRSG Michael Steiner Addresses University of Pristina on Privatization', UN Doc. UNMIK/PR718 (18 April 2002). See also Perritt, H. H., 'Economic Sustainability and Final Status for Kosovo', 25 *University of Pennsylvania Journal of International Economic Law* 270 (2004).

[575] Demekas, D. G., Herderschee, J. and Jacobs, D. F., *Kosovo: institutions and policies for reconstruction and growth* (Washington, DC: International Monetary Fund, 2002), p. 19.

[576] For a critique on this interpretation, see Perritt, *supra* note 574.

[577] See *in extenso* on privatization in Kosovo, and the question of the FRY's sovereignty, Zaum, *supra* note 75, pp. 155–168.

[578] See UNMIK Regulation 2002/12 on the Establishment of the Kosovo Trust Agency, UN Doc. UNMIK/REG/2002/12 (13 June 2002) and UNMIK Regulation 2005/18 amending UNMIK Regulation no. 2002/12 on the establishment of the Kosovo Trust Agency, UN Doc. UNMIK/REG/2005/18 (22 April 2005).

[579] European Commission, 'Kosovo (under UNSCR 1244) 2006 Progress Report', Doc. Nr. SEC (2006) 1386 (8 Nov. 2006).

[580] UNMIK Press Release, 'SRSG Michael Steiner Addresses University of Pristina on Privatization', UN Doc. UNMIK/PR718 (18 April 2002).

[581] Report of the Secretary-General on the United Nations Interim Administration Mission on Kosovo, UN Doc. S/2004/71 (26 Jan. 2004), para. 35.

on the capacity of the international administration effectively to implement its mandate. In this particular case, the temporary nature of authority could have been interpreted as an argument against the privatisation. This, however, would not have been in conformity with the EU's expectations, which had in addition been incorporated in a report of the Secretary-General.[582] In addition, according to Security Council Resolution 1244, the EU was mandated to "develop a comprehensive approach to the economic development and stabilization of the region affected by the Kosovo crisis, including the implementation of a Stability Pact for South Eastern Europe with broad international participation in order to further the promotion of democracy, economic prosperity, stability and regional cooperation".[583] This broadly formulated mandate gave the EU a large margin of appreciation in the reconstruction process. It should nevertheless be stressed that the mentioned Secretary-General's report, which envisaged the establishment of a market-based economy, could not in any event have superseded the Security Council Resolution.

Despite several setbacks, economic reconstruction in Kosovo has been described as a success,[584] although the private sector has apparently been more successful than the public sector.[585] Sustainability however is another issue,[586] and needs to be carefully monitored by international actors after withdrawal of the international administration. Kosovo has been and still is very dependent on external funding.[587] Kosovo's uncertain final status surely delayed many decisions in the economic reconstruction process mainly through the inability of Kosovar institutions to access international markets. In addition, the presence of international staff is economically advantageous, but the declining international presence since 2006 has already led to deflation.[588]

2. *'Timorising' the Economy*

As was the case in Kosovo, the physical infrastructure and economy of East Timor had suffered severely from underinvestment and damage following the years of occupation and conflict.[589] This had resulted in a complete collapse

---

[582] Report of the Secretary-General, UN Doc. S/1999/779, *supra* note 117, para. 103.

[583] SC Res. 1244, UN Doc. S/RES/1244 (1999), para. 17.

[584] Demekas, Herderschee and Jacobs, *supra* note 575, p. 21.

[585] Cf. European Commission, 'Kosovo (under UNSCR 1244) 2006 Progress Report', Doc. Nr. SEC (2006) 1386 (8 Nov. 2006), p. 20.

[586] *Ibid.*

[587] Dobbins *et al.*, *supra* note 521, p. 126.

[588] European Commission, 'Kosovo (under UNSCR 1244) 2006 Progress Report', Doc. Nr. SEC (2006) 1386 (8 Nov. 2006), p. 19.

[589] Apart from damage to buildings, the departure of Indonesian militias had led to damage to telephone cables and communication towers, and approximately half of the livestock were

of the public and private sectors and massive unemployment.[590] Even without the damage resulting from the conflict, East Timor had always been one of the poorest regions in Asia, with approximately 90 per cent of the population living in rural areas and depending on agriculture.[591] As with the judiciary, East Timor lacked competent managers to run the business sector, as the majority of them were Indonesian and had left East Timor.[592] Economy did not however enjoy a high priority in the UN mission,[593] as other key areas such as security and humanitarian issues had been identified as main concerns.[594]

The World Bank conducted a 'needs assessment' for the reconstruction in East Timor in which it identified several urgent measures to be taken by UNTAET.[595] Like UNMIK, UNTAET rapidly established a central fiscal authority,[596] a central payments office[597] and a new taxation regime,[598] as proposed in the World Bank's assessment report. UNTAET equally established the US dollar as the official currency of East Timor,[599] while permitting unrestricted use of foreign currencies in transactions.[600] In order rapidly to rehabilitate small business, the World Bank launched the 'Small Loans Enterprise Programme' to grant loans to small companies.[601] A 'Trust Fund for East Timor' was set up under the Bretton

slaughtered. See Dobbins, *et al., supra* note 550, p. 157. For an assessment of the pre-ballot economic situation of East Timor see Valdivieso, L. M., Endo T., Mendonça, L. V., Tareq, S. and López-Mejía, A., *East Timor: Establishing the Foundations of Sound Macroeconomic Management* (Washington: International Monetary Fund, 2000).

590 Report of the Secretary-General on the United Nations Transitional Administration in East Timor, UN Doc. S/1999/738 (26 July 2000), para. 24.

591 World Bank, 'Report of the joint assessment mission to East Timor', Summary (8 December 1999), para. 9.

592 *Ibid.*, para. 11.

593 Harrington, *supra* note 516.

594 Dahrendorf *et al., supra* note 496, para. 23.

595 World Bank, 'Report of the joint assessment mission to East Timor', Summary (8 December 1999), para. 13.

596 UNTAET Regulation 2000/1 on the establishment of the central fiscal authority of East Timor, UN Doc. UNTAET/REG/2000/1 (14 January 2000).

597 UNTAET Regulation 2000/6 on the establishment of a central payments office of East Timor, UN Doc. UNTAET/REG/2000/6 (22 January 2000).

598 UNTAET Regulation 2000/12 on a provisional tax and customs regime for East Timor, UN Doc. UNTAET/REG/2000/12 (8 March 2000).

599 UNTAET Regulation 2000/7 on the establishment of a legal tender for East Timor, UN Doc. UNTAET/REG/2000/7 (22 January 2000). Since November 2003, Timor-Leste started to replace the USD with equivalent Timorese coins. See Timor-Leste and Development Partners Meeting, 'Poverty Reduction and Economic Growth Background Document' (3–5 December 2003).

600 UNTAET Regulation 2000/2 on the use of currencies in East Timor, UN Doc. UNTAET/REG/2000/2 (14 January 2000).

601 Report of the Secretary-General, UN Doc. S/2000/738, *supra* note 493, para. 26.

Woods Institutions and funded several other projects, leading to the reparation of the infrastructure in several areas, such as agriculture, education and port facilities.[602] The Trust Fund could however only be used to allocate money to certain projects, whereas the mission was in need of funds to pay the salaries of civil servants. The slowness of payments into the Trust Fund and a strict UN policy of separating costs to support the mission from costs to assist the population led to many frustrations among UNTAET officials and the Timorese.[603]

In contrast to the very liberal interpretation of UNMIK's mandate, UNTAET officials on the contrary did not engage in wide-scale economic reforms. In light of its 'local capacity building' or 'Timorisation' approach, and because of the already mentioned problem of land registration and ownership which was left to the East Timorese Government, UNTAET decided not to engage in massive privatisation.[604] The question of the Timor Gap, which is essential in view of the country's natural resources, was equally only *negotiated* by UNTAET. The Treaty was eventually signed by the Timorese Government on the day of East Timor's independence.[605]

Although UNTAET managed fairly well to kick-start the economy upon arrival[606] and to create a functioning tax administration,[607] much of the immediate economic growth was attributed to international presence[608] and international donor assistance. Consequently, the departure of UN staff resulted in the stabilisation of growth. East Timor remains one of the poorest countries in Asia, with high poverty and unemployment rates.[609] Problems equally persist with regard to vague property rights. The sustainability and viability of East Timor's economy without foreign funding is uncertain and can be guaranteed only by

[602] For an overview of international assistance in this area see Parliament of Australia, Senate, Foreign Affairs, Defence and Trade Committee, 'Final report on the inquiry into East Timor' (1999–2002), Chapter 2.

[603] Chesterman, *supra* note 104, pp. 194–195.

[604] Caplan, *supra* note 467, p. 150.

[605] Timor Sea Treaty between the Government of East Timor and the Government of Australia, 2003 ATS 13 (20 May 2002).

[606] Dobbins *et al., supra* note 550, p. 175 and da Costa, H. and Soesastro, H., 'Building East Timor's Economy', in Soesastro, H. and Subianto, L. H. (eds.), *Peace Building and State Building in East Timor* (Jakarta: Centre for Strategic and International Studies, 2001), p. 16.

[607] Valdevieso, L. M. and Lopez-Mejia, A., 'East Timor: Macroeconomic Management on the Road to Independence', 38 *Finance and Development – An IMF Quarterly Magazine* (2001).

[608] da Costa, H. and Soesastro, H., 'Building East Timor's Economy', in Soesastro and Subianto, *supra* note 606, p. 11 and Valdevieso and Lopez-Mejia, *supra* note 607.

[609] Report of the Secretary-General, UN Doc. S/2007/134, *supra* note 490, para. 48.

an effective economic strategy with regard to East Timor's natural resources.[610] This was however, not addressed by UNTAET.

3. *Afghanistan: A 'Free for All Policy'?*

The economic situation of Afghanistan was as disrupted as those in the other cases, following decades of conflict, a military intervention and years of under-investment. Physical infrastructure was in addition heavily damaged. The international community's very limited role in the economic sector will be obvious throughout this analysis. In line with the 'light footprint' approach, the UN was mandated only to assist the provisional institutions in implementing the Bonn Agreement, and to coordinate UN activity in the field. Economic reconstruction was left to the initiative of donor states willing to fund individual economic reconstruction programmes. Immediate measures were taken by the Afghan Transitional Administration to re-launch the economy, such as the passing of a new law on private investments and the introduction of a new currency, the 'New Afghani'.[611] Obviously, the first signs of economic rehabilitation emerged in the reconstruction and services sectors.[612] Besides these relatively limited emergency measures, international efforts have focussed on emergency physical reconstruction. A World Bank administered 'Afghanistan Reconstruction Trust Fund' was created, in cooperation with the Islamic Development Bank and UNDP, in order to manage donor contributions and support investment activities.[613] The channelling of donor funds was however very problematic. Due to the absence of a UN-led administration, there was major disagreement between donors, the Afghan Transitional Administration and UNAMA on payments by donors. The Afghan Minister of Justice advocated the direct payment out of the funds to the administration or the Trust Fund, instead of through the UN, but third states were reluctant to direct funds straight to the inexperienced Afghan Transitional Administration.[614] UNAMA mediated between donors, UN agencies and the Afghan Transitional Administration, leading to a compromise on

610 Hasegawa, S., 'International Donor Coordination, Civil Society and Natural Resource Management', *Conference 'Beyond Cold Peace: Strategies for Economic Reconstruction And Post Conflict Management* (27–28 October 2004), and da Costa, H. and Soesastro, H., 'Building East Timor's Economy', in Soesastro and Subianto, *supra* note 606, p. 16.

611 Report of the Secretary-General, The situation in Afghanistan and its implications for international peace and security, UN Doc. A/57/487–S/2002/1173 (21 October 2002), para. 7.

612 Dobbins *et al., supra* note 521, p. 144.

613 Report of the Secretary-General, UN Doc. A/57/410, *supra* note 523, paras. 14–6.

614 The 'by-passing 'of the national authorities was based on the need to deliver emergency relief throughout the country, and to allow the Afghan Transitional Authority to build institutional capacities first. See Kapila, M., 'The Role of Donors in Afghanistan', in Azimi, Fuller and Nakayama, *supra* note 85, p. 206. See also on this issue: Dahrendorf, N. *et al.*, 'A Review of

the establishment of 'secretariats' led by UN agencies. These secretariats were to cooperate with the different ministries of the Afghan Transitional Administration on the use of funds for the implementation of sectoral programmes.[615]

Opium production remains the first and most serious impediment to economic reconstruction. In the aftermath of the foreign military intervention poppy cultivation increased enormously.[616] Despite clear and straightforward commitments by the official institutions on the prohibition of poppy cultivation,[617] the 2007 UN World Drug Report contained alarming figures on such cultivation in Afghanistan. The report showed that it had reached its highest peak in 2006, increasing Afghanistan's share in global opium production from 65 to 82 per cent.[618] The incapacity of the official institutions to deal with this issue is caused by several factors. First of all, the government's territorial control does not extend to all provinces, some of them being still largely ruled by local commanders.[619] Secondly, Afghanistan's limited economic growth and poverty have not facilitated the conversion of poppy cultivation to other agricultural products.[620] A third cause, until recently,[621] was the reluctance of the military to assist in crop destruction, whilst national law enforcement capacity is insufficient to tackle the issue.[622] Next to poppy cultivation, the security situation is the second cause of slow economic growth. Businessmen, for instance, cannot freely transport goods throughout the country. In addition, in the emergency

---

Peace Operations: A Case for Change: Afghanistan (A Snapshot Study)', *Conflict Security & Development Group, King's College London* (10 March 2003), para. 109.

615 See on the funding in Afghanistan, Costy, A., 'The Dilemma of Humanitarianism in the Post-Taliban Transition', in Donini, A., Niland, N. and Wermester, K. (eds.), *Nation-Building Unravelled? Aid, Peace and Justice in Afghanistan* (Bloomfield: Kumarian Press, 2004), pp. 152–153.

616 Poppy cultivation was indeed prohibited under the Taliban regime. The institutional breakdown in the aftermath of the conflict inevitably resulted in a vacuum leading to its resurgence.

617 See 'Statement of President Hamid Karzai on the Prohibition of Poppy Cultivation' (26 September 2002).

618 United Nations Office on Drugs and Crime, '2007 World Drug report' (2007).

619 The central government has nevertheless quite ironically relied on regional structures to address the issue (Dobbins *et al., supra* note 521, p. 145).

620 Farhang, A., 'Afghanistan: Questions/Comments' and Kapila, M., 'The Role of Donors in Afghanistan', in Azimi, Fuller and Nakayama, *supra* note 85, p. 230. Recently, several projects have been dedicated to conversion of poppy cultivation to other agricultural products, such as the pomegranate. For example, the USAID funded programme – the 'Alternative Development and Agriculture Program' – offers financial aid for the export of fruit. See: Robinson, S., 'Pomegranates: A Fruitful Trade', *Time* (5 December 2007).

621 In October 2008, the decision was taken to authorize NATO forces to attack opium factories and to help combating drug trafficking. See BBC News, 'NATO to attack Afghan opium labs' (10 October 2008), news.bbc.co.uk/1/hi/world/south_asia/7663204.stm.

622 Dobbins *et al., supra* note 521, p. 145.

phase, much of the foreign financial assistance was directed to emergency relief programmes, while only one major long-term project – the (re)construction of a highway – had been implemented.[623]

Economic reconstruction had been seriously underestimated by the international community. States were apparently convinced that reconstruction could be undertaken with a small amount of money, while it is now clear that what Afghanistan needed was a sort of 'Marshall plan'. In addition, it has generally been acknowledged that international donors were not as generous as in the other cases.[624] The concept of 'lead countries', in charge of specific areas of reconstruction, although no lead country was in charge of economic aspects, has also contributed to the low achievement with regard to the economic reconstruction in Afghanistan. Instead of adopting a comprehensive approach aimed at sustainable economic growth, the international community's involvement relied on a selective programmatic approach by international donors.[625] This has certainly created short-term growth in a few sectors, such as construction, but could not lead to the creation of a viable economy. What has been called the Afghan 'free for all' policy in economic reconstruction[626] can only confirm the need for all-inclusive post-conflict reconstruction mandates.

4. *Iraq: Economic Reconstruction and the Laws of Occupation*

The economic situation in Iraq was as disastrous as in the previous cases, although strict international sanctions had contributed even more to the deterioration of the Iraqi economy. Oil exports under the 'oil-for-food programme' had nevertheless created a small economic growth since its inception.[627] The UN was responsible for "promoting economic reconstruction and the conditions for sustainable development, including through coordination with national and regional organizations, as appropriate, civil society, donors, and the international financial institutions".[628] Security Council Resolution 1483 equally entrusted the CPA with a limited economic mandate, part of which was the management of the oil-for-food programme which was transferred to the CPA. The CPA nevertheless opted for a broad interpretation of its mandate and included several

---

[623] Saikal, A., 'Afghanistan's weak state and strong society', in Chesterman *et al., supra* note 5, p. 205.

[624] *Ibid.*, p. 206 and Kapila, M., 'The Role of Donors in Afghanistan', in Azimi, Fuller and Nakayama, *supra* note 85, p. 205.

[625] Ali, N., 'An Introduction to the Economic Reconstruction of Afghanistan', *Institute for Afghan Studies* (May 2003).

[626] Dobbins *et al., supra* note 521, p. 206.

[627] Report of the Secretary-General, UN Doc. S/2003/715 (17 July 2003), *supra* note 160, para. 84.

[628] SC Res. 1483, UN Doc. S/RES/1483 (2003), para. 8, e).

highly questionable economic measures in light of the mandate it was endowed with. The CPA based the adoption of regulations on economic issues on a very extensive interpretation of Security Council Resolution 1483, in which the authority was asked to "promote economic reconstruction and the conditions for sustainable development" and on its obligation to "provide for the effective administration",[629] combined with a report of the Secretary-General in which it was stated that "the development of Iraq and the transition from a centrally planned economy to a market economy needs to be undertaken".[630] The report from the Secretary-General cannot however in any case constitute an adequate legal basis for such measures, although one could argue that it represents a reliable interpretation of relevant Security Council resolutions. Despite the legal controversies on the conformity of this regulation with the international laws of occupation, and relevant Security Council Resolution, it has been claimed that these measures were undoubtedly mandatory to allow economic reconstruction in Iraq.[631]

With the aim of improving initial economic recovery the CPA took immediate measures, such as the distribution of new banknotes,[632] in cooperation with the World Bank and the IMF.[633] The Iraqi Central Bank was re-established as an independent authority in July 2003.[634] The CPA equally created an 'Iraqi Trade Bank' to "facilitate the importation and exportation of goods and services to and from Iraq in order to benefit the economy of Iraq".[635] In accordance with Security Council Resolution 1483, an Iraqi Development Fund, in essence intended to assemble the revenues from oil export, was set up under the auspices of the

---

629 Cf. the considerations of, for example, CPA Order 29 on Trade Bank of Iraq: "Recognizing the CPA's obligation to provide for the effective administration of Iraq, to ensure the well being of the Iraqi people and to enable the social functions and normal transactions of every day life, [...] Acting in a manner consistent with the Report of the Secretary General to the Security Council of July 17, 2003, concerning the need for the development of Iraq and its transition from a non-transparent centrally planned economy to a market economy characterized by sustainable economic growth through the establishment of a dynamic private sector, and the need to enact institutional and legal reforms to give it effect."

630 Report of the Secretary-General, UN Doc. S/2003/715 (17 July 2003), *supra* note 160, para. 84.

631 Wolfrum, *supra* note 159, p. 23. See also Report of the Secretary-General, UN Doc. S/2003/715 (17 July 2003), *supra* note 160, para. 84.

632 This is generally seen as authorised under the laws of occupation. See Benvenisti, *supra* note 450, p. 16.

633 Report of the Secretary-General, UN Doc. S/2003/715 (17 July 2003), *supra* note 160, para. 85.

634 CPA Order Number 18, 'Measures to Ensure the Independence of the Central Bank of Iraq', CPA/ORD/07 July 2003/18 (7 July 2003).

635 CPA Order Number 19, 'Trade Bank of Iraq', CPA/ORD/17 July 2003/20 (17 July 2003).

Iraqi Central Bank, while the CPA was authorised to make use of its revenues.[636] However, it should be stressed that the allocation of the exploitation of and responsibility over natural resources to the CPA is exceptional, as the laws of occupation provide only that the occupier is the administrator and usufructuary of public facilities.[637] The relevant Security Council resolution nevertheless authorised the use of the Fund only *in the interest of the local population.*

Perhaps the most controversial CPA measure was Order 39 on 'Foreign Investment'.[638] Whilst replacing all former Iraqi investment laws, the order allowed for the unlimited participation of foreign investors in the Iraqi economy, except in the oil sector. This foreign investment policy was subsequently extended to the banking sector.[639] Although the Central Bank of Iraq was to give clearance for a take-over in the banking sector, the CPA regulation limited refusal to only when the acquisition would "substantially lessen competition, jeopardize the financial soundness of the bank or endanger the interests of the bank's depositors".[640] This resulted in the complete take-over by foreign investors of six Iraqi banks by November 2003, leading to much criticism from Iraqis.[641] Although it is evident that the Bush Administration favoured a neo-liberal economic model in Iraq,[642] neither the laws of occupation nor Security Council Resolution 1483 provide a clear-cut legal basis for these kinds of intrusive transformation. In addition, the temporary nature of the CPA's authority should, in light of the ambiguities in the Security Council Resolution, have prevailed.

Although several promising measures were taken upon the CPA's take-over of the administration, reconstruction of the Iraqi economy can hardly be called a success. The CPA for instance failed to anticipate the effects of local traditions on its policy. The Authority had for example developed a tax system, but it

636 CPA Regulation Number 2, 'Development Fund for Iraq', CPA/REG/10 June 2003/02 (10 June 2003).

637 See Langenkamp, R. D. and Zedalis, R. J., 'What Happens to the Iraqi Oil? Thoughts on Some Significant, Unexamined International Legal Questions Regarding Occupation of Oil Fields', 14 *European Journal of International Law* 417 (2003). Contra: Perez, A. F., 'Legal Frameworks for Economic Transition in Iraq – Occupation under the Law of War vs. Global Governance under the Law of Peace', 18 *The Transnational Lawyer* 53 (2004–2005).

638 CPA Order Number 39, 'Foreign Investment (Amended by Order 46)', CPA/OR/20Dec 2003/35 (19 December 2003).

639 CPA Order Number 40, 'Bank Law with Annex A **Rescinded per Order 94 Sec 3**', CPA/OR/19 Sep 2003/40 (19 September 2003).

640 *Ibid.*, Art. 22, para. 3.

641 Murphy, M. A., 'A "World Occupation" of the Iraqi Economy? How Order 39 Will Create a Semi-Sovereign State', 19 *Connecticut Journal of International Law* 451 (2003–2004).

642 This had been proposed in a USAID classified document, which was leaked to the press. See King, N. Jr., 'Bush Officials Draft Broad Plan for Free-Market Economy in Iraq', *The Wall Street Journal* (1 May 2003).

completely lacked the capacity to collect tax revenues as the Iraqi economy was strongly cash-based.[643] Lack of consultation with Iraqi Interim structures has been a recurrent criticism of the CPA's work in this field. The adoption of intrusive measures, which go far beyond the promotion of economic reconstruction, was seen by many Iraqi officials as 'market fundamentalism'.[644] In addition to the growing suspicion on the United States' objectives, the main aim of the highly contested measure – foreign investment – was not achieved at all, except in the banking sector.[645] The CPA's liberal economic agenda was too important to be dealt with by an occupying force, which is limited by the legal framework of the laws of occupation, even with an extended Security Council mandate.

C. *Security Sector Reform: Building National Law Enforcement and Defence Capacity*

The most important characteristic of the security aspect of peace-building missions and post-conflict administrations is the multiplicity of the actors involved. The (foreign) military are often the primary actors in the re-establishment of law and order, as their presence on the ground in the very early post-conflict stage enables them to uphold the rule of law, based either on a *de facto* power[646] or, depending on the cases, a *de jure* power in accordance with the laws of occupation. Maintaining a secure environment is essential for a successful and sustainable reconstruction process. The re-establishment of law and order has to be a priority in post-conflict situations, as the ability rapidly to create a secure environment is an essential pre-condition to engaging in other reconstruction activities. In addition, the ability to restore law and order is indispensable for the international or national transitional administration's credibility and legitimacy.[647]

Throughout this analysis, we will continue to draw attention to the interrelation between various components. The security situation is a recurrent obstruction to progress in various fields. The swift restoration of a secure environment is also

---

643 United States Institute of Peace, 'The Coalition Provisional Authority's Experience with Economic Reconstruction in Iraq: Lessons Identified', *USIP Special Report 138* (April 2005), p. 13.

644 *Ibid.*

645 *Ibid.*

646 Stahn, C., 'Justice under Transitional Administration: Contours and Critique of a Paradigm', *Houston Journal of International Law* 2005 (27), p. 316.

647 Dodge, T., *Iraq's Future: The aftermath of regime change*, Adelphi Paper 372 (London: Routledge 2005), p. 9.

one of the main concerns of the population in post-conflict societies.[648] The rehabilitation of the security sector, commonly referred to as Security Sector Reform (SSR), has become one of the major challenges in peace-building mandates.[649] Although the concept of SSR has only very recently emerged in international literature, it is in our view a common denominator for various challenges when dealing with post-conflict reconstruction. It comprises the role and function of international police and defence forces in a post-conflict environment, the creation of a national law enforcement and defence capacity, and the 'disarmament, demobilisation, and reintegration' (DDR) of former military forces and militias.[650] The judiciary has sometimes been included in Security Sector Reform.[651] However, we view the reconstruction of the judiciary as a separate component in peace-building missions, although we acknowledge the close connection between the two. Judicial reconstruction nevertheless responds to different imperatives, and should not therefore be included in the security sector.[652]

Although UN missions in the past were usually accompanied by unarmed UN Police Officers (CIVPOL) to monitor the local police forces, CIVPOL officers in post-conflict peace-building missions have been put in charge of law and order. Kosovo and East Timor represent the first cases in which international police officers have been fully in charge of maintaining law and order.[653] Local capacity-building is of course one of the main aims of the civil component in post-conflict reconstruction missions, but has to be linked with the international security presence, as international police and defence forces will be in charge of maintaining law and order until local capacity is sufficient to take it over. This section will therefore both compare the policies for the creation of law enforcement and defence capacity in the territories, and establish the connection between civilian and military components.

---

648 See for example in Afghanistan: AIHRC, 'A Call for Justice, A National Consultation on Past Human Rights Violations in Afghanistan' (2004), pp. 16–17.

649 See the external study mandated by the UN Peacekeeping Best Practices Section of the Department of Peacekeeping Operations: Rees, E., 'Security Sector Reform (SSR) and Peace Operations: "Improvisation and Confusion" from the Field' (March 2006).

650 See for an extended list of key tasks: Schnabel, A. and Ehrhart, H.-G., 'Post-Conflict Societies and The Military: Challenged and Problems of Security Sector Reform', in Schnabel, A. and Ehrhart, H.-G. (ed.), *Security Sector Reform and Post-Conflict Peacebuilding* (Tokyo / New York / Paris: United Nations University Press, 2005), pp. 7–8.

651 *Ibid.*, p. 7 and OECD, 'Security System Reform and Governance', *A DAC Reference Document* (2005).

652 Cf. Rees, E., 'Security Sector Reform (SSR) and Peace Operations: "Improvisation and Confusion" from the Field', UN Peacekeeping Best Practices Section of the Department of Peacekeeping Operations (March 2006).

653 Although the majority of UNTAET CIVPOL officers were still unarmed upon arrival. See Caplan, *supra* note 467, p. 51.

1. *Kosovo: Re-establishing Law and Order*

As in other areas described elsewhere, Kosovo was left with no functioning police force.[654] The Security Council had explicitly mandated UNMIK to "[maintain] civil law and order, including establishing local police forces and meanwhile through the deployment of international police personnel to serve in Kosovo".[655] In the aftermath of NATO's intervention, and despite the presence of 20,000 KFOR troops since 12 June 1999[656] to ensure public order and safety until the international civil presence could take responsibility for this task,[657] the security situation deteriorated substantially because of wide-spread arms possession, looting, arson, revenge killings by Kosovo Albanians and cross-border incursions by the Yugoslav army.[658] The military presence was not capable of re-establishing law and order in the immediate post-conflict phase, notwithstanding joint efforts by KFOR and the international police force to patrol the whole of the territory.[659] KFOR did manage to complete the withdrawal of the Yugoslav forces from Kosovo within a few days after its arrival.[660]

The security situation in Kosovo remained precarious throughout the early years of UNMIK's presence.[661] Conflicting interpretations of KFOR's policing mandate by the different national contingents[662] and KFOR's over-broad focus on the military aspects of the mission and lack of preparation for dealing with policing activity[663] have been advanced as reasons for KFOR's incapacity to halt the escalating violence in Kosovo. In addition to this, the malfunctioning and ethnically biased judiciary often resulted in the immediate release of suspects arrested by either KFOR or CIVPOL. Although the only civilian detention facility was run by international police forces in the emergency phase,[664] CIVPOL could not prevent the release of suspects by the judiciary. In view of the deteriorating

---

654 O'Neill, W. G., *Kosovo: An Unfinished Peace* (Boulder / London: Lynne Rienner Publishers, 2002), p. 99.

655 SC Res. 1244, UN Doc. S/RES/1244 (1999), para. 11, i).

656 Williams, G. H., *Engineering Peace. The Military Role in Postconflict Reconstruction* (Washington: United States Institute of Peace, 2005), p. 126.

657 SC Res. 1244, UN Doc. S/RES/1244 (1999), para. 9, d).

658 Report of the Secretary-General, UN Doc. S/1999/779, *supra* note 117, para. 5 and Report of the Secretary-General, UN Doc. S/2000/177, *supra* note 474, para. 25.

659 Chesterman, *supra* note 104, p. 117.

660 A few days before the timetable established under the MTA. See Military Technical Agreement between the International Security Force ("KFOR") and the Governments of the Federal Republic of Yugoslavia and the Republic of Serbia, UN Doc. S/1999/682 (9 June 1999).

661 Report of the Secretary-General, UN Doc. S/2002/62, *supra* note 481, para. 22.

662 Caplan, *supra* note 467, p. 49.

663 Dahrendorf, N. *et al.*, 'A Review of Peace Operations: A Case for Change: Kosovo', *Conflict Security & Development Group, King's College London* (10 March 2003), paras. 45–6.

664 Report of the Secretary-General, UN Doc. S/1999/987, *supra* note 468, para. 27.

emergency situation in Kosovo and the already mentioned ineffective judiciary, KFOR decided to create its own detention system. As it was mandated by the Security Council to maintain law and order, and considering its distinct command structure, KFOR assumed the power to arrest and detain suspects.[665] In our view, and despite criticism of this working method,[666] the laws of occupation do in fact provide a useful framework for these types of situation. As a former human rights advisor to the Special Representative of the Secretary-General puts it, "UNMIK and KFOR should have declared martial law. If ever the conditions justified emergency rule, Kosovo from June to December 1999 was it".[667] In addition, the Special Representative of the Secretary-General issued executive detention orders to remedy the failures of the judicial system, based on the derogations provided for in the various human rights instruments.[668] The executive detention orders were rightly criticised, not because of their legality, but because of the absence of any mechanism for reviewing extra-judicial detentions based on executive orders. A Detention Review Commission was finally established for that purpose.[669] The Commission was designed for only a three-month period, which was not renewed. Its task has since then been taken over by the Kosovar Supreme Court.

The ineffectiveness of the military to rapidly re-establish law and order has nevertheless to be combined with the inability to rely on an international police force in the first few months, therefore placing the burden of maintaining law and order exclusively on the military presence. KFOR's presence remained an essential part of UNMIK's law enforcement strategy. KFOR troops were responsible for control over several regions in Kosovo, until CIVPOL's capacity enabled it to

---

665 See UNMIK Press Release, Statement on the right of KFOR to apprehend and detain, UN Doc. UNMIK/PR/7 (4 July 1999): "In accordance with United Nations Security Council resolution 1244 (1999) of 10 June 1999, KFOR has the mandate and responsibility to ensure both public safety and order as well as civil law and order until the United Nations Interim Administration Mission in Kosovo (UNMIK) itself can take full responsibility for maintaining civil law and order in Kosovo. In performing this task, KFOR has the right to apprehend and detain persons who are suspected of having committed offences against public safety and order, including the commission of such serious offences as murder, rape, kidnapping or arson, or war crimes." See also Hartmann, M. E., International Judges and Prosecutors in Kosovo: A New Model for Post-Conflict Peacekeeping, *United States Institute of Peace Special Report 112* (October 2003), p. 5.

666 OSCE Mission in Kosovo, 'Report 6: Extension of Custody Time Limits and the Right of Detainees: The Unlawfulness of Regulation 1999/6' (29 April 2000).

667 O'Neill, *supra* note 654, p. 75.

668 UNMIK Press Release, Background Note on Zeqiri Detention, UN Doc. UNMIK/PR/394 (18 October 2000).

669 UNMIK Regulation 2001/18 on the establishment of a Detention Review Commission for extra-judicial detentions based on executive orders, UN Doc. UNMIK/REG/2001/18 (25 August 2001).

take over that responsibility. The deployment of CIVPOL officers throughout the territory, in order to perform basic police services and observe the Kosovo borders, was very slow. The sluggish deployment had to do with many factors. The UN as such did not plan the police mission until after the end of NATO's intervention,[670] while the recruitment of civilian police officers is by definition time-consuming as, in contrast to the military, there are no national contingents prepared to engage rapidly in international missions. Although CIVPOL's total authorised strength had been established at around 4,700, this number had not yet been reached fifteen months after UNMIK's establishment.[671] The quality of CIVPOL officers has also been questioned.[672] Gradually, CIVPOL assumed responsibility over the entire territory, although, as of January 2002, CIVPOL was still in control of only four of the five Kosovo regions.[673]

In his first report, the Secretary-General considered the re-establishment of a functioning, credible, professional and impartial police force, while providing an interim police force, to be essential for UNMIK's law and order strategy.[674] UNMIK and the OSCE rapidly engaged in the creation of a Kosovo Police Service (KPS) and the training of Kosovo Police Officers. The OSCE training included new candidates, as well as former Kosovo police officers who had been expelled during Serb control over the territory. Soon after its arrival, the OSCE started rehabilitating the existing police academy, and the first training session began as early as September 1999.[675] Further training sessions were organised for managerial positions and trainers. The transfer of law enforcement responsibility from the international police to the Kosovo Police Service was envisaged to take place in several steps, from the partial transfer of patrol responsibility to the full transfer of senior management posts.[676] After the gradual take-over of managerial functions by the Kosovo Police Service, full authority was finally transferred to the local police force in January 2006.[677]

The 'Disarmament, Demobilisation, and Reintegration' programme (DDR) in Kosovo, with particular emphasis on the demilitarisation of the Kosovo Liberation Army (KLA/UCK), was seen as one of the most urgent issues to be dealt

[670] Caplan, *supra* note 467, p. 56.

[671] It was equally acknowledged that, even at full deployment, the UN police force would not be sufficient to maintain law and order. See Report of the Secretary-General, UN Doc. S/1999/987, *supra* note 468, para. 29.

[672] O'Neill, *supra* note 654, p. 100.

[673] Report of the Secretary-General, UN Doc. S/2002/62, *supra* note 481, para. 31.

[674] Report of the Secretary-General, UN Doc. S/1999/779, *supra* note 117, para. 60.

[675] Report of the Secretary-General, UN Doc. S/1999/987, *supra* note 468, para. 30.

[676] Report of the Secretary-General, UN Doc. S/2001/218, *supra* note 573, para. 35.

[677] Except for the ethnically divided town of Mitrovica. See Report of the Secretary-General on the United Nations Interim Administration Mission on Kosovo, UN Doc. S/2006/45 (25 January 2006), para. 29.

with in the security sector. UNMIK's approach consisted of creating a special 'force' for former KLA/UCK members, the 'Kosovo Protection Corps' (KPC).[678] The DDR programme started as early as June 1999 with the signature of an agreement between KFOR and the KLA/UCK Commander Hacim Thaci.[679] The 'Kosovo Protection Corps' was not a police force, nor was it responsible for law enforcement; its main task was to assist in disaster and rescue operations, demining activities and humanitarian assistance in isolated areas. The KPC functioned under the authority of the Special Representative, whereas KFOR remained in charge of the operational direction of the Corps. The KPC was in fact a *sui generis* response to the demilitarisation of the KLA/UCK, as Kosovo could not possess a national defence force. Although many of the former KLA/UCK members in fact saw the KPC as the predecessor of a Kosovo national army,[680] the Force had no offensive or defensive functions. The Agreement signed between KFOR and the KLA nevertheless envisaged the transformation of the KPC into a national army – "on the lines of the US National Guard" – as part of a political process designed to determine Kosovo's future status.[681]

Although the Secretary-General considered the demilitarisation of the KLA/UCK as "successfully completed on 20 September (1999)",[682] it became clear that the majority of KLA/UCK members had not disarmed.[683] In addition, even the integrated KPC officers continued to pose serious security threats to the Province, as they engaged in illegal law enforcement activities.[684] Several murders and human rights abuses have equally been attributed to the Kosovo Protection Corps.[685] Moreover, while the focus was laid on the integration of former KLA/UCK members, parallel security structures continued to exist in Kosovo, in particular the so-called 'Bridge Watchers', composed of Kosovo Serbs in the district of Mitrovicë/Mitrovica, and the Serbian Ministry of Interior Affairs Police (*Ministarstvo Unutrasnih Poslova* – MUP). Their integration into

678 UNMIK Regulation 1999/8 on the establishment of the Kosovo Protection Corps, UN Doc. UNMIK/REG/1999/8 (20 September 1999).

679 KFOR, 'Undertaking of demilitarisation and transformation by the UCK' (20 June 1999).

680 O'Neill, *supra* note 654, p. 117.

681 KFOR, 'Undertaking of demilitarisation and transformation by the UCK' (20 June 1999), para. 25, b.

682 Report of the Secretary-General, UN Doc. S/1999/1250, *supra* note 469, para. 10.

683 The KPC was composed of 5,000 members, while 18,500 former KLA members had applied for it. See Caplan, *supra* note 467, p. 155.

684 Report of the Secretary-General, UN Doc. S/2000/177, *supra* note 474, para. 32.

685 O'Neill, *supra* note 654, pp. 120–121.

the Protection Corps has not been successful.[686] The problem of parallel security forces in Kosovo persisted throughout UNMIK's administration.[687]

Nevertheless, the overall effort in reforming the security sector was described as successful, especially with regard to the creation of a functioning professional police service.[688] The several obstacles described above could have been avoided by what we argued earlier: a clear legal framework in respect of law enforcement. The application of the laws of armed conflict and a clear affirmation of the scope of application of human rights law in the emergency phase could have avoided much discussion on the legality of both KFOR and UNMIK action in respect of law enforcement. In addition, lack of preparation to meet the challenges posed by such comprehensive missions,[689] as well as an erroneous assessment of the security situation after NATO's intervention, equally delayed the re-establishment of law and order. This was especially true with regard to the protection of Kosovo Serbs. In its 'Responsibility to Protect' report, the International Commission on Intervention and State Sovereignty emphasised the need to plan security measures before deployment, as 'revenge killings' are to a certain extent inherent in post-conflict societies where parts of the local populations have frequently been targeted for their membership of a social group, race or religion.[690]

2. *Ensuring Sustainability in East Timor*

Before UNTAET's arrival in East Timor, the Australian-led INTERFET force had been authorised under Security Council Resolution 1264 to restore peace and security following the outbreak of violence after the popular consultation.[691] We argued in our second part that INTERFET was legally bound by the laws of occupation as the only applicable legal framework for its operations. In line with that analysis, and considering that no civilian authority existed to deal

---

686 OSCE Mission in Kosovo, Department of Human Rights and Rule of Law, 'Parallel Structures' in Kosovo (October 2003), p. 14.

687 For a recent overview see OSCE Mission in Kosovo, Department of Human Rights, Decentralization and Communities, 'Parallel Structures in Kosovo 2006–2007' (4 April 2007).

688 See International Crisis Group, 'An Army for Kosovo?', *Europe Report N° 174* (28 July 2006), p. 3.

689 Cf. paras. 118 *et s.*, Brahimi Report, *supra* note 175.

690 International Commission on Intervention and State Sovereignty, *supra* note 17, para. 5.8: "In post-conflict situations, revenge killings and even 'reverse ethnic cleansing' frequently occur as groups who were victimized attack groups associated with their former oppressors. It is essential that post-intervention operations plan for this contingency before entry and provide effective security for all populations, regardless of origin, once entry occurs. There can be no such thing as 'guilty minorities' in the post-intervention phase. Everyone is entitled to basic protection for their lives and property."

691 SC Res. 1264, UN Doc. S/RES/1264 (1999), para. 3.

with detainees, INTERFET created an emergency system to provide detainees with a temporary review process. A Detainee Management Unit (DMU) was created in October 1999. The INTERFET Detainee Ordinance indicated that it would apply Indonesian law and international humanitarian law, although Australia denied the *de jure* application of the Geneva Conventions.[692] By January 2000, at the handover of its detention-related functions to CIVPOL, the Detainee Management Unit had reviewed 60 detention cases. This emergency military regime permitted the swift restoration of peace and security, under a clear legal framework, emphasising in our view the necessity to apply international humanitarian law in the emergency phase. This approach should indeed prevail in the immediate post-conflict situation, as upon UNTAET's deployment security and law and order had already been normalised.[693] UNTAET's military component was integrated within the UN structure, and therefore fell within the Special Representative's responsibility. The transfer from INTERFET to the UNTAET military force was uncomplicated,[694] as six of the seven battalions were simply transferred to the new military force. The transfer was finalised in February 2000.[695]

Consistently with Security Council Resolution 1272, UNTAET deployed a UN civilian police force in order to re-establish law and order in East Timor. By January 2000, CIVPOL was present in all 13 districts,[696] although the force was composed of only 400 officers. In the same month, CIVPOL took over responsibility for arrest and detention from the INTERFET force.[697] Nevertheless, the overall reaction to CIVPOL's deployment has been rather negative. First of all, CIVPOL's transition from UNAMET – the UN mission deployed prior to UNTAET *inter alia* to oversee the popular consultation – to UNTAET was difficult, as the existing UNAMET police force had been criticised for its poor performance.[698] In addition, disagreement on whether the officers should be armed, inadequate resources, and unqualified staff contributed to the slow deployment of the civilian police force.[699] UNTAET's military component therefore continued to handle policing activities until the full deployment of CIVPOL.

Gradually, local police capacity was being bolstered though UN police officers who were in charge of both maintaining law and order and the training of the East Timor Police Force. This had not been planned by the UN Department

[692] For an extensive overview of the functioning of the DMU see Kelly, *supra* note 362.
[693] Report of the Secretary-General, UN Doc. S/2000/53, *supra* note 491, para. 14.
[694] Despite some logistical problems: Smith and Dee, *supra* note 496, p. 67.
[695] Report of the Secretary-General, UN Doc. S/2000/738, *supra* note 493, para. 51.
[696] Report of the Secretary-General, UN Doc. S/2000/53, *supra* note 491, para. 50.
[697] *Ibid.*, para. 45.
[698] Smith and Dee, *supra* note 496, pp. 74–75.
[699] *Ibid.* and Dahrendorf *et al.*, *supra* note 496, paras. 74–75.

of Peacekeeping Operations (DPKO), and it took some time for UNTAET to select trainers from within CIVPOL. Although the first cadets from the East Timor Police Service graduated in July 2000,[700] there was at that time no overall framework for the creation of a national police force. The legal framework for the East Timor Police Force, as well as for the Police Academy, was adopted only in August 2001.[701] The expected total strength of approximately 3,000 police officers was reached only in September 2003, more than a year after Timor-Leste's independence.[702] The Timorese Government therefore had to rely on the successor missions to enhance the capacity of the national police force. Under UNOTIL's mandate, 71 complementary training courses were conducted for the Timorese national police, training in total 2,556 Timorese police officers.[703] In addition, the current mission, UNMIT, deployed 1,070 international police officers in December 2006 to help restore and maintain law and order.[704]

The creation of the East Timor Defence Force was part of UNTAET's DDR programme, aimed at employing former FALINTIL members, the military wing of the political party FRETILIN. Although the Secretary-General had proposed the creation of a DDR programme in October 1999, its initiation had to wait for the creation of the East Timor Defence Force in January 2001.[705] The training of the East Timor Defence Force effectively started only in May 2001,[706] while East Timor's independence was scheduled just a year later. The main cause of this delay was the East Timorese leadership's view that the country would not need a defence force.[707] In addition, UNTAET's mandate did not explicitly include the creation of a national defence force, while many had expected the voluntary demobilisation of the FALINTIL.[708] The FALINTIL was finally disbanded in February 2001 with the creation of the East Timor Defence Force. The major-

---

700 Report of the Secretary-General, UN Doc. S/2000/738, *supra* note 493, para. 45.

701 UNTAET Regulation 2001/22 on the establishment of the East Timor police service, UN Doc. UNTAET/REG/2001/22 (10 August 2001).

702 Report of the Secretary-General on the United Nations Mission of Support in East Timor, UN Doc. S/2003/944 (6 October 2003).

703 End of mandate report of the Secretary-General on the United Nations Office in Timor-Leste, UN Doc. S/2006/251 (20 April 2006), para. 22.

704 Report of the Secretary-General on the United Nations Integrated Mission in Timor-Leste (for the period from 9 August 2006 to 26 January 2007), UN Doc. S/2007/50 (1 February 2007), para. 29.

705 See Report of the Secretary-General, UN Doc. S/1999/1024, *supra* note 310 and UNTAET Regulation 2001/1 on the establishment of a defence force for East Timor, UN Doc. (31 January 2001).

706 Interim report of the Secretary-General on the United Nations Transitional Administration in East Timor, UN Doc. S/2001/436 (2 May 2001), para. 32.

707 Dahrendorf *et al., supra* note 496, paras. 58–59.

708 Smith and Dee, *supra* note 496, p. 80.

ity of former FALINTIL members were integrated into the emerging Defence Force, whereas the remaining ex-combatants were helped through the 'Falintil Reinsertion Assistance Programme', led by the International Organisation for Migration.[709] The lack of capacity-building within the force can easily be illustrated by the severe security crisis in February 2006, when approximately 400 members of the armed forces demonstrated in front of the President's office, demanding a response to a petition submitted to him on alleged discrimination in promotions. The failure to respond adequately to the upheaval resulted in a decision by General Ruak to dismiss 591 soldiers, almost 40 per cent of the Force. President Gusmão acknowledged that the measure had "failed to address the root causes of the problems within the F-FDTL". He additionally requested the Secretary-General to authorise the deployment of civilian advisers to assist with capacity-building in the field of police and defence,[710] which was thus included in the follow-up mission's mandate.[711]

In addition to the upheaval in February–March 2006, the overall security situation in East Timor remains extremely precarious.[712] Nevertheless, when assessing the efficiency of maintaining law and order, in particular in the emergency phase, the rapid deployment of INTERFET and its capacity swiftly to restore a secure environment clearly were a success.[713] UNTAET's achievements with the creation of a national police force are however mixed. The Timorese police force is still embryonic, and lacks sufficient managerial experience, as well as adequate resources.[714] Despite the problems with regard to CIVPOL deployment, which are in fact similar to those faced by UNMIK, and the need to be addressed at the UN level, in our view the main shortcoming was the delay in boosting local capacity. The same mixed assessment is true with regard to the Defence Forces. The Secretary-General equally acknowledged such a failure: "[t]he absence of comprehensive regulatory frameworks has been particularly marked and detrimental in the security sector, where an overarching national defence policy, legislation, institutional mission statements and development plans, as well as mechanisms and procedures for coordination between the security forces, have all been absent".[715] The assessment can in our view only lead to the conclusion that

---

709 International Organisation for Migration, 'Falintil Reinsertion Assistance Programme. Final Evaluation Report' (June 2002), p. 10.

710 End of mandate report of the Secretary-General, UN Doc. S/2006/251, *supra* note 703, paras. 3–4.

711 SC Res. 1704, UN Doc. S/RES/1704 (2006), para. 4, f).

712 Report of the Secretary-General, UN Doc. S/2007/50, *supra* note 704, para. 30.

713 Dahrendorf *et al., supra* note 496, para. 43.

714 End of mandate report of the Secretary-General, UN Doc. S/2006/251, *supra* note 703, para. 27.

715 Report of the Secretary-General, UN Doc. S/2006/628, *supra* note 520, para. 33.

UNTAET withdrew too early. Despite continuing assistance from UNTAET's successor missions, the mandates of these follow-up missions are very limited and cannot on their own reinvigorate the security sector.

3. *Afghanistan: the Crucial Role of a Security Strategy*

The security situation in Afghanistan is characterised by the state's official institutions' inability effectively to preserve their monopoly on the use of force. Since the 1980s, the State had had no functioning national police force, while local commanders were in charge of providing security.[716] The security situation in Afghanistan was catastrophic, with no structure whatsoever. The Bonn Agreement had asked for the assistance of the international community in helping the new Afghan authorities to establish and train new Afghan security and defence forces. Following the 'light footprint' and 'lead nation' approaches, it was first recognised that the responsibility for security and law enforcement resided with the Afghans themselves, while international *assistance* in the security sector was delegated to lead nations. The establishment of a national army was led by the United States, police reform by Germany and the 'disarmament, demobilisation, and reintegration' programme by Japan. In addition to providing training to national police and defence forces, one of the major challenges was the restructuring of the Defence and Interior Ministries.

First, it should be noted that the international intervention in the country and the subsequent adoption of the Bonn Agreement resulted in a dual role for the foreign military presence. While the International Security and Assistance Force (ISAF) was mainly charged with the maintenance of security throughout the territory, the US-led military presence, 'Operation Enduring Freedom', continued to combat the remaining Taliban forces as self-defence in response to the 11 September attacks. The institutional framework for the international military presence and its mandate was set out in Annex I to the Bonn Agreement. That recognised "that the responsibility for providing security and law and order throughout the country resides with the Afghans themselves", but an international presence was deemed necessary "to assist the Afghan Interim Authority in the maintenance of security". Resolution 1683 at first limited the presence of the international forces to Kabul and its surroundings. The geographical limitation of ISAF's mandate was to ensure first a secure environment for the UN and the Interim Authority. However as early as 2002 requests were made to extend the military presence to other parts of Afghanistan, as was made possible under the Bonn Agreement.[717] The need to extend ISAF's mandate was reiterated by

---

[716] Jones, S. G., Wilson, J. M., Rathmell, A. and Riley, K. J., *Establishing Law and Order after Conflict* (Santa Monica: Rand Corporation, 2005), p. 66.

[717] Report of the Secretary-General, UN Doc. A/57/487–S/2002/278, *supra* note 2, para. 57.

the Secretary-General in July 2003.[718] Eventually, on 13 October 2003, the Security Council decided to expand ISAF's presence to outside Kabul,[719] but this was only achieved by the end of 2006.[720] In December 2002, the United States-led Coalition Forces and ISAF nevertheless also deployed a limited number of troops outside Kabul – the 'Provincial Reconstruction Teams'. These troops were charged with assisting reconstruction efforts, while maintaining security throughout the country.[721] The Teams equally provided a provincial platform for the training programme initiated by the United States.[722]

The expansion of ISAF throughout the territory was only completed more than four years after the Bonn Agreement. The limited deployment of international forces in the country from the start is one of the failures of the international community's involvement in Afghanistan. The possible threat to the peace process by not guaranteeing a security presence throughout the country had already been indicated by the Secretary-General in his March 2002 report on the situation in Afghanistan.[723] Drawing from the lessons of earlier peacekeeping operations, the international community should have been aware of the fact that effective control over the territory by a post-conflict administration is one of the preconditions for the success of the overall reconstruction process. Not only has the persisting control of local commanders hampered the official institutions in implementing reform in other areas; the international security force and the embryonic Afghan National Army have not been able to fill the security vacuum.[724]

The UN was not involved in the area of policing, although the Secretary-General decided to allocate one CIVPOL advisor to the UN mission. A special 'Law and Order Trust Fund for Afghanistan', managed by UNDP, was created to oversee and manage the physical reconstruction of police facilities and assure the payment of salaries.[725] A programme for the training of police officers was rapidly set up by Germany through the rehabilitation of the National Police

[718] Report of the Secretary-General, UN Doc. A/57/850–S/2003/754, *supra* note 530, para. 37.

[719] SC Res. 1510 UN Doc. S/RES/1510 (2003).

[720] Report of the Secretary-General to the UN Security Council on the Situation in Afghanistan and its Implications for International Peace and Security, UN Doc. A/61/799–S/2007/152 (15 March 2007), para. 33.

[721] Although their mandates have been interpreted differently. See Costy, A., 'The Dilemma of Humanitarianism in the Post-Taliban Transition', in Donini, Niland and Wermester, *supra* note 615, p. 57.

[722] Report of the Secretary-General, UN Doc. A/58/616, *supra* note 531, para. 34.

[723] Report of the Secretary-General, UN Doc. A/57/487–S/2002/278, *supra* note 2, para. 57.

[724] Cf. United States Institute of Peace, 'Unfinished Business in Afghanistan: Warlordism, Reconstruction, and Ethnic Harmony', *USIP Special Report 105* (April 2003).

[725] Report of the Secretary-General, UN Doc. A/57/487–S/2002/1173, *supra* note 611, para. 16.

Academy.[726] In October 2002, 80 trainers had already been trained; they in turn began the training of 1,549 police officers.[727] Nevertheless, as was the case with the creation of the Afghan National Army we will discuss below, the training programmes had not been supported by a wider institutional framework. The Presidential Decree on the establishment of a national police force in conjunction with a complete reform of the Ministry of Interior was signed only in April 2003. In spite of the necessary reforms, the training of police officers progressed slowly as it was Kabul-centred. The German Police Programme subsequently expanded its training sessions outside the capital, in cooperation with the Provincial Reconstruction Teams.[728] To date, there is still an insufficient number of police officers to maintain law and order, and the latest report of the United States Government Accountability Office considers that none of the Afghan police units is "fully capable".[729] In spite of the creation of a National Auxiliary Police and a National Civil Order Police, and short-term stop-gap measures to enhance police presence in the provinces, progress in the creation of an effective police force has been very poor.

The training and reform of the Afghan National Army began soon after the arrival of the international presence,[730] but obviously lacked an overall strategic framework. Next to parallel training initiatives undertaken by the United States, France and ISAF, no clear guidelines for recruitment were established, and the trained forces were often left with no instructions. The Defence Commission, established in order to propose a comprehensive framework for the rehabilitation and restructuring of the Afghan National Army, began its work only just before October 2002.[731] In December 2002 the President eventually signed a decree providing a legal basis for the reform of the Afghan National Army and of the Ministry of Defence.[732] The Defence Commission started implementing the Presidential Decree in January 2003. A first step towards the reform of the Ministry of Defence was taken in February of the same year, with a plan to provide a more ethnically-balanced ministry by the creation of several new

[726] Report of the Secretary-General, UN Doc. A/57/487–S/2002/278, *supra* note 2, para. 71.

[727] Report of the Secretary-General, UN Doc. A/57/487–S/2002/1173, *supra* note 611, para. 14.

[728] Report of the Secretary-General, The situation in Afghanistan and its implications for international peace and security, UN Doc. A/58/742–S/2004/230 (19 March 2004), para. 25.

[729] United States Government Accountability Office, 'Afghanistan Security: U.S. Efforts to Develop Capable Afghan Police Forces Face Challenges and Need a Coordinated, Detailed Plan to Help Ensure Accountability', Report Nr. GAO-08-883T (18 June 2008), p. 1.

[730] Report of the Secretary-General, UN Doc. A/57/487–S/2002/278, *supra* note 2, para. 62.

[731] Report of the Secretary-General, UN Doc. A/57/487–S/2002/1173, *supra* note 611, para. 12.

[732] Islamic Transitional Government of Afghanistan, Presidential Decree 174 (14 December 2002).

positions.[733] Implementation of the plan nevertheless started only in September 2003 and was "less sweeping than had been hoped".[734] In the meantime, various training programmes had been initiated. By July 2002 the United States had engaged in an 18-month training programme for an estimated 11,500 troops of the Afghan Army, while a parallel training programme was initiated by France, and the first battalion of the National Guard had been trained by ISAF.[735]

With regard to the existing armed groups, the Bonn Agreement provided that after the official transfer of power to the Interim Authority "all mujahidin, Afghan armed forces and armed groups in the country shall come under the command and control of the Interim Authority, and be reorganized according to the requirements of the new Afghan security and armed forces".[736] The risk of not entering into a parallel DDR programme when establishing national police and defence forces was immediately raised by the Secretary-General.[737] The DDR programme – the 'Afghan New Beginnings Programme' – was launched by UNAMA and the Afghan Administration only after the Tokyo Conference in January 2002. The programme was aimed at disarming 40,000 soldiers and reintegrating 35,000 former soldiers and combatants in the first year.[738] Japan was appointed as the lead nation for the implementation of the programme,[739] which programme was delayed until the necessary reforms in the Ministry of Defence had been undertaken, following the signature of two Presidential Decrees on the new Afghan Army and the reform of the Ministry of Defence in December 2002. The Ministry had indeed been charged with the collection of weapons, but former combatants and militias were reluctant to disarm, as they saw the current Ministry as representing factional instead of national interests.[740] Progress remained very slow, as the long-awaited reforms did not have the expected outcome, and could therefore not restore the population's confidence.[741] Despite

[733] Report of the Secretary-General, The situation in Afghanistan and its implications for international peace and security, UN Doc. A/57/762–S/2003/333 (18 March 2003), para. 27–!.

[734] Report of the Secretary-General, UN Doc. A/58/616, *supra* note 531, para. 20. See also International Crisis Group, 'Disarmament and Reintegration in Afghanistan', *ICG Asia Report No. 65* (30 September 2003), p. 6. The majority of the officials had remained in place or had simply been reassigned other posts within the Ministry.

[735] Report of the Secretary-General, UN Doc. A/56/1000–S/2002/737, *supra* note 523, para. 22.

[736] Section V, 1), Bonn Agreement.

[737] Report of the Secretary-General, UN Doc. A/57/487–S/2002/278, *supra* note 2, para. 63.

[738] Report of the Secretary-General, UN Doc. A/58/616, *supra* note 531, para. 22.

[739] Report of the Secretary-General, UN Doc. A/57/762–S/2003/333, *supra* note 733, para. 30.

[740] Report of the Secretary-General, UN Doc. A/57/850–S/2003/754, *supra* note 530, para. 26.

[741] Report of the Secretary-General, UN Doc. A/58/616, *supra* note 531, para. 20.

criticism, the reforms were deemed sufficient to start the pilot phase of the DDR programme in October 2003, which was expanded throughout other provinces in November and December of the same year.[742] The first phase of the programme was a failure. A very limited number of ex-combatants had effectively disarmed, while those who had opted for the reintegration packages were often subjected to extortion by local commanders, who in addition lacked the political will to encourage participation in the programme.[743] Disarmament and demobilisation were declared completed in October 2004 and April 2005 respectively, although illegal armed groups have still not been effectively disbanded.[744] The complete DDR programme eventually terminated in June 2006, when the last ex-combatant completed his reintegration.[745] In total, over 63,000 former combatants were disarmed, 62,000 were demobilised and almost 56,000 were reintegrated, while approximately 9,000 heavy weapons were collected.[746]

The failure rapidly to engage in a nation-wide demobilisation and reintegration programme from the start resulted in the persistence of parallel armed groups, especially in the provinces. The implementation of DDR programme could however have been feasible only if an effective National Army had been deployed throughout the country. Despite the relative success of certain parts of the DDR programme, many militias have still not been disarmed or dismantled.[747] In addition, the geographically limited presence of international troops, despite the many Provincial Reconstruction Teams who maintained a limited security presence, could not close the security gap, filled by local commanders. A recent report from the United States Government Accountability Office considers that, despite massive financial support by the United States, only 2 out of the 105 Army units are fully capable of performing their mission.[748] As a consequence,

[742] Report of the Secretary-General, The situation in Afghanistan and its implications for international peace and security, UN Doc. S/2003/1212 (30 December 2003), paras. 14–15.

[743] Report of the Secretary-General, UN Doc. A/58/742–S/2004/230, *supra* note 728, para. 24.

[744] Report of the Secretary-General, UN Doc. A/61/799–S/2007/152, *supra* note 720, para. 23.

[745] UNDP Press Release, 'DDR: Reintegration has been completed in time and within costs' (1 July 2006).

[746] Report of the Secretary-General, UN Doc. A/61/326–S/2006/727, *supra* note 534, para. 25.

[747] See for an overview International Crisis Group, 'Afghanistan: Getting Disarmament Back on Track', *Asia Briefing No. 35* (23 February 2005).

[748] United States Government Accountability Office, 'Afghanistan Security: Further Congressional Action May Be Needed to Ensure Completion of a Detailed Plan to Develop and Sustain Capable Afghan National Security Forces', Report Nr. GAO-08-661 (18 June 2008), p. 3.

the fiscal sustainability and effectiveness of the Afghan Army when the international presence withdraws is doubtful.[749]

The Afghanistan Compact reiterated the absolute necessity to engage in profound police and defence reforms. Although deadlines set *before* the Compact requested the completion of National Army reforms by 2005, the Compact postponed the time limit to the end of 2010, while agreeing on a continued ISAF presence, and its Provincial Reconstruction Teams, until the end of 2010, to "promote security and stability in all regions of Afghanistan, including by strengthening Afghan capabilities".[750] The same deadline was set for the creation of a "fully constituted, professional, functional and ethnically balanced Afghan National Police and Afghan Border Police with a combined force of up to 62,000 will be able to meet the security needs of the country effectively and will be increasingly fiscally sustainable".[751] Although training programmes had been initiated early, and progressed significantly throughout the country, the number of trained forces was not sufficient to enable the central government to address the deteriorating security situation. The lack of an effective strategy towards law enforcement[752] has clearly been detrimental to the reform of the security sector, and the overall security situation.

4. *Iraq: Demobilisation without Disarmament*

Security Council Resolution 1483 required the occupying powers to take on the effective administration of Iraq, "including in particular, working towards the restoration of conditions of security and stability and the creation of conditions in which the Iraqi people can freely determine their own political future".[753] The subsequent resolution also called "upon Member States and international and regional organizations to contribute to the training and equipping of Iraqi police and security forces", while authorising the deployment of a "multinational force under unified command to take all necessary measures to contribute to the maintenance of security and stability in Iraq".[754] The overall security situation in Iraq was disastrous and had not been anticipated.[755] The deteriorating security situation culminated in August 2003 when 22 people, including 15 UN staff members and Special Representative Sergio Vieira de Melo, were killed in one of

[749] International Crisis Group, 'Countering Afghanistan's Insurgency no Quick Fixes', *Asia Report No. 123* (2 November 2006).

[750] Annex I, Afghanistan Compact.

[751] Annex I, Afghanistan Compact.

[752] See 'Unfinished business in Afghanistan', *International Herald Tribune* (22 June 2008), p. 6.

[753] SC Res. 1483, UN Doc. S/RES/1483 (2003), para. 4.

[754] SC Res. 1511, UN Doc. S/RES/1511 (2003), paras. 13 and 16.

[755] Report of the Secretary-General, UN Doc. S/2003/1149, *supra* note 163, para. 23.

the most tragic attacks on UN personnel in the organisation's history, resulting in the complete withdrawal of almost all international personnel.

The UN mission was not mandated to take an active role in security issues. Although the idea of deploying an international civilian police force under UN leadership had been briefly envisaged, the idea has been quickly abandoned. The UN was asked only to "encourage international efforts to rebuild the capacity of the Iraqi civilian police".[756] In addition to the fact that under the laws of occupation maintaining law and order is the primary responsibility of the occupying forces, the Secretary-General feared that deploying an international police force would only lead to a parallel law enforcement system, detrimental to the re-establishment of security in Iraq.[757] It was therefore decided that the UN would limit its role to 'advising' the CPA and the Governing Council on the training curricula.[758] Unlike the Ministry of Defence, the Interior Ministry had not been disbanded, and could therefore be relied upon with regard to policing issues. Although an Iraqi Police Service existed at the CPA's arrival, it was ineffective and ill-equipped.[759] In addition, 'de-ba'athification' left both the police service and the Ministry without senior officials.

Training commenced rapidly, and in January 2004 the first 500 newly trained police officers graduated.[760] Training equally started for senior positions within the Police Force.[761] Police reform has nevertheless been described as inadequate, as the priority was placed upon quick training courses to enable trainees to replace foreign troops in the maintenance of law and order.[762]

One major blunder was the CPA's decision to disband the Iraqi army.[763] Soon after its arrival, the CPA decided on the dissolution of a wide list of formal entities, including the Army, the Air Force, the Navy, the Air Defence Force, and other regular military services, the Republican Guard, the Special Republican

---

756 SC Res. 1483, UN Doc. S/RES/1483 (2003), para. 8 (h).

757 Report of the Secretary-General, UN Doc. S/2003/715 (17 July 2003), *supra* note 160, para. 51.

758 *Ibid.*, para. 52.

759 Jones, Wilson, Rathmell and Riley, *supra* note 716, p. 44.

760 CPA Press Release, 'New Police Officers Join Ranks of Iraqis Protecting Iraq' (30 January 2004).

761 CPA Press Release, 'Thirty Iraqi Police Officers Graduate from Leadership Training Course' (29 May 2004).

762 Domisiewicz, R., 'Consolidating the Security Sector in Post-Conflict States: Polish Lessons from Iraq', in Ebnöter, A. H. and Fluri, P. H., *After Interventionism: Public Security Management in Post-Conflict Societies – From Intervention to Sustainable local Ownership* (Geneva: Geneva Centre for the Democratic Control of Armed Forces, 2005), p. 169.

763 See also Forman, J. M., 'Striking out in Bagdad. How Postconflict Reconstruction went Awry', in Fukuyama, *supra* note 543, p. 204. See also Kouchner, *supra* note 568, p. 437.

Guard, the Directorate of Military Intelligence and the Emergency Forces.[764] In complete disregard of experience gained in the other cases discussed, soldiers and Ministry employees were dismissed. This resulted in a complete security vacuum. In addition, since, obviously, these soldiers were neither demilitarised nor reintegrated into Iraqi society, this had serious consequences for both the economic and social status of former soldiers and arms possession throughout the country. Although some have argued that this decision was not as such unwise, as it could have facilitated the swift rehabilitation of the security sector,[765] the absence of an alternative security force to maintain security throughout the country resulted in a catastrophic deterioration in the already fragile security situation. The dissolution of the former Iraqi Army was not accompanied by a demilitarisation and reintegration programme, as the CPA opined that the defence institutions could not be transformed.[766] The advantages of a DDR programme were nevertheless obvious. Not only would it have permitted the security situation to be stabilised, but many of the former soldiers could also have been immediately reintegrated into the new Iraqi Army. The remaining former soldiers could then have been helped by a reintegration programme.

However, soon after the decision, the CPA somehow realised the disastrous effect of its decision, and announced both the start of recruitment procedures for the 'New Iraqi Army' and that former Iraqi career soldiers would receive a monthly interim stipend.[767] It immediately added that the responsibility for the creation of an entirely new Iraqi Defence Force would be left to the Iraqi Authorities. The Ministry of Defence had also been dissolved and needed to be rebuilt from scratch. Until the creation of a new ministry in March 2004, the CPA functioned as the *de facto* Ministry.[768] Recruitment and training centres were opened soon after the decision to create the 'New Iraqi Army'.[769] Many of the countries participating in the Multinational Force engaged in the training of Iraqi Security Forces. As in Afghanistan, the newly trained battalions nevertheless had a high desertion rate, caused by low salaries and the lack of a clear mission upon completion of the training programme. In addition, the engagement of the military in counter-insurgency activities led to revolt within the New Iraqi

---

764 CPA Order Number 2, 'Dissolution of Entities', CPA/ORD/23 May 2003/02 (23 May 2003).

765 See Jabar, F. A., 'Postconflict Iraq. A Race for Stability, Reconstruction, and Legitimacy', *United States Institute of Peace Special Report 120* (May 2004).

766 Dobbins *et al., supra* note 550, p. 198.

767 CPA Press Release, 'Good News for Iraqi Soldiers' (23 June 2003).

768 Jones, Wilson, Rathmell and Riley, *supra* note 716, p. 27.

769 CPA Press Release, 'First Steps towards Building the New Iraqi Army' (July 2003).

Army, which was not keen on fighting its fellow countrymen.[770] In order to fill the immediate security gap, an Iraqi Civil Defence Corps – renamed Iraqi National Guard – was set up, but its rapid deployment implied that personnel did not have time to complete their training.[771] Training is still continuing for the New Iraqi Army, although, as with the training of the police force, its effectiveness has not been great, as the majority of the courses were shortened to meet the continuing security challenge throughout the country.[772]

The CPA equally decided to adopt a DDR programme in June 2004, a few weeks before the announced, but questionable, 'end of occupation'.[773] The Order provides for either the integration of former soldiers in the Iraqi Armed Forces, or the retirement or reintegration into Iraqi society of individuals who did not enter the Armed Forces, the latter being limited to militias participating in the political process as identified by the CPA or the 'Transition and Reintegration Implementation Committee'. In August 2006, the Iraqi Government announced a National Reconciliation Plan, aimed at providing assistance to former members of dissolved entities.[774] The International Compact with Iraq further reiterated the Government's wish to implement the DDR programme contained in the National Reconciliation Plan.[775]

The lack of comprehensive planning seems to have been detrimental to the CPA's approach in the security sector. Obviously, the US-led coalition was not prepared to undertake reconstruction efforts with regard to the security sector. One of the key results of the lack of preparedness was the abovementioned decision taken by the military commander to completely disband the Iraqi military forces. Equally, the coalition did not prepare to take over police activity, which had been left to the unprepared and short-staffed military.[776] The impossibility of re-establishing law and order in Iraq is perhaps the biggest failure of the CPA and the Coalition military presence. The security vacuum created in the immediate aftermath of the military intervention can for a large part be attributed to the failure by the intervening powers to prepare for the reconstruction process

[770] Jones, Wilson, Rathmell and Riley, *supra* note 716, p. 6 and Dobbins *et al.*, *supra* note 550, p. 198.

[771] See Slocombe, W. B., 'Iraq's Special Challenge Security Sector Reform "Under Fire"', *Geneva Centre for the Democratic Control of Armed Forces* (2005). Slocombe was the security sector advisor to the CPA in 2003.

[772] Jones, Wilson, Rathmell and Riley, *supra* note 716, pp. 36 *et s.*

[773] CPA Order No 91, 'Regulation of Armed Forces and Militias within Iraq', CPA/ORD/02 June 2004/91 (6 June 2004).

[774] Government of Iraq, 'National Reconciliation Plan' (25 August 2006).

[775] Iraq Compact, section 3.2.3.

[776] Dobbins, J., 'Learning the Lessons from Iraq', in Fukuyama, *supra* note 543, p. 222. See also O'Brien, J. C., 'Lawyers, guns and money: Warlords and reconstruction after Iraq', 11 *University of California Davis Journal of International Law and Policy* 108 (2004–2005).

which would be needed afterwards. Similarly, the failure to integrate local officials within the newly created ministries from the start did not permit sufficient local capacity to be built.[777] As the Ministry of Defence had been dissolved in June 2003, and a full transfer of authority to national Institutions had been planned for June 2004,[778] the CPA and the Iraqis were left with little time to build a strong Ministry capable of guaranteeing effective control over the military.

The security situation remains the major concern in Iraq; in 2006, a total of 34,452 civilians were killed and 36,685 wounded.[779] The International Compact with Iraq restated the need to create functioning, professional and well-trained Police and Defence Forces,[780] although in the light of the worsening security situation it remains to be seen whether the Government, even with international assistance, will be able to succeed in this area.

D. *Emergency Relief, Refugees and Internally Displaced Persons*

The return of refugees and internally displaced persons (IDP) is an essential part of the reconstruction process. Often, years of conflict and international civil strife result in a massive refugee flow towards third countries, in addition to internally displaced persons who leave their homes or voluntarily or as a result of force. In addition to years of conflict and international civil strife, the cases under examination have all been preceded by military intervention and/or serious internal conflict. These interventions obviously have a direct influence on the increase in refugees and IDPs. In addition, after the end of a military intervention, third countries often engage in wide-scale forced repatriations of refugees residing in them.

This aspect of post-conflict reconstruction cannot be isolated from the other components. The return of refugees and IDPs necessitates not only immediate or emergency measures to provide adequate means for them to re-enter their country. In addition, the ability of international and national actors to provide a secure environment (physical safety), a functioning judiciary (legal safety) and a favourable economic environment (material safety)[781] will directly influence the

---

777 Jones, Wilson, Rathmell and Riley, *supra* note 716, p. 32.

778 Following the Agreement of 15 November 2003. See CPA and Iraqi Governing Council, 'The November 15 Agreement: Timeline to a sovereign, democratic and secure Iraq' (15 November 2003).

779 UNAMI, 'Human Rights Report (1 November–31 December 2006)', para. 6.

780 Iraq Compact, section 3.2.2.

781 Van Der Vaart, P., 'The Role of UNHCR in Helping Refugees Return ot Post-Conflict States', in Fischer, H. and Quenivet, N. (eds.), *Post-Conflict reconstruction: Nation- and/or State-Building* (Berlin: Berliner Wissenschafts-Verlag GmbH, 2005).

return of refugees and IDPs. Another factor that needs to be taken into account is their ability to return to their homes, which have often been destroyed, confiscated or are illegally occupied by others. This also underlines the necessity of creating claims commission relating to property rights, as discussed in the chapter on civil administration.

1. *Minorities in Kosovo*

Ensuring the safe and unimpeded return of all refugees and displaced persons to their homes in Kosovo was part of UNMIK's mandate under Security Council Resolution 1242.[782] The United Nations High Commissioner for Refugees (UNHCR) was in charge of Pillar I, the humanitarian component of UNMIK, responsible for emergency humanitarian assistance and the question of resettling refugees and IDPs. Besides the *return* of refugees and IDPs, UNHCR was also requested to ensure the *protection* of ethnic minority refugees.[783] UNHCR's role was mainly centred around the coordination of the activities of the main humanitarian agencies, including UNICEF, IOM, WFP, WHO, the EU's Humanitarian Office (ECHO), USAID, the IFRC and ICRC, as well as international and national NGOs.[784] Immediate emergency relief did not pose any real problems. As mentioned, essential services were quite rapidly restored, while humanitarian assistance has successfully been delivered throughout the country by either UN Agencies or local or international NGOs.[785] The return of refugees and IDPs was of course more complicated.

Prior to the NATO intervention, it had been estimated that that some 90 per cent of Kosovo Albanians were displaced from their homes.[786] By September 1999, the report of the Secretary-General presumed that some 770,000 refugees had already returned to Kosovo, while some 80,000 refugees were still in third countries awaiting return.[787] The number of IDPs was estimated at 500,000.[788] The problem however was that many houses had been damaged during and after the military operations, some of them beyond repair. Emergency measures, such as the carrying out of urgent repairs to houses, finding adequate shelters and

---

[782] Para. 11, k), SC Res 1244, UN Doc. S/RES/1244 (1999).

[783] Report of the Secretary-General, UN Doc. S/1999/779, *supra* note 117, para. 92.

[784] Estimated at approximately 300 in the early days of UNMIK's establishment (Report of the Secretary-General, UN Doc. S/1999/1250, *supra* note 469, para. 21).

[785] Report of the Secretary-General, UN Doc. S/2000/538, *supra* note 471, para. 66

[786] See International Crisis Group, 'Finding the Balance: The Scales of Justice in Kosovo', *ICG Balkans Report N° 134* (12 September 2002), p. 17.

[787] Report of the Secretary-General, UN Doc. S/1999/987, *supra* note 468, para. 9.

[788] By December of the same year, these numbers had been estimated at 810.000, 25,500 and 243.000 respectively (Report of the Secretary-General, UN Doc. S/1999/1250, *supra* note 469, para. 22).

providing food, were therefore necessary to ensure that the refugees and IDPs who had returned could be housed during the winter. UNHCR nevertheless successfully managed the emergency situation; the Humanitarian Assistance Pillar was phased out in June 2000, and was replaced by a UNHCR Humanitarian Coordinator.[789] After the emergency phase, UNMIK equally had to coordinate the return of refugees from third countries. While some of them had already voluntarily returned to Kosovo, UNMIK feared that it could not control wide-scale forced repatriations from host countries. UNMIK was particularly concerned that the return *en masse* of Kosovo Albanians would further strain the already precarious security, housing and economic situation, and limit the return of Kosovo Serbs. Several committees were therefore set up to coordinate and control returns from third countries.[790] UNMIK was nevertheless not able to postpone many of the planned forced repatriations.

The problem of IDPs in Kosovo stretches beyond the consequences of the NATO-led military intervention, emphasising the link between humanitarian issues and security.[791] In the summer of 1999, after UNMIK's arrival, a wave of revenge crimes caused the displacement of some 250,000 people, mainly from minorities.[792] The majority of these concerned Kosovo Serbs who had registered for assistance in Serbia.[793] As UNMIK was unable to ensure a secure and safe environment for minorities, especially Kosovo Serbs, UNHCR discouraged the return of minority populations in the early stages of the post-conflict period.[794] A 'Joint Committee on Return for Kosovo Serbs' in May 2000 and a 'Platform for Joint Action' to ensure a safe return for Kosovar minorities were established by UNMIK.[795] The first organised returns of Kosovo Serbs started in August 2001 following the identification of 'safe' sites and the organisation of 'go-and-see' visits by the Joint Committee on Return for Kosovo Serbs.[796] Despite these programmes, the continuing fragile security situation resulted in a very limited number of returns in the early years. The return of minorities progressed very slowly throughout the years. The resurgence of violence in March 2004, which mainly targeted Kosovo Serbs, resulted in the additional internal displacement

---

789 Report of the Secretary-General, UN Doc. S/2000/538, *supra* note 471, para. 66.

790 *Ibid.*, paras. 72–73.

791 Cf. Hochschild, F., 'It's Better to Leave, We Can't Protect You': Flight in the First Months of United Nations Transitional Administrations in Kosovo and East Timor', 17 *Journal of Refugee Studies* 286 (2004).

792 International Crisis Group, 'Finding the Balance: The Scales of Justice in Kosovo', *ICG Balkans Report N° 134* (12 September 2002), p. 3.

793 An estimated 150,000. Report of the Secretary-General, UN Doc. S/1999/987, *supra* note 468, para. 10.

794 Report of the Secretary-General, UN Doc. S/1999/1250, *supra* note 469, para. 23.

795 Report of the Secretary-General, UN Doc. S/2000/538, *supra* note 471, paras. 73–74.

796 Report of the Secretary-General, UN Doc. S/2001/926, *supra* note 482, paras. 36–38.

of minority community members. In these circumstances, many Kosovo Serbs questioned the sustainability of returning to Kosovo.[797] Following the events of March 2004, the returns process continued to progress very slowly throughout the years, and reconstruction of and compensation for the damage caused by the March 2004 incidents were finalised only by the end of June 2007.[798] In spite of the improvement of security in the Province, the poor economic conditions and the still uncertain final status of the Province continue to discourage many Kosovars from returning to their home country. Notwithstanding the success of emergency assistance provision,[799] neither UNMIK nor KFOR was able effectively to ensure the protection of minorities. Sustainable repatriations, especially of minorities, necessitate a favourable security, economic and legal environment. Even if the economic and legal environment somewhat exceeds UNMIK's direct control and necessitates long-term engagement, slow progress in the training of a national police force in conjunction with the sluggish deployment of CIVPOL and the inability of KFOR troops to maintain law and order seriously undermined the repatriation process. In addition, slow progress in the settlement of property claims, which in addition was not part of a framework programme on refugee returns, has not encouraged the return of minorities.[800]

2. *Refugees in West Timor*

The Security Council "welcomed" the "commitment of the Indonesian authorities to allow the refugees and displaced persons in West Timor and elsewhere in Indonesia to choose whether to return to East Timor, remain where they are or be resettled in other parts of Indonesia",[801] while emphasising Indonesia's responsibility to "take immediate and effective measures to ensure the safe return of refugees in West Timor and other parts of Indonesia to East Timor, the security of refugees, and the civilian and humanitarian character of refugee camps and settlements, in particular by curbing the violent and intimidatory activities of the militias there".[802] Humanitarian issues were handled by UNTAET's 'Humanitarian Assistance and Emergency Rehabilitation Pillar'. Again, UN effort concentrated on the coordination of the various UN and non-UN agencies and organisations engaged in humanitarian aid. UNTAET's emergency response to

---

[797] Report of the Secretary-General on the United Nations Interim Administration Mission in Kosovo, UN Doc. S/2004/348 (30 April 2004), paras. 21–23.

[798] Report of the Secretary-General, UN Doc. S/2007/395, *supra* note 487, Annex I, para. 45.

[799] Although some questioned this was due to the positive input of international agencies: see Dahrendorf *et al.*, *supra* note 663, para. 142.

[800] See on this aspect: Smit, R. A., 'Housing and Property Restitution and IDP Return in Kosovo', 44 *International Migration* 63 (2006).

[801] Para. 11, SC Res. 1272, UN Doc. S/RES/1272 (1999).

[802] *Ibid.*, para. 12.

the humanitarian crisis was adequate. Emergency aid could be delivered through various UN agencies. The rapid restoration of law and order by INTERFET forces and the smooth take-over by UNTAET's military component enabled the delivery of shelter packages and food and water supply in a timely manner.

In the aftermath of the 1999 popular consultation, an estimated 200,000 East Timorese were internally displaced.[803] In addition, 250,000 refugees were residing in West Timor,[804] although it has never been clear whether these refugees had voluntarily sought shelter across the border or had been forcibly displaced by pro-integration militias.[805] The problem of refugees in West Timorese camps was one of the major challenges for UNTAET. These camps were controlled by pro-integration militias, who obstructed UNHCR activity and influenced those who wished to return to East Timor. Despite the strong language used by the Security Council in Resolution 1272, Indonesia failed to meet its obligations. In October 2000, Indonesia announced it would no longer offer humanitarian aid to refugees.[806] The situation escalated in September 2000, when three UNHCR workers were murdered in the West Timorese camps, resulting in the total withdrawal from the camps of all UN personnel.[807] Eventually, the Indonesian Authorities decided to conduct a registration process to identify those refugees who wished to return to East Timor and those who wished to reside permanently in Indonesia. Approximately 98 per cent of the refugees in the West Timorese camps opted for permanent residence in Indonesia, although doubts were raised whether this high number was not the result of intimidation and misinformation by pro-Indonesian militias.[808] The cessation of food distribution by the Indonesian Authorities nevertheless led to an increase in the return of refugees in March 2002. At that time, the number of refugees residing in camps in West Timor was reduced to an estimated 50,000, while 202,000 had already returned to East Timor.

Refugees who had opposed East Timor's independence were generally well-received in East Timor, and their reintegration did not pose serious problems, but the population emphasised the need to engage in a national reconciliation and

---

[803] Strohmeyer, H., 'Making Multilateral Interventions Work: The U.N. and the Creation of Transitional Justice Systems in Kosovo and East Timor', 25 *The Fletcher Forum of World Affairs* 118 (2001).

[804] Report of the Secretary-General, UN Doc. S/2000/53, *supra* note 491, para. 29.

[805] McDowell, C. and Eastmond M., 'Transitions, State-building and the "residual" refugee problem: the East Timor and Cambodian repatriation experience', 8 *Australian Journal of Human Rights* 7 (2002).

[806] Report of the Secretary-General on the United Nations Transitional Administration in East Timor, UN Doc. S/2001/983 (18 October 2001), para. 36.

[807] Interim report of the Secretary-General, UN Doc. S/2001/436, *supra* note 706, para. 17.

[808] *Ibid.*, para. 45.

truth-finding exercise, while stressing that major crimes should result in criminal proceedings.[809] The problem of the refugee camps had not been completely solved by Timor-Leste's independence. By the end of 2002, all refugees remaining in the West Timorese camps lost their refugee status and became Indonesian citizens. Although sporadic returns still continue, the majority chose to stay in West Timor.[810] Another reason that has been advanced for the relatively slow return of refugees is UNTAET's failure to address the issue of land and property registration,[811] which to date has not been solved. In this environment, the return of refugees who have lost their property is not likely to increase. In addition, the political and security crisis of March 2006 led to the displacement of about two thirds of Dili's inhabitants due to fears for their safety and the destruction of their houses. Up to 80,000 people had fled to the countryside where they were sheltered by host families and in a very small number of camps.[812]

3. *Coordinating Returns in Afghanistan*

Te UN was explicitly mandated by the Security Council to coordinate all relief, recovery and reconstruction activities. The signatories to the Bonn Agreement had indeed asked the Security Council to authorise the establishment of a mission "to assist with the rehabilitation, recovery and reconstruction of Afghanistan, in coordination with the Interim Authority".[813] Before the military operation, the UN was already engaged in delivering humanitarian aid throughout the country.[814] Although aggravation of the disastrous humanitarian situation following military intervention could be prevented, approximately 70 per cent of the population was still dependent on international health assistance upon UNAMA's deployment.[815] Emergency aid was rapidly restored, but geographically limited, as the already described failure to maintain security in the Provinces had resulted in limited access of humanitarian agencies and NGOs. In addition to the security aspect, the much needed infrastructure for moving relief supplies to remote areas did not exist. The military was therefore rapidly employed in delivering humanitarian and

---

809 Interim report of the Secretary-General, UN Doc. S/2001/436, *supra* note 706, para. 18.

810 International Crisis Group, 'Managing Tensions on the Timor-Leste/Indonesia Border', *Asia Briefing N° 50* (4 May 2006), p. 2.

811 *Ibid.*, p. 2.

812 Report of the Secretary-General, UN Doc. S/2006/628, *supra* note 520, para. 26.

813 Annex III, Bonn Agreement.

814 Although no coordination whatsoever existed between UN agencies, States and NGOs. In addition, the UN's involvement was limited to providing emergency relief, without comprehensive framework. See Jazayery, L., 'The Migration-Development Nexus: Afghanistan Case Study', 40 *International Migration* 231 (2002).

815 Report of the Secretary-General, UN Doc. A/57/487–S/2002/278, *supra* note 2, para. 73.

reconstruction assistance through the creation of a Joint Civil-Military Operations Task Force.[816] In addition, the Provincial Reconstruction teams, already engaged in various physical reconstruction efforts, were invited to participate in delivering emergency relief. The UN equally created a 'Transitional Assistance Programme for Afghanistan', aimed at channelling humanitarian assistance and securing the Transitional Authority's participation in delivering humanitarian aid throughout the country.[817] Afghans nevertheless continue to be dependent on international aid. Factors external to the UN and Afghan authorities – six years of continuous drought followed by extensive flooding in 2005, again followed by drought – have hampered serious progress in the transition from emergency relief to long-term and sustainable recovery.

Upon UNAMA's deployment, an estimated 3.5 million Afghans were living as refugees in Iran and Pakistan, while approximately 1 million were estimated to be internally displaced.[818] Between March and November 2002, about 1.8 million Afghans returned from Pakistan and Iran under an 'assisted repatriation programme' organised by UNHCR and the Ministry of Refugees and Repatriation.[819] During 2002, more than 200,000 IDPs were helped to return to their homes.[820] A special 'Return Commission for the North' was established on 17 October 2002 to facilitate the return of Pashtun citizens who had been displaced by reason of ethnic violence in northern Afghanistan after the collapse of the Taliban.[821] Afghanistan rapidly engaged in negotiations with Iran and Pakistan to control the forced repatriation of refugees. Tripartite agreements were signed between UNHCR, Afghanistan, and Iran and Pakistan.[822] The high numbers of IDPs and refugees returning to their homes nevertheless decreased rapidly due to the deteriorating security situation and drought.[823] The number of returns continued to decline substantially throughout the years although many programmes have been set up to oversee and assist the repatriation and voluntary return of refugees.

Regardless of the natural disasters Afghanistan has faced, real progress in creating appropriate conditions for Afghans to recover from years of conflict was

---

816 See on this, Williams, *supra* note 656, p. 177.

817 Report of the Secretary-General, UN Doc. A/58/616, *supra* note 531, p. 58.

818 Report of the Secretary-General, UN Doc. A/57/487–S/2002/278, *supra* note 2, para. 81.

819 Report of the Secretary-General, UN Doc. A/57/410, *supra* note 523, para. 45 and UNAMA Fact Sheet, 'Refugee – IDP Return and Reintegration' (January 2003).

820 Report of the Secretary-General, UN Doc. A/56/1000–S/2002/737, *supra* note 523, para. 51.

821 Report of the Secretary-General, UN Doc. A/57/762–S/2003/333, *supra* note 733, para. 52.

822 *Ibid.*, paras. 51–53 and Report of the Secretary-General, UN Doc. A/57/850–S/2003/754, *supra* note 530, para. 48.

823 Report of the Secretary-General, UN Doc. A/57/850–S/2003/754, *supra* note 530, para. 47.

not made. Emergency relief was rightly a priority, but has been detrimental to long-term projects including ensuring viable conditions in which refugees and IDPs can return to their homes. While emergency aid appropriately provides essential and much-needed assistance to the population, it does not address the causes of the problem. The Afghan Administration, despite its rapid installation, did not control humanitarian aid in the emergency phase, and could not elaborate a comprehensive framework including transition from emergency measures to sustainable reconstruction.[824] Despite coordination efforts undertaken by UNAMA, critics argue that the various initiatives undertaken in parallel ways by donors, the military, NGOs and UN agencies were detrimental to enhancing national capacity to handle humanitarian and reconstruction issues.[825] This is however also partly owing to the lack of control outside the capital. Additionally, lack of security remains a major impediment to assisting the population in their needs. UN agencies have for instance not been able to provide aid in the southern provinces in recent years. With regard to refugees, the failure to address land property issues, deteriorating security and the incapacity of the Government to control and assist returning refugees and IDPs did not improve the situation of Afghans. While many of them are still returning, the economic and social conditions of the country remain a serious impediment.

4. *Iraq: the Prerequisite of Physical Safety*

In Iraq the UN was asked to "promot[e] the safe, orderly, and voluntary return of refugees and displaced persons".[826] The establishment of conditions in which refugees could return to Iraq remained the primary responsibility of the CPA as the occupying power. Emergency relief had been adequately managed in the immediate reconstruction phase. Various UN agencies were involved, and coordinated by UNAMI. Humanitarian aid restarted after the end of the major combat operations in March 2003, and cooperation with the Ministry of Trade was reactivated by June 2003.[827] The early reduction of international staff following the August 2003 attacks on the UN mission caused a serious delay in the implementation of several initiatives, although redeployment of UN staff in neighbouring countries permitted the limited continuation of emergency

---

824 McKechnie, A., 'Humanitarian Assistance, Reconstruction & Development in Afghanistan: A Practitioner's View', in Azimi, Fuller and Nakayama, *supra* note 85, pp. 223–225.

825 Cf. Costy, A., 'The Dilemma of Humanitarianism in the Post-Taliban Transition', in Donini, Niland and Wermester, *supra* note 615, p. 161. The input by the military was praiseworthy, although cooperation with NGOs seemed difficult and apparently resulted in duplication of efforts (Williams, *supra* note 656, p. 5).

826 SC Res. 1483, UN Doc. S/RES/1483 (2003), para. 8, b).

827 Report of the Secretary-General, UN Doc. S/2003/715 (17 July 2003), *supra* note 160, paras. 63–64.

assistance.[828] UN humanitarian presence to date remains limited and operations are mainly conducted from outside the country. The security situation, as well as continuing military operations, barred many international agencies, organisations and NGOs from conducting humanitarian and reconstruction activities. The UN therefore subcontracted many of its activities to local partners, while mandating national NGOs and consultants to oversee the implementation of the programmes.[829] Different ministries were directly involved in delivering humanitarian aid and promoting the return of refugees and IDPs, and training programmes were initiated to build local capacity to increase the involvement of the Iraqi Ministries in UN activities.[830]

The refugee and internally displaced persons situation in Iraq has evolved into a major humanitarian crisis. Prior to the conflict, approximately 400,000 refugees were located outside Iraq. The number of IDPs under the former regime was estimated at 1 million,[831] of whom 600,000 to 700,000 were Kurds in the north of Iraq.[832] Considering the catastrophic security conditions, UNHCR initially advised refugees not to return to the country, while assisting those who had nevertheless chosen to return. This UNHCR official position was maintained throughout 2004,[833] and in December 2006 UNHCR emphasised the impossibility for Iraqis from the Central and Southern Governorates to return to their homes.[834] The continuing violence throughout the country still does not permit the safe return of refugees or IDPs. UNHCR has estimated that since 2003 an *additional* 1.6 million Iraqis have become refugees.[835] By March 2007, 2 million refugees were still located outside Iraq; 1.9 million IDPs had not yet been resettled.[836] While resettlement is an essential part of solving the refugee

---

[828] Report of the Secretary-General, UN Doc. S/2003/1149, *supra* note 163, para. 34.

[829] Report of the Secretary-General, UN Doc. S/2005/373, *supra* note 553, para. 64. See also Qazi, A. J., 'UN's Role in Iraq', *Forced Migration Review* 5 (2007) (special issue).

[830] Report of the Secretary-General pursuant to paragraph 30 of Resolution 1546 (2004), UN Doc. S/2004/710 (3 September 2004), para. 47.

[831] Report of the Secretary-General, UN Doc. S/2003/715 (17 July 2003), *supra* note 160, para. 71.

[832] GA, Report of the United Nations High Commissioner for Human Rights and Follow-Up to the World Conference on Human Rights. The present situation of human rights in Iraq, UN Doc. E/CN.4/2005/4 (9 June 2004), para. 70.

[833] UNHCR, 'Iraq Operation Update' (9 March 2004).

[834] UNHCR, 'UNHCR Return Advisory and Position on International Protection Needs of Iraqis Outside Iraq' (18 December 2006).

[835] Report of the Secretary-General pursuant to paragraph 30 of Resolution 1546 (2004), UN Doc. S/2006/945 (5 December 2006), para. 36. Since the bombing in Samarra in February 2006 for instance, some 470,094 people have been forcibly displaced internally: UNAMI, Human Rights Report (1 November–31 December 2006), para. 13.

[836] Report of the Secretary-General pursuant to paragraph 30 of Resolution 1546 (2004), UN Doc. S/2007/126 (7 March 2007), para. 30.

and IDP crisis in Iraq, secure places in Iraq are limited and individuals remain vulnerable to sectarian violence. UNHCR therefore in December 2006 launched a programme to resettle many refugees outside Iraq.

The refugee and IDP question cannot indeed be solved without an overall improvement in security. Sectarian violence and military operations continue to cause the displacement of Iraqi citizens. Emergency relief cannot by itself offer a solution to the disastrous situation of refugees and IDPs. Although initial international financial assistance was generous, funds for emergency aid were rapidly exhausted as they had been envisaged only for the immediate post-conflict phase. The Iraqi Government proved to be unable to deal with the situation,[837] though, admittedly, building local capacity is hard to achieve under these circumstances. International assistance will nevertheless be needed for a much monger period than initially envisaged. The Compact with Iraq recognised the need for Iraqi leadership over humanitarian issues,[838] but the deteriorating situation will instead necessitate strong UN management of the humanitarian crisis.[839] Additionally, and although the need to settle property claims was rapidly raised as a precondition for sustainable returns,[840] no real progress has been made to date in that regard.

[837] Report of the Secretary-General on the United Nations Interim Administration Mission on Kosovo, UN Doc. S/2006/707 (1 September 2006), para. 28.

[838] Section 4.4.2. Iraq Compact.

[839] Cf. Report of the Secretary-General, UN Doc. S/2007/126, *supra* note 836, para. 34.

[840] Report of the Secretary-General, UN Doc. S/2003/715, *supra* note 160, para. 71.

Chapter 10

The Rule of Law and Judicial Reconstruction

Reforming the judiciary in order to ensure respect for the rule of law in post-conflict societies is a key element in their reconstruction. The strengthening of the rule of law has been supported by the international community for many years, and was part of post-conflict peace-building strategies prior to the most recent international administrations. Cambodia was in fact a major lesson in that regard. Rule of law elements, especially with regard to the creation of a functioning judicial system, were missing components in UNTAC's mandate.[841]

Re-establishing the rule of law in war-torn societies, often characterised by devastated institutions and infrastructure, an ethnically divided population, a lack of essential safety, and traumas resulting from decades of oppression and armed conflict, is without doubt an enormous task. Respect for the rule of law and the redefinition of the applicable laws in conformity with international human rights standards are thus paramount in rebuilding a country and the population's trust in the idea of a functioning democratic state.

The 'rule of law' is a broad and rather unclear concept.[842] International programmes containing rule of law elements have varied from delivering advice on constitution-making processes, reviewing national judicial systems and promoting respect for human rights to the latest cases of international administration and

---

[841] Cf. also International Commission on Intervention and State Sovereignty, *supra* note 17, para. 5.13.

[842] As defined by the UN Secretary-General, the rule of law "refers to a principle of governance in which all persons, institutions and entities, public and private, including the State itself, are accountable to laws that are publicly promulgated, equally enforced and independently adjudicated, and which are consistent with international human rights norms and standards. It requires, as well, measures to ensure adherence to the principles of supremacy of law, equality before the law, accountability to the law, fairness in the application of the law, separation of powers, participation in decision-making, legal certainty, avoidance of arbitrariness and procedural and legal transparency." (Report of the Secretary-General, 'The rule of law and transitional justice in conflict and post-conflict societies', *supra* note 15, para. 6).

complex peace-building. The growing importance of justice and the awareness of the international community in this respect have culminated in various recent UN documents. An explicit mention of the value of strengthening the rule of law was included in the Millennium Declaration.[843] The Secretary-General's report 'The Rule of Law and Transitional Justice in Conflict and Post-Conflict Societies' is another significant step. The 2004 report highlights the importance of rule of law programmes, tends to strengthen the UN's support in this area by enhancing the coordination of all UN efforts, and recommends a systematic analysis and application of the lessons learned in Security Council mandates, peace processes and the operations of United Nations peace missions.[844]

The importance of emphasising respect for the rule of law in post-conflict reconstruction lies in the close connection between justice and the restoration of security in these territories. Consequently, in the initial phase of the post-conflict environment, respect for the rule of law and the effective implementation of laws are perhaps the most important objectives. As Bernard Kouchner, the former Special Representative of the Secretary-General and head of UNMIK, said, "peacekeeping missions need a judicial or law-and-order 'kit' made up of trained police officers, judges and prosecutors, plus a set of potentially draconian security laws or regulations that are available on their arrival. This is the only way to stop criminal behaviour from flourishing in a post-war vacuum of authority".[845] Re-establishing the rule of law is a major part of restoring public order and security and works in two ways: it prevents the deterioration of the fragile public order and security situation and creates a safe and secure environment in which to address the root causes of the conflict.[846] The promotion of justice and the rule of law thus aim to address both the immediate post-conflict situation and the maintenance of peace and security in the long term.[847]

---

843 GA Res. 55/2, United Nations Millennium Declaration, UN Doc. A/RES/55/2 (8 September 2000).

844 Report of the Secretary-General, 'The rule of law and transitional justice in conflict and post-conflict societies', *supra* note 15, pp. 19–23.

845 See Smith, R. J., 'Kosovo Still Seethes as UN Official Nears Exit', *The Washington Post* (18 December 2000).

846 See Stahn, *supra* note 646, pp. 311–344.

847 As former Secretary-General Kofi Annan explained: "Our experience in the past decade has demonstrated clearly that the consolidation of peace in the immediate post-conflict period, as well as the maintenance of peace in the long term, cannot be achieved unless the population is confident that redress for grievances can be obtained through legitimate structures for the peaceful settlement of disputes and the fair administration of justice. At the same time, the heightened vulnerability of minorities, women, children, prisoners and detainees, displaced persons, refugees and others, which is evident in all conflict and post-conflict situations, brings an element of urgency to the imperative of restoration of the rule of law" (Report of

The starting point is necessarily an assessment of the specific needs of the host country with regard to the judicial system, taking into account the nature and causes of the underlying conflict, the history and scale of past abuses, the needs of vulnerable groups such as minorities and IDPs, the situation of women and children and especially the existing judicial system, traditions and culture. Every case is different, and although common features and programmes can be identified from recent post-conflict reconstruction missions, it should be kept in mind that the judiciary is closely related to local culture and tradition. The success of judicial reform programmes very much depends on in-depth knowledge of the local judicial structure and culture. We should therefore be careful when envisaging the mere transplantation of foreign legal systems. Although elements such as internationally recognised human rights unavoidably need to be introduced into the judicial system, maintaining and reforming existing legal structures can in some cases be more effective.

The reconstruction of the judicial system, including emergency measures, the applicable law and the reform of the judiciary, will be dealt with in the first section. The introduction of human rights will be addressed in the next section. 'Transitional justice', *i.e.* how a post-conflict society deals with the abuses of the past regime, will be analysed in the third section. Although a major part of the literature and a majority of commentators tend to focus only on the aspect of transitional justice in post-conflict societies, it remains part of the broader concept of the rule of law.

A. *Re-establishing the Judicial System*

A functioning judicial system and infrastructure is the starting point for any judicial reform. Introducing human rights and engaging in transitional justice mechanisms are inconceivable without a performing judicial system. The confidence of civilians in the idea of justice itself can equally be achieved only through a functioning judicial infrastructure. The economic revival of war-torn societies likewise requires a climate of functioning judicial mechanisms for potential investors, and thus implies both physical reconstruction of the infrastructure, and the (re-)establishment of judicial organisation, with a functioning court management *system*. Societies emerging from harsh and protracted conflicts are often faced with a deficient judicial system, in which physical infrastructure and judicial expertise are frequently lacking.

---

the Secretary-General, 'The rule of law and transitional justice in conflict and post-conflict societies', *supra* note 15, para. 2).

Especially when missions are established after armed intervention, as in Kosovo, Iraq or Afghanistan, severe damage is inevitably caused to the infrastructure of the country. The situation with regard to the infrastructure of the countries discussed was catastrophic.[848] However, the legal system of a state or a territory is equally part of its cultural heritage, and is therefore susceptible of creating tensions in the reconstruction process. The exercise is thus a difficult one. Often, there are no references to international human rights standards, and the existing legal systems contain discriminatory laws, sometimes used by the former regime to oppress the population. It is therefore necessary not just to indicate clearly which laws are applicable but also to introduce human rights standards and review the existing legislation in the light of those standards.

Judges and prosecutors in war-torn societies are often inadequately trained, especially in human rights law, some of them even lacking basic legal education because of politically and ethnically inspired appointments by former regimes. Training of judicial personnel remains fundamental and vital even after the rehabilitation of the judicial system. Building local capacity in the justice sector is one of the most important tasks in post-conflict reconstruction, as it improves sustainable local ownership over the process. On the other hand, relying only on local actors is not always possible in the immediate post-conflict phase. International judges and prosecutors are almost inevitably required to fill the gaps in the period between the establishment of the mission and the time needed for adequate training of the judiciary. The training of judges has therefore been a major part of the reconstruction processes in Kosovo, East Timor, Afghanistan and Iraq. In cases such as Kosovo and East Timor, local capacity was almost completely lacking due to years of ethnically motivated appointments,[849] whereas judges were largely available in Afghanistan and Iraq, although there they lacked education in human rights and other basic principles of law, such as due process and fair trial. In addition, the manifest lack of respect for the rule of law in recent years necessitates the focus of training programmes not only on the law *sensu stricto*, but also on the role of the judiciary in a democratic society.

---

[848] See for an overview of the situations upon arrival of the UN missions Dobbins *et al., supra* note 521 and Dobbins *et al., supra* note 550.

[849] In Kosovo for example, before the departure of the Kosovo Serbs, only 30 of the 756 judges and prosecutors were Kosovo Albanians (Report of the Secretary-General, UN Doc. S/1999/779, *supra* note 117, para. 66).

1. *Kosovo: From Emergency to Provisional Institutions*

Upon UNMIK's arrival in Kosovo, the formal justice system was almost non-existent, and unquestionably not functioning.[850] The NATO air strikes and the years of hostilities in Kosovo had caused major damage to the court infrastructure and facilities. Court equipment, legal materials, registers and records had been destroyed or stolen. Moreover, the departing Serb forces had mined or booby-trapped several courtrooms and destroyed other office equipment.[851] Kosovo was left with a devastated judicial infrastructure and UNMIK had the difficult task of providing immediate judicial assistance because of increasing ethnic violence and growing criminal activity. Security Council Resolution 1244 gave UNMIK a general mandate in the administration of the Province, with no explicit reference to the judiciary or judicial reconstruction. In line with this general mandate, the first UNMIK Regulation[852] adopted by the Special Representative of the Secretary-General vested in UNMIK all legislative and executive authority, including the administration of the judiciary.

(a) *The Applicable Law Dispute*

As Resolution 1244 explicitly maintained Serbian sovereignty over Kosovo, the first regulation included a provision stating that the law applicable in Kosovo prior to 24 March 1999 would still be applied provided it did not conflict with international human rights standards.[853] The principle underlying this regulation was the avoidance of a legal vacuum, and the avoidance of the introduction of an entirely new legal system which would have necessitated an immediate comprehensive training programme and would have jeopardised the security situation even more.[854] The incorporated provision immediately generated great opposition from the Kosovo Albanian community and judges, who viewed the application of this system of laws as a 'symbol of Serb discrimination'.[855] The Kosovo Albanians considered the law applicable in 1989, *i.e.* before the decision of the Serb Authorities to withdraw Kosovo's autonomy, to be the only legitimate system of

---

[850] OSCE Mission in Kosovo, 'Report 2: The Development of The Kosovo Judicial System (10 June Through 15 December 1999)' (17 December 1999). See also Jones, Wilson, Rathmell and Riley, *supra* note 716, p. 40.

[851] OSCE Mission in Kosovo, 'Report 1 – Material Needs of The Emergency Judicial System' (7 November 1999). See also Betts, W. S., Carlson, S. N. and Gisvold, G., 'The Post-Conflict Transitional Administration of Kosovo and the Lessons-Learned in Efforts to Establish a Judiciary and Rule of Law', 22 *Michigan Journal of International Law* 371 (2000–2001), p. 377.

[852] UNMIK Regulation 1999/1, *supra* note 118.

[853] *Ibid.* Section 3.

[854] Strohmeyer, *supra* note 803.

[855] Hartmann, *supra* note 665, p. 4. Michael Hartmann was the first international prosecutor appointed by the SRSG in Kosovo.

law. The result was that the many Kosovar judges resigned after the adoption of the regulation or simply refused to apply the 1999 law, basing their judgments instead on the law applicable in 1989.[856] The legality of the decisions based on the law applicable in 1989 was therefore highly questionable, as they were in manifest violation of UNMIK Regulation 1999/1.[857] Eventually, the Special Representative of the Secretary-General decided to amend the first regulation by altering the applicable law to the legal system in force in Kosovo on 22 March 1989.[858] The whole dispute and the eventual adjustment of the applicable legal framework of course harmed the reputation of the UN-led administration.[859] UNMIK eventually engaged in the drafting of an entirely new code of criminal law and criminal procedure, considering that many of the applicable criminal laws in Kosovo did not meet international human rights standards.[860]

(b) *The 'Emergency Judicial System'*

Within two weeks of its deployment, UNMIK established the 'Emergency Judicial System', which functioned from June to December 1999. The Emergency Judicial System focused on criminal cases and offences to support UNMIK and KFOR efforts to re-establish law and order. The Emergency Judicial System set up several emergency institutions to re-establish the judicial system. A 'Joint Advisory Council on Judicial Appointments'[861] was instituted to recommend the appointment of judges as part of an Emergency Judicial System mainly to hear suspects detained by KFOR in the immediate post-conflict phase. The Joint Advisory Council was composed of both local and international personnel, and recommended the provisional appointment of judges and public prosecutors for a three-month renewable term in order to conduct pre-trial hearings of

---

856 *Ibid.* This code had been adopted by the Kosovo Assembly before the withdrawal of Kosovo's autonomy.

857 In addition, the legal uncertainty caused by this dispute was further increased by the fact that the judges nevertheless applied several provisions of the Serb criminal code for crimes which were not covered by the 1989 Kosovo Criminal Code, such as drug-trafficking. See O'Neill, *supra* note 654, p. 80.

858 UNMIK Regulation 1999/24 on the law applicable in Kosovo, UN Doc. UNMIK/REG/1999/24 (12 December 1999), section 1.1.

859 Cf. O'Neill, *supra* note 654, pp. 80–81.

860 The drafting of the new codes started in 2000, and was finalised in November 2001 by the Joint Advisory Council on Legislative Matters. The new codes were promulgated by the Special Representative of the Secretary-General, and entered into force in April 2004. See UNMIK Regulation 2003/25, Provisional Criminal Code of Kosovo, UN Doc. UNMIK/REG/2003/25 (6 July 2003) and UNMIK Regulation 2003/26, Provisional Criminal Procedure Code of Kosovo, UN Doc. UNMIK/REG/2003/26 (6 July 2003).

861 UNMIK Emergency Decree No. 1999/1 (28 June 1999) (providing legal basis for the establishment of the Joint Advisory Council for Provisional Judicial Appointments (JAC/PJA)).

people detained by KFOR. The nine appointed judges and prosecutors served from 2 July 1999 as mobile units with jurisdiction throughout the territory of Kosovo. Between June and September 1999, the Special Representative of the Secretary-General appointed another 55 judges and public prosecutors following recommendations by the Joint Advisory Council, but the premature resignation of all Kosovo Serb judges and prosecutors rapidly brought the total number of judges and prosecutors appointed to 47.[862]

Provisional district courts and prosecutors' offices had been set up in the main districts; the mobile units of the Pristina District Court covered areas not served by the regular district courts. UNMIK also created an 'Ad Hoc Court of Final Appeal' to hear appeals against decisions of District Courts in the sphere of criminal law and also with regard to sentencing.[863] Very soon, the judicial system was administered by co-Ministers of Justice (one Kosovar and one international) in the UNMIK Judicial Affairs Office, established in August 1999. UNMIK established a Technical Advisory Commission on Judiciary and Prosecution Service, to advise the administrator on the structure and administration of the judiciary in Kosovo.[864] On 13 December 1999 the Technical Advisory Commission delivered to the Special Representative of the Secretary-General its recommendations on the establishment of the civil and criminal jurisdictions, the district and municipal courts, a Court of Appeal and a Supreme Court. The approval of the 'Constitutional Framework for Provisional Self-Government' in May 2001 was the start of a gradual transition from the Emergency Judicial System to permanent institutions. A definitive court structure along the lines of the recommendations of the Technical Advisory Commission gradually replaced the transitional system.[865] The Advisory Judicial Commission, which had replaced the Joint Advisory Council on Judicial Appointments in September 1999,[866] was in

---

862 OSCE Mission in Kosovo, 'Report 2 – The Development Of The Kosovo Judicial System (10 June Through 15 December 1999)' (17 December 1999), 3. See also OSCE Mission in Kosovo, 'Review of the criminal justice system (April 2003–October 2004): crime, detention, and punishment' (14 December 2004), p. 10.

863 UNMIK Regulation 1999/5 on the establishment of an ad hoc court of final appeal and an ad hoc office of the public prosecutor, UN Doc. UNMIK/REG/1999/5 (4 September 1999).

864 UNMIK Regulation 1999/6, on recommendations for the structure and registration of the judiciary and prosecution service, UN Doc. UNMIK/REG/1999/6 (7 September 1999).

865 UNMIK Regulation 2001/9 on the Constitutional Framework for Provisional Self-Government, UN Doc. UNMIK/REG/2001/9 (15 May 2001), section 9.4.4.

866 The Advisory Judicial Commission began its work on 27 October 1999, and was charged with recommending candidates for appointment as permanent judges and prosecutors. A gap of approximately six weeks between the dissolution of the first and the establishment of the second resulted in a critical delay in the appointment of judges, while the number of detainees waiting for pre-trial hearings and trials grew apace as a result of the alarming security situation in the Serb Province. The Advisory Judicial Commission interviewed approximately 500

turn dissolved and replaced by a permanent Kosovo Judicial and Prosecutorial Council.

(c) *Initial Training, Continuous Education and Practical Skills Training*

The OSCE, in charge of democratisation and institution building within the UNMIK administration, was responsible for the training of judicial personnel, the monitoring of trials and other judicial proceedings, and the development and/or improvement of institutions such as the law schools and bar associations.[867] Upon UNMIK's arrival, many of the judges and prosecutors who had worked in Kosovo during the previous ten years had left, while those remaining were seen as unacceptable to the population because of their role in the former Serbian dominated system. Others, mainly Kosovo Albanian lawyers, lacked appropriate knowledge and experience of the task as they had been educated by 'parallel' institutions and banned from exercising official legal functions.[868] The importance of the swift restoration of the judiciary, and therefore adequate training of judges holding office, was urgent by reason of growing ethnic violence and organised crime, and the consequent growing number of people detained by KFOR.[869] In addition, their training in international human rights law was imperative, as the applicable law in Kosovo required the judges to review the existing legislation in function of internationally recognised human rights standards.[870]

UNMIK's coherent approach to the training of the judiciary can been divided into three main categories: initial training programmes, continuous legal education and practical skills training. Within the Emergency Judicial System set up by UNMIK, the OSCE initiated training activities in August 1999 by its 'Judicial Training Section', which was replaced by the Kosovo Judicial Institute in February 2000.[871] The first step was a 'quick start' training course for the

applicants for appointment to the Kosovar judiciary, and on its recommendations the head of UNMIK had appointed 296 judges and prosecutors and 238 lay judges by the end of December 1999.

867 Cf. OSCE Mission in Kosovo, 'Report 1 – Material Needs Of The Emergency Judicial System' (7 November 1999), para. 1.

868 Report of the Secretary-General, UN Doc. S/1999/779, *supra* note 117, para. 69.

869 See for an overview OSCE Mission in Kosovo, 'Report 2 – The Development of the Kosovo Judicial System (10 June Through 15 December 1999)' (17 December 1999).

870 UNMIK Regulation 1999/24, *supra* note 858, para. 1.3.

871 OSCE Mission in Kosovo – Legal Systems Monitoring Section, 'Kosovo: Review of the criminal justice system 1999–2005 – Reforms and residual concerns' (March 2006), 16. In February 2006, the Assembly of Kosovo adopted a law establishing the Kosovo Judicial Institute as an independent body, which is therefore no longer part of the OSCE Mission on Kosovo. One representative of the OSCE and one UNMIK official still are full members of the Institute. See Provisional Institutions of Self Government, Assembly of Kosovo, Law No. 02/L-25 on Establishing The Kosovo Judicial Institute.

judges and prosecutors appointed, mainly focusing on criminal law and human rights laws.[872] These two-day training courses were intended to give the newly appointed personnel the capacity promptly to initiate hearings in accordance with international human rights standards. These initial training courses were however insufficient to guarantee the adequate functioning of the judiciary, considering the strong, although understandable, focus on criminal law, and the still very sensitive ethnic division.[873] As a consequence, the appointment of international judges in February 2000 became unavoidable. Although reluctant at first, the Special Representative of the Secretary-General in Kosovo decided to introduce international actors in the re-established judicial system in order to train the local judges and uphold the rule of law in the territory, as the courts and tribunals were generally seen as ineffective and biased.[874] This decision, which introduced the new concept of 'internationalised' courts and tribunal, was taken only several months after the establishment of UNMIK. Regulation 2000/6 first launched the possibility of appointing international judges and prosecutors in the Mitrovica District Court, which had been the scene of massive ethnic riots.[875] The possibility of appointing international judges and prosecutors was later extended to all other courts and tribunals in Kosovo,[876] following a massive strike by Kosovo Serbs, held in detention for several months without indictment.[877]

---

872 Report of the Secretary-General on the United Nations Interim Administration Mission in Kosovo, UN Doc. S/2000/1196 (15 December 2000), para. 49.

873 The initial training courses were completely restructured in 2005 to train candidates who passed the Judicial Entry Exam. A more comprehensive curriculum, covering all areas of legal practice, was developed to increase professional skills and enlarge the legal knowledge of future judges. The 'Initial Legal Education Program' was launched in April 2005 and is mandatory for candidates prior to their appointment.

874 Kosovo Albanian suspects arrested by KFOR (often former KLA members) were immediately released by the judges, while Serbian suspects were being detained in custody for identical crimes. See O'Neill, *supra* note 654, pp. 83 *et s.* and Hartmann, *supra* note 665, p. 5. See also Kouchner, *supra* note 568, pp. 304–305.

875 UNMIK Regulation 2000/6 on the appointment and removal from office of international judges and international prosecutors, UN Doc. UNMIK/REG/2000/6 (15 February 2000), para. 1.1.

876 UNMIK Regulation 2000/34 amending UNMIK Regulation 2000/6 on the appointment and removal from office of international judges and international prosecutors, UN Doc. UNMIK/REG/2000/34 (27 May 2000).

877 Hartmann, *supra* note 665, pp. 9–11. Soon, one of the problems relating to the limited number of international judges and prosecutors became clear: the international judges were often outvoted by the four other Kosovar panel judges, who nevertheless 'legitimised' their decision because of the presence of an international judge on the panel. A later regulation identified the possibilities for the competent prosecutor, the accused and the defence counsel to request the Special Representative to submit to the Department of Judicial Affairs a petition for the assignment of international judges/prosecutors "where this is considered necessary to ensure the independence and impartiality of the judiciary or the proper administration of justice"

A next step was to allow international prosecutors to reopen cases which had been abandoned by a Kosovar Prosecutor.[878]

After a needs assessment of priorities in the Kosovo Judicial System, and in consultation with officials and OSCE Rule of Law Officers in the different regions, the Kosovo Judicial Institute equally provided more specific courses on other legal issues. In approximately five years, the Kosovo Judicial Institute, occasionally in collaboration with other institutions such as the Council of Europe, the US Department of Justice, or the American Bar Association, organised more than 200 training programmes within the framework of the Continuous Legal Education Program. The majority of the judges and prosecutors have attended at least one programme. However, the courses organised under the Continuous Legal Education Programme were not mandatory and only an average of 25 judges attended all the special training courses.[879] The facultative character of the continuous legal training programme was probably not the best format for broadening the legal knowledge of the magistrates. Another facet of the training of magistrates was the launch by UNMIK in 2002 of the Practical Skills Training Programme, in collaboration with the US Agency for International Development (USAID). The training was offered by the International Development Law Organization and focused on improving management skills, decision-making, writing judgments and questioning of witnesses. However, these essential training programmes were initiated only three years after the first appointments to the judiciary. Especially considering that the main problem with the magistrates appointed was that they lacked any practical experience whatsoever, these indispensable courses should have ideally been initiated immediately upon the appointment of the judges and prosecutors.

Despite the setback with regard to the applicable law, the management of the emergency judicial reconstruction was handled rather well by UNMIK. In particular, its rapid consultation with the local population to appoint judges and prosecutors, and the creation of mechanisms to boost local capacity in the administration of justice were essential. Nevertheless, reliance on local judges

(UNMIK/REG/2000/64 on assignment of international judges/prosecutors and/or change of venue, UN Doc. UNMIK/REG/2000/64 (15 December 2000), para. 1.1). The same power was given to the Department of Judicial Affairs. (para. 1.2). After approval by the Special Representative, the Department of Judicial Affairs was empowered to designate an international judge or prosecutor or, in order to avoid the international judge being outvoted, a panel composed of only three judges, including at least two international judges, one of which was the presiding judge (*Ibid.*, para. 2.1).

[878] UNMIK Regulation 2001/2 amending UNMIK Regulation no. 2000/6, as amended, on the appointment and removal from office of international judges and international prosecutors, UN Doc. UNMIK/REG/2001/2 (12 January 2001).

[879] OSCE Mission in Kosovo – Legal Systems Monitoring Section, 'Kosovo: Review of the criminal justice system 1999–2005 – Reforms and residual concerns' (March 2006), p. 17.

did not always amount to the fair administration of justice. Local judges often lacked the capacity to handle difficult and sensitive cases, which fact, added to criticism about ethnic bias, resulted in the introduction of international judges and prosecutors. However, UNMIK's efforts should not be underestimated, as the judiciary was almost non-existent upon its arrival.

2. *Creating a Timorese Judiciary from Scratch*

The violence in East Timor in September 1999 after the popular consultation on the territory's future status resulted in the destruction of an estimated 70 per cent of the physical infrastructure.[880] Militias sympathetic to the integration of East Timor into Indonesia, backed by the Indonesian military, embarked on a large-scale, scorched earth campaign of reprisal, destroying virtually all the judicial infrastructure, including all court equipment, furniture, registers, records and law books during the hostilities.[881] The situation in East Timor required the judicial system to be completely rebuilt from scratch. UNTAET's mandate explicitly mentioned the administration of justice.[882] One of the first questions that needed to be addressed was which laws would be applied, which is, as rightly pointed out by the then Special Representative, a difficult question: "what law applies in a country that does not yet exist?".[883]

(a) *'What Law Applies in a Country That Does not yet Exist?'*

Like UNMIK's approach towards the definition of the applicable law and with the same rationale,[884] the first UNTAET Regulation adopted the principle that, until replaced by UNTAET regulations or subsequent legislation, the whole body of Indonesian law would apply in East Timor, as that was the law applied in East Timor before 25 October 1999. Indonesian law was nevertheless applicable only provided that it did not conflict with the internationally recognised human rights standards enumerated in the first UNTAET Regulation, the fulfilment of the mandate given to UNTAET under Resolution 1272, or the present or any

---

[880] World Bank, 'Report of the joint assessment mission to East Timor' (8 December 1999), p. 15.

[881] See in general for an overview of the situation upon arrival: Strohmeyer, H., 'Collapse and reconstruction of a judicial system: the United Nations Missions in Kosovo and East Timor', 95 *American Journal of International Law* 46 (2001), p. 50.

[882] SC Res. 1272, UN Doc. S/RES/1272 (1999), para. 1: UNTAET was 'endowed with overall responsibility for the administration of East Timor and [...] empowered to exercise all legislative and executive authority, including the administration of justice'.

[883] Vieira de Mello, S., 'How not to run a country. Lessons for the UN from Kosovo and East Timor' (June 2000).

[884] Strohmeyer, H., 'Policing the Peace: Post-Conflict Judicial System Reconstruction in East Timor', 24 *University of New South Wales Law Journal* 174 (2001).

other regulation or directive issued by the Transitional Administrator.[885] The choice of applying Indonesian law was based on practical considerations, taking into account that the few remaining lawyers were graduates of Indonesian universities, that the majority of the population was familiar with Indonesian law, and that Portuguese law had not been applied in the territory for almost 24 years.[886]

The East Timorese did not reject the legal system of the former regime, as the Kosovo Albanians did. Nevertheless, the problems with respect to the interpretation of the existing laws, especially the criminal and criminal procedure codes, in the light of international human rights proved difficult. The decision to apply Indonesian law equally encompassed an obligation for UNTAET to familiarise itself with Indonesian law. As UNTAET did not have the capacity to understand and implement Indonesian law, the problem was apparently sidestepped by UNTAET's decision to legislate extensively in various areas without actually taking into account conflicts with applicable Indonesian law.[887] For example, although several international and national actors had proposed using the Indonesian Code reviewed in the light of human rights standards, UNTAET decided to draft an entirely new Code of Criminal Procedure, which took almost a year. The result was naturally the difficult application of the existing Indonesian Code of Criminal Procedure, which was formally applicable in the transitional period, but required to be directly interpreted by local judges in the light of applicable human rights law.[888]

(b) *Emergency Measures*

The working method in the emergency phase was quite similar to that in the case of Kosovo, for the obvious reason that Vieira de Mello had been the interim Special Representative of the Secretary-General in Kosovo until 15 July 1999. Vieira de Mello created a 'Transitional Judicial Service Commission' to recommend candidates for provisional judicial or prosecutorial office, to provide advice on the removal of judges or prosecutors, and to prepare a 'Code of Ethics' for judges and prosecutors.[889] The Judicial Service Commission was composed of five individuals, three of East Timorese origin and two international experts.

As a result of the departure of Indonesian lawyers, judges, prosecutors and clerks and years of ethnic and political appointments in the judiciary, there

885 UNTAET Regulation 1999/1 on the Authority of the Transitional Administration in East Timor, UN Doc. UNTAET/REG/1999/1 (27 November 1999), section 3.

886 Morrow and White, *supra* note 390, p. 8 and Strohmeyer, *supra* note 881, p. 58.

887 See Morrow and White, *supra* note 390, p. 10.

888 *Ibid.*, pp. 11–12.

889 UNTAET Regulation 1999/3 on the Establishment of a Transitional Judicial Service Commission, UN Doc. UNTAET/REG/1999/3 (3 December 1999).

were almost no jurists left in East Timor who had sufficient experience in the application of the law. Upon its arrival, UNTAET began the difficult process of identifying qualified personnel for the judiciary. After a week, following a word of mouth campaign and voluntary action by INTERFET to drop leaflets from aeroplanes throughout the territory, 17 jurists had been identified. Only a few of them had had previous experience in legal practice, and none of them had served as judge or prosecutor.[890] On 7 January 2000, the Transitional Administrator appointed the first judges for an initial and probationary period of two years.[891] Prosecutors were appointed shortly thereafter. It is also interesting to note that, as in Kosovo, no international judges or prosecutors had initially been appointed, as the focus was on creating an exclusively East Timorese judiciary. This however, was not sustainable as the judges appointed lacked sufficient practical experience, and ultimately international judges were introduced into the Timorese judiciary, although these were principally appointed to handle sensitive cases dealing with past crimes. We will come back to this in a next section.

The re-establishment of the court structure was largely influenced by the availability of competent judicial personnel. Interestingly, the judges and prosecutors had been appointed prior to the establishment and design of the new judicial structure. At the time of their appointment, there was no court structure within which they and the lawyers could operate. An obvious lack of guidelines on working methods was also particularly problematic, especially for the investigating judges, an institution that did not exist in the Indonesian judicial system applicable until then. East Timor had to wait until March 2000 for a transitional court system to be established under an UNTAET Regulation.[892] The Court structure designed by UNTAET originally consisted of eight District Courts and one Court of Appeal. Due to a lack of competent judges and resources, the number of District Courts was subsequently reduced to four.[893] As in the Kosovo emergency phase, UNTAET Regulation 2000/11 provided that "[f]or a transitional period and until otherwise determined by the Transitional Administrator, the judges appointed to the District Court in Dili shall have jurisdiction throughout the entire territory of East Timor". The first hearings took place in the Dili District Court in May 2000, and as from June of the same year the

---

890 See for an overview of the emergency phase in East Timor: Strohmeyer, *supra* note 881, p. 54.

891 *Ibid.*, p. 54.

892 UNTAET Regulation 2000/11 on the organization of courts in East Timor, UN Doc. UNTAET/REG/2000/11 (6 March 2000).

893 Dili, Baucau, Suai and Oecussi. UNTAET Regulation 2000/14 amending Regulation No. 2000/11, UN Doc. UNTAET/REG/2000/14 (10 May 2000). The Oecussi district is in fact an enclave in West Timor.

three other district courts also started functioning. The existing court structure was largely maintained by Timor-Leste upon independence.

(c) *Mentoring and Mandatory Judicial Training*
UNTAET's approach was again fairly identical to the one UNMIK favoured. Following UNMIK's model, UNTAET officials equally preferred to rely on local capacity only, and established a three-tiered training programme consisting of initial training prior to or upon appointment, continuous training while in office, and a programme of mentoring by international experts. Before the appointed judges, prosecutors and public defenders took office, UNTAET organised a brief training course of one week in Indonesia and Darwin in Australia.[894] This was nevertheless clearly insufficient, as most of the appointed judges held law degrees from Indonesian universities but had no practical professional experience at all. In May 2000, the Director of Judicial Affairs launched a more comprehensive training programme to address both immediate and long-term needs with regard to the magistrates holding office, comprising both traditional teaching and a mentoring programme.[895] The mentoring programme introduced in May 2000 was intended to provide support and advice by international judges, who served as 'shadow' judges, prosecutors and public defenders for their East Timorese colleagues. This mentoring programme faced several difficulties mainly by reason of limited financial resources and the difficulty in finding experienced international lawyers to serve as mentors for the appointed magistrates.[896]

In order to provide a more coherent and comprehensive framework for the training of the judiciary, a Judicial Training Centre was established after the independence of East Timor. The Judicial Training Centre, mandated with the continuous training of already appointed judges and prosecutors, was formally instituted as an independent body in 2004. Its main purpose was to provide a two and a half year long training course to be undertaken by appointed magistrates in order to be eligible for permanent appointment and gradually take over the tasks of the international judges.[897] However, none of the 22 judges who participated in the first training programme managed to pass the exam and obtain

[894] See Dahrendorf *et al.*, *supra* note 496, para. 233.

[895] *Ibid.* The training programmes were subcontracted to the International Development Law Organisation which organised courses on criminal law. See on this: IDLO, 'Lessons learned on judicial & prosecutorial reform in post-conflict countries', 2 *Development Law Update* (June 2004).

[896] Dahrendorf *et al.*, *supra* note 496, para. 233.

[897] See Hasegawa, S., 'Speech Delivered at the Opening Ceremony for the Judicial Training Centre (JTC)' (7 September 2004).

the required qualification for conversion to permanent status.[898] A few months later, all Prosecutors and Public Defenders who had followed the training course equally failed the written test and were therefore obliged to stop acting in the courts.[899] Equally, several reports stated that in spite of their failure to pass the examinations after the training period, many of the judges and prosecutors were still handling cases, assisting the international judges and prosecutors.[900]

While the mandatory character of the post-appointment training was, in comparison to Kosovo, clear progress in ensuring the continuing training of appointed judges and prosecutors, it posed a great number of problems considering the already small number of magistrates. In addition, the Ministry of Justice favoured training in concentrated long periods, impeding the functioning of some of the District Courts.[901] In June 2002, for example, the entire judiciary was shut down as all judges and prosecutors had to attend a compulsory training course on the new constitution, leading to the release of suspects that were held in police stations because of unavailability of judicial review within the required time period.[902] The creation of a viable justice system was severely hampered by the absence of qualified magistrates.

3. *Afghanistan: Reconstruction in a Complex Legal Environment*

The Afghan judicial system's infrastructure was destroyed as a result of decades of war and political disorder. Basic office furniture and adequate court facilities did not exist and law books, legal decisions, studies and case reports were largely lost.[903] The focus therefore needed to be on a re-launch of the judiciary and reconstruction of the infrastructure. In reality, the reconstruction process began only in early 2003, after the identification of Italy as the lead donor, the constitution of an Afghan Transitional Authority, and the development of a strategic framework jointly developed by UNAMA and the Judicial Reform Commission.

---

[898] Hasegawa, S., 'The Development Perspective: Three Imperatives for Sustainable Peace and Nation-building in a Post-Conflict Society' (20 May 2005), para. B (1).

[899] Hasegawa, S., 'Lessons Learned from Peacekeeping and Peacebuilding Support Missions in Timor-Leste', *Berlin Centre for International Peace Operation* (27 January 2006), p. 17.

[900] See *e.g.* Human Rights Watch, *'World Report 2003: Asia – East Timor'* (2004) and Judicial System Monitoring Programme, 'Recent Developments in the Courts' *Justice Update Issue 22/2005* (October/November 2005), p. 1.

[901] See for the same critique GA, 'Interim report of the United Nations High Commissioner for Human Rights on the situation of human rights in Timor-Leste', UN Doc. A/57/446 (2 October 2002), para. 25.

[902] Human Rights Watch, *'World Report 2003: Asia – East Timor'* (2004), p. 3.

[903] See Judicial Reform Commission – UNAMA – UNDP, Rebuilding the Justice Sector of Afghanistan, Project Nr. AFG/03/001/01/34 (January 2003).

The Bonn Agreement paved the way for judicial reform, although it explicitly delineated the basis of such reform. Several elements in the reconstruction process, such as the definition of the applicable law, were thus very different from those in previous cases. The applicable Afghan laws and codes existed, but were largely unavailable to attorneys, judges and prosecutors. It was thus more a question of compiling, rather that defining, the applicable law.

(a) *Finding and Compiling the Applicable Law*

Afghanistan lacked a comprehensive judicial system, and laws differed substantially in the different provinces. The Afghan judicial system consists of state law, Sharia law and customary law, overlapping each other in the same subject areas.[904] The 1964 Constitution, which settled the applicable law in accordance with the Bonn Agreement, had a unified system of laws, but the various succeeding regimes adopted new laws, often creating inconsistencies with each other.[905] As the latter remained formally applicable, determining the applicable laws was not uncomplicated. Combined with the lack of training and education for judges, the lack of access to legal texts has resulted in a wider application of Sharia law throughout the country.[906] The revision and compilation of laws was therefore the main issue in post-conflict Afghanistan.

The Bonn Agreement provided that until Afghanistan's new constitution was adopted the country's basic legal framework would consist of the 1964 Constitution and existing laws and regulations to the extent that they accorded with the Bonn Agreement and with international treaties to which Afghanistan was a party.[907] The Afghan Interim Authority was also given the power to amend and repeal existing laws.[908] The International Development Law Organisation was mandated by the Government of Italy – the 'lead nation' in judicial reform – to issue a compilation of all Afghan laws that were applicable in accordance with the Bonn Agreement.

---

[904] For an overview see Wardak, A. and Spivack, D., 'Afghanistan's Domestic Legal Framework,' *The Senlis Council* (September 2005).

[905] Thier, J. A., 'Re-establishing the Judicial System in Afghanistan', *CDDRL Working Paper Number 19* (September 2004), p. 10. See in general on the applicable law and Afghanistan's legal background: International Commission of Jurists, 'Afghanistan's Legal System and its Compatibility with International Human Rights Standards' (November 2002), para. 16.

[906] See International Crisis Group, 'Afghanistan: Judicial Reform and Transitional Justice', *Asia Report N°45* (28 January 2003), p. 7; International Commission of Jurists, 'Afghanistan's Legal System and its Compatibility with International Human Rights Standards' (November 2002), paras. 11 and 59 and Thier, J. A., 'Re-establishing the Judicial System in Afghanistan', *CDDRL Working Paper Number* 19 (September 2004), p. 9.

[907] Section II, 1), Bonn Agreement.

[908] *Ibid.*

Revising existing laws and writing new ones was similarly imperative for the reform of the judiciary. Several new laws, such as the Law on the Organisation and Jurisdiction of the Courts, the Juvenile Justice Code and the Law on Prisons, were adopted in June 2005 after long consultations with the international community and UNAMA. The drafting of the interim Code of Criminal Procedure, which was promulgated by Presidential Decree in February 2004,[909] was probably one the major achievements of the Judicial Reform Commission, UNAMA and Italy. The new Code of Criminal Procedure replaced the former code throughout the country, but the difficulty in the effective implementation of the laws resurfaced. The Italian plan was to focus on some 20 District Courts and the training of 20 Judges and 20 Prosecutors, who would then be assigned to pilot District Courts. This plan was rightly criticised because of its partial focus on District Courts which would have caused inconsistency in the application of the interim code.[910] Effective implementation of the new Code was problematic as the rural areas continued to rely more on the traditional dispute settlement mechanisms. Even in the rest of the country, the lack of qualified judges and of the availability of amended and newly passed laws makes it hard to apply these laws. A review of the Civil and Criminal Codes has conversely not yet been undertaken, although they have remained unaltered since their adoption in the 1970s.

(b) *Institutional Reform and Physical Reconstruction*

Beside the complexity of the fragmented Afghan legal system,[911] the difficulty in rebuilding and proposing reforms in the justice sector in Afghanistan was mainly related to the many official institutions involved in the judiciary. The Minister of Justice, the Supreme Court and the Attorney General's Office all have competences with regard to the justice sector, and work in parallel. With the establishment of the Judicial Reform Commission, which we will discuss in the next paragraph, a fourth institution was added. The lack of coordination between the official institution, UNAMA and the Judicial Reform Commission,

[909] Report of the Secretary-General, UN Doc. A/58/742–S/2004/230, *supra* note 728, para. 27.

[910] See for a critique Miller, L. and Perito, R., 'Establishing the Rule of Law in Afghanistan', *United States Institute of Peace Special Report 117* (March 2004), p. 8.

[911] See in general on this, and the implications for the reconstruction process: International Crisis Group, 'Afghanistan: Judicial Reform and Transitional Justice', *Asia Report N°45* (28 January 2003), p. 5; Economic and Social Council, Commission on Human Rights, 'Final report on the situation of human rights in Afghanistan submitted by the Special Rapporteur, Mr. Felix Ermacora, in accordance with Commission on Human Rights resolution 1994/84', UN Doc. E/CN.4/1995/64 (20 January 1995) and International Commission of Jurists, 'Afghanistan's Legal System and its Compatibility with International Human Rights Standards' (November 2002), p. 15.

led to a focus on enhancing the coordination between these bodies instead of reforming the judiciary.[912]

The Bonn Agreement vested the judicial power of Afghanistan in the Afghan Supreme Court. The Interim Administration was also asked to "establish, with the assistance of the United Nations, a Judicial Commission to rebuild the domestic justice system in accordance with Islamic principles, international standards, the rule of law and Afghan legal traditions".[913] The first Judicial Commission was set up on 21 May 2002[914] and comprised 16 members appointed by President Karzai. As no progress had been made by the Judicial Commission and many criticisms had been expressed about its membership, which comprised only men linked to the ministries or the Supreme Court,[915] it was dissolved in August 2002. A second commission called the 'Judicial Reform Commission' was eventually set up in November 2002.[916] The Judicial Reform Commission's task was limited to reform *proposals*, as the Commission had no authority in the Administration of Justice.[917] Only the existing formal judicial institutions – the Minister of Justice, the Supreme Court headed by the Chief Justice, and the Attorney General's Office – could implement proposed reforms. The Judicial Reform Commission's tasks were nevertheless broad, from considering programmes for the selection and training of judicial professionals and prosecutors to proposing programmes for legal reform throughout the judicial system.[918] The Judicial Reform Com-

[912] See Report of the Secretary-General, UN Doc. S/2003/1212, *supra* note 742, (30 December 2003), para. 22.

[913] Art. II, 2), Bonn Agreement.

[914] Following the approval of its establishment by the President of the Interim Administration of Afghanistan (Interim Administration of Afghanistan, Presidential Decree 1243, 21 May 2002).

[915] International Crisis Group, 'Afghanistan: Judicial Reform and Transitional Justice', *Asia Report N°45* (28 January 2003), p. 12.

[916] Islamic Transitional Government of Afghanistan, Presidential Decree 153 (2 November 2002). The delays in the establishment – and working – of the Judicial Reform Commission had serious consequences, as many judicial appointments had already been made, especially to the Supreme Court which, in December 2002, comprised 137 members instead of 9, as provided for by the 1964 Constitution. Equally, the Chief Justice, Mawlawi Fazl Hady Shinwari, had created a *fatwa* council within the Supreme Court to issue extra-judicial religious decrees, without any legal basis and therefore in complete violation of the 1964 Constitution, the 1968 Law and Afghanistan's international legal obligations See International Crisis Group, 'Afghanistan: Judicial Reform and Transitional Justice', *Asia Report N°45* (28 January 2003), p. 10.

[917] Islamic Transitional Government of Afghanistan, Presidential Decree 153, Art. 3.

[918] *Ibid.*, Art. 2, 3, 4 and 5. The Judicial Reform Commission was composed of 12 prominent Afghan legal experts, including two women, who were added to the Commission's members only the day before the adoption of the presidential decree.

mission disbanded in June 2005 following a complete transfer of judicial reform responsibility to the three permanent judicial institutions.[919]

However, it is clear that in the first two years after the Bonn Agreement virtually no progress had been made in the Justice sector. Only in January 2003 did the Judicial Reform Commission publish the strategic framework, setting out the needs of and strategic plans for the reconstruction process.[920] More than a year later, UNAMA formulated a new 'Proposal for a Long-Term Strategic Framework'[921] expressing its views on improving the justice system and strengthening the permanent institutions by focusing on the reconstruction of the physical infrastructure, further training of judicial personnel, and law revision. Despite the proposed focus, physical reconstruction of the judiciary has been very sparse and has centred on Kabul and its surroundings.[922] A survey by the Judicial Reform Commission in February 2004 revealed that a majority of court buildings either did not exist or were severely damaged.[923] With regard to the court structure, and although the Bonn Agreement does not explicitly refer to the 1964 Constitution as the framework for the judiciary and the courts, the general provisions of the 1964 Constitution relating to the organisation of the judiciary and the courts were nevertheless seen as applicable.[924] In some districts, the Provincial Courts and/or Primary Courts had been established but were not functioning, while in other districts, most notably in the rural areas, the courts

919 Report of the Secretary-General, 'The situation in Afghanistan and its implications for international peace and security', UN Doc. A/59/744–S/2005/183 (18 March 2005), para. 38.

920 Judicial Reform Commissions – UNAMA – UNDP, Rebuilding the Justice Sector of Afghanistan, *Project Nr. AFG/03/001/01/34* (January 2003). The framework was officially supported by governmental officials, UN officials and the international community following the Rome Conference of December 2002 organised by the main donor and donor-coordinator. See: Final Statement of Rome Conference on Justice in Afghanistan (19–20 December 2002).

921 UNAMA – Rule of Law Unit, 'Securing Afghanistan's Future – Considerations on Criteria and Actions for Strengthening the Justice System: Proposal for a long-term strategic framework' (February 2004).

922 After almost three years, only the Ministry of Justice building, the Attorney General's offices and the Provincial Court Building in Kondoz had been restored. Report of the Secretary-General, The situation in Afghanistan and its implications for international peace and security, UN Doc. A/60/224–S/2005/525 (12 August 2005), para. 42.

923 See Islamic Republic of Afghanistan – Ministry of Justice, 'Justice for all – A Comprehensive Needs Analysis for Justice in Afghanistan' (May 2005) and UNAMA – Rule of Law Unit, Securing Afghanistan's Future – Considerations on Criteria and Actions for Strengthening the Justice System: Proposal for a long-term strategic framework (February 2004), p. 24.

924 That version of the Constitution as such only established the Supreme Court of Afghanistan as the administering, directing and representing authority of the judiciary (Article 107, 1964 Constitution), while the other courts were determined by the Law of the Jurisdiction and Organization of the Courts of Afghanistan of 1968.

had never been established.[925] The new Constitution, adopted in January 2004, and the new Law on the Organisation and Jurisdiction of the Courts largely maintained the courts' structure and competences. Nevertheless, there is a need to implement these structures effectively. In May 2006, for example, there was still only one Family and one Juvenile Court in the entire country,[926] while there were still some 308 vacancies to be filled at the level of the District and Provincial Courts.[927]

(c) *Continuous Education*

The training of magistrates holding office is of course the most important part in this process, considering that Afghanistan, especially compared to Kosovo or East Timor, could rely on an active group of magistrates. In 1992, there were approximately 1,800 judges, 1,100 prosecutors, 6,000 support staff for the courts, and 4,000 support staff for the offices of the Attorney General.[928] The majority of the judges and prosecutors had nevertheless been dismissed by the Taliban and by earlier governments, and replaced by theology graduates. This had resulted in a huge number of appointed magistrates lacking the required qualifications. In 2004, UNAMA's Rule of Law Unit estimated that only a third of the judges and prosecutors held university degrees,[929] while the Constitution clearly provided that in order to become a judge one must have a degree from the Faulty of Law or the Sharia Faculty. But the focus was laid too heavily on individuals who had no basic requirement for exercising the legal profession. Obviously, magistrates who did not have the required university degrees should have been replaced, but it was seen as politically unfeasible to disqualify unskilled personnel.[930] Instead, the training for sitting judges and prosecutors was seen as a method of giving officials who lacked the required basic legal education the minimum training they needed to do their job.

The main and largest training programme consists of providing continuous legal education to sitting judges and prosecutors. The programme was sponsored

925 UNAMA – Rule of Law Unit, 'Securing Afghanistan's Future – Considerations on Criteria and Actions for Strengthening the Justice System: Proposal for a long-term strategic framework (February 2004)', p. 7.

926 Basel, M., 'Judging in Countries in Conflict or Transition: An Afghan Perspective', *International Association of Woman Judges – 8th Biennial Conference* (3–7 May 2006).

927 Report of the Secretary-General, UN Doc. A/60/712–S/2006/145, *supra* note 152, para. 26.

928 World Bank – UNDP – Asian Development Bank, 'Afghanistan – Preliminary Needs Assessment for Recovery and reconstruction' (January 2002), para. 35.

929 UNAMA – Rule of Law Unit, 'Securing Afghanistan's Future – Considerations on Criteria and Actions for Strengthening the Justice System: Proposal for a long-term strategic framework (February 2004)', p. 18.

930 Miller and Perito, *supra* note 910, p. 9.

on a bilateral basis by Italy as the lead nation in coordination with UNAMA and the Judicial Reform Commission. The programme was subcontracted to the International Development Law Organisation (IDLO) and the equally Italian-based International Institute of Higher Studies in Criminal Sciences. The 16-month programme started in July 2003 and ended in October 2004.[931] Some 450 judges, selected by the Judicial Reform Commission, took part in the courses. Courses were given on all aspects of law, as well as on the role of the judiciary, court and case management and judicial drafting.[932] Although a clear focus on the principles of fair trial and human rights law seemed inevitable, the IDLO decided not to include human rights of women in its curriculum, nor questions on gender sensitivity, because this would be too sensitive for Afghans.[933] Even so, human rights law and gender equality are internationally recognised standards. The fact that these issues were or still are sensitive should not have precluded their inclusion in the training programmes. In fact, the training courses for local judicial actors in these fields of law were possibly the only opportunity to introduce these principles to the judiciary. The programme was however not repeated in the following years.

A recurring problem is the small percentage of women participating in these courses. In the first initial training sessions, only 20 participants were women,[934] and there does not seem to be any policy for improving women's participation in the training courses. No official figures or statistics exist on the percentage of women in the Afghan judiciary, but Amnesty International reports state that approximately 1.3 per cent of judges are women, which corresponds to 27 women out of a total of 2,006 sitting judges in August 2003.[935] On the other hand, the IDLO advanced that out of the 150 Kabul judges who followed the training courses approximately one third were women.[936] In any case, the inadequate representation of women in the judiciary is an alarming fact, and was reported by the Special Rapporteur of the Commission on Human Rights on violence

931 See International Institute of Higher Studies in Criminal Sciences (ISISC), 'Interim Training for the Afghan Judiciary', *Report on the Activities of ISISC during the first 6 months of the Project* (July 2003–January 2004).

932 An overview of the curriculum is available on IDLO's website: 'Interim Training Program for the Afghan Judiciary', www.idlo.int/Afg_interim_training.htm.

933 GA, 'Report of the Special Rapporteur of the Commission on Human Rights on violence against women, its causes and consequences, on the situation of women and girls on Afghanistan', UN Doc. A/58/421 (6 October 2003). See for a critique: Amnesty International, 'Afghanistan: Re-establishing the rule of law', *Report n° ASA 11/021/2003* (14 August 2003), p. 14.

934 *Ibid.*, p. 13.

935 *Ibid.*, pp. 13–14.

936 IDLO, *2003 Annual Report* (2004).

against women, who asked the Afghan Transitional Authority to take measures to increase the number of women in the judicial institutions.[937]

The setting up of an initial training programme for young lawyers, which commenced in May 2003, was an equally important step in re-establishing the judiciary. The successful completion of this course is a prerequisite for permanent appointment in the judiciary and other official institutions, such as the Ministry of Justice. The Legal Education Centre, established by the Judicial Reform Commission in April 2003, was mandated to oversee and organise the one-year training sessions.[938] The first training session, launched in May 2003, was attended by some 150 lawyers who graduated from the Faculty of Law and the Sharia Faculty. In May 2004, the first batch of 125 law students graduated after the one-year course at the Legal Education Centre.[939]

Notwithstanding the various efforts to re-create a sustainable judicial system, there was no clear coherence between the different programmes. Apparently, a separate training programme has been set up for every parcel of funding received by a state. Equally, considering the fundamental need to provide training and even basic education to the already appointed magistrates, especially in the Provinces, a mandatory training scheme following an assessment of all judges should have been envisaged. At present, more than six years after the signature of the Bonn Agreement, unqualified magistrates are still serving in many of the courts and tribunals. Many of the appointed judges still lack a university education, as required by the constitution and the laws. In addition to the problems relating to the qualification of judges, the judiciary is faced with considerable and deep-rooted corruption, mainly caused by very low salaries.[940]

---

[937] GA, 'Report of the Special Rapporteur of the Commission on Human Rights on violence against women, its causes and consequences, on the situation of women and girls on Afghanistan', UN Doc. A/58/421 (6 October 2003), para. 29.

[938] The course was divided into a nine-month theoretical part, including teaching on national, international and human rights law, followed by three months of practical training (Amnesty International, 'Afghanistan: Re-establishing the rule of law', *Report n° ASA 11/021/2003* (14 August 2003), p. 13).

[939] Judicial Reform Commission – UNAMA – UNDP, 'Rebuilding the Justice Sector of Afghanistan', *Project Nr. AFG/03/001/01/34* (January 2003). See also Press Briefing by Manoel de Almeida e Silva, Spokesman for the Special Representative of the Secretary General on Afghanistan, UN News Centre (13 May 2004).

[940] UNAMA – Rule of Law Unit, 'Securing Afghanistan's Future – Considerations on Criteria and Actions for Strengthening the Justice System: Proposal for a long-term strategic framework' (February 2004), p. 24. See also: Basel, *supra* note 926. An increase of 500% over a period of 12 years has however been envisaged by the latest 'Needs analysis' from the Ministry of Justice (See Islamic Republic of Afghanistan – Ministry of Justice, 'Justice for all – A Comprehensive Needs Analysis for Justice in Afghanistan' (May 2005), p. 7.

The international community's involvement in the reconstruction of the Afghan judiciary can in general be described as incomplete. Although strategic schemes and reform proposals have been developed by UNAMA and the Judicial Reform Commission, implementation of the proposed reforms has been deficient due to the abovementioned rivalry between the different formal institutions. Lack of financial resources also caused a slowdown in the progress of judicial reconstruction, especially with regard to the implementation of the Judicial Reform Commission's proposals and recommendations.[941]

4. *Limited Reforms in Iraq*

Before Saddam Hussein's regime, an independent and well-structured court and judicial system existed, established under the British Mandate. After the take-over by the Ba'ath Party, the judiciary's independence was ended and a significant number of Special and Military Courts, which supplanted the ordinary civil courts, were introduced.[942] The judicial system was outdated and more often used as an instrument of political repression than as an independent authority. Torture, inhumane and cruel punishment, as well as closed proceedings were widespread. Revolutionary Courts and other Special Courts, working independently of the regular judicial system, were often composed of party members, lacking any judicial training whatsoever. Women had been generally denied posts as judges or prosecutors since the 1980s. Additionally, severe damage had been caused to the Iraqi physical infrastructure, and many courtrooms were completely destroyed or damaged. The immediate needs in the reconstruction of the Iraqi judiciary were to support the effective implementation of the laws, the training of judges and prosecutors, especially with regard to international human rights standards, and the rebuilding and re-equipping of court buildings.[943] However, these tasks were difficult to undertake. The administration was, as already mentioned, quite unique in the sense that the occupying powers had to cooperate with the UN mission and with the existing Iraqi institutions. When UNAMI's mandate was reshaped in 2004, the mission was asked to "promote the protection of human rights, national reconciliation, and judicial and legal reform in order to strengthen the rule of law in Iraq."[944]

---

941 Report of the Secretary-General, The situation in Afghanistan and its implications for international peace and security, UN Doc. A/58/868–S/2004/634 (12 August 2004), para. 39.

942 See for an overview of the Tribunals and Courts under the regime of Saddam Hussein: United States Institute of Peace, 'Establishing the Rule of Law in Iraq, *Special Report 104* (April 2003), pp. 3–6.

943 See for an overview World Bank – United Nations, 'Joint Iraq Needs Assessment' (October 2003), p. 47.

944 SC Res 1546, UN Doc. S/RES/1546 (2004), para. 7 (b) (iii).

(a) *The Boundaries of Legal Reform under the Laws of Occupation*

The CPA had to work within the limits set by the Hague Regulations and the Geneva Conventions. In principle, Article 43 of the Hague Regulations implies a duty to restore and ensure public order and safety with respect for the laws in force in the country, unless absolutely impossible. This article is seen as a general rule on the legislative powers of the occupying force.[945] The CPA nevertheless had to carry out the administrative duties it was given by the Security Council Resolution 1483, which, with regard to the judiciary, were limited to "working towards the restoration of conditions of security and stability and the creation of conditions in which the Iraqi people can freely determine their own political future" and to "assist the people of Iraq through [...] encouraging international efforts to promote legal and judicial reform",[946] in coordination with UNAMI. Although obligations under a Chapter VII Resolution prevail, this provision cannot however be seen as an explicit derogation of article 43 of the 1907 Hague Regulations, and did not therefore give the CPA extensive legislative authority.[947] In essence, the CPA's mandate boiled down to guaranteeing the effective administration of justice and, where necessary, issue regulations to restore and reform the judiciary within the limits of ensuring the conditions of security and stability.

The first CPA Regulation vested in the CPA "all executive, legislative and judicial authority necessary to achieve its objectives, to be exercised under relevant U.N. Security Council resolutions, including Resolution 1483 (2003), and the laws and usages of war".[948] Consistently with its obligations under the laws of occupation, the CPA identified the applicable law in Section 2 of the same regulation: "[u]nless suspended or replaced by the CPA or superseded by legislation issued by democratic institutions of Iraq, laws in force in Iraq as of April 16, 2003 shall continue to apply in Iraq insofar as the laws do not prevent the CPA from exercising its rights and fulfilling its obligations, or conflict with the present or any other Regulation or Order issued by the CPA". The wording of both sections reveals major similarities with both UNMIK's and UNTAET's first regulations.

During occupation, the CPA undertook a review of the Iraqi Penal and Criminal Procedure Codes to evaluate compliance with international human rights standards, which can to a certain extent be regarded as a permitted exception to the Hague Regulations. However, due to the increase in serious crimes, like

---

945 Sassoli, *supra* note 433.

946 SC Res 1483, UN Doc. S/RES/1483 (2003), paras. 4 and 8 (i).

947 Also Sassoli, *supra* note 433.

948 CPA Regulation Number 1, 'The Coalition Provisional Authority', CPA/REG/16 May 2003/01 (16 May 2003), Section 1, 2).

kidnapping, rape, the theft of cars for use in explosive attacks against coalition forces and citizens, and sabotaging Iraqi infrastructure, most notably the oil infrastructure, the CPA adopted Order 31 which modified the penalties for such offences, bringing them up to a maximum punishment of life imprisonment.[949] Such reforms can also be seen as in line with the Hague Regulations, as they permit changes in the laws in force in order to maintain public order.[950] Based on the same provisions of the Hague Regulations concerning the use by the occupier of the occupied territory's public properties,[951] the CPA created an Iraqi public property management system[952] to facilitate the use and management of all public property, including the court buildings. This programme, headed by the CPA Facility Manager, allowed the rapid restoration of the judicial infrastructure and facilities. By November 2003, the capacity of the Iraqi courts and tribunals was restored to the pre-war level, and most of the courts were functioning. The further restoration, repair and refurbishment of the court buildings took place in the following years, although budget restrictions have hampered progress in that regard.[953]

(b) *Reorganising the Judiciary*

Although not a UN-led international administration, the steps undertaken by the CPA upon arrival were similar to the approach taken by the Special Representatives of the Secretary-General in Kosovo and East Timor. One of the first measures taken by the CPA related to the review and appointment of judicial personnel. Following the adoption of the first CPA order on the 'de-ba'athification' of Iraqi society,[954] CPA Order 15 established a Judicial Review Committee to investigate the suitability of the appointed judges and prosecutors, and consequently confirm their appointment, order their removal, and appoint judges to fill the vacancies.[955] In 2004, the Committee completed its work on the review of judges and prosecutors, after examining approximately 870 and removing

949 CPA Order Number 31, 'Modifications of Penal Code and Criminal Proceedings Law', CPA/ORD/10 Sep 2003/31 (10 September 2003).
950 Sassoli, *supra* note 433.
951 Art. 55 and 56, Hague Regulations.
952 CPA Order Number 9 (revised), 'Management and Use of Iraqi Public Property', CPA/ORD/27 June 2004/09 (23 June 2003, revised 27 June 2004).
953 United States General Accounting Office, 'Rebuilding Iraq. Resource, Security, Governance, Essential Services and Oversight Issues', *Report to Congressional Committee GAO-01–902R* (June 2004), p. 82.
954 CPA Order Number 1, *supra* note 543.
955 The Committee was composed of three Iraqi and three international members. See CPA Order Number 15, 'Establishment of the Judicial Review Committee', CPA/ORD/-Jun 2003/ – (23 June 2003), Section 3 and 4.

176 of them.[956] The Committee also appointed approximately 110 new judges and reinstated 80 who had been removed from office under the former regime.[957] The Iraqi 'Council of Judges' was equally reinstated by the CPA in September 2003 to nominate judges and prosecutors to fill the vacancies.[958]

The Court structure was largely maintained by the occupying forces. A complete reform of the Court structure would not have been in conformity with the CPA's mandate under the laws of occupation and the relevant Security Council Resolutions. However, the CPA dismantled the Revolutionary Courts and other Special Courts which had been established under Saddam Hussein' regime to try security related matters. Their abolition inevitably was the first step in restoring the court structure. The functioning of the Revolutionary and Special Courts, as well as their constitution, was an obvious violation of international human rights.[959] The establishment of a Central Criminal Court of Iraq on 11 July 2003[960] was the next step in establishing a secure environment in Iraq. The Central Criminal Court decides major criminal cases, such as those concerning terrorism, organised crime, race or religion based violence, government corruption, and acts intended to destabilise democratic institutions or processes, including cases of acts of violence against the Coalition forces occurring after 19 March 2003.[961] The establishment of this court to try crimes involving threats to public

---

956 See UNSC Press Release, 'Briefing to security council describes 'time of hope' for Iraq, with major accomplishments over past three months', UN Doc. SC/8006 (24 February 2004) and CPA Press Release, 'An Historic Review of CPA Accomplishments' (28 June 2004), p. 22.

957 United States General Accounting Office, 'Rebuilding Iraq. Resource, Security, Governance, Essential Services and Oversight Issues', *Report to Congressional Committee GAO-01–902R* (June 2004), p. 80.

958 CPA Order Number 35, 'Re-establishment of the Council of Judges', CPA/OR/13 SEP 2003/35 (13 September 2003). The Council of Judges had been abolished by Saddam Hussein's regime in 1979 and replaced by a 'Council of Justice', which was less independent because it was accountable to, and presided over by, the Minister of Justice. See Mahmoud, M., 'Judicial System in Iraq: A Review of the Legislation Regulating Judicial Affairs in Iraq', *Iraqi Judicial Forum: The Judicial System in Iraq: Facts and Prospects – Hashemite Kingdom of Jordan* (October 2004), pp. 21–22 and p. 33.

959 The Revolutionary and Special Courts were staffed by Ba'ath Party Members with no legal training, and their decisions were final and without appeal. See United States Institute of Peace, 'Establishing the Rule of Law in Iraq', *Special Report 104* (April 2003), p. 6. In addition, the members of these Courts were granted complete immunity for their private and public acts, which is a clear violation of the Iraqi Code of Criminal Procedure. See Bassiouni, M. C., 'Iraq Post-Conflict Justice: A Proposed Comprehensive Plan', *International Human Rights Law Institute*, DePaul University College of Law (28 April 2003 / Revised 2 January 2004), p. 4.

960 CPA Order Number 13, 'The Central Criminal Court of Iraq', CPA/ORD/11 Jul 2003/13 (11 July 2003).

961 CPA Order No. 13 (Revised), 'The Central Criminal Court of Iraq', CPA/ORD/11 July 2003/13 (22 April 2004), Sections 4 and 18. See also: Office of the Administrator of the CPA, Public

order and safety has been a crucial step in trying to provide for security in Iraq, although the Court alone could not fill the security vacuum. The Court was also intended to serve as a model for the other Iraqi Courts.

(c) *Building an Independent Judicial Capacity*

The presence of the CPA as administrative power, capable of issuing regulations in certain matters, helped the swift restoration of several judicial institutions. Equally, Iraq's situation had several advantages compared to that of Afghanistan. The availability of judges and prosecutors was far greater than in Afghanistan, although assistance was needed to update the magistrates' legal knowledge and provide training in human rights law and other principles of due process. In addition, the Iraqi judicial system was less fragmented throughout the country, and many of the institutions still existed, but had been corrupted and misused by the former regime.

The CPA established the 'Iraqi Judicial College', formerly called the Judicial Training Institute. Following the complete restoration of the building that housed the latter, the new College was officially opened on 17 June 2003.[962] The former Judicial Training Institute's curriculum has been reviewed to include due process norms and human rights. Following an assessment mission to Iraq, conducted by the International Legal Assistance Consortium (ILAC)[963] in cooperation with the UN and the CPA, a two-year training programme was launched to provide training on the independence of the judiciary, human rights and humanitarian law. Other assistance areas comprised a visit arranged for the leaders of the Iraqi Judicial Training College to observe judicial practice in other States, and the strengthening of institutions such as the Iraqi Bar Association.[964] These areas had been identified as major shortcomings in the Iraqi judicial system.[965] The management of the different training programmes had accordingly been outsourced to ILAC, while each branch of the judicial training programme was implemented by one of ILAC's members.

The training of Iraqi judges on the role of the judiciary in a democratic society, with an emphasis on judicial independence, was conducted by the American Bar Association and the Prague-based Central European and Eurasian Law Initiative (CEELI Institute).[966] The Human Rights training programme, funded by the UK

Notice Regarding the Creation of a Central Criminal Court of Iraq and Adjustments to the Criminal Procedure Code (18 June 2003).

[962] CPA, CPA Daily (7 July 2003).

[963] A consortium of human rights and legal assistance NGOs.

[964] ILAC, *ILAC Annual Report 2004* (2005), p. 2.

[965] ILAC, *Report from an ILAC Mission to Iraq 13–20 August 2003* (4 September 2003), p. 13.

[966] The institution organised two two-week training courses in 2004, for a total of 93 Iraqi judges (ILAC, *Annual Report 2004*, Stockholm (2005), p. 2). Another three training courses were

Department for International Development, was conducted by the International Bar Association's Human Rights Institute and lasted two years. The one-week training course started in February 2004, with the training of 50 judges, prosecutors and lawyers.[967] The training programme on international humanitarian law, funded by the Swedish Ministry of Foreign Affairs, was conducted by the International Bar Association. This component was aimed at providing a legal background for judges and prosecutors who may be faced with criminal charges for crimes against humanity, war crimes and other violations of international criminal law.[968] In addition to these general training courses, a special programme has been organised for the Tribunal which heard the cases against Saddam Hussein and other co-accused.

The CPA's accomplishments with regard to the reconstruction of the judiciary have been significant for trying to provide a secure environment for the reconstruction of Iraq, but the judiciary still has a long way to go. The vast majority of the courts and tribunals are operative, and the bases for an independent judiciary have been established. The presence of qualified judges did somewhat facilitate capacity building in the justice sector. While it can be argued that the training programmes have been efficient in reinforcing Iraqi capacity in the justice sector, several critical issues remain. Although judges have received training in human rights law, the continuing intimidation of them poses a real threat to the implementation of basis human rights.[969] The security situation in addition remains detrimental to the independence of the judiciary. Iraq is still confronted with daily attacks on officials, such as judges and prosecutors,[970] which of course do not facilitate the reconstruction of the judicial system. In addition, the inadequate number of judges – 700 out of a total need for 1,500 – undermines the proper functioning of the court system, and therefore respect for human rights. The continuing alarming security situation in the country has hampered the establishment of an effective rule of law-based society and has somewhat prevented the guaranteeing of the

again organised in 2005, and were attended by 121 judges and 14 prosecutors (ILAC, *ILAC Annual Report 2005* (2006), p. 2).

967 The first course was nevertheless held in Dubai, for security reasons. In 2004 and 2005, 103 judges, 55 prosecutors, 277 lawyers, 17 judicial investigators and 15 officials attended the courses. In addition, the International Bar Association trained 11 judges as trainers, who also conducted training courses on Human Rights. The number of judges who followed the courses however represents only a small percentage of the 700 Iraqi judges. See *ibid.* and United Kingdom, Department for International Development (DFID), 'Iraq Update Newsletter' (October 2004).

968 A total of 75 judges, 45 Prosecutors and 32 lawyers attended the courses, which were organised in 2004 and 2005. See ILAC, *ILAC Annual Report 2005* (2006), p. 3.

969 See Report of the Secretary-General, UN Doc. S/2006/945, *supra* note 835, para. 44.

970 UNAMI, 'Human Rights Report (1 May–30 June 2006)', para. 19.

security of judges as well as the independence of the judiciary, which have been directly targeted. Although the ingredients were laid out by the CPA during the transitional period, the question is of course whether the elected government will be able to maintain progress in that regard.

B. *Promoting and Introducing Respect for Human Rights*

Re-establishing the rule of law means not only that all actors in a State are accountable to law, but also that the laws need to be consistent with international human rights norms and standards. As the European Commissioner for External Relations puts it, "[r]espect for human rights is one of the most fundamental and universal values of our world. All of us, in our official capacity and in our private lives, have a responsibility to promote and protect the rights of our fellow members of the human family, be that at home or elsewhere in the world".[971] In each of the four cases under examination there was an explicit mandate either to introduce human rights in the territories or to promote human rights. This section will deal with the implementation of human rights under the international mandates, the issue of accountability of the international actors involved having been dealt with in the second part. Equally, the discussion of the implementation of human rights in relation to the introduction of democratic governance will be dealt with in the next chapter.

1. *The Kosovo Ombudsperson*

UNMIK was explicitly mandated to protect and promote human rights.[972] It was made clear from the start that international human rights instruments would be applicable in the territory. The first UNMIK Regulation provided that in exercising their functions "all persons undertaking public duties or holding public office in Kosovo shall observe internationally recognized human rights standards and shall not discriminate against any person on any ground such as sex, race, colour, language religion, political or other opinion, national, ethnic or social origin, association with a national community, property, birth or other status".[973] The regulation on the applicable law abolished the death penalty and listed the international human rights standards to be observed under the UNMIK administration.[974] Nevertheless, the supremacy of human rights over domestic laws was

---

[971] Ferrero-Waldner, B., Speech Delivered at the International Human Rights Day (10 December 2005), ec.europa.eu/external_relations/human_rights/intro/index.htm.

[972] SC Res. 1244, UN Doc. S/RES/1244 (1999), para. 11, j).

[973] UNMIK Regulation 1999/1, *supra* note 118, Section 3.

[974] UNMIK Regulation 1999/24, *supra* note 858, para. 1.3.

not explicitly confirmed by the Special Representative of the Secretary-General in Regulation 1999/24, although Regulation 1999/1 did state that the laws were applicable only insofar as they did not conflict with international human rights standards. Neither did any of the regulations provide that international human rights were directly applicable in Kosovo.[975] With the adoption of the Constitutional Framework for Provisional Self-Government, the doubts raised earlier were eliminated, as the Provisional Institutions were bound to observe international human rights standards, which "shall be directly applicable in Kosovo as part of the Constitutional Framework".[976]

The effective implementation of human rights under UNMIK's mandate proved difficult as the judges needed to interpret the existing laws in function of international human rights. In addition, the international judges brought in after several months were not always familiar with the local laws which could potentially violate human rights standards.[977] The regulation defining the applicable law indeed requested from the judges the application of the existing laws, in light of human rights standards. Some incompatibilities of existing provisions with human rights might seem obvious, but UNMIK was not able immediately to engage in an extensive analysis of each provision of the applicable law. The various superseding laws applicable throughout the territory – UNMIK regulations, the law in force prior to 1989, Yugoslav law which came into force after 1989 and which is applicable when the matter is not covered by the laws in force prior to 1989, and human rights law – makes it very hard for the Local and Municipal Courts clearly to establish the applicable legal provisions.[978] Eventually, considering that much of the criminal legislation applicable in Kosovo did not meet international human rights standards, the administration engaged in the drafting of a whole new code of criminal law and criminal procedure. The drafting of the new codes started in 2000, and was finalised in November 2001 by the Joint Advisory Council on Legislative Matters in cooperation with *inter alia* the OSCE and the American Bar Association.[979] The new codes were finally promulgated by the Special Representative of the Secretary-General and entered

[975] On this issue see OSCE Mission in Kosovo – Legal Systems Monitoring Section, 'Kosovo: Review of the criminal justice system 1999–2005 – Reforms and residual concerns' (March 2006), p. 27.

[976] UNMIK Regulation 2001/9, *supra* note 865, Article 3.3.

[977] Caplan, *supra* note 467, p. 64.

[978] For a critique see Ombudsperson Institution in Kosovo, Fourth Annual Report 2003–2004 (12 July 2004).

[979] OSCE Mission in Kosovo – Legal Systems Monitoring Section, 'Kosovo: Review of the criminal justice system 1999–2005 – Reforms and residual concerns' (March 2006), p. 28.

into force in April 2004.[980] During the drafting process, UNMIK adopted several regulations implementing human rights with respect to, for example, the protection of witnesses and the rights of detainees.[981]

An interesting feature of the implementation of human rights in Kosovo is the already briefly mentioned office of the ombudsperson, established to investigate complaints concerning human rights violations and actions constituting an abuse of authority by UNMIK or any other official institution.[982] The institution was incorporated in the Constitutional framework for Provisional Self-Government, and in February 2006 responsibility for the Ombudsperson Institution was transferred from UNMIK to the Kosovo Assembly.[983] The Ombudsperson is an independent institution *vis-à-vis* both the domestic and international institutions. It should nevertheless be reminded that the privileges and immunities of UNMIK personnel were not revoked, and that KFOR action initially fell outside the Ombudsperson's mandate. The Ombudsperson was allowed to give advice and make recommendations to any person or entity concerning the compatibility of domestic laws and regulations with recognized international standards.[984] The institution was generally seen as an effective supervision mechanism for human rights violations, either by advising people or by examining complaints, and can be regarded as the most important human rights institution in Kosovo. The various annual and thematic reports of the Ombudsperson reveal however that the human rights situation in Kosovo remained fragile. Apart from the recurrent criticism related to the immunities and alleged lack of accountability of both UNMIK and KFOR, the practical implementation of human rights law was, according to the Ombudsperson, "a myth".[985]

Nevertheless, the foundations of the respect for human rights were laid, although it has to be admitted that the main shortcoming was a lack of established institutions and procedures competent to engage in the review of the practical implementation of these rights.[986] The Ombudsperson in that regard was vital,

---

980 UNMIK Regulation 2003/25, Provisional Criminal Code of Kosovo, UN Doc. UNMIK/REG/2003/25 (6 July 2003) and UNMIK Regulation 2003/26, Provisional Criminal Procedure Code of Kosovo, UN Doc. UNMIK/REG/2003/26 (6 July 2003).

981 For an overview see OSCE Mission in Kosovo – Legal Systems Monitoring Section, 'Review 4: The Criminal Justice System in Kosovo: September 2001–February 2002' (29 April 2002), p. 15.

982 UNMIK Regulation 2000/38, *supra* note 400.

983 UNMIK Regulation 2006/6 on the Ombudsperson Institution n Kosovo, UN Doc. UNMIK/REG/2006/6 (16 February 2006).

984 UNMIK Regulation 2000/38, *supra* note 400, Section 4.3.

985 Ombudsperson Institution in Kosovo, Fourth Annual Report 2003–2004 (12 July 2004), p. 15.

986 See also Benedek, W., 'Final Status of Kosovo: The Role of Human Rights and Minority Rights', 80 *Chicago-Kent Law Review* 215 (2005), pp. 222–223.

although the institution did not have the power to engage in the judicial review of existing legislation or to ensure the correct application of human rights in courts and tribunals. This cannot but emphasise the need for and importance of the training of judges and prosecutors, and in the first stage the presence of international experts to ensure the correct application of international human rights standards.

2. *East Timor: Focusing on the Adoption of New Laws*

Security Council Resolution 1272 asked UNTAET to "carry out its mandate effectively with a view to the development of local democratic institutions, including an independent East Timorese human rights institution, and the transfer to these institutions of its administrative and public service functions."[987] Resolution 1272 underlined the "importance of including in UNTAET personnel with appropriate training in international humanitarian, human rights and refugee law",[988] but the Security Council did not specify the administration's obligations with respect to human rights law.

The first regulation adopted by the Special Representative of the Secretary-General provided that in exercising their functions all those undertaking public duties or holding public office in East Timor were to observe internationally recognised human rights standards.[989] Regulation 1999/1 equally contained an explicit reference to the prohibition of discrimination.[990] The next section of the regulation provided that Indonesian civil and penal law would continue to apply in East Timor insofar as they were not in contradiction with the listed human rights instruments. On that basis, several Indonesian laws were immediately repealed as they manifestly conflicted with these human rights standards.[991] The task of identifying those provisions of the applicable Indonesian law which violated human rights standards was obviously difficult, if not almost impossible, as there was no functioning judicial system, let alone experienced lawyers upon which to rely. This complication led UNTAET to focus on adopting new legislation compliant with international human rights standards, instead of trying to review the whole Indonesian legal system in function of international human rights standards.[992]

---

[987] SC Res. 1272, UN Doc. S/RES/1272 (1999), para. 8.

[988] *Ibid.*, para. 15.

[989] UNTAET Regulation 1999/1, *supra* note 885.

[990] *Ibid.*, Section 2.

[991] *Ibid.*, Section 3.2.

[992] See Morrow and White, *supra* note 390, pp. 9 *et s.*

UNTAET established a Human Rights Unit to advise the Special Representative on alleged human rights violations throughout the territory, but obviously the Human Rights Unit was not a court and could not enforce the correct application of human rights in East Timor.[993] As already briefly mentioned in the previous part, the (re)emergence of an ombudsperson institution as a method of examining human rights violations has led UNTAET, probably drawing on UNMIK's experience, to create a similar institution. The UNTAET Ombudsperson's official mandate was however not founded on an UNTAET Regulation. It can however be deduced from the UNTAET Daily Briefings that complaints against UNTAET, the Transitional Administration, the Cabinet, and agencies, programmes and institutions which collaborate with the Government could be accepted by the Ombudsperson, but the number of claims submitted proves that the local population was not fully aware of the mechanism.[994] The Ombudsperson in East Timor was generally described as ineffective, and it is clear that he did not have the same effect as in Kosovo.[995] Since independence, the concept of the Ombudsperson has nevertheless been incorporated into the State's constitution.

3. *The 'Afghan Independent Human Rights Commission'*

Afghanistan's international obligations in respect of human rights had already been explicitly established by the Bonn Agreement, which required respect for the international treaties the state was a party to.[996] Afghanistan had *inter alia* acceded to the Convention on the Elimination of All Forms of Discrimination against Women in 1980, the ICCPR in 1983 (although it had not acceded to the Optional Protocol), the Convention on the Elimination of All Forms of Racial Discrimination in 1983 and the Convention on the Rights of the Child in 1994. The Bonn Agreement equally envisaged the establishment of "an independent human rights commission, whose responsibilities will include human rights monitoring, investigation of violations of human rights, and development of domestic human rights institutions".[997] This Commission was effectively established as the Afghan Independent Human Rights Commission (AIHRC) by Presidential Decree in June 2002, and was charged with human rights monitoring, the investigation of violations of human rights, the development and implementation of a national programme of human rights education,

---

[993] Bongiorno, *supra* note 342, p. 652.
[994] *Ibid.*
[995] Chesterman, *supra* note 104, p. 150.
[996] Section II, 1, ii, Bonn Agreement.
[997] Section III, C), 6), Bonn Agreement.

and the development of domestic human rights institutions.[998] The AIHRC was incorporated into the 2004 Constitution and was mandated to monitor the observation of human rights in Afghanistan and to promote their advancement and protection. The AIHRC was equally granted the competence to receive complaints on human rights violations and to refer cases to the courts.[999] The AIHRC cooperated closely with UNAMA, which was granted the right to investigate human rights violations and recommend corrective action where necessary.[1000] However, as a result of the 'light footprint' approach, it was clear from the outset that the UN was reluctant to engage in a leading role in the field of human rights, which is *inter alia* illustrated by the fact that UNAMA did not include a 'Human Rights Pillar' in its structure.[1001] The fragmented approach in this area is also demonstrated by the fact that, even within UNAMA, some human rights staff report to Pillar I (Political Affairs), while others report to Pillar II (Economic Affairs) or directly to the Office of the High Commissioner for Human Rights (OHCHR).[1002]

One of Italy's achievements in the field of judicial reconstruction is the drafting of a new Interim Code of Criminal Procedure, which was adopted by presidential Decree in February 2004. The Interim Code was essentially aimed at eliminating human rights violations contained in the existing code. Despite its adoption by the Afghan Transitional Authority, approval of the new code was relatively controversial as there had been almost no input from Afghan jurists.[1003] However, it has to be emphasised that the main aim of this code was not to introduce an entirely civil-law-based code, but to ensure the correct application of fair trial standards and to protect the rights of defendants and witnesses. In addition, many of the provision of the new code were taken from the previous code.[1004] Along the same lines, a new Juvenile Code was drafted by the Italian authorities and adopted by the Interim Administration.[1005]

---

998 Interim Administration of Afghanistan, Decree of the Presidency of the Interim Administration of Afghanistan on the Establishment of an Afghan Independent Human Rights Commission (6 June 2002), Annex I.

999 Article 58, Constitution of Afghanistan 2004. See also Islamic Republic of Afghanistan, Law on Structure, Duties and Mandate of the Afghanistan Independent Human Rights Commission, No. 3471 (24/02/1384) (14 May 2005).

1000 Annex II, para. 6, Bonn Agreement.

1001 See also Chesterman, *supra* note 104, p. 176.

1002 See for a critique Dahrendorf *et al.*, *supra* note 614.

1003 Jones, Wilson, Rathmell and Riley, *supra* note 716, p. 78 and Miller and Perito, *supra* note 910, p. 8.

1004 See for an overview Tondini, M., 'The Role of Italy in Rebuilding the Judicial System in Afghanistan', 45 *Revue de droit militaire et de droit de la guerre* 79 (2006).

1005 *Ibid.*

Despite the presence of the AIHRC, the observance of and respect for human rights in Afghanistan has not progressed significantly. AIHRC and UNAMA monitoring throughout the country has revealed violations of time limits for pre-trial detention, access to counsel and even allegations of torture "in a significant proportion of cases", in addition to the situation of women and girls, which has not improved.[1006] One of the main criticisms is the remit of the AIHRC which in effect, and until its incorporation in the 2004 Constitution, was not intended to contribute actively to the enforcement of human rights. The AIHRC had the power to investigate violations, but these investigations did not result in legal claims brought against alleged perpetrators. Another reason is of course the specific situation in Afghanistan where effective administration and control are to a certain extent limited to Kabul and its surroundings, while more remote Provinces are still controlled by local commanders often imposing their own 'legal systems' on the population.[1007] Despite the limited results of legislative re-drafting, the enforcement of human rights remains rare. As already mentioned earlier, many Afghan courts and tribunals do not refer to written law when drafting judgments, and Islamic law is still applied throughout the country, creating a gap between the theory and practical reality.[1008] Arguably caused by the International Community's limited mandate, the effective implementation of human rights in Afghanistan has been neglected in the reconstruction process.

4. *Ensuring Effective Human Rights Implementation Iraq*

Before the military intervention, Iraq was a party to the main international human rights instruments,[1009] which were thus binding on the post-conflict Iraqi institutions. The CPA did not have an explicit mandate to engage in extensive human rights reforms. UNAMA, on the other hand, was tasked with promoting the protection of human rights,[1010] and therefore created a Human Rights Office within its structure, in coordination with the UN Office of the

---

1006 Report of the Secretary-General, UN Doc. A/61/799–S/2007/152, *supra* note 720, paras. 41–2.

1007 Cf. Bosi, T. D., 'Post-Conflict Reconstruction: The United Nations' Involvement in Afghanistan', 19 *New York Law School Journal of Human Rights* 819 (2003), p. 830.

1008 Lau, M., 'Afghanistan's Legal System and its Compatibility with International Human Rights Standards', *International Commission of Jurists, Final Report* (November 2002), p. 22.

1009 The International Covenant on Civil and Political Rights on 23 March 1976; the International Covenant on Economic, Social and Cultural Rights on 3 January 1976; the International Convention for the Elimination of All Forms of Racial Discrimination on 13 February 1970; the Convention on the Elimination of All Forms of Discrimination against Women on 12 September 1986 and the Convention on the Rights of the Child on 15 July 1994.

1010 SC Res. 1483, UN Doc. S/RES/1483 (2003), para. 8 (g), and SC Res. 1546, UN Doc. S/RES/1546 (2004), para. 7 (b) (iii).

High Commissioner for Human Rights. The fact that Iraq had already ratified the major human rights treaties limited the mandate of international actors to ensuring the correct application of human rights throughout the territory. Implementation however proved to be difficult, especially in view of the catastrophic security situation.

Although human rights were thus already binding upon the State's institutions, the applicable laws did not necessarily reflect these rights. During occupation, the CPA therefore undertook a review of the Iraqi Penal and Criminal Procedure Codes to evaluate compliance with international human rights standards, which can be regarded as a permitted exception to the Hague Regulations, since, as already mentioned, it can be argued that the occupying power has the right to abolish legislation which violates fundamental human rights.[1011] The Iraqi Criminal Code and the Code of Criminal Procedure, based on the French model, were drafted in 1969 and 1971 respectively, but were in need of review as various provisions were out-dated or had been amended by the former government and included manifest violations of human rights law. CPA Order Number 7 suspended several provisions of the 1969 Iraqi Penal Code which were inconsistent with fundamental human rights, such as provisions limiting the freedom of political association to the sole Ba'ath Party.[1012] In order to avoid the misuse of certain laws by judges, especially with regard to political human rights, CPA Order Number 7 equally reserved to the CPA Administrator the right to allow prosecutions for political crimes.[1013] The rationale of this provision is the exploitation of the aforementioned Penal Code provisions by the Ba'athist regime to try political opponents and disregard human rights. However, the margin of appreciation left to the CPA Administrator, as well as the guidelines or criteria under which these crimes could effectively lead to a trial, was unclear.[1014] The 1971 Iraqi Code of Criminal Procedure was equally revised in order to comply with human rights standards. CPA Memorandum 3 introduced the right to counsel, the right to avoid self-incrimination, the absolute exclusion of evidence obtained by torture and the right to be informed of these rights.[1015] The Transitional Administrative Law equally included several references to human rights,

---

1011 Also Sassoli, *supra* note 433.

1012 CPA Order Number 7, 'Penal Code', CPA/ORD/9 June 2003/07 (9 June 2003).

1013 Publication offences, offences against the internal security of the State, or against public authorities and insult to public officials. See CPA Order Number 7, 'Penal Code', CPA/ORD/9 June 2003/07 (9 June 2003), Section 2, para. 2.

1014 See for a critique Amnesty International, 'Memorandum on concerns related to legislation introduced by the Coalition Provisional Authority', *Report Nr. MDE 14/176/2003* (4 December 2003).

1015 CPA Memorandum No. 3 (Revised), 'Criminal Procedures', CPA/MEM/27 June 2003/03 (27 June 2003), sections 3, 4 and 7.

and the obligation for all official institutions to respect the rights of the Iraqi people.[1016] Nevertheless, the wide interpretation left to the legislators according to the Transitional Administrative Law raised serious doubts about the practical implementation of these rights.

Despite these efforts to introduce human rights provisions into the legal texts, the situation remains distressing. As stated in the UNAMI – OHCHR 'Human Rights Programme for Iraq', the problem is that, with respect to gender equality for example, the right is proclaimed at the constitutional level while discriminatory laws are established at the legislation level.[1017] As in Afghanistan, the implementation of and respect for human rights remain scarce,[1018] despite the creation of a Ministry of Human Rights, *inter alia* mandated to address past human rights atrocities and to safeguard the human rights and fundamental freedoms of all persons.[1019] Certain areas in the South and the North, such as the Region of Kurdistan, are relatively safer and therefore show fewer human rights violations.[1020] Despite Iraq's adherence to human rights treaties, the continuing application of tribal traditions and Islamic law causes serious violations of women's and girls' rights throughout the country.[1021] Needless to say, the worrying security situation in Iraq likewise involves a huge number of human rights violations, emphasising the urgent need to re-establish security and the rule of law in the country, an essential precondition to ensuring respect for fundamental human rights.

C. *Transitional Justice: How to Deal with Past Crimes?*

The notion of transitional justice as such is to a certain extent rather vague, and encompasses a whole range of mechanisms associated with a society's attempts to come to terms with a legacy of large-scale past abuses, in order to ensure accountability, serve justice and achieve reconciliation.[1022] Transitional justice

---

1016 CPA, 'Law of Administration for the State of Iraq for the Transitional Period' (8 March 2004), Chapter II. [Hereafter 'Transitional Administrative Law'].

1017 UNAMI-OHCHR, 'Building and Strengthening the National Human Rights Protection System in Iraq: The Human Rights Programme' (December 2004–December 2006), p. 13.

1018 See the various UNAMI Human Rights Reports since 2005.

1019 CPA Order Number 60, 'Establishment of the Ministry of Human Rights', CPA/ORD/19 Feb 2004/60 (22 February 2004).

1020 UNAMI, Human Rights Report (1 November–31 December 2006), para. 15.

1021 *Ibid.*, paras. 49–50.

1022 For an overview of the importance of transitional justice in post-conflict societies see Van Zyl, P., 'Promoting transitional justice in post-conflict societies', in Bryden, A. and Hänggi, H., *Security Governance in Post-Conflict Peacebuilding* (Geneva: Geneva Center for the Democratic Control of Armed Forces, 2005), p. 209.

needs to be undertaken after a careful analysis of the territory's needs, taking in to account the moral, political and legal problems. The major problem is that one tends to view transitional justice from the international criminal law perspective only,[1023] which implies that the perpetrators of past crimes should either be held accountable or acquitted.[1024] The overall objective of transitional justice is of course accountability, but truth-finding, truth-telling, reparation and reconciliation may also be part of the process. The instruments therefore vary widely from case to case, according to the expectations in the territories.

The most obvious method is of course to rely on tribunals, which may be national, international or 'mixed' with differing levels of international involvement, but these are not the only useful means as the instruments can be both judicial and non-judicial. Transitional justice needs to balance the past and the future: perpetrators of serious crimes in the past must be punished, but reconciliation and rebuilding the country are the overall objectives.[1025] Alternative means, such as a truth commission, have therefore frequently been established. Truth Commissions can be described as "official, temporary, non-judicial fact-finding bodies that investigate a pattern of abuses of human rights or humanitarian law committed over a number of years".[1026] This alternative and increasingly popular form of justice has already been used in more than 30 cases, especially in Central and South America.[1027] The shortcoming is naturally the risk that the conclusions of the commission will be ignored and filed away.[1028] On the other hand, one of the advantages of these Commissions is their capacity to engage is a wide-ranging investigation of a pattern of serious crimes, while criminal proceedings tend to focus on an individual charge. Amnesties can equally be an alternative.[1029] The UN has been very reluctant to use this alternative, although various UN participations in the negotiation of peace agreements did include

---

[1023] See for a critique on the criminal approach Dimitrijevic, N., 'Justice Beyond Blame: Moral Justification of (the Idea of) a Truth Commission', 3 *Journal of Conflict Resolution* 368 (2006).

[1024] Chesterman, *supra* note 104, p. 156.

[1025] Boraine, A., 'Transitional Justice', in Chesterman *et al., supra* note 5, p. 320.

[1026] Report of the Secretary-General, 'The rule of law and transitional justice in conflict and post-conflict societies', *supra* note 15, para. 50.

[1027] *Ibid.*

[1028] Mobekk, E., 'Transitional Justice in Post-Conflict Societies – Approaches to Reconciliation', in Ebnöther and Fluri, *supra* note 762, p. 269.

[1029] See on this issue Dugard, J., 'Dealing with Crimes of a Past Regime: Is Amnesty Still an Option?', 12 *Leiden Journal of International Law* 1002 (1999).

some form of amnesty.[1030] Both forms of transitional justice can of course work in parallel, as in the cases of East Timor and Sierra Leone.[1031]

1. *Kosovo: International and Mixed Trials*

The presence of the ICTY in the case of Kosovo somehow facilitated UNMIK's approach with respect to transitional justice. The issue of transitional justice in Kosovo is of course one of the most sensitive topics, as it is at the centre of the ethnic divisions in the Province. The Security Council had already established an international tribunal with jurisdiction for war crimes, genocide and crimes against humanity occurring in the Former Yugoslavia, including the Kosovo conflict. The ICTY has, according to its statute, concurrent jurisdiction with the national courts, although it has primacy over them.[1032] The ICTY's jurisdiction *ratione temporis* extends beyond the date of the establishment of UNMIK, therefore allowing the international tribunal to investigate crimes against humanity, war crimes and charges of genocide occurred after June 1999.[1033] Nevertheless, the ICTY Prosecutor stressed that only the principal perpetrators would be tried by the ICTY, therefore leaving the majority of trials to the Kosovar courts and tribunals.[1034] The majority of 'smaller' trials were therefore to be handled by the local courts.[1035]

Because of the continuing ethnic bias towards the prosecution of alleged perpetrators of crimes, UNMIK had seriously envisaged the creation of a special Kosovo court, the 'Kosovo War and Ethnic Crimes Court' (KWECC). The Court was envisaged as a mixed tribunal, including national and international judges and prosecutors. The idea was finally abandoned for several reasons, in particular the existence of the ICTY, which to a certain extent had overlapping jurisdiction, the costs of such a specialised court, and the presence of international judges and prosecutors in the 'regular' courts and tribunals.[1036] Ethnic sensitivity

---

1030 Stahn, C., 'United Nations Peace-Building, Amnesties and Alternative forms of Justice: A Change in Practice', 84 *International Review of the Red Cross* 191 (2002).

1031 See on the latter case Shabas, W. A., 'Truth Commissions and Courts Working in Parallel: The Sierra Leone Experience', 98 *American Society of International Law Proceedings* 189 (2004).

1032 Article 9, Statute of the ICTY.

1033 Article 8, Statute of the ICTY.

1034 ICTY Press Release, 'Address by the Prosecutor of the International Criminal Tribunal for the Former Yugoslavia, Carla del Ponte, to the UN Security Council', UN Doc. GR/P.I.S./642-e (27 November 2001).

1035 See on the relation between the ICTY and Kosovo's mixed tribunals Dickinson, L. A., 'The Relationship Between Hybrid Courts and International Courts: The Case of Kosovo', 37 *New England Law Review* 1059 (2002–2003).

1036 See International Crisis Group, 'Finding the Balance: The Scales of Justice In Kosovo', *ICG Balkans Report N°134* (12 September 2002), p. 20.

in Kosovo had led to the appointment of international judges and prosecutors in the tribunals and courts in order to try to avoid ethnic bias, especially with regard to cases concerning former KLA/UCK members. However, there was no specific court or tribunal within the national judicial structure which had exclusive jurisdiction over past serious crimes, as was the case in East Timor. The serious crimes trials therefore took place in the five regular District Courts, with a right to appeal to the Supreme Court of Kosovo. Only a small percentage of the trials dealt with by the regular courts and tribunals were related to serious crimes which occurred prior to the establishment of UNMIK.

Several suspects were arrested for crimes committed in 1998 and 1999.[1037] The majority of the trials conducted concerned Kosovo Serbs, and were handled by national as well as 'mixed' panels. By September 2002, only 17 cases concerning war crimes or crimes against humanity had been heard in the regular courts.[1038] Of these cases, only eight included actual charges of war crimes, crimes against humanity or genocide, whilst the charges in the others had often been withdrawn and requalified as murder. Other cases were solely related to charges of murder alleged to have taken place during the conflict.[1039] Interestingly, the majority of the verdicts of the regular panels in the district courts have been reversed by the Supreme Court, and consequent retrials by international or internationalised panels re-qualified the charges or resulted in acquittals. The Supreme Court has on the other hand been criticised for failing to make sufficient references to international jurisprudence. Even with the presence of international judges on the panels, critics argue that the standard of these trials remained very low, with regard to both language and the quality of the legal reasoning.[1040]

1037 *Ibid.* These included Kosovo Serbs and former KLA members, which led to a wave of protest by Kosovo Albanians who essentially saw the KLA members as 'freedom fighters' under Serb occupation. On the recent case of the indictment of the Kosovo Albanian Ramush Haradinaj by the ICTY Prosecutor and the problems relating to his release by UNMIK, see also Wood, N., 'Kosovo war crimes trial splits West and prosecutors', *International Herald Tribune* (8 April 2007).

1038 See for an overview of the 'war crimes trials' conducted until September 2002 OSCE Mission in Kosovo – Legal Systems Monitoring Section, 'Kosovo's War Crimes Trials: A Review' (September 2002).

1039 *Ibid.*, p. 53.

1040 *Ibid.* This report reproduces an excerpt of one of the Supreme Court Judgments which very clearly illustrates this critique: "Supreme Court found that factual state is wrongly verified concerning all the charges, since there is no direct evidence of final one that the accused acted personally or gave the orders that brought to crimes alleged or that he might be held responsible for duties of command responsibilities in connection with the above mentioned crimes, and there is no evidence that shows his aware intention in the case of attempted murder and neither unjustified conclusion of throwing out the window" (p. 50).

In general, the issue of transitional justice has received virtually no attention from the international authority in Kosovo. It is true that the presence of the ICTY somewhat relieved UNMIK of a part of its responsibility, but it seems that the majority of the cases which should have been dealt with in the regular courts have not led to the necessary reparation. In addition, truth-seeking or reconciliation mechanisms have not been established by UNMIK. Moreover, the judgments in trials conducted in the regular courts have so far not been published; the only overview of these trials was given by the OSCE as the organisation in charge of Human Rights and the Rule of Law in Kosovo.

2. *UNTAET's Comprehensive Approach*

UNTAET was explicitly mandated by the Security Council to bring to justice those responsible for serious violations of human rights and international humanitarian law after the 1999 popular consultation.[1041] Unlike in Kosovo, there was no parallel international tribunal to try alleged offences committed in East Timor prior to the UN take-over of the administration. Jurisdiction over serious crimes and offences was therefore integrated into the domestic legal system, although, as we will see, these cases were handled by special 'mixed' panels. Next to criminal investigations, UNTAET also relied on an extensive reconciliation exercise, as forgiveness is widely integrated in the Timorese cultural tradition.[1042] Although the creation of such a Commission has been criticised for lacking legitimacy as it was set up by international actors,[1043] it must be emphasised that the idea of such a commission was supported by the East Timorese themselves, notably the CNRT.[1044] This dual approach in addressing past crimes had also been proposed by the UN-led 'International Commission of Enquiry on East Timor', which had concluded that "it is fundamental for the future social and political stability of East Timor, that the truth be established and those responsible for the crimes committed be brought to justice".[1045]

The prosecution of serious crimes was left to the exclusive jurisdiction of a particular court within the regular court structure. Section 10 of Regulation 2000/11 provided that the Dili District Court had exclusive jurisdiction over 'serious criminal offences', such as genocide, war crimes, crimes against humanity,

---

1041 SC Res. 1338, UN Doc. S/RES/1338 (2001), para. 8.

1042 Strohmeyer, *supra* note 803, p. 119.

1043 Stahn, C., 'Accommodating Individual Criminal Responsibility and National Reconciliation: The UN Truth Commission for East Timor', 95 *American Journal of International Law* 952 (2001).

1044 Cf. UNTAET, Human Rights Unit Report (March 2001). The HRU organised two workshops with the East Timorese where the issue of transitional justice was raised and approved.

1045 OHCHR, Report of the International Commission of Inquiry on East Timor to The Secretary-General, UN Doc. A/54/726–S/2000/59 (31 January 2000), para. 155.

murder, sexual offences and torture.[1046] With regard to the crimes of torture, murder and sexual offences, the exclusive jurisdiction of the Dili District Court was limited to those offences which were committed between 1 January and 25 October 1999. Cases concerning the crimes listed above were to be handled by 'mixed' panels. A similar mixed composition was provided for the panels in the Court of Appeal in the event of an appeal on one of these matters. The so-called 'Special Panels' in the Dili District Court and the Court of Appeal were to be composed of two international judges and one East Timorese judge.[1047] With regard to the crime of genocide, war crimes, and crimes against humanity, the panels have "universal jurisdiction" which, according to Regulation 2000/15, is to be interpreted as "jurisdiction irrespective of whether the serious criminal offence at issue was committed within the territory of East Timor, the serious criminal offence was committed by an East Timorese citizen, or the victim of the serious criminal offence was an East Timorese citizen".[1048] For the investigation and prosecution of serious crimes the regulation on the organisation of the public prosecution created a separate department, the 'Serious Crimes Unit', headed by a Deputy General Prosecutor for Serious Crimes.[1049] The Serious Crimes Panels faced several difficulties in exercising their functions. In general, the lack of financial resources and the unavailability of sufficient international personnel led to some 700 unprocessed cases overall in 2001, and consequently the release of several alleged perpetrators while held on remand.[1050] Other general problems relating to the East Timorese judiciary, such as adequate translation and housing, have also hampered the effectiveness of 'serious crimes trials'.[1051] Despite these setbacks, the Special Panels conducted 55 trials involving 87 defendants, of whom 85 were found guilty.[1052]

1046 UNTAET Regulation 2000/11 on the organization of courts in East Timor, UN Doc. UNTAET/REG/2000/11 (6 March 2000), section 10.1.

1047 UNTAET Regulation 2000/15 on the establishment of panels with exclusive jurisdiction over serious criminal offences, UN Doc. UNTAET/REG/2000/15 (6 June 2000), section 22.1.

1048 *Ibid.*, section 2.2.

1049 UNTAET Regulation 2000/16 on the organization of the public prosecution service in East Timor, UN Doc. UNTAET/REG/2000/16 (6 June 2000), section 14.3.

1050 Beauvais, J., 'Benevolent Despotism: A Critique of U.N. State-Building in East Timor', 33 *New York University Journal of International and Law and Policy* 1101 (2000–2001), p. 1155 and Mobekk, E., 'Transitional Justice in Post-Conflict Societies – Approaches to Reconciliation', in Ebnöther and Fluri, *supra* note 762, p. 275.

1051 Cf. Linton, S., 'Prosecuting Atrocities at the District Court of Dili', 2 *Melbourne Journal of International Law* 414 (2001), pp. 418–419.

1052 Report of the Secretary-General on justice and reconciliation for Timor-Leste, UN Doc. S/2006/580 (26 July 2006), para. 9. For an extensive overview of the 'Serious Crimes Trials, see Cohen, D., 'Indifference and Accountability: The United Nations and the Politics of International Justice in East Timor', *East West Centre Special Report Number 9* (June 2006).

UNTAET established in parallel with these criminal proceedings the 'Commission for Reception, Truth and Reconciliation' (CRTR) in July 2001.[1053] The Commission was mandated to investigate the pattern of human rights violations and facilitate the 'acceptance' and 'reception' of East Timorese perpetrators of lesser crimes by undertaking community service instead of criminal prosecution.[1054] The Commission's work is therefore the complement of the criminal proceedings in the Dili District Court, although it must be emphasised that this alternative eased the task faced by the emerging judiciary in East Timor, which would have been unable to process all the waiting charges. The 'Commission for Reception, Truth and Reconciliation' was endowed with quasi-judicial powers, as Section 25.3 of Regulation 2001/10 provided that, when the Commission delegated the function of facilitating a 'Community Reconciliation Process' to a Regional Commissioner, the Public Prosecutor could no longer institute criminal proceedings. The regular courts retained a very limited right of control, in function of human rights standards and in order to ensure that the sanction was proportionate to the acts disclosed.[1055] The Commission's final report was submitted on 31 October 2005 after almost five years of its operation. The final report, containing more than 2,000 pages, revealed systematic and wide-spread human rights violations under Indonesian occupation. The main aim of the commission, truth-seeking, has therefore been achieved.[1056] According to the final report, the reconciliation and reception process has been a success.[1057] The final report of the Commission was disseminated in all Timorese districts by the Technical Secretariat, set up by the President in December 2005 to ensure the follow-up of the Commission's report.[1058]

The implication of Indonesia also led to the creation of special mechanisms for transitional justice. The vast majority of alleged perpetrators and indicted individuals still live in Indonesia, and therefore *de facto* outside the territorial jurisdiction of East Timor, despite the 'universal jurisdiction' of the Dili District Court. Indonesia established a 'Commission of Enquiry into Human Rights

[1053] UNTAET Regulation 2001/10 on the Establishment of a Commission for Reception, Truth and Reconciliation, UN Doc. UNTAET/REG/2001/10 (13 July 2001).

[1054] See on the goals of the Commission: UNTAET, Human Rights Unit Report (March 2001).

[1055] UNTAET Regulation 2001/10, *supra* note 1053, section 28.2.

[1056] The Commission received some 7,800 statements on crimes committed during the period between 1974 and 1999, while 1,400 low-level militia perpetrators were heard by the Commission. See Hasegawa, S., 'The Role of the International Community in New Nation Building. Case study of UN Experience in Timor – Leste', *Tokyo University International Symposium on Towards a New Paradigm of International Cooperation* (7 September 2005), p. 44.

[1057] Commission for Reception, Truth and Reconciliation in East Timor, Final Report, paras. 118–120.

[1058] Report of the Secretary-General, UN Doc. S/2007/134, *supra* note 490, para. 28.

Violations in East Timor' (KPP-HAM) in order to prepare a list of suspects for the Indonesian Ad Hoc Human Rights Court on East Timor. The Ad Hoc Court was generally seen as ineffective. Only 18 of 22 suspects were indicted before the Ad Hoc Court, and its trials led to the acquittal of the majority of Indonesian individuals.[1059]

An Indonesian nationwide 'Truth and Reconciliation Commission' was also set up in 2004, mandated to resolve past gross violations of human rights, although it has been widely condemned for its design and lack of capacity to contribute effectively to truth-telling.[1060] An additional joint commission, the 'Commission of Truth and Friendship between Indonesia and Timor-Leste', was set up in 2005 in order to promote reconciliation between the two countries.[1061] Both countries agreed that the results of the Commission's work would not lead to prosecution of the alleged perpetrators of past serious human rights violations, but only seek to reveal the truth about the violations which took place.[1062] The creation of the Joint Commission was disapproved on the ground that its work was already partly covered by the final report of the East Timorese Commission for Reception, Truth and Reconciliation and that the mandate contained provisions on a full amnesty for those who cooperated in revealing the truth.[1063]

Finally, a Commission of experts was mandated by the Security Council to examine the achievements of the various mechanism of transitional justice set up to investigate crimes committed in East Timor before 1999. The final report was submitted in May 2005 and contains an extensive overview and assessment of the effectiveness of the different processes.[1064] In general, the Commission found that the mechanisms put in place under UNTAET were effective although the critiques mentioned earlier have been reiterated by the commission. The Indonesian procedures have however been described as "manifestly inadequate",[1065] although the Commission approved the KPP-HAM report. The Commission found that the majority of suspects had not been held accountable for the serious human rights violations which occurred in East Timor. The Commission

---

1059 Hasegawa, *supra* note 1056, p. 44. See for a critique Human Rights Watch, 'Justice Denied for East Timor: Indonesia's Sham Prosecutions, the Need to Strengthen the Trial Process in East Timor, and the Imperative of U.N. Action'.

1060 See for a critique Linton, S., 'Accounting for Atrocities in Indonesia', 10 *Singapore Yearbook of International Law* 1 (2006).

1061 For the reasons leading to the establishment of the Commission see Babo Soares, D., 'East Timor: reconciliation and reconstruction', *East Timor Law Journal* 3 (2007).

1062 Report of the Secretary-General, *supra* note 1052, paras. 22–25.

1063 Report to the Secretary-General of the Commission of Experts to Review the Prosecution of Serious Violations of Human Rights in Timor-Leste (then East Timor) in 1999, UN Doc. S/2005/458 (26 May 2005), paras. 333–354.

1064 *Ibid.*

1065 *Ibid.*, para. 375.

therefore recommended, in the absence of positive action by either Indonesia or Timor-Leste, the adoption by the Security Council of a Chapter VII Resolution establishing an ad hoc international criminal tribunal for Timor-Leste.[1066] In the meantime, the follow-up mission UNMIT recruited experts to establish a new 'Serious Crimes Investigation Team' to work with the Prosecutor-General to complete the investigations into serious crimes committed in 1999, which were initiated by the Serious Crimes Unit. In addition, the records of the Serious Crimes Unit needed to be completely reconstructed as the May 2006 incidents had totally destroyed the documents collected so far.[1067]

3. *Afghanistan and the Marginalization of Past Crimes*

The reality of war crimes and crimes against humanity throughout Afghanistan's history and the persistence of these crimes under the Transitional Authority have been widely acknowledged by the international community and the Afghan Institutions.[1068] One of the difficulties in addressing accountability for past crimes was that many of the suspects had acted on the order and with the knowledge of political leaders and military commanders. Some of the suspects were present at the signature of the Bonn Agreement, and even part of the Interim Authority.[1069] The Bonn Agreement did not explicitly mention accountability for past crimes, although the UN was mandated to investigate human rights violations. Despite the Secretary-General's opinion that the issue of crimes of the past needed be addressed by the Afghans and the international partners,[1070] UNAMA was very reluctant to take the lead in retrospective investigations of serious human rights violations.[1071]

1066 *Ibid.*, para. 525.

1067 Report of the Secretary-General, UN Doc. S/2007/134, *supra* note 490, para. 28.

1068 See AIHRC, 'A Call for Justice, A National Consultation on Past Human Rights Violations in Afghanistan' (2004) and the speech delivered by President Karzai: 'A Vision of Human Rights in the New Afghanistan', Opening statement at the Afghan National Workshop on Human Rights: Toward Implementation of the Human Rights Provisions of the Bonn Agreement (22 March 2002). See also International Crisis Group, 'Afghanistan: Judicial Reform and Transitional Justice', *Asia Report N°45* (28 January 2003), p. 15.

1069 AIHRC, 'A Call for Justice, A National Consultation on Past Human Rights Violations in Afghanistan' (2004), pp. 41–42 and International Crisis Group, 'Afghanistan: Judicial Reform and Transitional Justice', *Asia Report N°45* (28 January 2003), p. 17. See also on the alleged implication of Rashid Dostum in the killing of Taliban detainees: Chesterman, *supra* note 104, p. 176.

1070 Report of the Secretary-General, The Situation in Afghanistan and its Implications for International Peace and Security, UN Doc. A/56/681–S/2001/1157 (6 December 2001), para. 83.

1071 Dahrendorf *et al.*, *supra* note 614, p. 35.

At the opening of a workshop on Human Rights, the President of the Interim Administration, Hamid Karzai, proposed the creation of a truth commission to deal with the serious crimes of the past.[1072] However, as was the case with the rebuilding of the justice sector in general, and human rights in particular, the crimes of the past were not considered a priority. As explicitly declared by Lakhdar Brahimi, Special Representative of the Secretary-General and Head of UNAMA, "our responsibility to the living has to take precedence and also you have to do what is possible. [...] It is not a question of condoning or forgetting about crimes, serious crimes. It is about moving the peace process in the interest of the people of Afghanistan".[1073] The Special Representative was obviously confident that bringing peace would evidently be followed by the re-establishment of the rule of law, although experience has shown that the rule of law is essential, for everything else depends on it. It has in addition been highlighted that in the so called 'chicken-and-egg dilemma of peace and justice' there is no need to postpone the latter if there is a political will to address the issue, especially with regard to transitional justice.[1074]

The aforementioned workshop on Human Rights nevertheless resulted in a clear mandate for the Afghan Independent Human Rights Commission to address the issue of transitional justice. The Presidential Decree on the establishment of the AIHRC mandated the Commission to "undertake national consultations and propose a national strategy for transitional justice and for addressing the abuses of the past".[1075] A nationwide consultation on transitional justice, directed by the AIHRC, revealed that the majority of the Afghans consulted demanded justice for past crimes.[1076] The national consultation equally revealed the extent of human rights violations by the various regimes and occupiers, and the population's distrust of the official institutions caused by the presence in them of suspects of serious crimes.[1077] The report resulted in the launch of an 'Action Plan on Peace, Reconciliation and Justice in Afghanistan', which was

[1072] Karzai, H., 'A Vision of Human Rights in the New Afghanistan', Opening statement at the Afghan National Workshop on Human Rights: Toward Implementation of the Human Rights Provisions of the Bonn Agreement (22 March 2002).

[1073] Transcript of the Press Conference by Lakhdar Brahimi the Special Representative of the Secretary-General for Afghanistan (27 August 2002).

[1074] International Crisis Group, 'Afghanistan: Judicial Reform and Transitional Justice', *Asia Report N°45* (28 January 2003), p. 17.

[1075] Article 9, Interim Administration of Afghanistan, Decree of the Presidency of the Interim Administration of Afghanistan on the Establishment of an Afghan Independent Human Rights Commission (6 June 2002).

[1076] AIHRC, 'A Call for Justice, A National Consultation on Past Human Rights Violations in Afghanistan' (2004), pp. 41–42.

[1077] *Ibid.*

adopted by the Government of Afghanistan.[1078] The Action Plan lists five 'Key Actions' to be taken by the Afghan Government to ensure accountability for past crimes: (1) the acknowledgement of the suffering of the Afghan people (2) the strengthening of state institutions through reform of the Civil Service Commission to ensure the integrity of civil servants (3) truth-seeking and documentation to establish the facts of the past conflict and atrocities (4) promoting reconciliation and national unity by initiating public debate on reconciliation and (5) the establishment of effective accountability mechanisms to bring to justice those responsible for grave human rights abuses. A subsequent international conference on transitional justice equally revealed the will of the population to create mixed mechanisms to address past violations, through criminal proceedings and reconciliation.[1079] The effective implementation of the Action Plan was however scheduled only for December 2006, and has recently been postponed until December 2009.

To date, apart from the different reports on the need for mechanisms to deal with transitional justice, no progress has been made. The issue remains sensitive, especially with regard to criminal accountability, as illustrated by the adoption of a 'Resolution on national reconciliation' by the Lower House on 20 February 2007, which highlighted the need for reconciliation but declared that all political parties and belligerent groups associated with the decades of conflict should be immune from prosecution.[1080] The resolution was approved by the Upper House. It was widely condemned for its attempts to provide amnesties in complete contradiction with the Action Plan and the AIHRC national consultation.[1081] President Karzai stated that he would not approve any bill that was unconstitutional or that contravened Sharia law, and affirmed that only victims of human rights violations had the right to forgive.

4. *The Iraqi Special Tribunal*

The CPA did not have a comprehensive transitional justice proposal. Next to the criminal proceedings against former leading members of the Ba'ath Party, there were no plans to create a truth-seeking Commission or to investigate past

[1078] Government of the Islamic Republic of Afghanistan, 'Action Plan on Peace, Reconciliation and Justice in Afghanistan' (14 December 2005).

[1079] AIHRC Press Release, 'Truth-seeking and Reconciliation in Afghanistan' (15 December 2005).

[1080] Report of the Secretary-General, UN Doc. A/61/799–S/2007/152, *supra* note 720, para. 14.

[1081] See for example International Center for Transitional Justice Press Release, 'President Karzai Must Resist Parliament's Attempt at Self-Amnesty' (3 February 2007).

crimes.[1082] The focus on individual criminal responsibility for past crimes, followed by the execution of Saddam Hussein and other high-ranking officials, left victims of other crimes without redress. To date, no comprehensive truth-seeking exercise has been launched, despite assertions by the CPA administrator that "[t]he leadership and workers of this Ministry will, through documentation and education, serve as the collective conscience of the Iraqi people. By documenting the fate of the hundreds of thousands of missing, by giving names and dates and places to those sacrificed to Saddam's lust for power, the dead will remind the living of what happens when government protects the powerful and not the powerless".[1083] The question of how to deal with past abuses had nevertheless already been raised when the UN's role in the reconstruction process was discussed.[1084] The then Special Representative of the Secretary-General argued that the international community should consider the "establishment of a mixed Iraqi and international panel of experts to consider in detail the options that would best suit Iraq".[1085] Nevertheless, a tribunal under leadership of the Iraqis was seen as the only immediate option, mainly aimed at restoring security throughout the country instead of seeking the truth about past crimes.[1086]

One of the first measures taken by the CPA with regard to judicial reform was the establishment in July 2003 of a Central Criminal Court of Iraq to try the most serious criminal cases. With regard to past crimes, the CPA assigned the task of identifying the measures to be taken to the 'Office of Human Rights and Transitional Justice', created in June 2003,[1087] and which recommended the creation of an Iraqi Special Tribunal to try senior members of the former regime

---

[1082] For a critique on this approach see Smith, A. M., 'Transitional justice in Iraq: the Iraqi Special Tribunal and the future of a nation' 14 *International Affairs Review* 5 (2005).

[1083] Bremer, L. P., 'Remarks at Official Opening of the Ministry of Human Rights Building' (14 February 2004).

[1084] See also the declaration by the German Representative to the Security Council: "The Iraqi people were forced to live for decades under a brutal regime with a complete disrespect for even the most basic principles of human rights. The almost daily new discovery of mass graves is only the most apparent evidence of the atrocities committed by the Saddam regime. Against this backdrop, it comes as no surprise that the issue of transitional justice and accountability for past crimes is a frequently cited priority area. We believe that this issue has to be dealt with under genuine Iraqi ownership in order to be accepted as impartial by the people of Iraq." (UNSC Meeting Record, UN Doc. S/PV.4791 (22 July 2003), p. 21).

[1085] Briefing by Sergio Vieira de Mello to the Security Council: UNSC Meeting Record, UN Doc. S/PV.4791 (22 July 2003), p. 7.

[1086] See CPA Briefing with Dan Senor, CPA Senior Advisor, and Brigadier General Mark Kimmitt, Deputy Director For Coalition Operations (9 March 2004).

[1087] GA, 'Report of The United Nations High Commissioner For Human Rights And Follow-Up To The World Conference On Human Rights. The present situation of human rights in Iraq', UN Doc. E/CN.4/2005/4 (9 June 2004), para. 119.

for war crimes, crimes against humanity and genocide. The Special Tribunal was effectively established by the Iraqi Governing Council on 10 December 2003.[1088] Although the Iraqi Special Tribunal allows international assistance for judges, prosecutors and investigators, the possibility of introducing international judges into the judiciary was never really envisaged.[1089] The law regarding the Iraqi Special Tribunal did not adopt a mixed composition for the tribunal, but allowed for the possibility of appointing international judges only after approval by the Iraqi Governing Council.[1090] The Tribunal's jurisdiction *ratione temporis* extended to acts committed between 17 July 1968 and 1 May 2003.[1091]

Apart from critiques of the Tribunal with regard to the appointment of judges and evidence-gathering,[1092] the main international concern was the reintroduction of the death penalty. Although the former Secretary-General had strongly opposed such a penalty, his successor stated that "we should never forget the victims of his crimes. The issue of capital punishment is for each and every Member State to decide".[1093] The Secretary-General nevertheless subsequently nuanced his statement. Entering into the debate on the death penalty would be outside the scope of this research, but we may just mention that the UN Special Rapporteur on the independence of judges and lawyers recently asked the Iraqi

---

1088 CPA Order Number 48, 'Delegation of Authority Regarding an Iraqi Special Tribunal', CPA/ORD/9 Dec 2003/48 (9 December 2003). The Special Tribunal was adopted by the Iraqi Governing Council on the same date: see 43 ILM 231 (2004). The law was subsequently re-adopted by the Iraqi parliament with some amendment, and published as a national law in the official gazette as the ''Law of the Supreme Iraqi Criminal Tribunal', Law Number 10 of 2005, 4006 *Official Gazette of the Republic of Iraq* (18 October 2005) [hereafter 'Statute of the Iraqi Special Tribunal]). For an extensive discussion of the Statute see Tarin, D., 'Prosecuting Saddam and Bungling Transitional Justice in Iraq', 45 *Vanderbilt Journal of International Law* 467 (2004–2005). On the legislative history see Olusanya, O., 'The Statute of the Iraqi Special Tribunal for Crimes Against Humanity – Progressive or Regressive?', 5 *German Law Journal* (2004).

1089 See however, Slaughter, A.-M. and Burke-White, W., 'Role for U.N. in War Crimes Trials', *The Washington Times* (21 May 2003) and Blum, V., 'Crafting Justice In Iraq: The Bush administration backs Iraqi court plan criticized by many in international legal community', *Legal Times* (22 December 2003).

1090 CPA Order Number 48, 'Delegation of Authority Regarding an Iraqi Special Tribunal', CPA/ORD/9 Dec 2003/48 (9 December 2003), section 2.

1091 Art. 1, Statute of the Iraqi Special Tribunal.

1092 See Newton, M. A., 'The Iraqi Special Tribunal: A Human Rights Perspective', 38 *Cornell International Law Journal* 863 (2005).

1093 UN News Centre, 'Ban Ki-Moon takes over as UN Secretary-General, calls for common action to face crises' (2 January 2007).

authorities to stop applying the death penalty, as the Iraqi Higher Tribunal could not guarantee strict due process standards.[1094]

At the time of the execution of Saddam Hussein and other Ba'ath Party officials, many of the cases brought against the former regime had not yet been tried. In addition to criminal proceedings, the CPA nevertheless established a Special Task Force on Compensation for the Victims of the Previous Regime in May 2004 to address the issue of reparation for past crimes, but compensation has not yet been awarded. In the May 2007 Compact, the Government of Iraq emphasised the necessity of providing reparation for past crimes, and committed itself to elaborating a comprehensive strategy for transitional justice, including the professionalisation of the 'De-ba'athification Committee', a possible law on amnesties and providing reparation for victims.[1095]

[1094] UN News Centre, 'UN independent expert calls for death penalties to cease in Iraq' (19 June 2007).

[1095] Section 3.3.3, Iraq Compact.

Chapter 11

Institution-building and Democratic Governance

An analysis of the mandates entrusted to the recent international administrations and the subsequent reconstruction missions in Afghanistan and Iraq reveals an unambiguous aim to introduce democracy into these states and territories.[1096] Democratic governance seems to be one of the primary, if not the most important, aims, and is for that reason not just an essential component of peace-building missions, but often one of the final objectives. The link between democracy and peace remains controversial,[1097] but was explicitly taken up by the former UN Secretary-General, Boutros Boutros-Ghali, in his Agenda for Democratisation, in which he considered that "[d]emocratic institutions and processes [...] minimize[e] the risk that differences or disputes will erupt into armed conflict or confrontation. [...] In this way, a culture of democracy is fundamentally a culture of peace."[1098] However, at the establishment of the UN the question of

---

1096 See Cogen, M. and De Brabandere, E., 'Democratic Governance and Post Conflict Reconstruction', 20 *Leiden Journal of International Law* 669 (2007) and d'Aspremont, *supra* note 242.

1097 See on the idea that democratic governance protects pluralistic and stable societies and enhances peaceful existence between social groups Diamond, L., 'Promoting Democracy in the 1990s: Actors and Instruments, Issues and Imperatives', *A Report to the Carnegie Commission on Preventing Deadly Conflict*, Carnegie Corporation of New York (December 1995). This idea of 'democratic peace' and the question of democratic governance enjoy high priority in foreign policy. See for example the speech delivered by the former EU External Relations Commission, Chris Patten, at a plenary session in Brussels: "Free societies tend not to fight one another or to be bad neighbours. [...] That is why, over the last twenty years, we have made human rights and democratisation in other countries a matter of European concern". (SPEECH/99/193 (30 November 1999)). See also the declaration made by the ASEAN spokesman to the BBC following the adoption of the Bali Concord II: "Through the Bali Concord 11, ASEAN has subscribed to the notion of democratic peace, which means all member countries believe democratic processes will promote regional peace and stability" (Luard, T., 'Asean: Changing, but only slowly', *BBC News Online* (8 October 2003)).

1098 Report of the UN Secretary General, 'An Agenda for Democratisation', UN Doc. A/51/761 (20 December 1996), para. 7.

democracy was only indirectly addressed by the then newly accepted concept of human rights.[1099] Several UN resolutions and declarations have since further specified the contents of democracy and the level of a state's obligations in that respect.[1100]

Within the mandates aimed at reconstructing states one can easily distinguish both the short-term and long-term objectives. Providing basic civil administration and economic and physical reconstruction can be seen as short-term objectives, although they paradoxically may require a long-term engagement. The overarching and long-term objective is however the creation of a viable and democratic entity.[1101] Previous peace-building cases already showed a commitment to introducing democracy. In Somalia for example, the Security Council emphasised the need to establish "representative democratic institutions".[1102] In the case of Cambodia, the Security Council underlined the importance of free and fair elections in settling the internal conflict.[1103] The Cambodian experience nevertheless already extended beyond the mere holding of elections, with a clear commitment to include other aspects of democratic capacity-building. The enshrinement in Cambodian laws of the right to create and organise political parties, and therefore to hold legitimate multi-party elections, has for instance been one of the major achievements of UNTAC. The number of political parties in Cambodia rose from 19 in 1993 to 39 in the 1998 election.[1104]

A brief look at the mandates of current peace-building missions is sufficient to identify the continuation of this trend and the weight of democracy in these recent missions. Security Council Resolution 1244, establishing the interim administration in Kosovo, is of particular relevance in that respect, as it determines one of the basic functions of the civil presence as "organizing and overseeing the development of provisional institutions for democratic and autonomous self-

1099 See Rich, R., 'Bringing Democracy into International Law', 12 *Journal of Democracy* 22 (2001).

1100 See for example GA Res 52/18 'Support by the United Nations system of the efforts of Governments to promote and consolidate new or restored democracies', UN Doc. A/RES/52/18 (21 November 1997); GA Res. 55/2, United Nations Millennium Declaration, UN Doc. A/RES/55/2 (8 Sep. 2000); GA Res. 55/96, UN Doc. A/RES/55/96 (28 February 2001). Report of the Secretary-General, Support by the United Nations system of the efforts of governments to promote and consolidate new or restored democracies, UN Doc. A/52/513 (21 October 1997) and Economic and Social Council, Commission on Human Rights, Resolution 1999/57, UN Doc. E/CN.4/1999/L.55/Rev.2 (27 April 1999).

1101 Although this objective can be detected even outside the scope of post-conflict reconstruction. See d'Aspremont, *supra* note 242.

1102 SC Res. 814, UN Doc. S/RES/814 (1993), preamble.

1103 SC Res. 745, UN Doc. S/RES/745 (1992), preamble.

1104 Peou, S., 'The UN's modest impact on Cambodia's democracy', in Newman and Rich, *supra* note 82, p. 264.

government pending a political settlement, including the holding of elections".[1105] At the establishment of UNTAET the Security Council adopted similar provisions, asking the international administration to "carry out its mandate effectively with a view to the development of local democratic institutions [...] and the transfer to these institutions of its administrative and public service functions".[1106] As far as Afghanistan is concerned, the Bonn Agreement established a Special Independent Commission for the Convening of an 'Emergency Loya Jirga' to decide on a Transitional Authority to govern the State until "a fully representative government can be elected through free and fair elections".[1107] The Agreement equally acknowledged "the right of the people of Afghanistan to freely determine their own political future in accordance with the principles of Islam, democracy, pluralism, and social justice".[1108] In Iraq, the Security Council did not explicitly refer to democracy, although it asked the UNAMI to work with the CPA to "restore and establish national and local institutions for representative governance".[1109] The CPA was moreover asked to work towards the "creation of conditions in which the Iraqi people can freely determine their own political future".[1110] The Security Council recently acknowledged that "a democratically elected and constitutionally based Government of Iraq is now in place."[1111]

We will start with an analysis of the transitional process in the institutional sphere, to examine the setting up of local or mixed institutions in the emergency stage. In the second section, we will analyse to what extent the principles of democratic governance have been implemented in the four cases, in particular in the conversion from transitional or interim institutions to entirely national ones. We will focus on the organisation of free and fair elections, in conjunction with the implementation of freedom of expression and association in particular in respect of political parties.

A. *From Interim to Elected Institutions*

In the past, the UN has been a major actor in providing assistance in the organisation and overseeing of elections. Electoral assistance by the UN varied from acting as observer of the election campaign, the guarantee of adequate media access for all political parties, the prevention of possible misuse of government resources

---

1105 SC Res. 1244, UN Doc. S/RES/1244 (1999), para. 11(c).

1106 SC Res. 1272, UN Doc. S/RES/1272 (1999), para. 8.

1107 Article I(4), Bonn Agreement.

1108 *Ibid.* Preamble.

1109 SC Res. 1483, UN Doc. S/RES/1483 (2003), para. 8(c).

1110 *Ibid.*, para. 4.

1111 SC Res. 1830, UN Doc. S/RES/1830 (2008), preamble.

by one of the parties and verification of the results to the actual organisation and conduct of elections. The UN's first involvements in electoral assistance were mainly centred on the self-determination and decolonisation processes. The supervision of Namibian elections in 1989 following a *de jure* take-over by the UN of the administration of the territory marked a decisive stage in future UN activities, beginning with the first comprehensive electoral observation mission in Nicaragua in 1990,[1112] followed by the election-monitoring mission in Haiti in 1990, which was far more than merely counting votes.[1113] From that time onwards, the UN has been actively involved in giving electoral assistance, observation and verification in a large number of states in Africa, Asia and Latin America. In the cases under consideration, the UN's role with regard to free and fair elections has been paramount. When the UN was not directly mandated to perform administrative functions, the organisation's role was limited to provide assistance and advice, and to supervising the electoral process, without however organising the elections.

The transfer of power to elected institutions must always be regarded as the goal of a reconstruction process, but the participation of local actors in the transition process is crucial. Obviously, this is the aspect which has been influenced the most by the different approaches, as it was in particular the level of 'internationalisation' of the interim or transitional structures which differed substantially. In the case of Afghanistan, purely national institutions were set up as a part of the Bonn Agreement, while the full administration technique resulted in exclusively international transitional administrations in Kosovo and East Timor. In Iraq on the other hand, the US- and UK-led CPA was established as the principal executive and legislative organ. In addition, various local interim structures were equally created to assist, advise or even exercise limited administrative or legislative power. Gradually, elections were organised to establish national institutions to which full authority was transferred.

1. *A Constitutional Framework for Kosovo*

UNMIK's mandate was both explicit and imprecise. Since Kosovo's final status was left in an indeterminate state, the administration's main task was to facilitate the transfer of all authority to "provisional institutions for democratic and autonomous self-government", but the actual substance and timetable for such a transfer were uncertain. Having established that the UN mission would exercise all legislative, executive and judicial authority in the province, the Special Representative upon his arrival established a 'Kosovo Transitional Council'

1112 SC Res. 637, UN Doc. S/RES/637 (1989).

1113 GA Res. 45/21 Electoral Assistance to Haiti, UN Doc. A/45/490 (1990), para. 12.

(KTC), as a consultative, legislator-like organ. The Council was convened for the first time in July 1999.[1114] A few months later it was expanded and integrated into the first Kosovar multi-ethnic governmental structure: the 'Joint Interim Administrative Structure' (JIAS).[1115]

The JIAS comprised, besides the Kosovo Transitional Council, an Interim Administrative Council (IAC) and administrative departments, co-headed by local and international officials. The Kosovo Transitional Council and the Interim Administrative Council were both advisory organs with no real powers. However, the setting up of intermediary structures was important in order to replace all parallel structures at the same time as creating a single authority in the province. While some of the functions had already been transferred to the administrative departments, UNMIK's pillars remained the principal organs of the transitional administration. Unlike the Kosovo Transitional Council which was an institution comprising only Kosovars, the Interim Administrative Council was composed of four UNMIK and four Kosovar representatives. The Interim Administrative Council's main task was to propose amendments to the applicable laws and the adoption of new regulations.[1116] The Special Representative who presided over the Council had no voting power, but could nevertheless refuse to take account of the recommendations provided that his refusal was reasoned. The Interim Administrative Departments were co-headed by a Kosovar national and a senior international UNMIK staff member, under the overall supervision of a Deputy Special Representative who retained the final authority to take a decision if there was no agreement between the co-heads. These governing bodies were the first step towards the transfer of the legislative and executive competences to Kosovar institutions. This transitional solution lasted for more than a year and was abandoned after the adoption of the 'Constitutional Framework for Provisional Self-Government'.[1117] The promulgation of the Constitutional Framework was criticised by both Kosovo Albanians and Serbs. The former protested because the structures did not challenge the fact that Kosovo belonged to Serbia, while the latter interpreted the structure as paving the way for independence as it included a Kosovar Presidency.[1118]

Under the Constitutional Framework large areas of executive and legislative power were transferred to the local institutions, while reserving powers to the

---

1114 UNMIK Press Release, UNMIK Convenes First Meeting of Kosovo Transitional Council, UN Doc. UNMIK/PR/12 (16 July 1999).

1115 UNMIK Regulation 2000/1, *supra* note 476.

1116 *Ibid.*, section 3.

1117 UNMIK Regulation 2001/19, *supra* note 477. See Annex VI, Structure of the Provisional Institutions of Self-Government.

1118 See Derens, J.-A., 'Le plan Haekkerup inquiète les Serbes', *La Libre Belgique* (16 May 2001).

Special Representative to ensure the implementation of Resolution 1244.[1119] The Special Representative retained final authority on various competences transferred to the Kosovar institutions. The Constitutional Framework provided *inter alia* that it is the task of the Special Representative to promulgate the laws adopted by the Assembly.[1120] The Special Representative could therefore veto any law considering that the Constitutional Framework did not specify an *obligation* for the Special Representative to promulgate all the laws adopted by the Assembly. It was nevertheless understood that this right should be exercised only in order to prevent the adoption of legislation which conflicted with, for example, Resolution 1244 or international human rights obligations. In the early years of the Assembly's work the Special Representative of the Secretary-General did not promulgate several of these laws since these impinged on the Special Representative's reserved competences.[1121]

While UNMIK immediately included local actors in the decision-making process, it has nevertheless been very reluctant to transfer competences to the local institutions. First, one must remember that the security situation in which politicians were often targeted and the ethnic divisions within Kosovar society were not favourable to a complete handover. In addition, parallel structures persisted,[1122] and the Serb minority was unwilling to participate in the functioning institutions. Moreover, the uncertain final status of the Province was an important obstruction to a complete transfer of competences, as Resolution 1244 requested UNMIK only to work towards the establishment of substantial autonomy and self-government in Kosovo.

UNMIK decided to hold the first local elections on 28 October 2000, following the creation of "provisional institutions for democratic and autonomous self-government at the municipal level" in August 2000.[1123] The preference for holding *municipal* elections first has to be considered in the context of Kosovo's uncertain final status. National elections were not yet feasible in 2000 as there was no agreement on the provisional national institutions. Moreover, UNMIK feared that early elections would be beneficial to radical parties such as the UCK/

[1119] UNMIK Regulation 2001/19, *supra* note 477, consideration 9 and Chapter 12.

[1120] *Ibid.*, para. 9.1.44.

[1121] For example, the Assembly adopted a Resolution on the protection of the territorial integrity of Kosovo which challenged borders which had been defined in a treaty concluded in 2001 between the Federal Republic of Yugoslavia and the former Yugoslav Republic of Macedonia. See: UNSC Presidential Statement, UN Doc. S/PRST/2002/16 (24 Mai 2002).

[1122] See on this issue: OSCE Mission in Kosovo, Department of Human Rights, Decentralization and Communities, 'Parallel Structures in Kosovo 2006–2007 (4 April 2007).

[1123] UNMIK Regulation 2000/45 on Self-Government of Municipalities on Kosovo, UN Doc. UNMIK/REG/2000/45 (11 Aug 2000), Section 1.1.

KLA.[1124] In addition, and more generally, the UN has learned that the holding of national elections can no longer be a mere exit strategy by itself, but needs to be considered as no more than a part of the long-term institution-building process. The requirement of a stable political environment can therefore necessitate the postponement of national parliamentary or presidential elections.[1125] A similar gradual approach towards the holding of elections has been taken in the other cases.

The elections for the municipal assemblies were generally seen as free and fair, and despite some logistical problems[1126] no serious incidents have been reported.[1127] However, due to the boycott of the three Serb-dominated municipalities in the north of the Province, only 27 of the 30 municipalities successfully elected a Municipal Assembly. As far as the three other municipalities are concerned, the outcome was not certified as a result of the insignificant voter turnout,[1128] and the Special Representative of the Secretary-General decided to appoint the members of the Municipal Assemblies in these three municipalities.[1129] The next municipal elections were held on 26 October 2002, and were similarly, according to the observers, in accordance with international standards.[1130] Again, the turnout of Kosovo Serb voters was very low as a result of mixed signals from the Yugoslav authorities with regard to participation, and, secondly, because of doubts among the Serbs themselves concerning the benefits of participation.[1131]

The Constitutional Framework established a Parliamentary Assembly, a Government and a President of Kosovo as the new Kosovar institutions. These institutions were effective from the organisation of elections on 17 November 2001, resulting in the successful transfer of large parts of the executive and legislative authority. Again, the elections were considered a success, in spite of some

---

1124 Caplan, *supra* note 467, p. 123.

1125 See Chesterman, *supra* note 104, pp. 208–210 and Ludwig, R., 'The UN's Electoral Assistance: Challenges, Accomplishments, Prospects', in Newman and Rich, *supra* note 82, p. 169.

1126 Report of the Secretary-General on the United Nations Interim Administration Mission on Kosovo, UN Doc. S/2000/196 (15 Dec. 2000), para. 3.

1127 See Hysa, Y., 'Kosovo: A permanent international protectorate?', in Newman and Rich, *supra* note 82, p. 296 and Yannis, A., 'The UN as Government in Kosovo', 10 *Global Governance* 67 (2004), p. 76.

1128 Report of the Secretary-General, UN Doc. S/2000/196, *supra* note 1126, para. 4 and OSCE Mission in Kosovo, 'Kosovo Municipal Elections 2000 – Final Results' (8 November 2000).

1129 Report of the Secretary-General on the United Nations Interim Administration Mission on Kosovo, UN Doc. S/2003/113 (29 January 2003), para. 18.

1130 Council of Europe, 'Final report of the Election Observation Mission for the 2002 Kosovo Municipal Assembly Elections (CEEOM III)', Doc. Nr. SG/Inf(2002)49 (26 November 2002), paras. 140–145.

1131 Report of the Secretary-General, UN Doc. S/2000/196, *supra* note 1126, para. 3.

reports of voter intimidation in the northern part of Kosovo.[1132] As provided for by the 2004 Kosovo Standards Implementation Plan,[1133] the 2004 elections to the National Assembly were organised by the people of Kosovo themselves, under the supervision of the Central Election Commission.[1134] The Kosovo Serb turnout in the 2004 National Assembly elections was again 'negligible',[1135] and resulted in the reduction of their available seats to the ten set aside for Kosovo Serbs in the Assembly.[1136] Finally, following the declaration of independence by the Assembly on 17 February 2008, a new Constitution came into effect on 15 June 2008 which is principally based on the February 2007 Ahtisaari settlement proposal.[1137]

2. *Consultation in East Timor*

Soon after UNTAET's arrival, the Transitional Administrator established the National Consultative Council (NCC), a political body consisting of 11 East Timorese and four UNTAET members, to oversee the decision-making process during the transitional period leading to independence.[1138] The National Consultative Council was chaired by the Transitional Administrator. The Council's primary responsibility was to make policy recommendations on significant executive and legislative matters, and to consult with the Timorese on all aspects of UNTAET's involvement. The Council therefore had no legislative or executive power. Review of UNTAET regulations was included in the Council's advisory mandate. All UNTAET regulations adopted during the National Consultative Council's tenure were endorsed by the Council.[1139] Within the National Consultative Council, 'sectorial committees' were established in the areas of macroeconomics and finance, civil service, local administration, infrastructure, agriculture, health and education.[1140] In April 2000, a 'District Advisory Council', comprising

1132 Report of the Secretary-General, UN Doc. S/2002/62, *supra* note 481, paras. 3–4.

1133 UNMIK, Kosovo Standards Implementation Plan (31 March 2004), p. 8.

1134 UNMIK Regulation 2004/9 on the Central Election Commission, UN Doc. UNMIK/REG/2004/9 (27 April 2004).

1135 Special Representative of the Secretary-General for Kosovo, Annex 1 to the Report of the Secretary-General on the United Nations Interim Administration Mission on Kosovo, UN Doc. S/2004/907 (17 November 2004), para. 6.

1136 See European Commission, 'Kosovo (under UNSCR 1244) 2005 Progress Report', Doc. Nr. SEC (2005) 1423 (9 November 2005), p. 9.

1137 Comprehensive Proposal for the Kosovo Status Settlement, UN Doc. S/2007/168, Add. 1 (26 March 2007).

1138 UNTAET Regulation 1999/2, *supra* note 499.

1139 Report of the Secretary-General, 'Financing of the United Nations Transitional Administration in East Timor', UN Doc. A/54/769 (7 March 2000), para. 14.

1140 *Ibid.*, para. 16.

community leaders and chaired by the UNTAET District Administrator, was established in each district to decide on district-level policy.[1141] A few months later, UNTAET's 'Governance and Public Administration Pillar' was replaced by the 'East Timor Transitional Administration', divided into nine portfolios, four of them being run by UNTAET officials, while the remaining five were entrusted to the East Timorese.[1142] The Special Representative continued to head the East Timor Transitional Administration. The next step in the transition process was the establishment of the National Council in October 2000[1143] to replace and expand the former National Consultative Council as the basis of a future legislative assembly, while in the meantime increasing local participation.[1144]

The political situation of East Timor differed substantially from that of Kosovo, but the holding of free and fair elections for the creation of democratic institutions was approached in a similar way. As in Kosovo, elections were not seen as the priority at UNTAET's arrival and the first elections were held only some 18 months after the setting up of the operation.[1145] Evidently, the fact that East Timor's independence was a clear objective of the transition process influenced the institution-building process, and accelerated the handover to East Timorese institutions. In addition, in UNTAET's view, the size of the country meant that the creation of local municipal institutions was unnecessary.[1146] Notwithstanding the absence of an explicit reference in the relevant Security Council Resolutions to the holding of elections, the setting up of democratic institutions based on free and fair elections was seen as a part of UNTAET's mandate.[1147]

On 30 August 2001, exactly two years after the popular consultation leading to UNTAET's creation, the first elections were held. The 30 August 2001 Constituent Assembly elections were certified as free and fair by key international observers[1148] and by the Independent Electoral Commission set up to oversee to

1141 UNTAET Daily Press Briefing, 'UNTAET Establishes Advisory Councils In The Districts' (5 April 2000).

1142 Report of the Secretary-General, UN Doc. S/2000/738, *supra* note 493, para. 3. See also Smith and Dee, *supra* note 496, p. 65.

1143 UNTAET Regulation 2000/24 on the establishment of a National Council, UN Doc. UNTAET/REG/2000/24 (14 July 2000).

1144 Report of the Secretary-General, UN Doc. S/2000/738, *supra* note 493, para. 2.

1145 For a critique see Chopra, *supra* note 10.

1146 See Chesterman, *supra* note 104, p. 208.

1147 Report of the Secretary-General, UN Doc. S/1999/1024, *supra* note 310. See also d'Aspremont, *supra* note 242, p. 900.

1148 European Union Election Observations Mission, 'Final Report of the European Union Election Observations Mission in East Timor – 30 August 2001 Constituent Assembly Elections' (2001), p. 37. See also Report of the Secretary-General, UN Doc. S/2001/983, *supra* note 806, para. 5 and Juvenal Dos Reis, M., 'East Timor and the Role of International Assistance', in Azimi, Fuller and Nakayama, *supra* note 85, p. 182.

fairness of the election process.[1149] The elected 88-member Constituent Assembly was tasked with writing and adopting a new Constitution and establishing the framework for future elections to complete the transition to full independence. In conjunction with the election of the Assembly, the Special Representative appointed a second, exclusively Timorese, Transitional Government based on the results of the 2001 Constituent Assembly elections. The Special Representative nevertheless included several independents and members of minority parties in the Transitional Government.[1150] The elaborated Constitution was signed on 22 March 2002 and provided for the direct election of a President and a National Parliament.[1151]

The first Presidential elections were held on 14 April 2002, and were equally viewed as free and fair by international observers.[1152] The Constituent Assembly was transformed into the country's parliament on 20 May 2002. Whereas the relevant UNTAET Regulation authorised such a transformation if so provided by the Constitution,[1153] this raised serious doubts about the democratic nature of such a conversion. Although the transitional process might have necessitated the creation of un-elected governmental bodies while awaiting the creation of a stable political environment, this transformation was seen as a violation of the right to free and fair elections, given that elections had already been held in the state and that democratic institutions been provided for in the adopted Constitution. Ideally, a second round of elections should have been organised in order to elect the Parliamentary Assembly, as the Constituent Assembly was elected only for the purpose of *drafting* a Constitution, but not to function as a legislative body.[1154]

1149 UNTAET Press Release, East Timor: certified voting results presented to head of UN mission (10 September 2001) and UNSC Press Release, Security Council Hears Details of Free and Fair Elections in East Timor, UN Doc. SC/7139 (10 September 2001). On the Independent Electoral Commission, see UNTAET Regulation 2001/2, *supra* note 701, section 11.

1150 Cliffe, S., 'The East Timorese Reconstruction Programme: Successes, Problems and Tradeoffs', in Azimi, N. and Chang, L. L. (eds.), *The United Nations Transitional Administration in East Timor (UNTAET): debriefing and lessons* (Leiden / Boston: Martinus Nijhoff Publishers, 2003), p. 104.

1151 For an overview of the drafting of the Constitution see Morrow and White, *supra* note 390.

1152 European Union Election Observations Mission, 'East Timor Presidential Elections – 14 April 2002, European Union Election Observations Mission Final Report' (2002), p. 12. See also the Report of the Secretary-General, UN Doc. S/2002/432, *supra* note 516, para. 7.

1153 UNTAET Regulation 2001/2, *supra* note 701, para. 206 and Constitution of the Democratic Republic of Timor-Leste, section 167.

1154 Saldanha, J. M. and Magno, M. X., 'UNTAET: Mandate, East Timorese Role, and Exit Strategy', in Azimi and Chang, *supra* note 1150, p. 165.

Despite these and other limited concerns with regard to the electoral process,[1155] the UN achieved one of the primary goals of the administration, namely a successful transition to independence through the creation of democratic institutions based on free and fair elections.[1156] The question remains however whether the success of the elections just discussed will be repeated in the years to come. One of the critiques of the UN's involvement has indeed been the failure to create sufficient capacity to strengthen the governmental institutions.[1157] In the meantime, the National Assembly adopted new laws to regulate the presidential and parliamentary elections which took place respectively in April and June 2007.[1158] The recent elections can be seen as an evaluation of the institution-building process. The overall impression of the April 2007 Presidential elections was positive, with a high degree of voter participation. Despite several 'clashes' in the campaign, no major incidents were reported.[1159] On the technical side, the Timorese authorities managed to conduct the elections in a peaceful manner, although questions were raised about the late adoption of the Electoral Law (December 2006), the registration of voters, and identity checking on Election Day.[1160] The impression given by the subsequent parliamentary elections in June 2007 was similar. Despite some isolated but serious incidents during the campaign, the elections were peaceful.[1161] The same logistical problems as arose in the April 2007 Presidential elections were highlighted by the EU's observer mission. Although the legal framework was seen as in accordance with international standards for democratic elections, it nevertheless contained significant gaps and was finalised late.[1162]

1155 Especially in respect of the registration process. UNTAET faced the difficult task of defining the electoral *system* and, in fact, used different systems in the different elections. With regard to the 2001 elections for the Constituent Assembly, UNTAET engaged in the nationwide registration process to identify voters. Conversely, as certain independent experts had questioned the accuracy of the registry, the Independent Electoral Commission decided not the use the same registry for the 2002 Presidential Elections and relied on a system where voters were free to choose their place of voting upon presentation of certain identity documents. See on this issue: Juvenal Dos Reis, M., 'East Timor and the Role of International Assistance', in Azimi, Fuller and Nakayama, *supra* note 85, p. 182.

1156 Valenzuela, C. 'Towards elections', in Azimi and Chang, *supra* note 1150, p. 180 and p. 182.

1157 See for example: Saldanha, M. and Magno, M. X., 'UNTAET: Mandate, East Timorese Role, and Exit Strategy', in Azimi and Chang, *supra* note 1150, p. 164.

1158 See SC Res. 1745, UN Doc. S/RES/1475 (2007), para. 7.

1159 European Union Election Observation Mission, 'Presidential Elections – 9 April 2007, Preliminary Statement' (11 April 2007), p. 6.

1160 *Ibid.*

1161 European Union Election Observation Mission, 'Parliamentary Elections – 30 June 2007, Preliminary Statement' (2 July 2007), p. 2.

1162 *Ibid.*

3. *'Relatively Fair' Elections in Afghanistan*

The first step in the political transitional process was the establishment of a Special Independent Commission for the Convening of an 'Emergency Loya Jirga' to decide on a Transitional Authority.[1163] The Bonn Agreement established an 'Interim Authority', chaired by Hamid Karzai, to govern Afghanistan until the appointment of the Transitional Authority. The Interim Authority was inaugurated a few weeks after the signature of the Agreement. The Emergency Loya Jirga was finally held in June 2002, and appointed the Afghan Transitional Authority, designed to govern the State until "a fully representative government can be elected through free and fair elections".[1164] From that time on, the focus was on the drafting of a constitution. The Bonn Agreement equally contained detailed provisions in that regard. Within 18 months a 'Constitutional Loya Jirga' had to be convened to adopt a new constitution for Afghanistan, prepared by a Constitutional Commission established by the Transitional Authority. The 'Constitutional Loya Jirga' was effectively convened on 14 December 2003 and the Constitution of Afghanistan was finally adopted in January 2004.[1165] The Constitution as elaborated provided for a bicameral National Assembly, consisting of a directly elected *Wolesi Jirga* (House of People or Lower House), an indirectly elected *Meshrano Jirga* (House of Elders or Upper House), and a directly elected President, laying the basis for a democratic political system. Apart from the national institutions, the 2004 Constitution equally created provincial, district and village councils to be elected by free election.

Despite the different situation, the timeline for the holding of elections was very similar to those in Kosovo and East Timor. As said, the Bonn Agreement expressly asked the Afghan Transitional Authority to "lead Afghanistan until such time a fully representative government can be elected through free and fair elections to be held no longer than two years from the date of the convening of the Emergency Loya Jirga",[1166] which was to have been June 2004. Again, the agreed two-year period has to be seen in the context of creating a stable democratic environment in which elections could take place without jeopardising the entire peace process.[1167] Presidential elections were held with a few months delay on

---

1163 For an overview of the transitional political processes see Saikal, A., 'Afghanistan's weak state and strong society', in Chesterman *et al.*, *supra* note 5, p. 357.

1164 Section I (4), Bonn Agreement.

1165 Report of the Secretary-General, UN Doc. A/58/742–S/2004/230, *supra* note 728, para. 2. For a critique of the 'democratic' nature of the Constitutional Loya Jirga and the constitutional developments in Afghanistan see Arjomand, S. A., 'Constitutional Developments in Afghanistan: A Comparative and Historical Perspective', 53 *Drake Law Review* 943 (2005).

1166 Art. I, para. 4, Bonn Agreement.

1167 Cf. Johnson, C., Maley W., Their, A. and Wardak, A., 'Afghanistan's political and constitutional development', *Overseas Development Institute* (January 2003), p. 32.

9 October 2004,[1168] and were monitored by the Joint Electoral Management Body (JEMB), an Afghan–UN body established to oversee the electoral process. The presidential elections were relatively peaceful, despite some shortcomings relating to logistical problems and complaints of violation of the electoral rules and procedure by candidates' representatives and even JEMB staff.[1169]

It soon became clear that the time limit set by the Bonn Agreement would be impossible to meet for the elections to the *Wolesi Jirga* and the Provincial Councils because of technical (seat allocation, population figures and voter registration), legal (delays in the drafting of the Electoral Law) and security (disarmament of militias) problems.[1170] The elections to the *Wolesi Jirga* and Provincial Councils were finally held on 18 September 2005.[1171] As the elections for the District Councils had not yet taken place due to problems with regard to the determination of district boundaries, the 34 members of the *Meshrano Jirga*, which had to be selected by the District Councils, were appointed by the Provincial Councils. The *Wolesi Jirga* and Provincial Council elections were seen as 'relatively fair', although the main observer, the EU, did not send its staff to 'high-risk' areas and reported the killing of several voters during and after the election process.[1172] The JEMB, which monitored the electoral process, nevertheless did report several cases of intimidation by agents and attempts at fraud, which however did not, in the view of the JEMB, undermine the legitimacy of the results.[1173]

Although UNAMA was not mandated to participate principally and actively in the administration of the territory, it provided efficient support to the Interim Authority and afterwards to the Transitional Authority. Pillar I was critically efficient in the convening of the emergency *Loya Jirga*.[1174] UNAMA participated in the elaboration of the rules for selection of the roughly 1,500 delegates to the

[1168] Report of the Secretary-General, 'The situation in Afghanistan and its implications for international peace and security', UN Doc. A/59/581–S/2004/925 (26 November 2004), para. 7.

[1169] See AIHRC-UNAMA, 'AIHRC's Report on 2004 Presidential Elections and its Recommendations [sic]' (November 2004).

[1170] See the following reports of the Secretary-General on 'The situation in Afghanistan and its implications for international peace and security': UN Doc. A/58/742–S/2004/230 (19 March 2004), paras. 14–15, UN Doc. A/58/868–S/2004/634 (12 August 2004), para. 9 and UN Doc. A/60/224–S/2005/525 (12 August 2005).

[1171] Joint Electoral Management Body, 'Final Report. National Assembly and Provincial Council Elections 2005' (December 2005).

[1172] European Union Election Observations Mission, 'Afghanistan Parliamentary and Provincial Council Elections – 18 September 2005, European Union Election Observations Mission Final Report' (2005), p. 28.

[1173] Joint Electoral Management Body, 'National Assembly and Provincial Council Elections 2005, Final Report', 16.

[1174] Dahrendorf *et al., supra* note 614, para. 52.

emergency Grand Council from nearly 400 districts. UNAMA equally provided technical support and advice during the emergency *Loya Jirga*, as well as election monitoring. The same assistance was given for the preparation of the Constitutional Loya Jirga. UNAMA also participated actively in the election process by supporting the Electoral Commission appointed by the Afghan Transitional Authority and assisting in the registration of voters and in the organisation of the elections.

Following the holding of parliamentary and provincial elections the Bonn process ended formally on 19 December 2005 with the inauguration of the National Assembly.[1175] In less than four years, the Bonn process had managed to lead to the election of a president and, with more than a year's delay, a bicameral National Assembly. Despite the relative 'successes' of the Bonn process, obstacles to a sustainable peace remain. Several critical aspects included in the Bonn Agreement have not been met: voter registration, civil service reform, judicial reform and the holding of district council elections. Despite the existing formal governmental structure, traditional structures are often the only source of legitimate power in rural areas.[1176] These local structures re-emerged after the fall of the Taliban regime, and the central authority still has many difficulties in gaining control over these parallel power holders.

4. *Iraq: from Foreign Occupation to National Institutions*

The creation of democratic institutions based on free and fair elections was not expressly included in the relevant Security Council Resolutions or in the first CPA regulations. One of the first indications of the holding of elections is contained in Resolution 1546, in which the Security Council confirmed the importance of holding direct democratic elections and welcomed the effort of the Interim Government in working toward democratic institutions.[1177] As in Afghanistan, the political transition process was characterised by two phases: an interim and a transitional phase. The first interim phase comprised the establishment of a 'Governing Council of Iraq', while an Iraqi 'Interim Government' would be created in a second stage. Two months after the formation of the CPA, the appointed 'Governing Council of Iraq' was recognised as the principal body of the Iraqi interim administration pending the establishment of an internationally recognised representative government.[1178] The CPA immediately included in the regulation a provision that the Governing Council and the CPA would consult and coordinate on all matters involving the temporary governance of Iraq. The

1175 Report of the Secretary-General, UN Doc. A/60/712–S/2006/145, *supra* note 152, para. 7.
1176 See Report of the Secretary-General, UN Doc. A/61/799–S/2007/152, *supra* note 720.
1177 SC Res. 1546, UN Doc. S/RES/1546 (2004).
1178 CPA Regulation Number 6, CPA/REG/13 July 2003/06 (13 July 2003).

creation of an interim Iraqi Government was a necessary intermediate step for the legitimacy of the entire operation and the institution-building process. It was unimaginable for the CPA to have been solely responsible for the administration of the territory pending the organisation of free and fair elections.

On 8 March 2004, the Governing Council of Iraq adopted the 'Law of Administration for the State of Iraq for the Transitional Period' (the 'Transitional Administrative Law' or TAL),[1179] aimed at establishing the legal framework for the Iraqi Government during transition and until the election of the government. The TAL came into force on 28 June 2004, the date on which, according to Security Council Resolution 1546, the Coalition occupation of Iraq came to an end. The CPA, which had administered Iraq since the fall of the Ba'athist regime, was consequently dissolved. The TAL was designed to function as a sort of interim constitution[1180] and contained details of further political developments. The 'interim' phase was the formation of an 'Iraqi Interim Government', appointed by the 'Iraqi Governing Council' and the CPA to assume authority in June 2004, after the dissolution of the CPA. The 'Iraqi Interim Government' assumed authority over the country, and governed Iraq between June 2004 and January 2005 until the holding of direct elections leading to the second 'transitional' phase.

On 30 January 2005, elections were held for the National Assembly, which was mandated to draft the permanent constitution by no later than 15 August 2005. The overall conduct of the election was in accordance with international standards, although the overall turnout was low, especially among Arab Sunnis.[1181] Following these elections, the 'Iraqi Interim Government' was replaced by the 'Iraqi Transitional Government' and the Transitional Assembly was convened to draft the constitution.[1182] Following the positive outcome of the referendum on the constitution, general elections were held on 15 December 2005 for a permanent 275-member Iraqi Council of Representatives.[1183] The overall turnout was far larger than in the January 2005 elections and no 'major' incidents

[1179] CPA, 'Law of Administration for the State of Iraq for the Transitional Period' (8 March 2004).

[1180] Critics nevertheless disapproved the incorporation of provisions relating to Islam as a source of legislation, while providing that no law could be adopted which contradicted the universally agreed tenets of Islam (see: UNAMI-OHCHR, 'Building and Strengthening the National Human Rights Protection System in Iraq: The Human Rights Programme' (December 2004–December 2006), p. 13).

[1181] Report of the Secretary-General, UN Doc. S/2005/141, *supra* note 553, para. 5.

[1182] Report of the Secretary-General pursuant to paragraph 30 of Security Council Resolution 1546 (2004), UN Doc. S/2005/585 (7 September 2005), para. 4.

[1183] Report of the Secretary-General pursuant to paragraph 30 of Security Council Resolution 1546 (2004), UN Doc. S/2006/137 (3 March 2006), para. 3.

were reported on Election Day, apart from several reports of violence.[1184] An Independent Electoral Commission charged with ensuring the fairness of the process supervised the elections.[1185]

The main criticisms of the electoral process concerned the timetable and the involvement of local actors. A stable environment is indeed a prerequisite to the holding of elections, but the reliance on various interim or transitional institutions caused great distrust among the local population. In addition, no local or provincial elections were held before the nation-wide parliamentary elections.[1186] Nevertheless, the bases of a democratic system, as well as the principle of holding elections on a regular basis, were laid. The major issue in the Iraqi institutional reconstruction process remains the security aspect which, of course, greatly influences the capacity of the population to participate freely in the electoral process. Indeed, the general perception of the fairness of the elections conducted has to be considered with regard to human rights such as the freedoms of association and expression, the respect of which inevitably influences the fairness of the electoral process.

B. *The Context of Elections: Freedom of Expression and Freedom of Association*

The practice pertaining to institutional reconstruction in post-conflict situations also demonstrates that the freedoms of expression and of association are basic pillars of democratically elected institutions.[1187] This is not entirely surprising since both freedoms are important conditions of the holding of free and fair elections. The freedom of association and the freedom of expression have been considered by one author as "essential preconditions for an open electoral process".[1188] The respect of these rights cannot therefore be disconnected from free and fair elections.[1189] The General Assembly reaffirmed that, "determining the will of the

1184 *Ibid.*, paras. 4 and 11.

1185 CPA Order No. 92, 'The Independent Electoral Commission of Iraq', CPA/ORD/31 May 2004/92 (31 May 2004).

1186 See for a critique on the election timetable Diamond, L., 'Building Democracy after Conflict: Lessons from Iraq', 16 *Journal of Democracy* 9 (2005).

1187 See in general: Cogen and De Brabandere, *supra* note 1096.

1188 Franck, *supra* note 335, p. 61.

1189 See Human Rights Committee General Comment 25 (57), The right to participate in public affairs, voting rights and the right of equal access to public service (Art. 25), UN Doc. CCPR/C/21/Rev.1/Add.7 (1996). In its General Comment 25, the Human Rights Committee confirms, in order to ensure the full enjoyment of rights protected by Article 25, the importance of "free communication of information and ideas about public and political issues between citizens, candidates and elected representatives, [which] implies a free press and other media

people requires an electoral process that provides an equal opportunity for all citizens to become candidates and put forward their political views, individually and in co-operation with others".[1190] The European Court of Human Rights has similarly emphasized the importance of the respect of these rights in an electoral process, especially in relation to political parties.[1191]

In fact, already in the case of West Irian, the Agreement concluded between Indonesia and the Netherlands placed an emphasis on these rights, as it provided that "[t]he UNTEA and Indonesia will guarantee fully the rights, including the rights of free speech, freedom of movement and of assembly, of the inhabitants of the area".[1192] This could be seen as an early form of emphasising the importance of these rights in the context of democratic governance under foreign administration, as the West Irianese were asked to vote for the future status of the territory in a referendum. The subsequent practice which we will discuss further below provides evidence of the weight of these rights in the current context.

1. *Freedoms and Ethnic Sensitivities in Kosovo*

Besides the confirmation by the Transitional Administrator that, in exercising their functions, all people undertaking public duties or holding public office in Kosovo must observe internationally recognised human rights standards,[1193] Chapter 2(b) of the 2001 'Constitutional Framework for Provisional Self-Government' imposes on the Provisional Institutions of Self-Government the duty "to promote and

able to comment on public issues without censorship or restraint and to inform public opinion" (§ 26). The Human Rights Committee equally considered the "right to freedom of association, including the right to form and join organizations and associations concerned with political and public affairs, [as] an essential adjunct to the rights protected by article 25" (§ 27). The 1993 Vienna Declaration and Programme of Action adopted at the World Conference on Human Rights in Vienna, 14–25 June 1993, equally confirmed the interdependency between democracy and human rights (Vienna Declaration and Programme of Action, UN Doc. A/CONF.157/23 (12 July 1993)). See also Langlois, A. J., 'Human Rights without Democracy? A Critique of the Separationist Thesis', 25 *Human Rights Quarterly* 990 (2003).

1190 GA Res. 45/150, 'Enhancing the effectiveness of the principle of periodic and genuine elections', UN Doc. A/RES/45/150 (18 December 1990), para. 3.

1191 See e.g. European Court of Human Rights, 'United Communist Party of Turkey v Turkey', 30 January 1998, 1998 ECHR 1, paras. 25 and 43: "political parties are a form of association essential to the proper functioning of democracy", and "political parties make an irreplaceable contribution to political debate, which is at the very core of the concept of a democratic society". See also European Court of Human Rights, 'Socialist Party and others v Turkey', 25 May 1998, 1998 ECHR 45, para. 43: "[t]he protection of opinions and the freedom to express them [...] applies all the more in relation to political parties in view of their essential role in ensuring pluralism and the proper functioning of democracy. [...] Their activities form part of a collective exercise of freedom of expression".

1192 Article XXII, Agreement concerning West Irian.

1193 UNMIK Regulation 1999/24, *supra* note 858, para. 1.3.

fully respect the rule of law, human rights and freedoms, democratic principles and reconciliation".[1194] Next to these general tools of human rights protection, several more specific instruments on the relationship between human rights and the holding of elections were adopted under UNMIK's administration.

Regulation 2000/16 on the registration and operation of political parties established the right to create political parties and initiated a whole regime of registration, organisation and dissolution of political parties. A similar regulation was adopted governing the founding, registration, activities and dissolution of all legal persons organised as NGOs.[1195] The regulation, drafted with the assistance of national and international NGOs, fully recognised the right of individuals to associate and work together in the common interest and for the public good. The regulation also declared that it did not seek to limit the right of individuals to the freedom of association by providing simple procedures for associations to form a legal entity separate from the legal personality of its members. In a few years, the number of registered NGOs in Kosovo had risen to 2,800, with some 300 representing Kosovo Serbs.[1196] However, on 23 February 2005, the Kosovo Assembly passed a 'Law on Freedom of Association in NGO', which raised concern since the draft law incorporated amendments which would in a way limit the right to free association through mandatory registration. Registration could indeed have been refused on certain grounds, which could thus generate obstacles to the formation of associations.[1197] The former UNMIK Regulation merely offered the opportunity to be registered to form a separate legal entity. The proposed law has not been promulgated by the Special Representative.[1198]

The Ombudsperson Institution mentioned above and created by UNMIK to receive complaints with regard to *inter alia* the observance of fundamental human rights and freedoms by the Kosovar official institutions, also played a vital role in safeguarding human rights. Although its powers were merely recommendatory, it was for a year the only human rights institution in the territory. Since its establishment, the office of the Ombudsperson has dealt with various cases of alleged human rights violations by Kosovo official institutions. One of the first

---

1194 UNMIK Regulation 2001/9, *supra* note 865.

1195 UNMIK Regulation 1999/22 on the registration and operation of non-governmental organizations in Kosovo, UN Doc. UNMIK/REG/1999/22 (15 November 1999).

1196 Report of the Secretary-General on the United Nations Interim Administration Mission on Kosovo, UN Doc. S/2005/88 (14 February 2005), para. 10.

1197 See on this issue Council of Europe, Advisory Committee on the Framework Convention for the Protection of National Minorities, 'Opinion on the Implementation of the Framework Convention for the Protection of National Minorities in Kosovo', Doc. Nr. ACFC/OP/I(2005)004 (25 November 2005), para. 60.

1198 See Provisional Institutions of Self-Government, Assembly of Kosovo, 'Evidence of the processed and adopted Laws'.

cases concerned the freedom of association with regard to political participation. The Ombudsperson found that the 'arbitrary' removal by the Special Representative of the Secretary-General of three people from the list of candidates of their respective political parties for the 2001 elections to the Kosovo Assembly violated *inter alia* the right to freedom of association guaranteed under Article 11 of the ECHR. The Ombudsman recommended that the Special Representative of the Secretary-General reinstate them for the elections to the Kosovo Assembly to take place on 17 November 2001.[1199]

With regard to the implementation of the right to freedom of expression, the climate in Kosovo was at least worrying at the time of the establishment of UNMIK. Intolerance had emerged within the Kosovo Albanian community, and the rights of the Kosovars to freedom of association and expression were generally challenged. As the KLA/UCK controlled most of the municipal administrations which had meanwhile been re-established and self-appointed, opposition to these new institutions led to several reports of intimidation and harassment.[1200] The main problem in Kosovo is the complexity of maintaining peaceful coexistence and tolerance amongst all ethnic groups and of creating an environment in which freedom of opinion and expression can be exercised to the full. In that regard, the fact that defamation was still a part of criminal law seems to play a vital role in the initiation of legal action, in particular against journalists, and resulted in approximately 300 libel actions between 2000 and 2004.[1201] The Kosovo Ombudsperson reminded the Special Representative of the negative effects of these provisions of the criminal code and urged him to remove criminal insult and libel from the code.[1202] UNMIK's presence was however indispensable for encouraging efforts to resolve these issues,[1203] especially considering the years of oppression under the previous regime.

1199 Ombudsperson Institution in Kosovo, Ex Officio Investigation No 19/01: Report Regarding the Removal of Emrush Xhemajli, Gafurr Elshani and Sabit Gashi from the List of Candidates for the November 2001 Elections.

1200 OSCE Mission in Kosovo, 'Human Rights in Kosovo: As Seen, As Told', Volume II (October 1999).

1201 Human Rights Committee, 'Concluding Observations of the Human Rights Committee: Serbia and Montenegro', UN Doc. CCPR/CO/81/SEMO (12 August 2004), p. 22.

1202 Ombudsperson Institution in Kosovo Press Release, 'The Ombudsperson asks the SRSG to decriminalize defamation cases to safeguard freedom of expression' (7 March 2005).

1203 Economic and Social Council, Commission on Human Rights, Report submitted by the Special Rapporteur on the promotion and protection of the right to freedom of opinion and expression – Addendum 4 – Mission to the State Union of Serbia and Montenegro, UN Doc. E/CN.4/2005/64/Add.4 (8 February 2005).

2. *Defamation Laws in East Timor*

UNTAET took an important first step in adopting Regulation 1999/1, which affirmed on the one hand that all legislative and executive authority, including the administration of the judiciary, was vested in UNTAET, and on the other hand that in exercising their functions all those undertaking public duties or holding public office in East Timor had to observe internationally recognised human rights standards. UNTAET reaffirmed the importance of the freedoms of association and expression in the drafting of the regulation on the election of the Constituent Assembly: "persons in East Timor have the right to freedom of association, the right to peaceful assembly, the right to freedom of expression, the right to vote and to be elected and to take part in the conduct of public affairs, directly or through freely chosen representatives".[1204]

The difficulties in fully achieving the freedom of association in a post-conflict setting can be illustrated by the discussion that arose concerning the provisions of this regulation relating to the registration of political parties. Some local actors had requested that parties that had opposed East Timor's independence be excluded. UNTAET refused to accede to this demand, mainly inspired by ethnic and post-conflict reactions, and finally introduced a general right to form political parties,[1205] leading to the registration of 16 political parties participating in the election for the Constituent Assembly.[1206] This highlights the necessity of having a neutral actor in the post-conflict process to ensure the correct implementation of fundamental political human rights with far-reaching implications for the introduction of democratic governance.

In the meantime, the right to freedom of association, in conjunction with the protection of human rights as one of the State's main objective, was enshrined in the Constitution, adopted in March 2002. The Constitution guarantees that everyone has the right to freedom of association, with the important proviso that the association be not intended to promote violence and be in accordance with the law.[1207] The Constitution also includes the prohibition on establishing armed, military or paramilitary associations, including organisations of a racist or xenophobic nature or those promoting terrorism. A specific provision was introduced concerning the right of every citizen to participate in the political life and public affairs of the country, and to establish and participate in political

---

1204 UNTAET Regulation 2001/2, *supra* note 701, section 20.3.

1205 See on this issue Morrow and White, *supra* note 390, p. 15.

1206 Progress Report of the Secretary-General on the United Nations Transitional Administration in East Timor, UN Doc. S/2001/719 (24 July 2001), para. 2.

1207 See Constitution of Timor-Leste, section 43.

parties. Such a provision was also included concerning the freedom to form and to join trade unions.[1208]

In East Timor, freedom of expression had been severely restricted in the past, not just during the Indonesian occupation, but also under the former Portuguese administration of the territory. The right to freedom of expression was explicitly incorporated into the State's Constitution with explicit reference to the basic human right treaties.[1209] UNTAET had few problems regarding freedom of expression during the administration of the territory, but since independence some problems have risen, especially with regard to harsh defamation laws which are a significant assault to the freedom of expression. While defamation laws are an accepted restriction on the freedom of expression, reparation should be a matter of civil rather that criminal law.[1210] Whilst Timor Leste's Press Law contains a basic regime guaranteeing the right to freedom of expression for journalists, in complete accord with international standards and treaties, the Penal Code includes a hard regime for defamation which can be applied concurrently with the Press Law. In February 2005, the parliament adopted new draft articles of the Penal Code providing for imprisonment of up to two years for defamation if committed through the media, and three years for defamation against individuals performing public, religious or political duties,[1211] although international case law established that public officials should tolerate a higher degree of criticism.[1212] In addition, the draft articles did not provide maximum levels for fines. Eventually, the President declined to sign the decree which was to criminalise defamation and referred it back to the parliament.[1213] Although this incident has not caused any real problems except major unease and concerns, it does show that freedom of expression, particularly in relation to the media and the press, is often targeted and needs to be fully implemented. Defamation laws in particular, which are as such not an insurmountable problem, can cause attacks on the freedom of expression in countries where there is no established tradition of democracy and where courts and politicians may react excessively to media criticism.

1208 *Ibid.*, Section 52.

1209 Constitution of Timor-Leste, sections 40 and 41.

1210 See for example the Joint declaration by the UN Special Rapporteur on Freedom of Opinion and Expression, the OSCE Representative on Freedom of the Media and the OAS Special Rapporteur on Freedom of Expression: "Criminal defamation is not a justifiable restriction on freedom of expression; all criminal defamation laws should be abolished and replaced, where necessary, with appropriate civil defamation laws" (11 December 2002).

1211 For an overview of the issue see USAID's Timor Leste Media Assessment (February 2006).

1212 See for example European Court of Human Rights, 'Lingens v. Austria', 8 July 1986, 1986 ECHR (Ser. A).

1213 End of mandate report of the Secretary-General, UN Doc. S/2006/251, *supra* note 703.

3. *Afghanistan: Ensuring Implementation*

Afghanistan acceded to the ICCPR on 24 January 1983. The 2004 Constitution provides that the citizens of Afghanistan shall have the right to form associations and political parties in accordance with the law,[1214] but the constitution also provided that these associations or parties cannot be "contrary to the provision of the sacred religion of Islam, and the provisions and values of this Constitution", and that they cannot "be affiliated to foreign political parties or sources".[1215] The formation and operation of a party on the basis of ethnicity, language, religion or region is equally prohibited.[1216] While some restrictions on the right to form associations, such as mandatory registration and the exclusion of military or paramilitary activities, are obvious and even necessary to guarantee the efficient exercise of the right freely to form associations, some of the restrictions contained in the Afghan constitution are in our view a direct threat to the right itself and go far beyond the internationally accepted restriction contained, for example, in the ICCPR.[1217]

Freedom of association in Afghanistan remains fragile, especially in respect of political parties and religion-related issues. By June 2005, the Ministry of Justice had registered 72 political parties. But the registration process for the *Wolesi Jirga* elections was more difficult. Parties were barred from registration on ideological grounds.[1218] Another worrying factor was that only 12 per cent of the candidates for the *Wolesi Jirga* elections had recorded affiliation to a political party, because political party candidates feared to be negatively influenced by the role played by some parties in the Afghan civil war during the 1990s.[1219]

Freedom of expression requires more than inclusion in the Constitution and adherence to international human right treaties. During the presidential election campaign, for instance, the Supreme Court issued a statement asking for the disqualification of a presidential candidate because of anti-Sharia statements.[1220] Although the Afghan constitution has explicitly incorporated the freedom of expression,[1221] the Supreme Court did not seem effectively to interpret and apply this right. In general, Kabul province remains the most open in terms of freedom

---

1214 Article 35, Constitution of Afghanistan.

1215 *Ibid.*

1216 *Ibid.*, para. 2.

1217 See art. 23 ICCPR.

1218 AIHRC-UNAMA, Joint Verification of Political Rights, 'Wolesi Jirga and Provincial Council Elections, First Report (19 Apr.–3 June 2005)', p. 4.

1219 *Ibid.*

1220 United States Commission on International Religious Freedom Press Release, 'Afghanistan: Freedom and Electoral Democracy Stifled by Supreme Court Chief Justice' (13 September 2004).

1221 Constitution of Afghanistan, Art. 34.

of expression due to active and diverse media reporting.[1222] In other provinces the main problem remains the lack of independent media, in conjunction with reprisals against journalists for criticising officials.[1223] In the election process, critical remarks against official institutions or local commanders caused local officials to interfere in media content and the censoring of statements made by candidates which were deemed 'sensitive'.[1224]

Overall, the UN mission in Afghanistan has made major efforts to promote freedom of expression, especially during elections. The verification exercise made by the Afghan Independent Human Rights Commission and UNAMA, to which we have referred, is to ensure that the commitments with regard to the basic human rights are in fact implemented throughout the country. This is an important aspect of democratic governance, since fundamental freedoms are effective only when they are applied throughout the country. However, the tangible effect of the Commission's and UNAMA's work is less obvious. Although the presence of the Commission as such is supposed to be one of the major goals of the exercise,[1225] its presence did not stop violations from taking place during the presidential and *Loya Jirga* elections. The Commission, as mentioned, has a verification mandate, and the results of its verifications are published. However, to be effective, the Commission should not only be in charge of verification, but clear violations of fundamental freedoms should be followed by legal investigations, and eventually lead to judicial proceedings.

4. *Iraq: The Gap between Theory and Practice*

The ICCPR was ratified by Iraq on 25 January 1971. The freedom to establish political organisations and parties is guaranteed by Article 39 of the Constitution, without any limitation. Article 39 equally prohibits the forcing of any person to join any party, society or political entity or to continue his membership of it. Although these rights have been enshrined in the Constitution, their effective implementation seems rather difficult. With regard to trade unions for example, the Iraqi Government failed to respond to a request made by the ILO to amend its Decree no. 16 of 28 January 2004, which imposed a trade union monopoly

---

1222 AIHRC-UNAMA Joint Verification of Political Rights, 'First Report (15 June–7 July 2004)', p. 3.

1223 *Ibid.*, 4–5. A private magazine, for example, had its office shut down after it published a satirical piece on the Governor (AIHRC-UNAMA Joint Verification of Political Rights, 'Wolesi Jirga and Provincial Council Elections First Report (19 Apr.–3 June 2005)', p. 4.

1224 AIHRC-UNAMA Joint Verification of Political Rights, 'Wolesi Jirga and Provincial Council Elections, Second Report (4 June–16 Aug. 2005)', para. 38.

1225 Joint press conference by Jean Arnault, Special Representative of the Secretary-General for Afghanistan and Dr. Seema Samar, Chairperson of the Afghan Independent Human Rights Commission (23 June 2004).

situation by recognising the Iraqi Federation of Workers' Trade Unions as the only legitimate and legal trade union in Iraq. The ILO rightly considered that such monopoly imposed by law was contrary to democracy and freedom of association.[1226]

Similar concerns have arisen with regard to the freedom to establish NGOs. A draft law on civil society organisations was proposed by the Minister in charge of civil society affairs, whereby the executive would be authorised to interfere in the internal management of NGOs, thereby violating international regulations on the issue.[1227] At UNAMI's insistence, the Minister finally agreed to redraft the proposed law.[1228] Freedom of association in respect of political parties and NGOs seems to be difficult to implement, notwithstanding clear and precise legal instruments. The advisory role of the UN in Afghanistan and Iraq has, in some cases, been helpful in drawing the attention of officials to manifest violations of the freedom of association. The long-term effects of the emphasis on freedom of association are however not evident. Similar concerns have arisen with regard to the freedom of expression, which in its application is closely connected with the freedom of association.

Iraq had and still has many restrictive laws with regard to freedom of expression, most of them dating back to the Ba'athist regime. Again, harsh defamation laws contained in the Iraqi Penal Code are a major concern for journalists and the media. Soon after its installation, the CPA suspended some of the restrictions on the right to freedom of expression and the right of peaceful assembly imposed by the 1969 Iraqi Penal Code, considering that they were inconsistent with Iraq's human rights obligations. The CPA also adopted regulations to implement the freedom of expression. Criticism has nevertheless been heard with regard to some of the CPA's regulations restricting the freedom of assembly and publications which are provocative.[1229] Although far-reaching restrictions on fundamental freedoms have been adopted, some of which might not be permissible, measures restricting, for example, the freedoms of expression and assembly can be in conformity with international obligations, especially if we take into account the very worrying security situation in Iraq. Article 19(3) of the ICCPR, for example, considers that freedom of expression may be subject to certain restrictions for the protection of national security or of the public. In any event, it is generally admitted that freedom of expression does not cover situations of incitement to crimes or hatred.

[1226] Statement by Mr. Ulf Edström (Sweden) on behalf of the Workers Group on the 338th Report of the Committee on Freedom of Association (CFA) (16 November 2005).

[1227] UNAMI, 'Human Rights Report (1 September–31 October 2006)', p. 23.

[1228] UNAMI, 'Human Rights Report (1 March–30 April 2006)', p. 24.

[1229] See for example: Article 19 Press Release, 'Iraqi laws threaten democracy' (5 February 2004).

The present situation in Iraq is still disturbing, but the legal foundation has been laid to smooth progress towards democratic governance. Adhering to human rights treaties and adopting a constitution which guarantees the right to freedom of expression, and the freedom of association for that matter, are without doubt a first step, but as in Afghanistan, effective implementation nevertheless remains a recurrent problem in Iraq.

Part IV

Improving Post-conflict Administration. A Legal Framework for Comprehensive Post-conflict Reconstruction

Several critical aspects of the different reconstruction processes analysed, and in particular in respect of the international legal obligations of international actors, can be identified from this research. The challenges and difficulties encountered when administering foreign territory are to a certain extent inherent in the exercise of such intrusive powers by international organisations. However, the post-conflict context has also to be taken into account, since, obviously, the main and recent purpose of the exercise is linked to this particular situation. The critical issues can be synthesised and grouped into several overarching principles which need to be addressed when assessing the use of international administrations or alternative forms in these particular post-conflict scenarios.

The first of these aspects is the need to have adequate exit strategies, which is closely linked to the concept of post-conflict administration itself, and its inherent features such as its temporary nature. However, it is also this particular feature which distinguishes these recent cases from previous examples of foreign administration. In cases such as Danzig or Trieste, the purpose was not to rebuild territories or states by establishing democratic institutions. Rather, these precedents were internationalised merely to solve certain territorial issues. The question which will need to be addressed is thus where post-conflict peacebuilding eventually leads, and how this end can and should be envisaged. We will then turn to the question of internationalisation and local ownership over the transition process. Although these concepts seem closely connected to the question of the nature of authority, internationalisation and local ownership are nevertheless distinct in the sense that internationalisation and local ownership constitute overarching principles, applied in very different ways in the cases examined. Ownership must however not be linked to the scale of authority exercised by international actors, although obviously the 'light footprint' approach drew on the extensive application of local ownership. The last chapter will evaluate the concept of post-conflict administration. While it would be impossible to draw from this research definitive conclusions on the effectiveness of one approach as compared to the other, certain trends can nevertheless be identified. Besides the extent to which the nature of authority and the involvement of the UN have influenced the reconstruction process, we will address the need for a comprehensive approach including all aspects of state reconstruction. Finally, the international legal framework will be analysed, to measure whether a new emerging 'jus post bellum' can be identified.

Chapter 12

Exit Strategies and Post-conflict Administration

The conditions which are necessary for scaling down a mission are as vital as those for its setting up. The need to have a genuine exit *strategy* was highlighted by the Secretary-General in his report to the Security Council on the closure of UN peacekeeping missions.[1230] The Report had been requested by the Security Council following a debate on exit strategies, aimed at improving the Security Council's performance in decision-making in respect of the termination of peace operations or transition to another (follow-up) mission.[1231] We will first address the question of the appropriate exit strategy when dealing with post-conflict reconstruction. Subsequently, we will evaluate the difference between initial and sustainable successes in the examined cases.

A. *Focussing on 'Getting the Job Done Right Rather than on Getting Out'?*

Exit strategies are necessary for two reasons. First, a clear exit strategy at the establishment of an international administrative mission will directly influence the conduct of the administration itself. Post-conflict administrations and peace-building missions indeed need to work towards the achievement of a specific goal, and the lack of a clear exit strategy therefore poses a real problem to the conduct of operations. Secondly, exit strategies need to be carefully examined and planned, as an inadequate exit strategy may have serious deleterious effects on the future of the state or territory concerned, which in turn may necessitate a much longer period of international assistance. Experience in Somalia

1230 Report of the Secretary-General, 'No exit without strategy: Security Council decision-making and the closure or transition of United Nations peacekeeping operations', UN Doc. S/2001/394 (20 April 2001).

1231 SC Meeting Record, 'No exit without strategy', UN Doc. S/PV.4223 (15 November 2000).

highlighted, besides the need for an adequate mandate, that simple withdrawal cannot be an option; experience in Bosnia proved that setting arbitrary deadlines for the withdrawal of international staff cannot be an efficient exit strategy. The following statement of the former High Representative in Bosnia reflects the former UN approach towards peacekeeping where elections were considered the highest priority in post-conflict situations:

> in Bosnia we thought that democracy was the highest priority, and we measured it by the number of elections we could organize. The result seven years later is that the people of Bosnia have grown weary of voting. In addition, the focus on elections slowed our efforts to tackle organized crime and corruption, which have jeopardized quality of life and scared off foreign investment. [...] In hindsight, we should have put the establishment of the rule of law first, for everything else depends on it: a functioning economy, a free and fair political system, the development of civil society, public confidence in police and the courts. We would do well to reflect on this as we formulate our plans for Afghanistan and, perhaps, Iraq.[1232]

The exit strategies in the post-conflict administrations examined were very different. In Kosovo, UNMIK was left with an uncertain final status, while nevertheless mandated to promote substantial autonomy with Serbia. In East Timor, the UN to an extent fell back on the holding of (presidential) elections as the primary exit for the mission, while envisaging a follow-on mission comprising certain limited peace-building components. In Afghanistan and Iraq, elections and the completion of the transitional process were apparently seen as sufficient to reduce international involvement in those countries. The question is, however, which strategy needs to be adopted when dealing with post-conflict peace-building.

The United States representative rightly pointed out that there is a need to focus on "getting the job done right rather than on getting out",[1233] and identified as the "the ultimate exit strategy', [...] accountable governance and stability, and the fact that international forces can leave without their departure triggering a return to the very things that caused the initial intervention".[1234] The International Commission on Intervention and State Sovereignty considered that there should be a commitment to "helping to build a durable peace, and promoting good governance and sustainable development. Conditions of public safety and order have to be reconstituted by international agents acting in partnership with local authorities, with the goal of progressively transferring to them authority and responsibility to rebuild."[1235] The main exit strategy of

---

1232 Ashdown, P., 'What I Learned in Bosnia', *The New York Times* (28 October 2002).

1233 Statement by Mr Holbrooke, Representative of the Unites States, SC Meeting Record, 'No exit without strategy', UN Doc. S/PV.4223 (15 November 2000), p. 5.

1234 *Ibid.*, p. 4.

1235 International Commission on Intervention and State Sovereignty, *supra* note 17, para. 5.1.

a transitional administration is thus transfer of authority to local institutions.[1236] The central question is therefore whether the territory under administration is sufficiently prepared to assume such power. Elections will in general not be sufficient to evaluate local capacity. In addition, in light of what we established with regard to the introduction of democratic governance, the question of exit strategy has to be linked with the setting up of democratic institutions. A combination of these elements gives a main purpose and thus exit strategy to international administrations, namely the transfer of authority to functioning, democratic and stable institutions, capable of ensuring an effective administration. In operations such as Iraq and Afghanistan, the transfer of authority cannot by definition take place, but the requirement of functioning, democratic and stable institutions, capable of ensuring effective administration needs to be retained as the ultimate goal of the process. Follow-on missions are therefore unavoidable, especially considering the long-term nature of democratic institution-building, which is essential to the exit strategy.

In respect of the creation of democratic institutions, the limitation of the exit strategy to the holding of free and fair elections is certainly not sufficient. The context in which such elections are organised, respect for the freedoms of expression and association, and progress in the institution-building process are paramount to assessing the democratic character of the institutions and the fairness of the elections. In most cases, the fairness as such of elections has been largely met, but the conditions in which elections were held and the stage in which the institutions were left after withdrawal of the international presence often emphasised the need for a long-term engagement. Initial success must not be confused with sustainable success.[1237]

B. *In Practice: Carefully Balancing Initial and Sustainable Success*

The inadequacy of exit strategies is perhaps best illustrated by Kosovo, as no final status for the Province had been identified at the start of the mission. Despite this unclear final status, the mission was to work towards the creation of functioning and democratic institutions and substantial autonomy and self-government. The transfer to local capable institutions was thus one of the major goals of the mission, but the problem was that full transfer of authority could not take place until the decision on the final status of the Province had been made, despite the already extensive transfer of legislative and executive powers to local institutions. UNMIK was also under an obligation not to prejudge the

[1236] Chesterman, *supra* note 104, p. 223.
[1237] Smith and Dee, *supra* note 496, p. 100.

final outcome, making it very difficult for the administration to work towards something that was not yet defined.

The Province's uncertain final status had many consequences for policy choices which had to be made in various areas. Economic reconstruction is one example we have mentioned extensively. In addition, it has been stressed by some authors that Kosovo could not access credits from the international market because of its non-sovereign status, leading to the inability of institutions to support the expansion of private companies. The creation of the Kosovo Protection Corps, as a substitute national army and an ad hoc solution to the demilitarisation of the KLA, the applicable law discussions which partly resulted from the confirmation of Serbia's *de jure* sovereignty, and the slow transfer of powers to local institutions were also clearly linked to the final status of the Province. The uncertain final status not only impeded progress in the various areas, but also unnecessarily prolonged the interim administration. Although the holding of elections was one of the early achievements of the UNMIK administration, this was only a step in a long-term exit strategy. The holding of elections nevertheless permitted the mission to be scaled down, although in reality, this was only a perception of exit mainly aimed at satisfying the calls for independence by the Kosovo Albanians.[1238] The adoption of the 'Standards for Kosovo' was a second move to delay the final exit of the UN administration. Although the implementation of these standards was seen as a necessary pre-condition to the start of the political process to determine Kosovo's final status,[1239] it was eventually decided that the definitive settlement of Kosovo's status could no longer be postponed.[1240] Although the proposal drafted by Martti Ahtisaari might have been an interesting and constructive exit strategy, conditional 'independence' was not accepted by the actors involved in the discussions. However, many of the items contained in the settlement proposal have been retained, in particular in respect of the follow-on missions and the adopted Constitution.

East Timor is perhaps the best example to highlight to need to carefully balance initial and sustainable successes. The mission's success in leading East Timor to independence is undeniable. The different elections organised under UNTAET and the creation of democratically elected institutions which have assumed power in the country have been achieved without too many problems. The question is nevertheless whether East Timor can be seen as a success as regards the creation of sustainable structures beyond independence. The answer

---

1238 Chesterman, *supra* note 104, p. 229.

1239 Cf. SC, 'Report of the Special Envoy of the Secretary-General on Kosovo's future status', UN Doc. S/2007/168 (26 March 2007).

1240 See Statement by the President of the Security Council, UN Doc. S/PRST/2005/51 (24 October 2005).

to this question needs to be more balanced. Several issues were not solved by UNTAET. Several setbacks have in addition arisen since UNTAET's withdrawal and its subsequent replacement by the smaller follow-on missions. Reform of the civil service had not been adequately completed. The national army and police force, economic capacity and the judiciary prove the necessity of a close follow-up. The objective of transferring power to national institutions has been largely met, but local capacity was not sufficient to maintain stability upon independence.[1241] This underlines the need for long-term UN engagement in these types of operations. The fact that the current UNMIT mission contains expanded peace-building mandates, as compared to the former UNOTIL and UNMISET missions, confirms this. The much smaller UNMISET and UNOTIL missions were not capable of providing sufficient support to the nascent authorities, although UNMISET's mandate had been extended and expanded following a request by the Secretary-General.[1242] The requirement of a close follow-up of the reconstruction process was highlighted by the creation of UNMIT, following an appeal by the national authorities. The current UNMIT mission has a more extensive mandate than the previous missions, and would have been ideal as a follow-on mission to UNTAET instead of the two previous limited missions. The Secretary-General equally recognised the failure of previous UN missions to strengthen local capacity, especially in the security sector.[1243]

Iraq and Afghanistan reveal major similarities with regard to exit strategies. Indeed, in both cases, the exit strategies, if these actually formally existed, were completely flawed and relied on the false assumption that elections and the creation of a national government would be sufficient. Besides the inadequate planning of the post-conflict phase by the intervening states, it appears that no exit strategy at all was developed by the occupying coalition in Iraq[1244] or in Afghanistan.[1245] In both territories, the military victory and the rapid but merely formal restoration of institutions perhaps led the international actors to believe that reconstruction would be smooth and uncomplicated. In Iraq, the withdrawal of American troops was envisaged very early but was never really finalised as a

---

[1241] Chesterman described the exit strategy in East Timor as "far from ideal" (Chesterman, *supra* note 104, p. 233.

[1242] Special report of the Secretary-General on the United Nations Mission of Support in East Timor, UN Doc. S/2004/117 (13 February 2004), para. 16.

[1243] Report of the Secretary-General, UN Doc. S/2006/628, *supra* note 520, para. 33.

[1244] See on this Williams, H. R., 'The Reconstruction of Iraq amid the Realities of Failed Assumptions: Consequences of the Actions of a Trusteeship of the Powerful', in Fischer and Quenivet, *supra* note 781, p. 186.

[1245] See for example the statement of the Belgian Minister of Defence Castle, S., 'NATO urged to plan Afghanistan exit strategy as violence soars', *The Independent* (27 November 2006). See also CBC News, 'No early exit strategy' from Afghanistan' (7 February 2004).

result of the escalating violence. It was only after the Baker – Hamilton report that the United States seriously started to envisage an exit strategy.[1246] Both cases highlight that a purely political process, aimed at organising elections and creating national institutions while not providing sufficient support for these intuitions, cannot be sufficient to reduce international presence. Although the US representative to the Security Council clearly indicated that exit deadlines are not similar to exit strategies,[1247] in both cases clear deadlines for withdrawal were indicated from the start.

The adoption of the compacts with Iraq and Afghanistan nevertheless provided some form of exit strategy, although they were formulated at a very late stage. In addition, both compacts are confirmations of certain failures in the reconstruction processes in many areas, or at least a failure in exit strategy. The Iraqi compact is explicitly intended "to complete the reconstruction of Iraq and to set it firmly on the path to self-sufficiency and prosperity in a society with a pluralistic political, democratic and federal system", whereas the compact with Afghanistan acknowledges that "Afghanistan's transition to peace and stability is not yet assured, and that strong international engagement will continue to be required to address remaining challenges".[1248] Both instruments can therefore be seen as useful tools in providing sufficient international support for enhancing local capacity.

In contrast with the findings we made above, the exit strategies in both cases relied on the assumption that transferring power to national institutions would be sufficient to scale down international assistance. The question of the capacity of the institutions to govern the countries effectively had not been posed. Both compacts nevertheless set clear benchmarks, linked with deadlines. The question remains, however, whether these compacts will provide sufficient support for the creation of functioning institutions. The compacts are not treaties and thus not legally binding, and it is thus unclear how they need to be interpreted. The question has also been raised whether turning these cases into successes would necessitate both a multilateral approach and a radical policy shift.[1249] The minimal involvement of the UN and other international actors in these cases has not brought the necessary results and it is therefore questionable whether the adoption of the compacts, relying again on national actors only, will be sufficient.

1246 Iraq Study Group, 'The Iraq Study Group Report' (2006).

1247 Statement by Mr Holbrooke, Representative of the Unites States, SC Meeting Record, 'No exit without strategy', UN Doc. S/PV.4223 (15 November 2000), p. 5.

1248 See the preamble of both Compacts.

1249 See on Iraq: International Crisis Group, 'After Baker-Hamilton: What to do in Iraq', *Middle East Report No. 60* (19 December 2006). The recommendation contained in the ICG report reflects in our view an effective assessment of the situation and could equally be envisaged in the case of Afghanistan, although admittedly, the situation presents many differences.

Chapter 13

Internationalisation, Consultation and Local Ownership

Ownership has often been described as the key to successful reconstruction.[1250] The question is, however, how local ownership can be ensured in the absence of a functioning government and administration. UN-led administrations as well as foreign (military) occupation are generally considered as contravening local ownership, as they lack democratic legitimacy, whereas the Afghanistan 'light footprint' approach is generally perceived as enhancing local ownership. The observation however is erroneous. Such a statement is inaccurate since, if ownership were possible, there would not be a need to establish an international administration.[1251] We will analyse what needs to be understood by local ownership, before turning to an examination of the question of local ownership and internationalisation in the judicial sector.

A. *Local Ownership: Aim or Method?*

When discussing the post-conflict scenario in Iraq, Vieira de Mello emphasised that democracy needed to evolve from within Iraqi society. He stressed that the empowering of the provisional institutions was essential to ensure ownership of the reconstruction process until the election of a representative Iraqi Government.[1252] While it is true that democracy is difficult to impose on a society, it is questionable whether the creation of national transitional authorities is sufficient

---

[1250] See e.g. Chopra, J. and Hohe T., 'Participatory Intervention', 10 *Global Governance* 289 (2004).

[1251] Chesterman, *supra* note 104, p. 239.

[1252] Presentation of the report of the Secretary General by Mr Sergio Vieira de Mello: UNSC Meeting Record, UN Doc. S/PV.4791 (22 July 2003) and Report of the Secretary-General, UN Doc. S/2003/1149, *supra* note 163, para. 2.

to ensure local ownership. This is the major problem in post-conflict settings. In the cases of Kosovo and East Timor there was simply no Government. In the cases of Afghanistan and Iraq authorities had emerged from the post-conflict peace agreements, but they obviously lacked experience, financial resources and arguably the necessary legitimacy among the population. Empowering national institutions to take a leading role in reconstruction while they lack legitimacy is therefore not always the solution, although they certainly have more legitimacy than purely international or foreign administrations. In general, we saw that the national interim or transitional institutions have not necessarily been more able to maintain control over the territory and that they often lacked the capacity to implement much-needed reforms. As observed in the case of Afghanistan, reliance on purely national institutions which have little legitimacy – in this case the Ministries of Defence and Interior – may delay the implementation of important measures such as DDR programmes and security sector reform.

In line with our discussion on the exit strategies, ownership must be the goal of international administration. This does not preclude the consultation of local actors during the administration, be it UN-led or based on occupation. Local ownership must indeed not be confused with consultation. The lack of consultation with local actors has been a recurrent and perhaps well-founded criticism. Former UNTAET transitional administrator Vieira de Mello explained that "[t]he more powers conferred on local representatives, the closer power is to the people and thus the more legitimate the nature of the administration. But conferring power on non-elected local representatives can also have the undesired effect of furthering a particular party. The inclination of the UN is thus to be cautious about delegating power in the interest of avoiding furthering any particular political party. There is consultation, but all essential decision making and executive authority remains with the UN."[1253] But the former transitional administration questioned the appropriateness of such an approach.[1254]

For these reasons, consultation aimed at taking into consideration the local context in which reconstruction is conducted is paramount, and the necessary local institutions have been created in all four cases. However, this has not always led to the *effective* inclusion of local actors in the decision-making process. Consultation with the Kosovars would, for instance, have avoided an uncomfortable applicable law dispute under UNMIK. In the case of East Timor on the other hand, the Timorese National Consultative Council had endorsed all UNTAET regulations.

[1253] Vieira de Mello, S., 'How not to run a country. Lessons for the UN from Kosovo and East Timor' (June 2000).

[1254] *Ibid.*

One area in which the balance between ownership and consultation can best be evidenced is the inclusion of international elements in the judicial systems of the territories and states under administration.

B. *Internationalisation vs. Ownership: Internationalising the Judiciary*

Providing adequate judicial assistance appropriate to the territory's own context in post-conflict situations is complicated, and the reconstruction process often involves assistance from foreign experts and the importation of foreign judicial models. In the short term relying only on local capacity is often unrealistic. The presence of international experts is thus regularly a necessary step towards judicial reconstruction, but the participation of local actors through consultation and meaningful involvement remains indispensable. This delicate balance between internationalisation and relying only on local capacity is perhaps one of the most obvious differences in the UN-led international administrations and the 'light footprint' approach. In the first scenario, despite early assumptions that relying on local staff only would be more beneficial for the reconstruction process, international staff were gradually inserted into the judicial structures, mainly in an effort to improve respect for the rule of law and the ensure the correct application of human rights law.

The 'internationalisation' of domestic courts, by which we mean the participation of international judges and/or prosecutors in purely domestic courts, is a recent trend in international law and has emerged from the experiences in Kosovo and East Timor. Prior to UNMIK, international judges and prosecutors had been employed only in the International Criminal Tribunals for the Former Yugoslavia and Rwanda. Courts and tribunals have since been 'internationalised' in Cambodia, Sierra Leone and Lebanon. The appointment of international judges and prosecutors in peace-building missions and international administrations therefore set a precedent of what has been referred to as 'hybrid', 'mixed' or 'internationalised' courts or tribunals,[1255] composed of both local and international judges, as opposed to national and international courts and tribunals, respectively composed of local and international judges only. The concern to create exclusively local institutions has to be weighed against the creation of an effective and sustainable judicial system. Although local ownership is important,

[1255] See on the emergence of 'hybrid' or 'internationalized' criminal courts: Romano, C. and Boutruche, T., 'Tribunaux pénaux internationalisés: état des lieux d'une justice "hybride"', 107 *Revue Générale de Droit International Public* 109 (2003); Boutruche, T., 'Les tribunaux pénaux internationalisés ou l'émergence d'un modèle de justice hybride', *Jusletter* (2002) and Romano, C. P. R., Nollkaemper, A. and Kleffner, J. K. (eds.), *Internationalized Criminal Courts: Sierra Leone, East Timor, Kosovo and Cambodia* (Oxford: Oxford University Press, 2004).

transferring full authority to the local institutions should be evaluated with caution, as the main aim is to establish workable structures in the long term.[1256] Additional training and the presence of international experts to assist local actors should therefore not be seen as an obstruction to local ownership of the reconstruction process, but as a means of facilitating a fully functioning and lasting judiciary. Nevertheless, although international judges are experts in international law or their own national legal systems, they often lack the necessary familiarity with the applicable local law. Equally, language barriers, necessarily implying the translation of domestic laws and the presence of interpreters at court hearings, hamper the extensive deployment of international judges.

The appointment of international judges and prosecutors nevertheless serves several purposes. First, they can ensure the correct application of international law, and particularly human rights law and the basic principles of due process,[1257] thus filling the gap until local judges have undertaken sufficient training. International judges therefore also serve as 'examples' and mentors to their local colleagues.[1258] This is especially true in the case of insufficient number of judges and prosecutors who, in addition, have been lost to the judicial system for many years. Appointing international magistrates can therefore be used as a training method for newly appointed judges and prosecutors, who often, have never before undertaken these functions.[1259] However, the heavy costs related to the hybridisation of national courts and tribunals, and the short-term availability of international actors have severely weighed down the reconstruction process. The presence of such actors is thus valuable, especially with regard to the aforementioned need to ensure respect for human rights and fair trial principles, but two conditions need to be fulfilled. International actors need to be appointed for longer terms and need to have certain qualifications, such as extensive experience in their field. In addition, the necessary funding needs to be provided to ensure a certain level of internationalisation to avoid such situations as occurred in East Timor where the international panels were frequently unable to sit because of the unavailability of international judges.

The 'internationalisation' of the domestic courts and tribunals in the cases under consideration has served the various purposes described above. UNMIK decided to introduce international judges and prosecutors after several months of trying to rely solely on local capacity. The effectiveness of the internationalisa-

---

1256 Brandt, M., 'International Intervention and Post-Conflict Reconstruction I: Capacity Building and training in post-conflict countries', in Azimi, Fuller and Nakayama, *supra* note 85.

1257 Cassesse, A., 'The Role of Internationalized Criminal Courts and Tribunals in the Fight Against International Criminality', in Romano, Nollkaemper and Kleffner, *supra* note 1255, p. 6.

1258 See also Betts, Carlson and Gisvold, *supra* note 851.

1259 Cassesse, A., 'The Role of Internationalized Criminal Courts and Tribunals in the Fight Against International Criminality', in Romano, Nollkaemper and Kleffner, *supra* note 1255, p. 6.

tion of the Kosovo courts and tribunals has however been described as marginal, as their contribution to the training of local judges was limited due to their appointment on a case-by-case basis.[1260] Nevertheless, others have stressed the efficient support provided by international judges and prosecutors in handling sensitive cases[1261] which, without their presence, could have undermined the rule of law in the territory, and therefore destabilised the already fragile peace process. Their presence equally halted the perceived ethnic bias of the judiciary, and restored the perception of an independent and functioning one.[1262]

As in Kosovo, no international judges or prosecutors were initially appointed in East Timor, as the focus was on the creation of exclusively Timorese institutions. The appointment of local judges was seen as a symbolic step towards a long-awaited self-determination and self-government, and was seen as necessary to avoid the future disruption of the judiciary after the withdrawal of the international judges.[1263] Practical concerns, such as the urgency in reviewing the detention of suspects by INTERFET after the dissolution of the Detention Management Unit and the unavailability of international jurists, seem to have influenced this policy.[1264] The necessity of focussing on building an East Timorese judiciary was also expressed by the Secretary-General in his October 1999 report, in which the Secretary-General asked to recruit professionals from among the East Timorese to the largest extent possible.[1265] However, this quite rapidly became unsustainable, given the limited availability of qualified judges and prosecutors. In addition, the failure of the judiciary to re-establish the rule of law has led to criticism of the choice of this policy. Despite the clear

---

1260 OSCE Mission in Kosovo – Legal Systems Monitoring Section, 'Kosovo: Review of the criminal justice system 1999–2005 – Reforms and residual concerns' (March 2006), pp. 66–67; Cerone, J. and Baldwin, C., 'Explaining and Evaluating the UNMIK Court System', in Romano, Nollkaemper and Kleffner, *supra* note 1255, p. 52 and Shraga, D. 'The Second Generation UN-Based Tribunals: A Diversity of Mixed Jurisdiction', in Romano, Nollkaemper and Kleffner, *supra* note 1255, p. 34.

1261 Cerone, J. and Baldwin, C., 'Explaining and Evaluating the UNMIK Court System', in Romano, Nollkaemper and Kleffner, *supra* note 1255, p. 52.

1262 Perriello, T. and Wierda, M., 'Lessons from the Deployment of International Judges and Prosecutors in Kosovo', *International Centre for Transitional Justice* (March 2006), pp. 31–32.

1263 On the rationale behind the 'Timorization' of the judiciary, see the various contributions of Strohmeyer who was subsequently Acting Principal Legal Advisor and Deputy Principal Legal Advisor to UNTAET from October 1999 until June 2000. Strohmeyer was had previously worked as Legal Advisor to UNMIK, and participated in UNTAC. See in particular Strohmeyer, H., 'Building a New Judiciary for East Timor: Challenges of a Fledgling Nation', 11 *Criminal Law Forum* 259 (2000), p. 262 and Strohmeyer, *supra* note 884, p. 177. See also Beauvais, *supra* note 1050, pp. 1155–1156.

1264 Katzenstein, S., 'Hybrid Tribunals: Searching for Justice in East Timor', 16 *Harvard Human Rights Journal* 245 (2003), p. 255.

1265 Report of the Secretary-General, UN Doc. S/1999/1024, *supra* note 310, para. 51.

policy decision to rely on local capacity only, a decision was eventually made to introduce international judges and prosecutors for a limited number of crimes, mainly past crimes. It has been argued that the alternative approach, consisting of introducing international judges and prosecutors from the start with the appointment of East Timorese judges and prosecutors as deputies, could have avoided many difficulties the judiciary faced in the early years.[1266] The outcome of a research project, funded by four major donors to peace-building operations, confirmed this criticism. The researchers argued that "while the symbolic value of an indigenous judiciary was a worthy aspiration, this should not have overridden the immediate demands of the situation which were to create an emergency judicial regime".[1267] However, this assessment and critique can be made only with hindsight, and only emphasises the need for the availability of international experts to be deployed rapidly in these kinds of civilian operations.[1268]

In spite of the growing tendency to create internationalised courts and tribunals, no international judges and prosecutors have been appointed in Afghanistan as a result of the 'light footprint' approach. The main aim of the UN's presence was to assist in the implementation of the Bonn Agreement. The Special Representative of the Secretary-General in Afghanistan, Lakhdar Brahimi, who favoured this approach, relied on the assumption that the reconstruction of the judiciary could be viable only if the process was led by Afghans.[1269] This policy was in complete contrast to the experience in Kosovo and East Timor, where the actors involved recognised the urgency of creating an environment with respect for the rule of law. Considering the weakness of the judiciary in Afghanistan, as well as the unavailability of sufficient competent judges and prosecutors, the arguments for relying upon a purely Afghan judiciary were highly questionable.[1270] Similar reasoning was used with regard to the reconstruction process in Iraq. The continuing malfunctioning of the judiciary with regard to the implementation of human rights could equally have been prevented by the introduction of international experts into the judicial system. As mentioned, the possibility of introducing international judges into the judiciary was only raised by some with

---

[1266] Linton, *supra* note 414, p. 134. See also Katzenstein, *supra* note 1264, p. 256.

[1267] Dahrendorf *et al., supra* note 496, para. 241.

[1268] Cf. para. 145, Brahimi Report, *supra* note 175.

[1269] See 'Address of Mr. Lakhdar Brahimi, Special Representative of the Secretary-General for Afghanistan', Conference of Rome on Justice in Afghanistan (19 December 2002).

[1270] Chesterman, *supra* note 104, p. 179. See also on a proposal for the creation of mixed tribunals in Afghanistan: Dickinson, L., 'Transitional Justice in Afghanistan: The Promise of Mixed Tribunals', 31 *Denver Journal of International Law and Policy* 23 (2002–2003); Amnesty International, 'Afghanistan: Addressing the past to secure the future', *Report n° ASA 11/003/2005* (7 April 2005) and Human Rights Watch, 'Blood-Stained Hands: Past Atrocities in Kabul and Afghanistan's Legacy of Impunity' (2005).

regard to the Iraqi Special Tribunal, charged with the trial of Saddam Hussein.[1271] The law regarding the Iraqi Special Tribunal did not, however, permit the mixed composition of the tribunal, but allowed for the possibility of appointing international judges only after approval by the Iraqi Governing Council.[1272]

A second, and complementary, area in which the equilibrium between internationalisation and ownership is difficult to maintain is the applicable law. The various issues which have arisen with respect to the definition of the applicable law, and more specifically, with regard to the interpretation of the laws in light of human rights standards have been a severe impediment in the reconstruction of the judiciary in many cases. In theory, various alternatives could have been chosen by international actors, although very often practical issues, such as staffing, are more likely to influence the decision than concerns of efficiency. The question was often raised how human rights, and in particular the essential trial-related human rights, could best be introduced into a post-conflict environment. In Kosovo, East Timor and Afghanistan the choice was made to rely in the first place on the existing codes but applied though a human rights lens, while at the same time starting the process of drafting a new code.

The difficulty of the exercise and the lessons learned from judicial reconstruction led to one of the most tangible results of these recent reconstruction missions, namely the proposal to elaborate a model code of criminal law, the so-called 'Brahimi code', named after the proposal made by the Panel on United Nations Peace Operations chaired by Lakhdar Brahimi. The report of the Panel recommended the Secretary-General to "invite a panel of international legal experts, including individuals with experience in United Nations operations that have transitional administration mandates, to evaluate the feasibility and utility of developing an interim criminal code, including any regional adaptations potentially required, for use by such operations pending the re-establishment of local rule of law and local law enforcement capacity".[1273] The United States Institute of Peace recently published the model criminal code and the model code for criminal procedure as part of its 'Model Codes for Post-Conflict Criminal Justice Project' launched in 2001, with the Irish Centre for Human Rights, the Office of the UN High Commissioner for Human Rights and the UN Office on Drugs and Crime.

The four cases examined do prove the necessity to at least consider the application of such interim criminal codes.[1274] The question is, however, whether

---

1271 See *supra* note 1089.

1272 CPA Order Number 48, 'Delegation of Authority Regarding an Iraqi Special Tribunal', CPA/ORD/9 Dec 2003/48 (9 December 2003), Section 2.

1273 Para. 83, Brahimi Report, *supra* note 175.

1274 See Fairlie, *supra* note 418. See for a proposal in the context of economic reconstruction: Valdevieso and Lopez-Mejia, *supra* note 607. The authors argue that an "[e]arly adoption of

this exercise is useful. It seems to overlook the fact that it will require a major input from international judges and prosecutors from the start, while often the necessary instruments are available but need to be revised in accordance with human rights standards. It would not, in our view, eradicate the problems engendered by post-conflict situations. Such a solution might however be used as an interim measure, and *complement* the review of existing legislation. It seems more appropriate to rely on the immediate creation of a law review or reform commission, which would be in charge of the review of existing legislation in light of human rights standards and of the compilation and identification of the applicable laws.[1275] This technique, however, does not exempt the administration in place to define the legal framework, which, as seen in Kosovo, can be a sensitive issue. The advantages of such a commission are evident, and could have boosted respect for the rule of law in the cases examined. However, this is of course easy to argue in retrospect, and we acknowledge the difficult circumstances in which the various missions had to operate. In addition, the practical problems relating to the implementation of such a commission are obvious, as it would require the availability of both international experts, familiar with the local laws, and a translated set of applicable laws, and the presence of national experts familiar with the local laws.

a basic and easily enforceable legal and regulatory framework helps to reduce uncertainty. The framework must be simple but sufficiently comprehensive to minimize the scope for discretion in its applicability".

1275 See for a proposal on the creation of such a commission in East Timor: Morrow and White, *supra* note 390, p. 10.

Chapter 14

International Administration, the Light Footprint and Beyond

Although the level of UN participation in these cases was very different, the components of the reconstruction process were largely identical. The powers entrusted to the UN in the case of Kosovo and East Timor were manifestly far more comprehensive than in Afghanistan or Iraq. The Afghan light-footprint approach encompassed a very limited mandate for the UN, but the Bonn Agreement and its annexes nevertheless revealed many similarities with the reconstruction process in the other cases. The same is true for the reconstruction process in Iraq, where the first phase resembled that in Kosovo and East Timor, while the second stage, after the dissolution of the CPA, was very similar to the Afghan scenario.

The nature of authority will of course directly influence the capacity of the actors to engage in the reconstruction process. It is in particular the exercise of vast administrative powers by unelected international administrations which has been the subject of many criticisms of their 'autocratic' character.[1276] However, although such a critique is founded on the inherent paradox between the means and the ends of international administration, condemning the autocratic nature of international administrations does not take into account the context of these missions, or the practical consequences of one approach as opposed to the other in terms of achieving the objectives of post-conflict reconstruction. From a legal point of view however, such as critique is unfounded. As noted in a previous chapter, the granting of administrative powers to international actors is not only in conformity with the UN Charter, it can be argued that it also does not violate other international legal rules, such as that of self-determination.

There are nevertheless inherent problems associated with these types of administrations and missions. The question of centralising executive and legislative

[1276] See e.g. Chopra, *supra* note 10; Beauvais, *supra* note 1050 and Ombudsperson Institution in Kosovo, 'Fourth Annual Report 2003–2004' (12 July 2004).

powers within one institution indeed raises some questions with regard to, for example, accountability. Chopra for instance compared the status of UNTAET to that of a "pre-constitutional monarch in a sovereign kingdom".[1277] In the case of Afghanistan, the nature of international authority can of course not be criticized, but in Iraq the critique of the 'autocratic' character of the authority can be reiterated with regard to the CPA in the first stage of the process. An analysis of these critiques nevertheless reveals that they are directed at more the way in which the administration was exercised than the concept of international or foreign administration itself. One should indeed be aware of the setbacks which have occurred in UN-led international administrations, which are however mostly related to the prerequisite of adequate planning. We will therefore start with an overview of the influence of planning and the nature of authority on the reconstruction process, before turning to the necessity of having a comprehensive approach and the question whether the evolutions we described in this book can be interpreted as leading to a new international legal framework.

A. *UN Involvement, Planning and the Nature of the Transitional Authority*

The analysis conducted did reveal many inconsistencies and deficiencies in UN-led administrations. Several critical issues have not or have been insufficiently addressed in the cases of Kosovo and East Timor. Lack of planning at the UN level, especially with regard to the deployment of CIVPOL officers and international staff, is to certain extent inherent in international administrations, and should be addressed at the UN level. In East Timor, the early planning of the withdrawal of the mission and the programmed independence resulted in the reluctance of the international administration to address certain issues. The need for adequate planning is equally one of the main conclusions of the Brahimi report:

> The struggles of the United Nations to set up and manage those operations are part of the backdrop to the narratives on rapid deployment and on Headquarters staffing and structure in the present report. [...] No other operations must set and enforce the law, establish customs services and regulations, set and collect business and personal taxes, attract foreign investment, adjudicate property disputes and liabilities for war damage, reconstruct and operate all public utilities, create a banking system, run schools and pay teachers and collect the garbage – in a war damaged society, using voluntary contributions, because the assessed mission budget, even for such "transitional administration" missions, does not fund local administration itself. In addition to such tasks, these missions must also try to rebuild civil society

---

[1277] Chopra, *supra* note 10, p. 29.

> and promote respect for human rights, in places where grievance is widespread and grudges run deep.[1278]

The Brahimi report further states that, "if the Secretariat anticipates future transitional administrations as the rule rather than the exception, then a dedicated and distinct responsibility centre for those tasks must be created somewhere within the United Nations system."[1279] The lack of knowledge about the local environment, including minority issues in Kosovo, and the need to protect minorities from revenge killings are equally evidence of insufficient preparation. The prerequisite of serious planning is essential in the security sector in particular. As noted by the International Commission on Intervention and State Sovereignty:

> complaints are regularly heard from military officers around the world that in interventions and their aftermath they are all too often given functions for which they are not trained and which are more appropriate to police. The simple answer is that civilian police are really only able to operate in countries where functioning systems of law and courts exist. Although the presence of some police in any military operation may be necessary from the start, including for the purpose of training local police, there is probably little alternative to the current practice of deploying largely military forces at the start, but as conditions improve and governmental institutions are rebuilt, phasing in a civilian police presence.[1280]

In Afghanistan, the UN was not directly involved in the administration or governance of the territory. Although UNAMA's role has not always been very clear, the mission, through its influence, proved to be quite efficient with regard to the political process. However, this approach was certainly apposite to the UN's assistance mandate to the Afghan Transitional and Interim Authority, but the long-term objectives for the creation of viable democratic institutions was not guaranteed and lies solely in the hands of the Afghan authorities. This was intended, as the Special Representative of the Secretary-General, Lakhdar Brahimi, was convinced that Afghan leadership was the key to the success of the reconstruction process.[1281] The fact that Afghanistan was a large sovereign State while Kosovo's and East Timor's international status was uncertain during the international administration undoubtedly played a role in defining the approach towards reconstruction. The same can be said with regard to Iraq although, in that case, the United States' role and expectations have led to a more comprehensive mandate than in Afghanistan.

Nevertheless, and although it may be too early to draw conclusions from this 'light footprint' and 'lead nation' approach, especially compared to UNTAET,

---

1278 Paras. 76–77, Brahimi Report, *supra* note 175.

1279 *Ibid.*, para. 78.

1280 International Commission on Intervention and State Sovereignty, *supra* note 17, para. 5.11.

1281 See Chesterman, *supra* note 131, p. 3.

which was concluded at the same time as the beginning of the political transition in Afghanistan, the establishment of a democratic society in Afghanistan still has a long way to go. Relying principally on local actors is probably an efficient way of improving local ownership of the process, but the effectiveness of this approach has not always proved very successful. This can be exemplified by the slow progress in economic reconstruction, which was seriously underestimated by the international community. While it is generally acknowledge that international donors have not been as generous as in the other cases, the concept of 'lead countries', leading to involvement in a selected number of programmes, has contributed to the low achievement in Afghan economic reconstruction, as there was in fact no economic strategy aimed at sustainable economic growth. Arguably, the centralisation of authority in an international entity could have remedied this. Another area in which the approach failed was the reform of the justice sector. Numerous institutions were in charge of parts of the judicial reconstruction process – the Minister of Justice, the Supreme Court headed by the Chief Justice and the Attorney General's Office. The Judicial Reform Commission's task was limited to making reform proposals and the UN was mandated only to serve as an advisor. There were similar considerations with regard to the DDR programme and the training of the Afghan police forces which has been clearly insufficient to create of functioning police and military forces, capable of maintaining security.

The failure of the United States adequately to prepare a post-conflict scenario is at the heart of the problems Iraq is facing today. Paul Wolfowitz, the former Deputy Secretary of State, admitted that the US – quite erroneously – compared post-conflict Iraq to the liberation of France.[1282] As noted by the International Commission on Intervention and State Sovereignty, "if military intervention is to be contemplated, the need for a post-intervention strategy is also of paramount importance".[1283] The prospect of a smooth transfer was completely flawed, and could have been avoided with adequate planning, taking into account the experiences from other post-conflict reconstruction efforts in the past. The lack of planning is perhaps more obvious in the security sector. The abovementioned decision taken by the military commander to completely disband the Iraqi military forces and the Ministry of Defence, in conjunction with the short-staffed military which was unprepared to take over policing activity, provides sufficient evidence. The excessive centralisation of power in the CPA administrator[1284] equally gave rise

1282 Kouchner, *supra* note 568, p. 428.

1283 International Commission on Intervention and State Sovereignty, *supra* note 17, para. 5.3.

1284 See for a critique Stapel, O., 'Experiences with democracy building in the Local Governance Project in Iraq', in Musch, A. (ed.), *Post-Conflict reconstruction of local government* (The Hague: VNG International, 2005), p. 28.

to suspicion in the Iraqi people.[1285] This has in addition been amplified by the intrusive and highly questionable measures taken in the economic sector, such as the 'foreign investment' order. This is however equally due to the fact that this authority was exercised by occupying powers instead of a neutral international organisation. The question here is thus whether such operations can only be undertaken by a body which has international legitimacy. The violent attacks on UNAMI's headquarters question whether full UN administration would have been more acceptable to the Iraqi population. In addition, the existing Iraqi institutions and the availability of qualified Iraqi people, in contrast to the other three cases examined did not require such centralisation of power within the occupier. The failure to include Iraqis during the transitional period was detrimental to the much-needed legitimacy of the foreign presence. An advisory Governing Council was established only three months after the arrival of CPA administrator Bremer, and was composed of a majority of exiled political leaders who also lacked the necessary legitimacy among the population. The need to create such a body in order to legitimise the interim structures for the Iraqi people was not part of Ambassador Bremer's structural design, but required the interference of the then Special Representative Vieira de Melo.[1286] The creation of national interim institutions to consent to the measures adopted by the CPA, and therefore to add a perception of legitimacy to the CPA's activities did not provide adequate capacity-building within the Iraqi institutions, nor could it 'legitimise' the CPA's role in the reconstruction process. Close cooperation with the national institutions would have been productive if it had been effective, based on a clear mandate and division of tasks between the international and national authorities.

Inherent characteristics of the states and territories in question play an important role in achieving sustainable success in several areas. Starting from scratch can in certain cases be easier to handle than reforming existing structures, as witnessed in Afghanistan and Iraq. In addition, the size of the states of Afghanistan and Iraq surely contributed to slower progress in various areas, due to a more limited security presence, the difficulty in eradicating parallel structures and the lack of implementation power outside the secure areas. In addition, the fact that Afghanistan and Iraq were sovereign states probably hindered the creation of a purely international administration in these territories. However, we need to admit that effective implementation of necessary reforms can be achieved only by an effective administration and institutions, which was obviously not available in Afghanistan, or in Iraq after the CPA's dissolution. In addition, we consider that in these cases fragmented or partial approaches were

1285 Diamond, L., 'What Went Wrong in Iraq', in Fukuyama, *supra* note 543, p. 186.

1286 Dodge, *supra* note 647, p. 33.

detrimental to the whole reconstruction process, emphasising the necessity of having all-inclusive mandates.

B. *A Comprehensive Approach*

The interrelation between the analysed components is clearly identifiable. Economic reconstruction, for instance, influences security aspects and vice versa; regenerating a functioning judiciary is paramount for civil administration, law enforcement and democratic institution-building. An all-inclusive approach is thus the only viable solution to the reconstruction process, and is in fact a lesson learned from previous experience, which led to the establishment of these recent missions. Each issue needs to be addressed and dealt with, even if some areas demand higher priority. In the short term, the rule of law and security are fundamental, for everything else depends on it. The question of democratic governance equally highlights the importance of respect for political human rights in addition to free and fair elections.

In Afghanistan, the reliance on a maximum local participation and a minimal international involvement has not permitted a comprehensive and overall institution-building approach. The approach favoured in Afghanistan – a focus on political transition, with limited international involvement in the reconstruction – has been disadvantageous to the process as a whole. The Afghan Minister for Reconstruction identified four dimensions to reconstruction: economic, political, social and psychological. Successful reconstruction, according the Minister, can take place only when these four aspects are dealt with more or less simultaneously.[1287] Political reconstruction, in the sense of implementation of the Bonn Agreement, can indeed be described as successful, but was detrimental to the other components of reconstruction. Little attention was given to the other aspects of reconstruction, which have been dealt with by lead nations with variable success. Afghanistan proved that a sectoral approach is not viable in the long term. The failure rapidly to engage in a nation-wide demobilisation and reintegration programme from the start for example resulted in the persistence of parallel armed groups, especially in the provinces. In addition, the DDR programme could only have been envisaged in conjunction with the creation of an effective National Army, which again necessitated reform of the Ministry of Defence by the Transitional Authority, which apparently lacked the capacity to initiate these reforms. The limited geographic presence of international troops could not close the security gap, filled by local commanders, emphasising the need for control over the territory, but economic and civil reconstruction cannot be achieved

[1287] Farhang, A., 'Afghanistan', in Azimi, Fuller and Nakayama, *supra* note 85, p. 199.

without a secure environment. In Afghanistan the reconstruction process preceded the establishment of the rule of law and security.[1288] The reconstruction process favoured in Afghanistan has revealed several weaknesses, especially with regard to the capacity to engage in a comprehensive reconstruction process, but it has been argued that, possibly, Afghanistan's unique situation made that approach the only viable and appropriate one.[1289] Nevertheless, transferring authority to local institutions can be envisaged only when they actually have the ability to exercise that power, in an environment which respects the rule of law.

The same criticism can be made of the reconstruction process in Iraq, under both the CPA administration and the subsequent 'light footprint'. The focus was too much on political transition. The security situation was largely underestimated. The delay in the creation of national law enforcement capacity was detrimental to stability in the country. In addition, important issues such as improving local capacity in the civil service, and most notably in the judiciary, have not been adequately addressed. The need to cover all areas when dealing with post-conflict reconstruction is perhaps most obvious in the problem of refugees and internally displaced persons. In Iraq, we stressed that the refugee and IDP question cannot be solved without an overall improvement in security, emergency relief, and the settlement of property claims. The CPA did not manage to solve the refugee and IDP problems, while the violence resulted in additional refugees, although the same can however be said for UNMIK, where the inability of KFOR troops to maintain law and order in the emergency phase and the slow progress of the Property Claims Commission seriously undermined the return process.

C. *An International Legal Framework for Post-conflict Reconstruction*: Jus Post Bellum?

A clear legal framework applicable in post-conflict reconstruction is not only necessary in order to untangle the issue of accountability of international actors and clearly to delineate their respective obligations, but also to establish a clear structure in which the mission has to operate. Recently, several authors suggested that the legal framework applicable to international administration and post-conflict reconstruction might be put under the umbrella of *jus post bellum*.[1290]

1288 McKechnie, A., 'Humanitarian Assistance, Reconstruction & Development in Afghanistan: A Practitioner's View', in Azimi, Fuller and Nakayama, *supra* note 85, p. 220.

1289 Cf. the discussion leading to the 'light footprint' approach in Afghanistan in Chesterman, *supra* note 131, p. 3.

1290 See Stahn, C. and Kleffner, J., *Jus Post Bellum. Towards a Law of Transition from Conflict to Peace* (The Hague: T.M.C. Asser Press, 2008).

That category of legal rules would then be the third of three distinct frameworks applicable to armed conflicts, together with the *jus ad bellum* and the *jus in bello*.[1291] The starting point of such an assertion is often the negotiated peace treaties and the conditions laid down in them.

In general, the idea of a *jus post bellum* can be seen either as a normative notion or as a corollary of the *jus ad bellum*.[1292] In the first case, it is then used as a legal framework of the laws or rules applicable after an armed conflict. In the second case, when *jus post bellum* is used as the 'third' part of a tripartite conception of the use of armed force together with *jus ad bellum* and *jus in bello*, it implies that the outcome or result of an armed conflict cannot be detached from the very reasons or legality of the use force. In that case, it has an intrinsic link with the notion of 'just war'.[1293]

Before the recent re-emergence of the concept, theorists and political philosophers such as Saint Augustine, Saint Isidore of Seville, Saint Thomas Aquinas, Francisco de Vitoria, Francisco Suarez, Alberico Gentili, Hugo Grotius and later on Immanuel Kant had included a 'just' post-war arrangement in their conception of a 'just war' as a necessary corollary of the just cause of the war.[1294] Grotius, in his discussion of 'The Law of War and Peace' in which both *jus ad bellum* and *jus in bello* issues were addressed, added several legal rules pertaining to the period *after* war, such as how to treat enemy property.[1295] However, the

1291 See e.g. Boon, K., 'Legislative Reform in Post-conflict Zones: Jus Post Bellum and the Contemporary Occupant's Law-Making Powers', 50 *McGill Law Journal* 285 (2005); Stahn, C., 'Jus ad bellum', 'jus in bello'…'jus post bellum'? – Rethinking the Conception of the Law of Armed Conflict, 17 *European Journal of International Law* 921 (2007); Cohen, J. L., 'The Role of International Law in Post Conflict Constitution-Making: Toward a *Jus post Bellum* for "Interim Occupation", 51 *New York Law School Law Review* 497 (2006–2007).

1292 See also Bellamy who, although rejecting these, identifies two approaches to this notion, a 'minimalist' approach which sees *jus post bellum* as a set of moral principles derived from *jus ad bellum*, and a 'maximalist' approach which focuses on the responsibilities of the victors of a war (Bellamy, A. J., 'The Responsibilities of victory: *Jus Post Bellum* and the Just War', 34 *Review of International Studies* 601 (2008)) and Stahn, who sees two uses for this concept, namely to close either a 'normative gap', or a 'systemic gap' (Stahn, C., '*Jus Post Bellum*: Mapping the Discipline(s)', 23 *American University International Law Review* 311 (2007–2008), p. 327).

1293 See DiMeglio, R. P., 'The Evolution of the Just War Tradition: Defining Jus Post Bellum', 186 *Military Law Rev*iew 116 (2005).

1294 See for an overview Grewe, W. G., *The Epochs of International Law* (Berlin/New York: Walter de Gruyter, 2000), in particular Part I, Chapter 7 (Law Enforcement: The Idea and Reality of the "Just War") and Part II, Chapter VII (Law Enforcement: The Genesis of the Classical Law of War).

1295 See for example Chapter 13 'On Moderation in Making Captures in War' of Book III, Grotius, H., *De jure belli ac paci libri tres* (1625), translation by Campbell, A. C. (Kitchener: Batoche Books, 2001), p. 328.

rules set out by Grotius all result from the just cause of the war, which was, according to the author, the only valid source for the rules on the conduct of war.[1296] In the eighteenth century, Kant argued that the rights of the victor were different according to whether the vanquished was either a just, or an unjust enemy. Kant was one of the first to establish a three-tiered framework for war: "The Right of Nations in relation to the State of War may be divided into: 1. The Right of *going to* War; 2. Right *during* War; and 3. Right *after* War, the object of which is to constrain the nations mutually to pass from this state of war, and to found a common Constitution establishing Perpetual Peace."[1297] The underlying reason for this theory was thus to further eternal peace, as a continuation of the right to resort to force, which was seen as lawful if aimed at establishing this eternal peace.[1298]

The fundamental problem of a *jus post bellum* is this inevitable link with the 'just war' theory. The recent re-emergence of the notion has also been principally the work of a new generation of just war theorists.[1299] This intrinsic[1300] link with the justness of an armed conflict is the inherent flaw in this conception of *jus post bellum*. In times where international law is moving from a *jus ad bellum* to a *jus contra bellum*,[1301] it seems even more unwise to assess the legality of an armed conflict in function of its effects. In addition, actors operating in the post-conflict situation are not necessarily the same as those who resorted to the use of force. In Kosovo, the military operation was launched by NATO, while the civil part of the reconstruction process was handled by other international organisations as well; in Afghanistan and Iraq, the military intervention was principally carried out by the United States, but the reconstruction process involved other actors such as the UN and NATO. One should on the contrary move to a neutral approach towards the post-conflict reconstruction process, as distinct from the issues of both *jus ad bellum* and the *jus in bello*. The recent practice shows that, notwithstanding clear controversies as to the legality of the use of force, there was almost unanimity about the need to have a genuine reconstruction process.[1302] The only quandary related to the scale of UN and United States involvement in

1296 *Ibid.* Chapter I, section III, p. 7.

1297 Kant, *I., The Philosophy of Law: An Exposition of the Fundamental Principles of Jurisprudence as the Science of Right,* translation by W. Hastie (Edinburgh: Clark, 1887), p. 214.

1298 *Ibid.*, p. 221 *et s.*

1299 See for example Orend, B., 'Jus Post Bellum: The Perspective of a Just-War Theorist', 20 *Leiden Journal of International Law* 572 (2007).

1300 See for example Stahn arguing that "*jus post bellum* is to some extent inherent in the conception of *jus ad bellum*" (Stahn, *supra* note 1292, p. 328.

1301 See for example: Corten, O., *Le droit contre la guerre. L'interdiction du recours à la force en droit international contemporain* (Paris: Pedone, 2008).

1302 In the case of Iraq, see the statements after the adoption of Security Council Resolution 1441: UNSC Meeting Record, UN Doc. S/PV.4791 (22 July 2003).

this process. To link post-conflict reconstruction to the legality of the intervention, or to change the rights and obligations of actors in post-conflict reconstruction according the (il)legality of the intervention is thus not only unacceptable, also runs contrary to current international law and practice.

If one uses *jus post bellum* as a legal framework of the law or rules applicable after an armed conflict, the question is whether the whole legal framework of post-conflict interventions can be categorised as a distinct set of legal rules and, if not, whether the use of such new terminology has some added value. As discussed in the second part of this book, post-conflict administrations and peace-building missions have international legal obligations, resulting *inter alia* from Security Council resolutions, customary human rights law, and the laws of armed conflict. Clearly, and contrary to what some authors have claimed, post-conflict administrations and peace-building missions do not operate in a legal vacuum. The problems discussed in the second part in respect of the application of human rights law to UN-led or foreign operations, are not a question of applicable law, but rather a question of accountability. The need to improve the accountability of the UN when involved in these types of operations is distinct from the rules applicable to international actors. There does not therefore, seem to be a need for additional legal obligations in that regard.[1303] The only additional set of legal rules which could be envisaged would be a consequence of the application of the fiduciary nature of authority of post-conflict administrations, which we considered to be only applicable in a subsidiary manner. In any case, practice shows that the exercise of administrative powers in the different cases has not been greatly influenced by the temporary nature of authority. In Iraq, we took as an example the introduction of intrusive measures in the economic sector, which in our view went far beyond the promotion of economic reconstruction, and we raised doubts about the conformity of such measures with the international laws of occupation. In the case of Kosovo, the massive privatisation of public companies resulted in objections from both the UN Legal Advisor and the Serb Authorities. UNMIK and the EU nevertheless decided to implement their plans notwithstanding the legal ambiguity. However, in that particular case, the uncertainty about Kosovo's final status greatly influenced the dispute. UNTAET was more careful in taking measures that would affect the country in the longer term, such as the signature of the Timor Gap Treaty and UNTAET's reluctance to address the issue of property rights.

Besides the application of those legal rules in a post-conflict situation, it is doubtful that international actors operating in the post-conflict situation are

[1303] See in general on the link between enhancing the accountability of non-state actors and their respective human rights obligations, De Brabandere, E., 'Non-state Actors, State-centrism and Human Rights Obligations', 22 (1) *Leiden Journal of International Law* (2009).

bound by other legal obligations than those discussed in the second part of this book. Often suggestions as to additional obligations inevitably lead to an attempt of *ex post facto* justification of the intervention. Some authors for instance suggest that the conduct of war crimes trials and compensatory reparation should be incorporated into *jus post bellum* obligations of the 'aggressor'.[1304] Such additional obligations then amount to either linking the results of an armed conflict to the legality of the use of armed force, or they add obligations according to whether or not the use of force was in conformity with international law, thus again linking post-conflict arrangements to the (il)legality of the use of force.

If one thus takes the notion of 'jus post bellum' as a 'law after conflict', or to fill an alleged 'normative gap',[1305] with no reference to the resort to force, then the added value of the notion seems rather limited.[1306] It is then used only as an alternative for the existing legal framework.

1304 See for example Bass, G. J., 'Jus Post Bellum', 32 *Philosophy and Public Affairs* 384 (2004), pp. 404 *et s.*

1305 Stahn, *supra* note 1292, p. 327.

1306 See also Molier, G., 'Rebuilding after armed conflict: towards a legal framework of the responsibility to rebuild or a *ius post bellum*?', in Molier, G. and Nieuwenhuys, E. C. (eds.), *Peace, Security and Development in an Era of Globalization. The Integrated Security Approach Viewed from a Multidisciplinary Perspective* (Leiden: Martinus Nijhoff, 2009).

Conclusion

From a historical viewpoint, the concept of conferring administrative powers on international actors is not as revolutionary as sometimes argued in legal and political doctrine. However, the first cases of administrative powers conferred on international actors need to be seen in a different context, as they were mainly aimed at resolving territorial disputes or at guaranteeing a certain international status for the territories concerned. The administration of the Saar Basin was a means of guaranteeing the international status of the territory through an international administration, while the Administration of the Free City of Danzig was explicitly aimed at 'protecting' the Free City's status in the transition towards independence. The analysis of the historical context in which the current missions have grown determined that the revival of international administrations and the expansion of peace-building missions are in fact the result of an evolution in addressing post-conflict scenarios. The recent missions encompassed a clear commitment by the international community to engage in wide-scale and comprehensive reforms in all governmental sectors, aimed at creating sustainable democratic institutions, as a technique to maintain international peace and security. This evolution is logical, since the UN learned from its experiences in former peace-keeping and peace-building operations. The current cases can be seen as evidence of the growing awareness of the international community not only of intervening in an actual threat to international peace and security but also of helping in the longer term to avoid the recurrence of similar situations.

Many of the precedents discussed revealed several imperfections, which have however not always led to a satisfactory 'lessons learned' exercise. Lessons from cases such as The Congo and Cambodia evidenced the need for long-term and comprehensive international assistance to create a sustainable peaceful environment, which can be seen as embodied in the international administrations of Kosovo and East Timor. The Bosnian experience reaffirmed that the holding of elections cannot as such be sufficient to ensure sustainable peace. However, this exit strategy has resurfaced in both Afghanistan and Iraq, and to a lesser extent in East Timor, as the holding of elections, and therefore the transfer of authority to elected institutions, was seen as the starting point for decreasing international involvement. International administration is thus a flexible instrument, used for very different purposes, from the settlement of territorial disputes, the transition towards independence in the decolonisation context, to the recent cases of post-conflict peace-building. The post-conflict scenario in which these recent missions need to be situated is thus paramount, not only because of the need to situate them in the evolution of peace-building missions, but also in terms of applicable legal framework. The post-conflict context equally shows that the cases of Kosovo and East Timor bear many resemblances with the operations in Afganistan and Iraq, although the level of internationalisation of the interim or transitional structures was of course very different.

The Legal Framework

If we consider the historical context of the current peace-building missions and their main objective, it becomes evident that the application of notions such as protectorate and trust territories cannot be upheld, since they do not consider the objective, but merely the administration *sensu stricto*. An analysis of these previous cases does not lead to the conclusion that the concept of international administration is an independent institution with a specific inbuilt normative framework. On the other hand, the situation of these recent cases in a historical perspective enables one to draw important lessons for the legal framework of international involvement in post-conflict reconstruction. Current debates on issues such as the capacity of the UN to engage in post-conflict peace-building and the legal status of the state or territories under administration are largely influenced by these precedents.

The Security Council's capacity to engage in such missions is beyond doubt, since several provisions of the UN Charter can be invoked as legal bases. One of the most important consequences of the Security Council's Chapter VII powers is the temporary nature of the administration, which is an essential feature of the various recent forms of international administration. However, the fiduciary nature of authority can only be a useful but subsidiary method of interpretation of the mandate. In addition, practice shows that the temporary nature of authority did not greatly influence the exercise of administrative powers in the different cases. The introduction of intrusive measures in the economic sector in Iraq and the massive privatisation of public companies in Kosovo support this conclusion, the conformity of these measures with both the mandates and the temporary character of the missions is questionable. In practice, missions have often referred only to the mandate conferred on them by the Security Council as the primary source for the exercise of powers. UNMIK's declarations on the detention orders issued by KFOR, for instance, did not refer to the laws of occupation, but principally to Security Council Resolution 1244. The Security Council resolutions remain the ultimate guidelines for the exercise of powers.

Security Council action in this field nevertheless raises several closely related questions. In respect of the scope of measures the Security Council can resort to, the 'domestic jurisdiction' principle does not rule out the establishment of comprehensive peace-building missions and the grant of administrative powers to international actors. The non-application of the 'domestic jurisdiction' principle can be either based on the exception provided in Article 2, para. 7 of the UN Charter, or on the fact that certain issues no longer fall within the domestic jurisdiction of states. Certain changes in the internal political structure of a state can thus be part of Security Council measures. Imposing a particular form of government can however in certain scenarios contravene the internal right of self-determination, if the existence of such an internal right should be confirmed. Nevertheless, an approach in which the maintenance of international peace and security and the rights of minorities is balanced against the right of self-determination should be favoured.

The need for a distinct legal qualification of the territories placed under international administration is questionable. Given the reasonable alternatives, the concept of 'internationalised territory' would best fit the territories under international administration, considering the neutrality of the concept, but its neutrality then again raises the question of its usefulness. Indeed, the 'internationalisation' of a state's or a territory's administration, by transferring the exercise of administrative powers to an international organisation or foreign states does not result in the transfer of sovereignty over that state or territory. A clear distinction between the exercise of state competences and the concept of sovereignty permits to conclude that the international organisation or state exercises state competences only in place of the sovereign. In addition, despite arguments in favour of limited legal personality, the exercise of administrative functions by the UN does not automatically amount to limited international legal personality. The limited exercise of treaty-making power by international actors can often be explained by existing forms of legal personality, without having to resort to the creation of a distinct legal person as the result of the internationalisation of a territory's or a state's administration. The limited practice discussed in the third part of the book provided sufficient support for this.

Besides the implementation of the mandate in accordance with relevant Security Council resolutions and the other defined applicable rules, additional legal obligations of international and foreign actors can be found in both human rights law and the laws of occupation, the latter being of particular importance in the case of Iraq. The activity in question, namely the administration can entail an obligation for civilian components of peace-building missions to respect customary human rights norms. It is however unquestionable that the *accountability* of international organisations when performing civil administration still needs to be improved, but there is no reason to simply abolish the system of immunities or the change the human rights obligations of international actors. Rather, establishing alternative mechanisms to provide a certain form of review is preferable. Review mechanisms of the compatibility of certain official acts with internationally recognised human rights standards, in particular with regard to executive or military detention orders, should be put in place. Local mechanisms introduced into territories under administration did not have the expected results; neither did the judicial review of official acts by national courts and tribunals.

The above-established legal framework did not lead to a comprehensive set of rules applicable to peace-building missions and international administrations. This however, is a consequence of the fact that international administrations and other post-conflict peace-building operations cannot be seen as a self-regulating institution in international law, with inherent normative implications. It does not seem necessary to resort to new legal rules for such operations, since international actors are clearly bound by various existing rules of international law. A straightforward indication of the applicable legal framework by for instance the Security Council, would nevertheless not only clear up ambiguities as to the application of certain rules of international law, such as human rights norms, to international actors, but could also facilitate the interpretation of the mandates conferred on peace-building missions.

A Comprehensive Approach towards Post-conflict Reconstruction

Despite the different approaches of the reconstruction processes in Kosovo, East Timor, Afghanistan and Iraq, the areas in which reforms and reconstruction have been addressed, or at least need to be addressed are similar. The importance of civil administration in a reconstruction process is beyond doubt. Not only is delivering basic civil services to the population paramount in general, its importance is highlighted in cases of emergency. The UN has been relied upon in each of the cases, either within the international administrations or with a coordination mandate in the cases of Afghanistan and Iraq.

A recurrent issue remains the need to build local capacity. In East Timor, this need highlighted that for a long-term engagement, while in Afghanistan and Iraq it showed that it is often pointless to envisage reconstruction without addressing the reform of the civil service. In addition, the case of Afghanistan proved that, even if the intention exists, as witnessed by the inclusion of a Civil Service Reform Commission in the Bonn Agreement, effective reforms require political will and capacity in order to be implemented.

Reform of the Security Sector and the re-establishment and maintenance of a secure environment also need to be a high priority in a post-conflict scenario. This has been one of the major achievements of INTERFET in East Timor, deployed prior to the establishment of UNTAET, which thus had the advantage of taking over an already existing emergency administrative system concerning detainees and law and order. Sustainable progress in all areas can be achieved only in a secure environment, the lack of which was perhaps the most obvious in Afghanistan and Iraq. The decision to geographically limit ISAF in Afghanistan clearly was an error. In Iraq the consequences of military intervention were seriously underestimated, especially as regards the deteriorating security situation. When security cannot be maintained by international actors relying on local capacity becomes the only alternative, but this is of course highly problematic in every post-conflict societies.

The rule of law had an overall weight in the reconstruction processes. It is also the sector in which progress has been very slow, regardless of the differing approaches. The lack of capable judicial personnel is of course a matter which transcends the direct responsibility of the international administrations and the efforts of the international community. All territories were characterised by an insufficient number of judges and prosecutors, or by unqualified personnel. This certainly necessitates long-term investment in education and training. The reliance on a maximum local participation from the start, with no or limited international presence in Afghanistan and Iraq certainly added legitimacy to the reconstruction process, but it is questionable whether it was effective in the long term in reconstructing the judicial system in Afghanistan. Competition between local actors hampered the execution of reform proposals and, as no implementing power had been granted to UNAMA or the Judicial Reform Commission, the process was inevitably slowed down. The judicial reconstruction processes in Kosovo, East Timor and Iraq have been far more intrusive, arguably by reason of the greater powers of UNMIK, UNTAET and the CPA, and the presence of international experts. As far as human rights are concerned, although often the foundations have been laid, as human rights have been explicitly incorporated into the Constitutions, ensuring respect for human rights can be ensured only through effective review mechanisms and functioning courts.

The emphasis of democratic governance in the institution-building process is one of the primary objectives and strategies of current missions. Ensuring that democratic institutions are capable of effectively exercising authority is seen as the solution to addressing the causes of the problems. The interim institutions were, of course, mainly aimed at improving consultation with the local population, although in the case of Iraq it is questionable whether this was in fact the best option, considering their perceived lack of legitimacy of the foreign presence. The formal political transition from interim to permanent institutions was completed successfully in all cases. The fairness of the various elections was in general acknowledged by international observers. However, when one considers respect for the freedoms of expression and association, the overall impression is more modest. In the end, the texts inserted into the Constitution and the laws are only affirmations of the fundamental freedoms, but the implementation and effective exercise of these rights in public life is another question, stressing the need to go beyond the mere holding of elections as an exit strategy.

It is important to rely on a comprehensive mandate in a post-conflict environment. Although the components of the reconstruction process were largely identical, the capacity to implement reforms was very different. The relationship between the analysed components of post-conflict reconstruction can be clearly detected. Regenerating a functioning judiciary is imperative for the civil administration, law enforcement and democratic institution-building. Democratic governance is for instance essential to the civil service and security sector reform. A focus on political transition in the cases of Afghanistan, with limited international involvement in reconstruction has been disadvantageous to the process as a whole. The same criticism can be made of the entire reconstruction process in Iraq. The focus was too much on political transition, and other aspects post-conflict reconstruction were to a certain extent not taken into account. The security situation was largely underestimated. The delay in the creation of national law enforcement capacity was detrimental to stability in the country. In addition, important issues such as improving local capacity in the civil service, and most notably in the judiciary, have not been adequately addressed. The interdependence of all aspects of post-conflict reconstruction analysed can thus only lead to the conclusion that post-conflict reconstruction needs a comprehensive mandate.

Ownership, Consultation and International Authority

The question of 'ownership' needs to be divided into the end of international administration and the need to consult local actors. Local ownership is indeed the ultimate target of post-conflict reconstruction, *i.e.* the full transfer of authority to national institutions. However, relying on international actors does not as such preclude 'local ownership'. Consultation, aimed at taking into consideration the local context in which reconstruction is conducted by including local actors in the decision-making process, is paramount. The creation of national transitional authorities is not sufficient to ensure local ownership. In the cases of Afghanistan and Iraq, authorities had emerged from the post-conflict peace agreements, but they obviously lacked the necessary legitimacy. Empowering national institutions to take a leading role in the reconstruction is not *the* solution. Of course, in the cases of Kosovo and East Timor there was simply no government, which somewhat facilitated the task of establishing an international administration. Nevertheless, the aim of peace-building missions and international territorial administration is the re-establishment of functioning, democratic and stable institutions capable of ensuring effective administration. Therefore, the transfer of authority to these institutions has to be seen as the final objective of international administrations, provided that local capacity has been sufficiently bolstered. In the cases where no international administration has been set up this transfer cannot by definition take place. The major objective is nevertheless identical. However, in Afghanistan and Iraq, the political transition was seen as the major exit strategy, in spite of the incapacity of the established authorities effectively to implement reforms and continue the reconstruction efforts.

The centralisation of executive and legislative powers in the Special Representative of the Secretary-General raises questions of accountability, especially when compared to the preferred 'participatory' model in Afghanistan and Iraq after dissolution of the CPA. However, it seems that it is more the way in which the administration was exercised than the concept of full administration itself which led to criticism, emphasising the need to have adequate review mechanism for the actions of such international missions. From a legal point of view, such missions do not necessarily breach international law, although the exercise of certain activities might of course have amounted to the violation of an international legal obligation. The need to enhance the conduct of such missions should not, however, be used in support of criticism on the concept of international administration in post-conflict scenario's. Ownership should be the final goal of post-conflict reconstruction, rather than a method to achieve this. The needed internationalisation of national institutions in certain areas, such as the judiciary, should thus not necessarily be seen as contravening ownership, but as an element to work towards ownership.

One should nevertheless bear in mind that the circumstances of the four cases were very different and have very much influenced the type of mission set up, and the conduct and achievements of the reconstruction process. Obviously, there is no 'blueprint' for a successful transition, applicable in every post-conflict scenario and in every state. In addition, problems inherent in the territories or states concerned are difficult to solve, such as ethnic violence, parallel structures and lack of local capacity, and are important matters to be addressed, but the question is how laying the foundations for democratically elected institutions capable of effectively governing and administering the state or the territory can best be achieved. The establishment of a UN-led international administration over a territory can be seen as a useful tool for addressing the reconstruction of states and territories after conflict, considering that they embody an all-inclusive approach and that they have the power effectively to implement necessary reforms according to their mandates.

This task the international community embarked upon in the context of post-conflict reconstruction unquestionably fits into the evolution of the 'traditional' peace-keeping mandates. This evolution equally shows that post-conflict administration clearly needs to be placed in this operational context, since it evidences the very reason of its revival in international law, and since it is that context which will particularly influence the applicable legal framework, and thus the rights and obligations of the parties.

Selected Literature

I. *Books*

Azimi, N. and Chang, L. L. (eds.), *The reform process of United Nations peace operations: debriefing and lessons* (The Hague: Kluwer Law International, 2001).

Azimi, N. and Chang, L. L. (eds.), *The United Nations Transitional Administration in East Timor (UNTAET): debriefing and lessons* (Leiden / Boston: Martinus Nijhoff Publishers, 2003).

Azimi, N., Fuller, M. and Nakayama, H. (eds.), *Post Conflict Reconstruction* (New York / Geneva: United Nations Publications, 2003).

Aznar Gomes, M. J., *La administración internacionalizada del territorio* (Barcelona: Atelier, 2008).

Bakarat, S. (ed.), *Reconstructing war-torn societies: Afghanistan* (New York: Pallgrave McMillan, 2004).

Basdevant, J., *Dictionnaire de la terminologie du Droit International* (Paris: Sirey, 1960).

Benvenisti, E., *The International Law of Occupation* (Columbia / Princeton: University Presses of California, 2004).

Bergling, P., *Rule of Law on the International Agenda* (Antwerpen: Intersentia, 2006).

Bernhardt, R. (ed.), *Encyclopedia of Public International Law* (Amsterdam / London / New York / Tokyo: Elsevier – North-Holland, 1996).

Bledsoe, R. and Boczek, B., *The International Law Dictionary* (Santa Barbara: ABC-Clio, 1987).

Blokker, N. M. and Schermers, H. (eds.), *Proliferation of International Organizations – Legal Issues* (The Hague / London / Boston: Kluwer Law International, 2001).

Bowett, D. W., *United Nations Forces. A Legal Study of United Nations Practice* (London: Stevens & Sons, 1964).

Brownlie, I., *Principles of Public International Law* (Oxford: Oxford University Press, 2003).

Bryden, A. and Hänggi, H., *Security Governance in Post-Conflict Peacebuilding* (Geneva: Geneva Centre for the Democratic Control of Armed Forces, 2005).

Caplan, R., *A new trusteeship? The international administration of war-torn territories* (Oxford: Oxford University Press, 2002).

Caplan, R., *International Governance of War-Torn Territories: Rule and Reconstruction* (Oxford: Oxford University Press, 2005).

Cassesse, A., *Self-Determination of Peoples. A Legal Appraisal* (Cambridge: Cambridge University Press, 1995).

Chesterman, S., *You the People – The United Nations, Transitional Administration, and State-Building* (Oxford: Oxford University Press, 2004).

Chesterman, S., Ignatieff, M. and Thakur, R. (eds.), *Making States Work: State failure and the crisis of governance* (Tokyo / New York / Paris: United Nations University Press, 2005).

Clapham, A., *Human Rights Obligations of Non-State Actors* (Oxford: Oxford University Press, 2006).

Cogen, M., *The Comprehensive Guide to International Law* (Brugge: Die Keure, 2008).
Colliard, C. A. and Manin, A., *Droit International et Histoire Diplomatique, Documents Choisis, Tome I et II* (Paris: Montchrestien, 1970).
Conforti, B., *The law and practice of the United Nations* (The Hague / London / Boston: Kluwer Law International, 2000).
Conte, A., *Security in the 21st Century: The United Nations, Afghanistan and Iraq* (Aldershot: Ashgate, 2005).
Cot, J. P. and Pellet, A. (eds.), *La charte des Nations Unies* (Paris: Economica 2005).
Cousens, E. M. and Cater, C. K., *Towards Peace in Bosnia: Implementing the Dayton Accords* (Boulder: Lynne Riener Publishers, 2001).
Crawford, J., *The creation of states in International Law*, 2nd edition (Oxford: Clarendon Press, 2006).
d'Aspremont, J., *L'état non démocratique en droit international* (Paris: Pedone, 2008).
David, E., *Principes de droit des conflits armés* (Bruxelles: Bruylant, 2002).
Delcourt, B., Duez, D. and Remacle, E. (eds.), *La guerre d'Irak. Prélude d'un nouvel ordre international?* (Bern: PIE Peter Lang, 2004).
de Montfort, H., *Danzig, Port de Pologne dans le passé et dans le présent* (Paris: Pedone, 1939).
Demekas, D. G., Herderschee, J. and Jacobs D.F., *Kosovo: institutions and policies for reconstruction and growth* (Washington, DC: International Monetary Fund, 2002).
De Pover, M.-F., *Trust – Fiducie* (Brussel: Larcier, 2001).
de Wet, E., *The Chapter VII powers of the United Nations Security Council* (Oxford: Hart Publishers, 2004).
di Marzo, L., *Component Units of Federal States and International Agreements* (Alphen aan den Rijn / Rockville: Sijthoff & Noodhoff, 1980).
Dobbins, J. *et al., America's Role in Nation-Building: from Germany to Iraq* (Santa Monica: Rand, 2003).
Dobbins, J. *et al., The UN's Role in Nation-Building: from the Congo to Iraq* (Santa Monica: Rand, 2005).
Dodge, T., *Iraq's Future: The aftermath of regime change* (London: Routledge 2005).
Donini, A., Niland, N. and Wermester, K. (eds.), *Nation-Building Unravelled? Aid, Peace and Justice in Afghanistan* (Bloomfield: Kumarian Press, 2004).
Dunoff, J. L., Ratner, S. R. and Wippman, D., *International Law: norms, actor, process – A problem-Oriented Approach* (New York / Gaithersburg / Aspen: Law & Business, 2002).
Dupuy, P. M., *Droit international Public* (Paris: Dalloz, 2000).
Dupuy, R.-J. (ed.), *Manuel sur les organisations internationales – A Handbook on International Organizations* (Dordrecht / Boston / London: Martinus Nijhoff Publishers, 1998).
Ebnöter, A. H. and Fluri, P. H., *After Interventionism: Public Security Management in Post-Conflict Societies – From Intervention to Sustainable local Ownership* (Geneva: Geneva Centre for the Democratic Control of Armed Forces, 2005).
European University Institute (ed.), *Kosovo 1999–2000, The Intractable Peace* (Florence: European University Institute, 2001).
Fischer, H. and Quenivet, N. (eds.), *Post-Conflict reconstruction: Nation- and/or State-Building* (Berlin: Berliner Wissenschafts-Verlag GmbH, 2005).
Fleck, D. (ed.), *The Handbook of The Law of Visiting Forces* (Oxford: Oxford University Press, 2001).
Fox, G. H., *Humanitarian Occupation* (Cambridge: Cambridge University Press, 2008).
Fukuyama, F. (ed.), *Nation-Building beyond Afghanistan and Iraq* (Baltimore: John Hopkins University Press, 2006).
Grewe, W. G., *The Epochs of International Law* (Berlin / New York: Walter de Gruyter, 2000).

Grotius, H., *De jure belli ac paci libri tres* (1625), translation by Campbell, A. C. (Kitchener: Batoche Books, 2001).
Hannum, H. (ed.), *Documents on Autonomy and Minority Rights* (Dordrecht / Boston / London: Martinus Nijhoff Publishers, 2002).
Henkin, L. (ed.), *The International Bill of Right. The Covenant on Civil and Political Rights* (New York: Columbia University Press, 1981).
Henkin, A. H. (ed.), *Honouring Human Rights under International Mandates. Lessons from Bosnia, Kosovo and East Timor. Recommendations to the United Nations* (Washington D.C.: The Aspen Institute, 2003).
Henzelin, M. and Roth, B. (eds.) *Le droit pénal à l'épreuve de l'internationalisation* (Paris / Brussels / Geneva: LGDJ / Bruylant / Georg, 2002).
Higgins, R., *United Nations Peacekeeping 1946–1967. Documents and Commentary. Volume II: Asia* (London / Bombay / Karachi / Kuala Lumpur: Oxford University Press, 1970).
Jones, S. G., Wilson, J. M., Rathmell, A. and Riley, K. J., *Establishing Law and Order after Conflict* (Santa Monica: Rand Corporation, 2005).
Kant, I., *The Philosophy of Law: An Exposition of the Fundamental Principles of Jurisprudence as the Science of Right*, translation by W. Hastie (Edinburgh: Clark, 1887).
Kelly, M. J., *Restoring and Maintaining Order in Complex Peace Operations. The Search for a Legal Framework* (London / The Hague / Boston: Kluwer Law International, 1999).
Kelsen, H., *The Law of the United Nations* (London: Stevens & Sons Limited, 1951).
Knoll, B., *The Legal Status of Territories Subject to Administration by International Organisation* (Cambridge: Cambridge University Press, 2008).
Kolb, R., *Ius in bello, le droit international des conflits armés* (Bruxelles: Bruylant, 2003).
Kolb, R., Porretto, G. and Vité, S., *L'application du droit international humanitaire et des droits de l'homme aux organisations internationales: Forces de paix et administrations civiles transitoires* (Bruxelles: Bruylant, 2005).
Kohen, M. (ed.), *Secession* (Cambridge: Cambridge University Press, 2006).
Kreijen, G. (ed.), *State, Sovereignty, and International Governance* (Oxford: Oxford University Press, 2004).
Kumar, K. (ed.), *Rebuilding Societies after Civil War* (Boulder: Lynne Rienner Publishers, 1997).
Lagrange, E., *Les opérations de maintien de la paix et le chapitre VII de la Charte des Nations Unies* (Paris: Montchrestien, 1999).
Le Fur, L. and Chklaver, G., *Recueil de textes de Droit International public* (Paris: Dalloz, 1935).
Leprette, J., *Le Statut International de Trieste* (Paris: Pedone, 1949).
Macmillan, M., *Paris 1919: Six months that changed the world* (New York: Random House Trade, 2002).
Mayall, J. (ed.), *The new interventionism 1991–1994: United Nations experience in Cambodia, former Yugoslavia and Somalia* (Cambridge: University Press, 1997).
McCoubrey, H. and White, N. D., *The Bleu Helmets: Legal Regulation of United Nations Military Operations* (Aldershot / Brookfield USA / Singapore / Sydney: Dartmouth, 1995).
Mendez, J. E., 'In defence of transitional justice', *in* McAdams, A. J. (ed.), *Transitional Justice and the Rule of Law in New Democracies* (London: University of Notre Dame, 1997).
Meron, T., *Human Rights and Humanitarian Norms as Customary Law* (Oxford: Clarendon Press, 1989).
Musch, A. (ed.), *Post-Conflict reconstruction of local government* (The Hague: VNG International, 2005).
Newman, E. and Rich, R. (eds.), *The UN Role in Promoting Democracy – Between Ideals and Reality* (Tokyo / New York / Paris: United Nations University Press, 2004).
Nguyen Quoc Dinh, Dallier, P. and Pellet, A., *Droit International Public* (Paris: L.G.D.J., 1999).

O'Neill, W. G., *Kosovo: An Unfinished Peace* (Boulder / London: Lynne Rienner Publishers, 2002).

Orakhelashvili, A., *Peremptory Norms in International Law* (Oxford: Oxford University Press, 2006).

Pictet, J. (ed.), *Les conventions de Genève du 12 août 1949: commentaire. IV La Convention de Genève Relative à la Protection des Personnes Civiles en Temps de Guerre* (Geneva: International Committee of the Red Cross, 1956).

Rathmell, A., Oliker, O., Kelly, T. K., Brannan, D. and Crane, K., *Developing Iraq's Security Sector. The Coalition Provisional Authority's Experience* (Santa Monica: Rand, 2005).

Reichel, S., *Transitional Administrations in former Yugoslavia* (Berlin: Wisschenschaftzentrum für Socialforschung, 2000).

Romano, C. P. R., Nollkaemper, A. and Kleffner, J. K. (eds.), *Internationalized Criminal Courts: Sierra Leone, East Timor, Kosovo and Cambodia* (Oxford: Oxford University Press, 2004).

Rotberg, R. I. (ed.), *When States Fail: Causes and Consequences* (Princeton / Oxford: Princeton University Press, 2003).

Rotberg, R. I. (ed.), *State Failure and State Weakness in a Time of Terror* (Harvard: World Peace Foundation, 2003).

Rousseau, C., *Droit International Public, Tome II – Les sujets de droit* (Paris: Sirey, 1974).

Salamun, M., *Democratic Governance in International Territorial Administration* (Baden-Baden: Nomos Verlagsgesellschaft, 2005).

Salmon, J. (ed.), *Dictionnaire de droit international public* (Brussel, Bruylant, 2001).

Sands, P. and Klein, P., *Bowett's Law of International Institutions* (London: Sweet & Maxwell, 2001).

Sarooshi, D., *The United Nations and the Development of Collective Security. The Delegation by the UN Security Council of its Chapter VII Powers* (Oxford: Clarendon Press, 1999).

Shraga, D., 'The UN as an actor bound by international humanitarian law', in *Les Nations Unies et le droit international humanitaire, Actes du Colloque international à l'occasion du 50ième anniversaire de l'ONU* (Paris: Pedone, 1996), p. 326.

Schnabel, A. and Thakur, R. (ed.), *Kosovo and the challenge of humanitarian intervention: Selective indignation, collective action, and international citizenship* (Tokyo / New York / Paris: United Nations University Press, 2000).

Schnabel, A. and Ehrhart, H.-G. (ed.), *Security Sector Reform and Post-Conflict Peacebuilding* (Tokyo / New York / Paris: United Nations University Press, 2005).

Schwarzenberger, G., *International Law as Applied by International Courts and Tribunals. Volume I.* (London: Steven & Sons Limited, 1957).

Schwarzenberger, G., *International Law as applied by International Courts ad Tribunals. Volume II: The Law of Armed Conflict* (London: Steven & Sons Limited, 1968).

Seyersted, F., *United Nations Forces in the law of peace and war* (Leyden: A. W. Sijthoff, 1966).

Shaw, M. N., *International Law* (Cambridge: Cambridge University Press, 2003).

Siekmann, R. C. R., *Basic Documents on United Nations and Related Peace-keeping Forces* (Dordrecht: Martinus Nijhoff Publishers, 1985).

Simma, B. (ed.), *The Charter of the United Nations* (Oxford: Oxford University Press, 1994).

Smith, M. G. and Dee, M., *Peacekeeping in East Timor. The Path to Independence* (Boulder: Lynne Rienner Publishers, 2003).

Soesastro, H. and Subianto, L. H. (eds.), *Peace Building and State Building in East Timor* (Jakarta: Centre for Strategic and International Studies, 2001).

Spillmann, K. R. and Krause, J. (éd.), *Kosovo: Lessons Learned for International Cooperative Security* (Bern / Berlin / Bruxelles / Frankfurt a.M. / New York / Oxford / Wien: Peter Lang, 2000).

Stahn, C., *The Law and Practice of International Territorial Administration. Versailles to Iraq and Beyond* (Cambridge: Cambridge University Press, 2008).

Stahn, C., and Kleffner, J., *Jus Post Bellum. Towards a Law of Transition From Conflict to Peace* (The Hague: T.M.C. Asser Press, 2008).
Strupp, K., *Documents pour servir à l'histoire du droit des gens* (Berlin: Sack, 1923).
Swinarski, C. (ed.), *Etudes et essais sur le droit international humanitaire et sur les principes de la Croix-rouge/studies and essays on international humanitarian law and Red Cross principles, en l'honneur de/in honour of J. Pictet* (Geneva / The Hague: ICRC / Martinus Nijhoff, 1984).
Thakur, R. and Schnabel, A. (eds.), *United Nations Peacekeeping Operations: Ad Hoc Missions, Permanent Engagement* (Tokyo / New York / Paris: United Nations University Press, 2001).
Thakur, R. and Sidhu, W. P. S. (eds.), *The Iraq Crisis and World Order: Structural, Institutional and Normative Challenges* (Tokyo / New York / Paris: United Nations University Press, 2006).
The Independent International Commission on Kosovo, *The Kosovo Report: Conflict, international response, lessons learned* (Oxford: Oxford University Press, 2001).
Tomuschat, C. (ed.), *Kosovo and the International Community* (The Hague: Kluwer Law International, 2002).
Tomuschat, C. (ed.), *Modern Law of Self-Determination* (Dordrecht: Martinus Nijhoff Publishers, 1993).
Toussaint, C., *The trusteeship system of the United Nations* (London: Stevens & Sons Limited, 1956).
UK Ministry of Defence, *The Manual of the Law of Armed Conflict* (Oxford: Oxford University Press, 2004).
Valdivieso, L. M., Endo T., Mendonça L. V., Tareq S. and López-Mejía, A., *East Timor: Establishing the Foundations of Sound Macroeconomic Management* (Washington: International Monetary Fund, 2000).
Verzijl, J. H. W., *International Law in Historical Perspective, Part II – International Persons* (Leyden: A. W. Sijthoff, 1969).
Virally, M., *L'administration internationale de l'Allemagne du 8 mai 1945 au 24 avril 1947* (Paris: Pedone, 1948).
Walters, F. P., *A History of the League of Nations* (London / New York / Toronto: Oxford University Press, 1952).
Wambaugh, S., *The Saar Plebiscite with a Collection of Official Documents* (Cambridge: Harvard University Press, 1940).
Warner, D. (ed.), *New Dimensions of Peacekeeping* (Dordrecht: Martinus Nijhoff Publishers, 1995).
Weiss, T. G. and Daws, S., *The Oxford Handbook on the United* Nations (Oxford: Oxford University Press, 2007).
White, N. D., *Keeping the peace. The United Nations and the maintenance of international peace and security* (Manchester: Manchester University Press, 1997).
White, N. D. and Klaasen, D. (eds.), *The UN, Human Rights and Post-Conflict Situations* (Manchester: Manchester University Press, 2005).
Whiteman, M. M. (ed.), *Digest of International Law* (Washington: Department of State Publications, 1963).
Wilde, R., *International Territorial Administration. How Trusteeship and the Civilizing Mission Never Went Away* (Oxford: Oxford University Press, 2008).
Williams, G. H., *Engineering Peace. The Military Role in Postconflict Reconstruction* (Washington: United States Institute of Peace, 2005).
Yannis, A., *Kosovo under International Administration. An Unfinished Conflict.* (Athens: ELIAMEP / PSIS, 2001).
Ydit, M., *Internationalised Territories: from the "Free city of Cracow" to the "Free city of Berlin". A study in the Historical Development of a modern Notion in International Law and International relations (1815–1960)* (Leyden: A. W. Sijthoff, 1961).

Zartman, W. I., *Collapsed States: The Disintegration and Restoration of Legitimate Authority* (Boulder / London: Lynne Rienner Publishers, 1995).

Zaum, D., *The Sovereignty Paradox: The Norms and Politics on International Statebuilding* (Oxford: Oxford University Press, 2007).

II. *Articles*

Abraham, E., 'The Sins of Saviour: Holding the United Nations Accountable to International Human Rights Standards for Executive Order Detentions in its Mission in Kosovo', 52 *American University Law Review* 1291 (2003).

Afshar, M. K. R., 'The Case of an Afghan Apostate – The Rights to a Fair Trial between Islamic Law and Human Rights in the Afghan Constitution', 10 *Max Planck Yearbook of United Nations Law* 591 (2006).

Bain, W., 'The idea of Trusteeship in International Society', 368 *The round Table* 67 (2003).

Bass, G. J., 'Jus Post Bellum', 32 *Philosophy and Public Affairs* 384 (2004).

Bassiouni, M. Ch., 'Post-Conflict Justice in Iraq: An Appraisal of the Iraq Special Tribunal', 38 *Cornell International Law Journal* 101 (2005).

Baxter, R., 'The Role of Law in Modern War', 58 *Proceedings of the American Society for International Law* 90 (1953).

Beauvais, J., 'Benevolent Despotism: A Critique of U.N. State-Building in East Timor', *New York University Journal of International and Law and Policy* 1101 (2000–2001).

Bellamy, A. J., 'The Responsibilities of victory: *Jus Post Bellum* and the Just War', 34 *Review of International Studies* 601 (2008).

Betts, W. S., Carlson, S. N. and Gisvold, G., 'The Post-Conflict Transitional Administration of Kosovo and the Lessons-Learned in Efforts to Establish a Judiciary and Rule of Law', 22 *Michigan Journal of International Law* 371 (2000–2001).

Bongiorno, C., 'A culture of impunity: applying international human rights law to the United Nations in East Timor', 33 *Columbia Human Rights Law Review* 643 (2001–2002).

Boon, K., 'Legislative Reform in Post-conflict Zones: Jus Post Bellum and the Contemporary Occupant's Law-Making Powers', 50 *McGill Law Journal* 285 (2005).

Bosi, T. D., 'Post-Conflict Reconstruction: The United Nations' Involvement in Afghanistan', 19 *New York Law School Journal of Human Rights* 819 (2003).

Bothe, M. and Marauhn, T., 'The United Nations in Kosovo and East Timor – Problems of a Trusteeship Administration', 6 *International Peacekeeping* 152 (2000).

Boutruche, T., 'Les tribunaux pénaux internationalisés ou l'émergence d'un modèle de justice hybride', *Jusletter* (2002).

Brahimi L., 'Afghanistan: Prospects for the Future', 4 *Georgetown Journal of International Affairs* 75 (2003).

Brand, M. G., 'Institution-Building and Human Rights Protection in Kosovo in the Light of UNMIK Legislation', 70 *Nordic Journal of International Law* 460 (2001).

Buzzini, G., 'La théorie des sources face au droit international général', 106 *Revue Générale de Droit International Public* 582 (2002).

Cameron, L., 'Human Rights Accountability of International Civil Administrations to the People Subject to Administration', 1 *Human Rights & International Legal Discourse* 267 (2007).

Cerone, J., 'Minding the gap: outlining KFOR accountability in post-conflict Kosovo', 12 *European Journal of International Law* 469 (2001).

Cerone, J., 'The Application of Regional Human Rights Law Beyond Regional Frontiers: The Inter-American Commission on Human Rights and US Activities in Iraq', *ASIL Insights* (2005).

Chesterman, S., 'East Timor in Transition: Self-Determination, State-Building and the United Nations', 9 *International Peacekeeping* 45 (2002).
Chesterman, S., 'From Kabul to Baghdad: Unfinished Business', 1 *The National Interest* 3 (2002).
Chesterman, S., 'Walking Softly in Afghanistan: the Future of UN State-building', 44 *Survival* 37 (2002).
Chopra, J., 'The UN's Kingdom of East Timor', 42 *Survival* 27 (2000).
Chopra, J. and Hohe T., 'Participatory Intervention', 10 *Global Governance* 289 (2004).
Cochetel, V., 'Resettlement', *Forced Migration Review* 21 (2007) (special issue).
Cogen, M. and De Brabandere, E., 'Democratic Governance and Post Conflict Reconstruction', 20 *Leiden Journal of International Law* 669 (2007).
Cohen, J. L., 'The Role of International Law in Post Conflict Constitution-Making: Toward a *Jus post Bellum* for "Interim Occupation", 51 *N. Y. L. Sch. L. Rev.* 497 (2006–2007).
d'Aspremont, J., 'La création internationale d'Etats démocratiques', 109 *Revue générale de droit international public* 889 (2005).
d'Aspremont, J., 'Legitimacy of Governments in the Age of Democracy', 38 *New York University Journal of International Law and Politics* 877 (2006).
d'Aspremont, J., 'Post-Conflict Administrations as Democracy-Building Instruments', 9 *Chicago Journal of International Law* 1 (2008).
Day, A., 'No exit without judiciary: learning a lesson from UNMIK's transitional administration in Kosovo', 23 *Wisconsin International Law Journal* 183 (2005).
De Brabandere, E., 'Non-state Actors, State-centrism and Human Rights Obligations', 22 *Leiden Journal of International Law* (2009).
Delbez, L., 'Le concept d'internationalisation', *Revue générale de droit international public* 5 (1967).
de Wet, E., 'The Direct Administration of Territories by the United Nations and its Member States in the Post Cold War Era: Legal Basis and Implications for National Law', 8 *Max Planck Yearbook of United Nations Law* 291 (2004).
Desautels-Stein, J., 'Rites and Rights in Afghanistan: The Hazara and the 2004 Constitution', 29 *Fletcher Forum of World Affairs* 157 (2005).
Diamond, L., 'Building Democracy after Conflict: Lessons from Iraq', 16 *Journal of Democracy* 9 (2005).
Diamond, L., 'Promoting Democracy in Post-Conflict and Failed States: Lessons and Challenges', 2 *Taiwan Journal of Democracy* 93 (2006).
Diamond, L., 'What went wrong in Iraq', 84 *Foreign Affairs* (2004).
Dickinson, L. A., 'The Promise of Hybrid Courts: Notes and Comments, 97 *Proceedings of the American Society for International law* 295 (2003).
Diamond, L., 'Accountability for War Crimes: What Roles for National, International, and Hybrid Tribunals?', 98 *Proceedings of the American Society for International law* 181 (2004).
Diamond, L., 'The Relationship Between Hybrid Courts and International Courts: The Case of Kosovo', 37 *New England Law Review* 1059 (2002–2003).
Diamond, L., 'Transitional Justice in Afghanistan: The Promise of Mixed Tribunals', 31 *Denver Journal of International Law and Policy* 23 (2002–2003).
DiMeglio, R. P., 'The Evolution of the Just War Tradition: Defining Jus Post Bellum', 186 *Military Law Review* 116 (2005).
Dreyer, R., 'The United Nations and Namibia: an overview (1946–1990)', 5 *International Geneva Yearbook* 26 (1991).
Dugard, J., 'Dealing with Crimes of a Past Regime: Is Amnesty Still an Option?', 12 *Leiden Journal of International Law* 1002 (1999).

Englebert, P. and Tull, D. M., 'Postconflict Reconstruction in Africa. Flawed Ideas about Failed States', 32 *International Security* 106 (2008).

Everly, R., 'Reviewing Governmental Acts of the United Nations in Kosovo', 8 *German Law Journal* 21 (2007).

Fairlie, M. A., 'Affirming Brahimi: East Timor makes the Case for a Model Criminal Code', 18 *American University International Law Review* 1059 (2003).

Fox, G. H., 'The Occupation of Iraq', 36 *Georgetown Journal of International Law* 195 (2004–2005).

Franck, T., 'The Emerging Right to Democratic Governance', 86 *American Journal of International Law* 46 (1992).

Franckx, E., Pauwels, A. and Smis, S., 'An international trusteeship for Kosovo: attempt to find a solution to the conflict', 52 *Studia Diplomatica* 155 (2001).

Gordon, R. E., 'Saving Failed States: Sometimes a Neocolonialist Notion', 12 *American University Journal of Internal Law and Policy* 903 (1997).

Grant, T. D., 'Extending Decolonisation: How the United Nations Might Have Addressed Kosovo', 28 *Georgia Journal of International and Comparative Law* 8 (1999).

Gill, T. D., 'Legal and Some Political Limitations on the Power of the UN Security Council to Exercise its Enforcement Powers under Chapter VII of the Charter', 26 *Netherlands Yearbook of international Law* 33 (1995).

Halderman, J. W., 'United Nations Territorial Administration and the Development of the Charter', *Duke Law Journal* 95 (1964).

Hall, B., 'Using Hybrid Tribunals as Trivias: Furthering the Goals of Post-Conflict Justice While Transferring Cases from the ICTY to Serbia's Domestic War Crimes Tribunal', 13 *Michigan Journal of International Law* 39 (2005).

Han, S. K., 'Building a Peace that Lasts: The United Nations and Post-Civil War Peace-Building', 26 *NYU Journal of International Law and Politics* 837 (1993–1994).

Hannum, H., 'The Status of the Universal Declaration of Human Rights in National and International law' 25 *Georgia Journal of International & Comparative Law* 287 (1995–1996).

Harper, E., 'Delivering Justice in the Wake of Mass Violence: New Approaches to Transitional Justice', 10 *Journal of Conflict and Security Law* 149 (2005).

Harrington, A., 'Ethnicity, Violence, & Land and Property Disputes in Timor-Leste', 2 *East Timor Law Journal* (2007).

Helman, G. B. and Ratner, S. R., 'Saving Failed States', 89 *Foreign Policy* 3 (1993).

Henkin, L., Restatement of the Foreign Relations Law of the United States (Revised): Tentative Draft No. 3, 76 *American Journal of International Law* 653 (1982).

Henkin, L., 'Human Rights and State "Sovereignty",' 25 *Georgia Journal of International and Comparative* 31 (1995–1996).

Hochschild, F., 'It's Better to Leave, We Can't Protect You': Flight in the First Months of United Nations Transitional Administrations in Kosovo and East Timor', 17 *Journal of Refugee Studies* 286 (2004).

Horsington, H., 'The Cambodian Khmer Rouge Tribunal: The Promise of a Hybrid Tribunal', 5 *Melbourne Journal of International Law* 462 (2004).

Iasiello, L. V., 'Jus Post Bellum: The Moral Responsibilities of Victors in War', 57 *Naval War College Review* 33 (2004).

Irmscher, T. H., 'The Legal Framework for the Activities of the United Nations Interim Administration Mission in Kosovo: The Charter, Human Rights, and the Law of Occupation', 44 *German Yearbook of International Law* 353 (2001).

Islami, I., 'The Insufficiency of International Legal Personality of Kosova as Attained Through the European Court of Human Rights: A Call for Statehood', 80 *Chicago-Kent Law Review* 83 (2005).

Isoart, P., 'L'O.N.U. et le Cambodge', 97 *Revue Générale de Droit International Public* 645 (1993).

Kaikobad, K. H., 'Problems of Belligerent Occupation: The Scope of Powers exercised by the Coalition Provisional Authority in Iraq', 54 *International and Comparative Law Quarterly* 253 (2005).

Katzenstein, S., 'Hybrid Tribunals: Searching for Justice in East Timor', 16 *Harvard Human Rights Journal* 245 (2003).

Kelly, M. J., McCormack, T. L. J., Muggleton, P. and Oswald, B. M. 'Legal aspects of Australia's involvement in the international force for East Timor', 841 *International review of the Red Cross* 101 (2001).

Kirgis, F. L., 'Security Council Governance of Postconflict Societies: A Plea for Good Faith and Informed Decision Making', 3 *American Journal of International Law* 579 (2001).

Klabbers, J., 'The Right to be Taken Seriously: Self-Determination in International Law', 28 *Human Rights Quarterly* 186 (2006).

Knoll, B., 'From Benchmarking to Final Status? Kosovo and The Problem of an International Administration's Open-Ended Mandate', 16 *European Journal of International* 637 (2005).

Kondoch, B., 'The United Nations Administration of East Timor', 6 *Journal of Conflict and Security Law* 245 (2001).

Korhononen, O., 'International Governance in Post-Conflict Situations', 14 *Leiden Journal of International Law* 495 (2001).

Koskenniemi, M., 'The Lady Doth Protest Too Much, Kosovo and the Turn to Ethics in International Law', 65 *The Modern Law review* (2002).

Koskenniemi, M., 'The Police in the Temple Order, Justice and the UN: A Dialectical View', 6 *European Journal of International Law* 1 (1995).

Kreilkamp, J. S., 'U.N. Postconflict Reconstruction', 35 *New York University Journal of International Law and Politics* 619 (2003).

Lagrange, E., 'La mission intérimaire des Nations Unies au Kosovo, nouvel essai d'administration directe d'un territoire', 45 *Annuaire Français de Droit International* 335 (1999).

Langenkamp, R. D. and Zedalis, R. J., 'What Happens to the Iraqi Oil? Thoughts on Some Significant, Unexamined International Legal Questions Regarding Occupation of Oil Fields', 14 *European Journal of International Law* 417 (2003).

Langlois, A. J., 'Human Rights without Democracy? A Critique of the Separationist Thesis', 25 *Human Rights Quarterly* 990 (2003).

Lattman, T., 'Legal status and protection of people deprived of their freedom by U.S. forces in Iraq', 2 *Miskolc Journal of International Law* 85 (2005).

Lauterpacht, E., 'The contemporary practice of the United Kingdom in the field of International law – Survey and comment', 5 *International and Comparative Law Quarterly* 405 (1956).

Leininger, J., 'Democracy and UN Peace-Keeping-Conflict Resolution through State Building and Democracy Promotion in Haiti', 10 *Max Planck Yearbook of United Nations Law* 465 (2006).

Levrat, N., 'Le droit International Humanitaire au Timor Oriental: entre Théorie et Pratique', 841 *International Review of the Red Cross* 77 (2001).

Linton, S., 'Rising From The Ashes: The Creation Of A Viable Criminal Justice System In East Timor', 25 *Melbourne University Law Review* 122 (2001).

Linton, S., 'Prosecuting Atrocities at the District Court of Dili', 2 *Melbourne Journal of International Law* 414 (2001).

Linton, S., 'Accounting for Atrocities in Indonesia', 10 *Singapore Yearbook of International Law* 1 (2006).

Marshall, D. and Inglis, S., 'The Disempowerment of Human Rights – Based Justice in the United Nations Mission in Kosovo', 16 *Harvard Human Rights Journal* 95 (2003).

Matheson, M. J., 'United Nations governance of postconflict societies', 95 *American Journal of International Law* 76 (2001).

Maziau, N. and Pech, L., 'L'administration internationale de la Bosnie-Herzégovine: un modèle pour le Kosovo?', 4 *Civitas Europa* 51 (2000).

McLaughlin, R., 'East Timor, Transitional Administration and the Status of the Territorial Sea', 4 *Melbourne Journal of International Law* 323 (2003).

Megret, F. and Hoffmann, F., 'Fostering Human Rights Accountability: An Ombudsperson for the United Nations', 11 *Global Governance* 43 (2005).

Megret, F. and Hoffmann, F., 'The UN as a Human Rights Violator? Some Reflections on the United Nations Changing Human Rights Responsibilities', 25 *Human Rights Quarterly* 330 (2003).

Meron, T., 'Extraterritoriality of Human Rights Treaties', 89 *American Journal of International Law* 78 (1995).

Moloney, R., 'Incompatible reservations to Human Rights Treaties: severability and the problem of State consent', 5 *Melbourne Journal of International Law* 155 (2004).

Morrow, J. and White, R., 'The United Nations in Transitional East Timor: International Standards and the Reality of Governance', 22 *Australian Yearbook of International Law* 1 (2002).

Mortimer, E., 'International Administration of War-Torn Societies', 10 *Global Governance* 7 (2004).

Murphy, M. A., 'A "World Occupation" of the Iraqi Economy? How Order 39 Will Create a Semi-Sovereign State', 19 *Connecticut Journal of International Law* 445 (2003–2004).

Nevelev, B., 'Legal authority over occupied territory', 42 *German Yearbook of international law* 337 (1999).

Newton, M. A., 'The Iraqi Special Tribunal: A Human Rights Perspective', 38 *Cornell International Law Journal* 863 (2005).

Nouwen, S. M. H., 'Hybrid Courts' The Hybrid Category of a New Type of International Crimes Courts', 2 *Utrecht Law Review* 190 (2006).

O'Brien, J. C., 'Lawyers, guns and money: Warlords and reconstruction after Iraq', 11 *University of California Davis Journal of International Law and Policy* 99 (2004–2005).

O'Sullivan, D., 'Is the Declaration of Human Rights Universal', 4 *International Journal of Human Rights* 25 (2000).

Oosthuizen, G. H., 'Playing the Devil's Advocate: The United Nations Security Council is Unbound by Law, 12 *Leiden Journal of International Law* 549 (1999).

Patterson, M., 'Who's got the Title? Or, The Remnants of Debellatio in Post-Inviasion Iraq', 47 *Harvard International Law Journal* 467 (2006).

Pellet, A., 'The opinions of the Badinter Arbitration Committee. A Second Breath for the Self-Determination of Peoples', 3 *European Journal of International Law* 178 (1992).

Perez, A. F., 'Legal Frameworks for Economic Transition in Iraq – Occupation under the Law of War vs. Global Governance under the Law of Peace', 18 *The Transnational Lawyer* 53 (2004–2005).

Perritt, H. H., 'Economic Sustainability and Final Status for Kosovo', 25 *University of Pennsylvania Journal of International Economic Law* 259 (2004).

Pritchard, S., 'United Nations Involvement in Post-Conflict Reconstruction Efforts: New and Continuing Challenges in the Case of East Timor', 24 *University of New South Wales Law Journal* 183 (2001).

Qazi, A. J., 'UN's Role in Iraq', *Forced Migration Review* 5 (2007) (special issue).
Rapoza, P., 'Hybrid Criminal Tribunals and the Concept of Ownership: Who owns the process?', 21, *American University International Law Review* 525 (2006).
Ratner, S. R., 'Foreign Occupation and International Territorial Administration: The Challenges of Convergence', 16 *European Journal of International Law* 697 (2005).
Reidy, A., 'The approach of the European Commission and Court of Human Rights to international humanitarian law'. 324 *International Review of the Red Cross* 513 (1998).
Reinhart, A. K. and Merritt, G. S., 'Reconstruction and Constitution Building in Iraq', 37 *Vanderbilt Journal of Transnational Law* 765 (2004).
Rich, R., 'Bringing Democracy into International Law', 12 *Journal of Democracy* 22 (2001).
Riordan, K., 'Peacekeeping Operations in East Timor', *New Zealand Armed Forces Law Review* 19 (2001).
Roberts, A., 'What is a military occupation?', 55 *British Yearbook of International Law* 291 (1984).
Roberts, A., 'The End of Occupation: Iraq 2004', 54 *International and Comparative Law Quarterly* 27 (2005).
Roberts, A., 'Transformative Military Occupation: Applying the Laws of War and Human Rights', 100 *American Journal of International Law* 580 (2006).
Romano, C. and Boutruche, T., 'Tribunaux pénaux internationalisés: état des lieux d'une justice hybride', 107 *Revue Générale de Droit International Public* 109 (2003).
Root, E., 'The Effect of Democracy on International Law', 4 *International Conciliation* 153 (1917).
Ruffert, M., 'The administration of Kosovo and East-Timor by the International Community', 3 *International and Comparative Law Quarterly* 613 (2001).
Sassoli, M., 'Legislation and Maintenance of Public Order and Civil Life by Occupying Powers', 16 *European Journal of International Law* 688 (2005).
Schabas, W. A., 'The Relationship Between Truth Commissions and International Courts: The Case of Sierra Leone', 25 *Human Rights Quarterly* 1035 (2003).
Schrijver, N., 'Some aspects of the UN involvement with Indonesia, West Irian and East Timor', 2 *International Law Forum* 26 (2000).
Schrijver, N., 'Commentary on the Lecture 'The Complex Role of the Legal Adviser when international Organisations Administer Territory' by R. Wilde', 95 *Proceedings of the American Society for International law* 259 (2001).
Senier, A., 'Rebuilding the Judicial Sector in Afghanistan: The Role of Customary Law', *Al Nakhlah – The Fletcher School Online Journal for issues related to Southwest Asia and Islamic Civilization* (2006).
Seyersted, F., 'United Nations Forces: Some Legal Problems', 37 *British Yearbook of International Law* 351 (1961).
Smit, R. A., 'Housing and Property Restitution and IDP Return in Kosovo', 44 *International Migration* 63 (2006).
Smoljan, J., 'Socio-economic aspects of peacebuilding: UNTAES and the organisation, of employment in Eastern Slavonia', 10 *International Peacekeeping* 27 (2003).
Spencer, W. H., 'Establishing the Rule of Law in Post-Taliban Afghanistan', 17 *Connecticut Journal of International Law* 445 (2001–2002).
Stahn, C., 'International Territorial Administration in the former Yugoslavia: Origins, Developments and Challenges ahead', 61 *Zeitschrift für ausländisches öffentliches Rechts und Völkerrechts* 107 (2001).
Stahn, C., 'The United Nations Transitional Administrations in Kosovo and East Timor: a First Analysis, 5 *Max Planck Yearbook of United Nations Law* 105 (2001).

Stahn, C., 'Constitution without a State? Kosovo under the United Nations Constitutional Framework for Self-Government', 14 *Leiden Journal of International Law* 531 (2001).

Stahn, C., 'Accommodating Individual Criminal Responsibility and National Reconciliation: The UN Truth Commission for East Timor', 95 *American Journal of International Law* 952 (2001).

Stahn, C., 'Justice under Transitional Administration: Contours and Critique of a Paradigm', 27 *Houston Journal of International Law* 311 (2005).

Stahn, C., 'Jus ad bellum', 'jus in bello'…'jus post bellum'? – Rethinking the Conception of the Law of Armed Conflict, 17 *European Journal of International Law* 921 (2007)

Stahn, C., '*Jus Post Bellum*: Mapping the Discipline(s)', 23 *American University International Law Review* 311 (2007–2008), p. 327).

Strohmeyer, H., 'Building a New Judiciary for East Timor: Challenges of a Fledgling Nation', 11 *Criminal Law Forum* 259 (2000).

Strohmeyer, H., 'Collapse and reconstruction of a judicial system: the United Nations Missions in Kosovo and East Timor', 95 *American Journal of International Law* 46 (2001).

Strohmeyer, H., 'Policing the Peace: Post-Conflict Judicial System Reconstruction in East Timor', 24 *University of New South Wales Law Journal* 171 (2001).

Strohmeyer, H., 'Making Multilateral Interventions Work: The U.N. and the Creation of Transitional Justice Systems in Kosovo and East Timor', 25 *The Fletcher Forum of World Affairs* 107 (2001).

Tarin, D., 'Prosecuting Saddam and Bungling Transitional Justice in Iraq', 45 *Vanderbilt Journal of International Law* 467 (2004–2005).

Thier, A. and Chopra, J., 'The Road Ahead: Political and Institutional Reconstruction in Afghanistan', 23 *Third World Quarterly* 893 (2002).

Thurer, D., 'The Failed State and International Law', 836 *International Review of the Red Cross* 731 (1999).

Tittemore, B. D., 'Belligerents in Blue Helmets: Applying International Humanitarian Law to United Nations Peace Operations', 33 *Stanford Journal of International Law* 61 (1997).

Tolbert, D. and Solomon, A., 'United Nations Reform and Supporting the Rule of Law in Post-Conflict Societies', 19 *Harvard Human Rights Journal* 29 (2006).

Tomuschat, C., 'International Law: Ensuring the Survival of Mankind on the Eve of a New Century: General Course on Public International Law, 281 *Recueil des Cours de l'Académie de Droit International* (2001).

Tondini, M., 'The Role of Italy in Rebuilding the Judicial System in Afghanistan', 45 *Revue de droit militaire et de droit de la guerre* 79 (2006).

Valdevieso, L. M. and Lopez-Mejia, A., 'East Timor: Macroeconomic Management on the Road to Independence', 38 *Finance and Development – An IMF Quarterly Magazine* (2001).

Vité, S., 'L'applicabilité du droit international de l'occupation militaire aux activités des organisations internationales', 86 *International Review of the Red Cross* 9 (2004).

Wheatley, S., 'The Security Council, Democratic Legitimacy and Regime Change in Iraq', 17 *European Journal of International Law* 531 (2006).

Wilde, R., 'Accountability and international actors in Bosnia and Herzegovina, Kosovo and East Timor', 7 *ILSA Journal of International and Comparative Law* 455 (2001).

Wilde, R., 'From Danzig to East Timor and Beyond: The Role of International Territorial Administration', 3 *American Journal of International Law* 583 (2001).

Wilde, R., 'Taxonomies of International Peacekeeping: an alternative Narrative', 9 *ILSA Journal of International & Comparative Law* 391 (2003).

Wilde, R., 'The Skewed responsibility Narrative of the 'Failed States' Concept', 9 *ILSA Journal of International & Comparative Law* 425 (2003).

Wilde, R., 'Representing International Territorial Administration: A Critique of Some Approaches', 15 *European Journal of International Law* 71 (2004).

Wilde, R., 'The Applicability of International Human Rights Law to the Coalition Provisional Authority (CPA) and Foreign Military Presence in Iraq', 11 *ILSA Journal of International and Comparative Law* 489 (2005).

Wilde, R., 'Legal "Blackhole"? Extraterritorial State Action and International Treaty Law on Civil and Political Rights', 26 *Michigan Journal of International Law* 739 (2005).

Williams, P. R. and Jannotti Pecci, F., 'Earned Sovereignty: Bridging the Gap Between Sovereignty and Self-Determination', 40 *Stanford Journal of International law* 347 (2004).

Wright, W., 'Some Land Tenure Issues in Post-Conflict East Timor', 1 *East Timor Law Journal* (2006).

Yannis, A., 'State Collapse and Prospects for Political Reconstruction and Democratic Governance in Somalia', 5 *African Yearbook of International Law* 23 (1997).

Yannis, A., 'The Concept of Suspended Sovereignty in International Law and its Implications in International Politics', 13 *European Journal of International Law* 1037 (2002).

Zimmermann, A. and Stahn, C., 'Yugoslav Territory, United Nations Trusteeship or Sovereign State? Reflections on the Current and Future Legal Status of Kosovo', 70 *Nordic Journal of International Law* 423 (2001).

III. *Treaties*

Convention (IV) respecting the Laws and Customs of War on Land and its annex: Regulations concerning the Laws and Customs of War on Land, The Hague, 18 October 1907, 187 CTS 227 (1907).

Versailles Peace Treaty, 28 June 1919, 225 CTS 188 (1919).

Convention concerning Upper Silesia, 15 May 1922, 9 LNTS 466.

Montevideo Convention on the Rights and Duties of States, 26 December 1933, 165 LNTS 19.

Convention on the Privileges and Immunities of the United Nations, 13 February 1946, 1 UNTS 15.

Treaty of Peace with Italy, signed at Paris, 10 February 1947, 49 UNTS 126.

ILO Convention (No 87) concerning freedom of association and protection of the right to organize, 9 July 1948, 68 UNTS 17.

European Convention for the Protection of Human Rights and Fundamental Freedoms and its protocols, 4 November 1950, 213 UNTS 222.

Memorandum of Understanding (with annexes and exchange of notes) regarding the Free Territory of Trieste, 5 October 1954, 235 UNTS 99.

Convention on the Rights and Obligations of Foreign Forces and Their Members in the Federal Republic of Germany, with annexes, 26 May 1952, as amended by the Paris Protocol (23 October 1954), 332 UNTS 3.

Agreement (with annex) concerning West New Guinea (West Irian), 15 August 1962, 437 UNTS 274.

International Covenant on Economic, Social and Cultural Rights, 16 December 1966, 993 UNTS 3.

International Covenant on Civil and Political Rights, 16 December 1966, 999 UNTS 171.

Agreement between the United Republic of Tanzania and the United Nations Council for Namibia concerning the Issuance by the Council of Travel and Identity Documents to Namibians, Signed in Dar es Salaam, 5 December 1972, in *Yearbook of International Law Commission*, Vol. II, Part Two (1974).

Protocol Additional to the Geneva Conventions of 12 August 1949, and relating to the Protection of Victims of International Armed Conflicts (Protocol I) (8 June 1977), 1125 UNTS 3.

European Charter of Local Self-Government (15 October 1985), conventions.coe.int/treaty/en/Treaties/Html/122.htm.

The Charter of Paris for a New Europe, (1991) SIPRI Yearbook 603.

Agreement on the Comprehensive Political Settlement of the Cambodia Conflict, UN Doc. A/46/608–S/23177 (23 October 1991); 31 ILM 174 (1992).

Addis Ababa Agreement concluded at the first session of the Conference on National Reconciliation in Somalia (27 March 1993), in *The United Nations and Somalia 1992–1996*, United Nations Blue Books Series, vol. VIII. (New York: United Nations, Dept. of Public Information, 1996).

Basic Agreement on the Region of Eastern Slavonia, Baranja and Western Sirmium, UN Doc. S/1995/951 (12 November 1995).

Statement by the Chairman on the conclusion of the meeting of the G-8 Foreign Ministers held at the Petersberg Centre on 6 May', UN Doc. 1999S/1999/516 (6 May 1999).

Agreement on the principles (peace plan) to move towards a resolution of the Kosovo crisis presented to the leadership of the Federal Republic of Yugoslavia by the President of Finland, Martti Ahtisaari, representing the European Union, and Viktor Chernomyrdin, Special Representative of the President of the Russian Federation, UN Doc. S/1999/649 (3 June 1999).

Interim Agreement for Peace and Self-Government in Kosovo, UN Doc. S/1999/648 (7 June 1999).

Military Technical Agreement between the International Security Force ("KFOR") and the Governments of the Federal Republic of Yugoslavia and the Republic of Serbia, UN Doc. S/1999/682 (9 June 1999).

Agreement on Provisional Arrangement of Afghanistan pending the Re-establishment of Permanent Government Institutions, UN Doc S/2001/1154 (5 December 2001).

Military Technical Agreement between the International Security Assistance Force (ISAF) and the Interim Administration of Afghanistan ("Interim Administration") (4 January 2002), 41 ILM 1032 (2002).

Timor Sea Treaty between the Government of East Timor and the Government of Australia (20 May 2002), (2003) ATS 13.

Free Trade Agreement between The United Nations Interim Administration Mission in Kosovo (UNMIK) on behalf of the Provisional Institutions of Self-Government in Kosovo and The Council of Ministers of the Republic of Albania, UN Doc. UNMIK/FTA/2003/1 (4 July 2003).

Agreement between the United Nations Interim Administration Mission in Kosovo and the Council of Europe on technical arrangements related to the European Convention for the Prevention of Torture and Inhuman or Degrading Treatment or Punishment (23 August 2004), www.cpt.coe.int/documents/scg/2004–08–23–eng.htm.

Interim Free Trade Agreement between The United Nations Interim Administration Mission in Kosovo (UNMIK) on behalf of the Provisional Institutions of Self-Government in Kosovo and the Government of FYROM, UN Doc. UNMIK/FTA/2005/1 (31 August 2005).

IV. *Cases*

A. *Permanent Court of International Justice*

Nationality Decrees Issued in Tunis and Morocco (French Zone) on November 8th, 1921, Advisory Opinion, 7 February 1923, 1922 PCIJ Reports 7.
Case of the S.S. "Wimbledon", Judgment, 17 August 1923, 1923 PCIJ Reports 25.
Free City of Danzig and International Labour Organization, Advisory Opinion, 30 August 1930, 1930 PCIJ Reports 4.
Treatment of Polish National and other Persons of Polish Origin or Speech on the Danzig Territory, Advisory Opinion, 4 February 1932, 1932 PCIJ Reports 23.
Interpretation of the Statute of the Memel Territory, Judgement, 11 August 1932, 1932 PCIJ Reports 294–339.

B. *International Court of Justice*

Reparation for injuries suffered in the service of the United Nations, Advisory Opinion, 11 April 1949, 1949 ICJ Reports 174.
International Status of South West Africa, Advisory Opinion, 11 July 1950, 1950 ICJ Reports 128. Separate opinion by Sir Arnold McNair, 1950 ICJ Reports 146.
Effect of Awards of Compensation Made by the United Nations Administrative Tribunal, Advisory Opinion, 13 July 1954, 1954 ICJ Reports 47.
Certain Expenses of the United Nations (Article 17, paragraph 2, of the Charter), Advisory Opinion, 20 July 1962, 1962 ICJ Reports 151.
Barcelona Traction, Light and Power Company, Limited (Belgium v. Spain), Judgment, 5 February 1970, 1970 ICJ Reports 3.
Legal Consequences for States of the Continued Presence of South Africa in Namibia (South West Africa) notwithstanding Security Council Resolution 276 (1970), Advisory Opinion, 21 June 1971, 1971 ICJ Reports 16. Dissenting opinion of Judge Sir Gerald Fitzmaurice, 1971 ICJ Reports 220.
Interpretation of the Agreement of 25 March 1951 between the WHO and Egypt, Advisory Opinion, 20 December 1980, 1980 ICJ Reports 73.
Case concerning East Timor (Portugal v. Australia), Judgment, 30 June 1995, 1995 ICJ Reports 90.
Legality of the Threat or Use of Nuclear Weapons, Advisory Opinion, 8 July 1996, 1996 ICJ Reports 226.
Difference relating to immunity form Legal Process of a Special Rapporteur of the Commission on Human Rights, Advisory opinion, 29 April 1999, 1999 ICJ Reports 66.
Legal Consequences of the Construction of a Wall in the occupied Palestinian Territory, Advisory Opinion, 9 July 2004, 2004 ICJ Reports 136.
Application of the Convention on the Prevention and Punishment of the Crime of Genocide (Bosnia and Herzegovina v. Serbia and Montenegro), Judgement, 26 February 2007, www.icj-cij.org.

C. *European Court of Human Rights*

Lingens v. Austria, 8 July 1986, [1986] ECHR (Ser. A).
Loizidou v. Turkey, 23 February 1995, 1995 ECHR Series A No. 310.
United Communist Party of Turkey v Turkey, Decision of 30 January 1998, 1998 ECHR 1.

Socialist Party and others v Turkey, Decision of 25 May 1998, 1998 ECHR 45.
Incal v Turkey, Decision of 9 June 1998, 1998 ECHR 48.
Waite and Kennedy v. Germany, Decision of 18 February 1999, 1999 ECHR 13.
Jerusalem v Austria, Decision of 27 January 2001, 2001 ECHR 122.
Agim Behrami and Bekir Behrami against France and Ruzhdi Saramati against France, Germany and Norway, Decision on the admissibility, 2 May 2007, Application n[os] 71412/01 and 78166/06.

D. *Other*

Island of Palmas Case (Netherlands v. U.S.), Arbitral Award, 4 April 1928, 22 *American Journal of International Law* 967 (1928).
International Criminal Tribunal for the Former Yugoslavia, 'Prosecutor v. Dusko tadic a/k/a "Dule", Decision on the Defence Motion for Interlocutory Appeal on Jurisdiction', Case n° IT-95-9-PT, 2 October 1995.
International Criminal Tribunal for the Rwanda, *Prosecutor v. Kenyabashi*, Case n° ICTR-96-15-T, 18 June 1997.
Constitutional Court Of Bosnia And Herzegovina, Decision U9/00 (3 Nov. 2000), www.ustavnisud.ba/eng/odluke/.

V. *Official Documents and Publications*

United Nations official documents used in this book can be obtained, through their official number, from the UN website: www.un.org/documents/.

Official documents from other international organisations can also be obtained from these organisations' official websites. The Official Documents from the administrations, missions and official institutions in Kosovo, East Timor, Afghanistan and Iraq can be obtained from the following websites:

Kosovo

www.unmikonline.org
www.nato.int/kfor/docu/docs/index.htm
www.ombudspersonkosovo.org
www.assembly-kosova.org

East Timor

www.un.org/peace/etimor/UntaetN.htm
www.timor-leste.gov.tl
www.eueomtimorleste.org

Afghanistan

www.unama-afg.org
www.aihrc.org.af
president.gov.af

www.jemb.org
www.moj.gov.af

Iraq

www.uniraq.org
www.cpa-iraq.org
www.iraqcoalition.org
www.iraqigovernment.org
www.iraqcompact.org

Other

Office of the High Representative (Bosnia): www.ohr.int

VI. *Reports, Research Papers and Conference Papers*

Documents from frequently cited non-governmental organisations are not reproduced in the list of selected documents below, and can be obtained from these organisations' official websites:

Amnesty International: web.amnesty.org.
Human Rights Watch: www.hrw.org.
International Crisis Group: www.crisisgroup.org.
International Legal Assistance Consortium: www.ilac.se.

Adamson, R. and Vamos-Goldman, A., 'Internationalization of Post-Conflict Justice in Iraq: Ensuring a Rule for the United Nations and International Justice', *LIU Institute for Global Issues, University of British Columbia* (July 2003), www.ligi.ubc.ca.

Aita, J., 'United Nations' Brahimi says Afghanistan will need help for years', *United States Mission to the European Union* (9 September 2002), www.useu.be.

Ali, N., 'An Introduction to the Economic Reconstruction of Afghanistan', *Institute for Afghan Studies* (May 2003), unpan1.un.org/intradoc/groups/public/documents/APCITY/ UNPAN015700 .pdf.

Article 19, 'Freedom of Expression and the Media in Timor Leste' (December 2005), www .article19.org/pdfs/publications/timor-leste-baseline-study.pdf.

Bain, W., 'Trusteeship: A Response to Failed States?', *Paper Presented at the Conference on Failed States and Global Governance, Perdue University* (10–14 April 2001), www.comm.ucsb.edu/ Research/mstohl/failed_states/2001/papers/bain.pdf.

Baker, J. A., Hamilton, L. H. *et al.*, 'The Iraq Study Group Report', www.usip.org/isg/iraq_study_ group_report/report/1206/index.html.

Basel, M., 'Judging in Countries in Conflict or Transition: An Afghan Perspective', *International Association of Woman Judges – 8th Biennial Conference* (3–7 May 2006), www.iawj.org/what/ Session1–Basel.doc.

Bassiouni, M. C., 'Iraq Post-Conflict Justice: A Proposed Comprehensive Plan', *International Human Rights Law Institute*, DePaul University College of Law (28 April 2003 / Revised 2 January 2004), www.law.depaul.edu/institutes_centers/ihrli/_downloads/Iraq_Proposal_04.pdf.

Boisson de Chazournes, L., 'Taking the International Rule of Law Seriously: Economic Instruments and Collective Security', *International Peace Academy Policy Paper* (October 2005), www .ipacademy.org.

Brahimi, L., 'Address of Mr. Lakhdar Brahimi, Special Representative of the Secretary-General for Afghanistan', *Conference of Rome on Justice in Afghanistan* (19 December 2002), www.unama-afg.org/docs/_nonUN%20Docs/_Internation-conferences&Forums/RC/Address%20of%20SRSG.doc.

Brahimi, L., "Address by Mr. Lakhdar Brahimi, the Special Representative of the Secretary-General for Afghanistan to The International Conference on Reconstruction Assistance to Afghanistan' (21 January 2002), www.un.org/News/dh/latest/afghan/brahimi-tokyo21.htm.

Bremer, L. P., Remarks at Official Opening of the Ministry of Human Rights Building (14 February 2004), www.cpa-iraq.org/transcripts/20040214_HR_Opening.html.

Chesterman, S., 'Kosovo in Limbo: State-Building and Substantial Autonomy', *International Peace Academy*, New York (August 2001), www.ipacademy.org.

Chesterman, S., 'Tiptoeing through Afghanistan: The Future of UN State-Building', *International Peace Academy – Report from the Transitional Administrations Project* (September 2002), www.ipacademy.org.

Chesterman, S., 'Justice under International Administration: Kosovo, East Timor and Afghanistan' (September, 2002), www.ipacademy.org.

Dahrendorf, N. *et al.*, 'A Review of Peace Operations: A Case for Change: East Timor', *Conflict Security & Development Group, King's College London* (10 March 2003), www.jsmp.minihub.org/Reports/otherresources/Peace4Timor_10_3_03.pdf.

Dahrendorf, N. *et al.*, 'A Review of Peace Operations: A Case for Change: Kosovo', *Conflict Security & Development Group, King's College London* (10 March 2003), ipi.sspp.kcl.ac.uk/peace-operationsreview.

Dahrendorf, N. *et al.*, 'A Review of Peace Operations: A Case for Change: Afghanistan (A Snapshot Study)', *Conflict Security & Development Group, King's College London* (10 March 2003), ipi.sspp.kcl.ac.uk/peaceoperationsreview.

Dahrendorf, N. *et al.*, 'A Review of Peace Operations: A Case for Change: Overall Introduction and Synthesis Report', *Conflict Security & Development Group, King's College London* (13 March 2003), ipi.sspp.kcl.ac.uk/peaceoperationsreview.

Diamond, L., 'Promoting Democracy in the 1990s: Actors and Instruments, Issues and Imperatives', *A Report to the Carnegie Commission on Preventing Deadly Conflict*, Carnegie Corporation of New York (December 1995), wwics.si.edu/subsites/ccpdc/pubs/di/fr.htm.

Halchin, L. E., 'The Coalition Provisional Authority (CPA): origin, characteristics, and institutional authorities', *Congressional Research Service report for Congress- RL32370*, Washington D.C. (2005), www.fas.org/man/crs/RL32370.pdf.

Hartmann, M. E., 'International Judges and Prosecutors in Kosovo: A New Model for Post-Conflict Peacekeeping', *United States Institute of Peace Special Report 112* (October 2003), www.usip.org/pubs/specialreports/sr112.html.

Hasegawa, S., 'Justice and/or Reconciliation: the key to successful transition from post-conflict peacekeeping to peace and nation-building', *Victoria University of Wellington* (19 July 2004), www.unmiset.org.

Hasegawa, S., 'Speech Delivered at the Opening Ceremony for the Judicial Training Centre (JTC)' (7 September 2004), www.unmiset.org.

Hasegawa, S., 'International Donor Coordination, Civil Society and Natural Resource Management', *Conference 'Beyond Cold Peace: Strategies for Economic Reconstruction And Post Conflict Management* (27–28 October, 2004), www.unmiset.org.

Hasegawa, S., 'The Development Perspective: Three Imperatives for Sustainable Peace and Nation-building in a Post-Conflict Society' (20 May 2005), www.unmiset.org.

Hasegawa, S., 'The Role of the International Community in New Nation Building. Case study of UN Experience in Timor – Leste', *International Symposium on Towards a New Paradigm of International Cooperation* (7 September 2005), www.unmiset.org.

Hasegawa, S., 'Lessons Learned from Peacekeeping and Peacebuilding Support Missions in Timor-Leste', *Berlin Centre for International Peace Operation* (27 January 2006), www.unmiset.org.

International Commission of Jurists, 'Afghanistan's Legal System and its Compatibility with International Human Rights Standards' (November 2002), www.icj.org/IMG/pdf/doc-51.pdf.

International Commission of Intervention and State Sovereignty, 'The Responsibility to Protect' (December 2001), www.iciss.ca/pdf/Commission-Report.pdf.

International Institute of Higher Studies in Criminal Sciences (ISISC), 'Interim Training for the Afghan Judiciary', *Report on the Activities of ISISC during the first 6 months of the Project* (July 2003–January 2004), www.isisc.org.

Jabar, F. A., 'Postconflict Iraq. A Race for Stability, Reconstruction, and Legitimacy', *United States Institute of Peace Special Report 120* (May 2004), www.usip.org/pubs/specialreports/sr120.pdf.

Johnson, C., Maley W., Their, A. and Wardak, A., 'Afghanistan's political and constitutional development', *Overseas Development Institute* (January 2003), www.odi.org.uk/hpg/papers/evaluations/afghandfid.pdf.

Judicial System Monitoring Programme, 'Justice in the Districts' (December 2003), www.jsmp.minihub.org.

Judicial System Monitoring Programme, 'Recent Developments in the Courts' *Justice Update Issue 22/2005* (October/November 2005), www.jsmp.minihub.org.

Judicial System Monitoring Programme, 'Overview of Timor Leste Justice Sector 2005' (January 2006), www.jsmp.minihub.org.

Karzai, H., 'A Vision of Human Rights in the New Afghanistan', *Opening statement at the Afghan National Workshop on Human Rights: Toward Implementation of the Human Rights Provisions of the Bonn Agreement* (22 March 2002), www.unama-afg.org/news/_statement/Others/2002/_gov/02mar22–Karzai.htm.

Karzai, H., 'Statement of President Hamid Karzai on the Prohibition of Poppy Cultivation' (26 September 2002), www.unama-afg.org/news/_statement/Others/2002/_gov/02sep26–Karzai.htm.

Katzman, K., 'Iraq: Post-Saddam Governance and Security', *Congressional Research Service Report for Congress – RL31339*, Washington D.C., The Library of Congress (29 March 2006), fpc.state.gov/documents/organization/64963.pdf.

Kelly, M. J., 'INTERFET Detainee Management Unit in East Timor', *Paper presented at the Swiss Seminar on the Law of Armed Conflict, Chavannes-de-Bogis*,(27 October 2000), www.jsmp.minihub.org/Resources/2000/INTERFET%20DETAINEE%20MANAGEMENT%20UNIT%20(e).pdf.

Lau, M., 'Afghanistan's Legal System and its Compatibility with International Human Rights Standards', *International Commission of Jurists, Final Report* (November 2002), www.icj.org/IMG/pdf/doc-46.pdf.

Mahmoud, M., 'Judicial System in Iraq: A Review of the Legislation Regulating Judicial Affairs in Iraq', *Iraqi Judicial Forum: The Judicial System in Iraq: Facts and Prospects – Hashemite Kingdom of Jordan* (October 2004), www.worldbank.org/publicsector/legal/Iraq.htm.

Miller, L. and Perito, R., 'Establishing the Rule of Law in Afghanistan', *United States Institute of Peace Special Report 117* (March 2004), www.usip.org/pubs/specialreports/sr117.html.

Mobekk, E., 'Identifying Lessons in United Nations International Policing Missions', *Policy Paper nº 9, Geneva Centre for the Democratic Control of Armed Forces* (DCAF) (November 2005), http://www.dcaf.ch.

Norwegian Refugee Council / UNHCR, 'A Guide to Property Law in Afghanistan' (2005), www.internal-displacement.org/8025708F004CE90B/(httpDocuments)/86A7E9B3EE11392EC125716F002D49E8/$file/PropertyLawManual(EngVer).pdf.

Nowicki, M.A., 'Kosovo Pro Memoria', *Paper presented at the 2006 NGO Coalition OSCE Conference*, Brussels (February 2006), unpublished (copy on file with the author).

Parker, T., 'The Ultimate Intervention: Revitalising the UN Trusteeship Council for the 21st Century', *Centre for European and Asian Studies, Norwegian School of Management, Report 3/2003* (April 2003), www.bi.no/dep2/ceas.

Pegg, S., 'De Facto States in the International System', *Institute of International relations, The University of British Columbia, Working Paper No. 21* (February 1998), www.iir.ubc.ca/pdffiles/webwp21.pdf

Perito, R., 'Establishing the Rule of Law in Iraq', *United States Institute of Peace Special Report 104* (April 2003), www.usip.org/pubs/specialreports/sr104.html.

Perriello, T. and Wierda, M., 'Lessons from the Deployment of International Judges and Prosecutors in Kosovo', *International Centre for Transitional Justice* (March 2006), www.ictj.org.

Rees, E., 'Security Sector Reform (SSR) and Peace Operations: "Improvisation and Confusion" from the Field', *UN Peacekeeping Best Practices Section of the Department of Peacekeeping Operations* (March 2006), www.peacekeepingbestpractices.unlb.org/pbpu/view/viewdocument.aspx?id=2&docid=750.

Sedra, M. (ed.), 'Confronting Afghanistan's Security Dilemma: Reforming the Security Sector', *Bonn International Center for Conversion Brief 28* (September 2003), www.bicc.de/publications/briefs/brief28/content.php.

Slocombe, W. B., 'Iraq's Special Challenge Security Sector Reform 'Under Fire', *Geneva Centre for the Democratic Control of Armed Forces* (DCAF) (2005), www.dcaf.ch/mena/_publications.cfm?navsub1=10&navsub2=3&nav1=3.

Thier, J. A., 'Re-establishing the Judicial System in Afghanistan', *CDDRL Working Paper Number 19* (September 2004), cddrl.stanford.edu/.

United Kingdom, Department for International Development (DFID), 'Iraq Update Newsletter' (October 2004), www.dfid.gov.uk/news/default.asp?move=0&CountryID=c108.

United Kingdom, Department for International Development (DFID), 'Iraq Programme Update Newsletter' (October 2006), www.dfid.gov.uk/news/default.asp?move=0&CountryID=c108.

United Kingdom, Department for International Development (DFID), House of Commons, Defence Committee, 'Iraq: An Initial Assessment of Post Conflict Operations: Government Response to the Committee's, *Sixth Report of Session 2004–2005* (20 July 2005).

United States Agency for International Development (USAID), United States Office Pristina (USOP), & Organisation for Security and Cooperation in Europe (OSCE), *'Judicial Assessment Mission II'* (December 2001), www.state.gov/documents/organization/7652.pdf.

United States Agency for International Development (USAID), 'Commercial Legal and Institutional Reform Assessment. Diagnostic Assessment Report for Kosovo' (September 2004), www.usaid.gov/.

United States Agency for International Development (USAID), 'Postconflict Elections and Democratization: an Experience Review', *Issue Paper No. 8* (May 2005), www.dec.org.

United States Agency for International Development (USAID), *USAID's Timor Leste Media Assessment* (February 2006), pdf.usaid.gov/pdf_docs/PNADF898.pdf.

United States Department of Defence, 'Measuring Stability and Security in Iraq', *Report to Congress in accordance with the Department of Defense Appropriations Act 2006* (August 2006), www.defenselink.mil/news/August 006.

United States Department of State, 'Kosovo Judicial Assessment Mission Report' (April 2000), pristina.usmission.gov/jud.pdf.

United States General Accounting Office, 'Rebuilding Iraq. Resource, Security, Governance, Essential Services and Oversight Issues', *Report to Congressional Committee Nr. GAO-01-902R* (June 2004), www.gao.gov/new.items/d04902r.pdf.

United States Government Accountability Office, 'Afghanistan Security: Further Congressional Action May Be Needed to Ensure Completion of a Detailed Plan to Develop and Sustain Capable Afghan National Security Forces', *Report Nr. GAO-08-661* (18 June 2008), www.gao.gov/docsearch/featured/oif.html.

United States Government Accountability Office, 'Afghanistan Security: U.S. Efforts to Develop Capable Afghan Police Forces Face Challenges and Need a Coordinated, Detailed Plan to Help Ensure Accountability', *Report Nr. GAO-08–883T* (18 June 2008), www.gao.gov/docsearch/featured/oif.html.

United States Institute of Peace, 'Unfinished Business in Afghanistan: Warlordism, Reconstruction, and Ethnic Harmony', *USIP Special Report 105*, (April 2003), www.usip.org/pubs/index.html.

United States Institute of Peace, 'The Coalition Provisional Authority's Experience with Economic Reconstruction in Iraq: Lessons Identified', *USIP Special Report 138* (April 2005), www.usip.org/pubs/index.html.

Vieira de Mello, S., 'How not to run a country. Lessons for the UN from Kosovo and East Timor' (June 2000), www.jsmp.minihub.org/Resources/2000/INTERFET%20DETAINEE%20MANAGEMENT%20UNIT%20(e).pdf.

Wardak, A. and Spivack, D., 'Afghanistan's Domestic Legal Framework,' *The Senlis Council* (September 2005), www.senliscouncil.net/modules/publications/008_publication/domestic_law_exec_summ.

Index